Milton, Marvell, and the Dutch Republic

The tumultuous relations between Britain and the United Provinces in the seventeenth century provide the backdrop to this book, striking new ground as its transnational framework permits an overview of their intertwined culture, politics, trade, intellectual exchange, and religious debate. How the English and Dutch understood each other is coloured by these factors, and revealed through an imagological method, charting the myriad uses of stereotypes in different genres and contexts. The discussion is anchored in a specific context through the lives and works of John Milton and Andrew Marvell, whose complex connections with Dutch people and society are investigated. As well as turning overdue attention to neglected Dutch writers of the period, the book creates new possibilities for reading Milton and Marvell as not merely English, but European poets.

Esther van Raamsdonk is a British Academy Postdoctoral Researcher at the Centre for the Study of the Renaissance, University of Warwick, examining the politics of biblical narrative in the Dutch Republic and England. She previously worked on the digital humanities project *Networking Archives*, and completed a Ph.D. on Milton and Marvell at the University of Exeter. She has published articles on Milton's and Marvell's poetry, Dutch language acquisition, demonology, and travelogues.

Routledge Studies in Renaissance and Early Modern Worlds of Knowledge

Series Editors: Harald E. Braun
University of Liverpool

Emily Michelson
University of St Andrews

This series explores Renaissance and Early Modern Worlds of Knowledge (c.1400-c.1700) in Europe, the Americas, Asia and Africa. The volumes published in this series study the individuals, communities and networks involved in making and communicating knowledge during the first age of globalisation. Authors investigate the perceptions, practices and modes of behaviour which shaped Renaissance and Early Modern intellectual endeavour and examine the ways in which they reverberated in the political, cultural, social and economic sphere.

The series is interdisciplinary, comparative and global in its outlook. We welcome submissions from new as well as existing fields of Renaissance Studies, including the history of literature (including neo-Latin, European and non-European languages), science and medicine, religion, architecture, environmental and economic history, the history of the book, art history, intellectual history and the history of music. We are particularly interested in proposals that straddle disciplines and are innovative in terms of approach and methodology.

The series includes monographs, shorter works and edited collections of essays. The Society for Renaissance Studies (www.rensoc.org.uk) provides an expert editorial board, mentoring, extensive editing and support for contributors to the series, ensuring high standards of peer-reviewed scholarship. We welcome proposals from early career researchers as well as more established colleagues.

SRS Board Members: Erik DeBom (KU Leuven, Belgium), Mordechai Feingold (California Institute of Technology, USA), Andrew Hadfield (University of Sussex, UK), Peter Mack (University of Warwick, UK), Jennifer Richards (University of Newcastle, UK), Stefania Tutino (UCLA, USA), Richard Wistreich (Royal College of Music, UK)

Milton, Marvell, and the Dutch Republic
Esther van Raamsdonk

Staging Favorites
Theatrical Representations of Political Favoritism in the Early Modern Courts of Spain, France, and England
Francisco Gómez Martos

For more information about this series, please visit: www.routledge.com/
Routledge-Studies-in-Renaissance-and-Early-Modern-Worlds-of-Knowledge/
book-series/ASHSER4043

Milton, Marvell, and the Dutch Republic

Esther van Raamsdonk

Routledge
Taylor & Francis Group

LONDON AND NEW YORK

First published 2021
by Routledge
2 Park Square, Milton Park, Abingdon, Oxon OX14 4RN

and by Routledge
52 Vanderbilt Avenue, New York, NY 10017

Routledge is an imprint of the Taylor & Francis Group, an informa business

© 2021 Esther van Raamsdonk

British Library Cataloguing-in-Publication Data
A catalogue record for this book is available from the British Library

Library of Congress Cataloging-in-Publication Data
Names: Van Raamsdonk, Esther, author.
Title: Milton, Marvell, and the Dutch republic / Esther van
   Raamsdonk.
Description: First edition. | New York : Routledge, 2020. | Series:
   Routledge studies in Renaissance and early modern worlds of
   knowledge | Includes bibliographical references and index.
Identifiers: LCCN 2020014184 (print) | LCCN 2020014185
   (ebook) | ISBN 9780367520571 (hardback) | ISBN
   9781003056218 (ebook)
Subjects: LCSH: Great Britain—Relations—Netherlands. |
   Netherlands—Relations—Great Britain. | Great Britain—Foreign
   relations—17th century. | Netherlands—Foreign relations—
   17th century. | Marvell, Andrew, 1621–1678—Appreciation—
   Netherlands. | Milton, John, 1608–1674—Appreciation—
   Netherlands. | Dutch literature—17th century—History and
   criticism. | Stereotypes (Social psychology) in literature.
Classification: LCC DA47.3 .V36 2020 (print) | LCC DA47.3
   (ebook) | DDC 303.48/241049209032—dc23
LC record available at https://lccn.loc.gov/2020014184
LC ebook record available at https://lccn.loc.gov/2020014185

ISBN: 978-0-367-52057-1 (hbk)
ISBN: 978-1-003-05621-8 (ebk)

Typeset in Sabon
by Apex CoVantage, LLC

To Michael 'where my extended soul is fixt'.

Contents

Figures

Poetry Editions

All poetry of John Milton is from the following editions:

> *Paradise Lost*, ed. by Alastair Fowler (London: Longman Pearson, 2007).
> *The Complete Shorter Poems*, ed. by John Carey (London: Longman Pearson, 2007).

All poetry of Andrew Marvell is from the following edition:

> *The Poems of Andrew Marvell*, ed. by Nigel Smith (London: Longman Pearson, 2007).

All poetry of Joost van den Vondel is from the following edition:

> *De werken van Vondel*, ed. by J.F.M. Sterck, et al., 10 vols. (Amsterdam: Wereldbibliotheek, 1927–1937).

All poetry and plays of John Dryden are from the following editions:

> *The Works of John Dryden*, ed. by Edward Niles Hooker and H.T. Swedenberg, 20 vols. (Los Angeles: University of California Press, 1974).

Preliminary Remarks

I have used modern editions for quotations from English primary sources when available. When unavailable, I have retained the original spellings.

All Dutch, Latin and French quotations used in the book are translated by myself, unless otherwise stated in the endnotes. I have decided to include all Dutch (and other languages) sources within the text itself (with some minor exceptions) rather than presenting them in the endnotes. Having the translations side by side, especially with poetry, enables the reader to make direct comparisons. Frequently the availability of similar expressions and images illustrates lines of connection between the Dutch and the English. It was also important to display the alexandrine form and robust enjoyment of full rhyme that almost all of Dutch poetry shares (an interesting contrast with Milton's iambic blank verse, which also raised eyebrows in England). Hopefully, the original sense and rhyme scheme can still be followed.

Acknowledgements

Several brilliant early modernists have offered advice over the duration of this project, read chapters, shared unpublished works, and made valuable suggestions that hugely contributed to the book as it stands, for which I am very grateful. I am cheerfully indebted to Ruth Ahnert, Jack Avery, Jan Bloemendal, Gordon Campbell, Thomas Corns, Jörgen Dahlberg, Martin Dzelzainis, Stephen Fallon, Ola Gustavsson, Johanna Harris, Helmer Helmers, Ineke Huysman, Edward Jones, Jason Kerr, Ad Leerintveld, Sjoerd Levelt, Miranda Lewis, Alan Moss, Henk Nellen, James Parente Jr., Henry Power, Yolanda Rodríguez Pérez, Cornelis W. Schoneveld, Nigel Smith, Kees Teszelsky, Gary K. Waite, Helen Wilcox, and Rachel Willie. I need to thank Nicholas McDowell in particular, as a source of inspiration and support over several years of this book's gestation. Thanks also to the editors of this series Harald Braun and Emily Michelson, the editors of Routledge for their unstinting positivity, and the anonymous reviewer(s) for their helpful suggestions. Throughout the research and writing of this book, I have been grateful for the financial support offered by research grants from the Arts and Humanities Research Council and the British Academy.

I acknowledge *Milton Quarterly*, and their editor Edward Jones, who allowed the reproduction of sections from my article 'Creation in John Milton's *Paradise Lost* and Joost van den Vondel's *Adam in Ballingschap*', 51.2. (2017): 97–110. Thanks also to the editors of *Renaissance Studies*, Jennifer Richards and Kevin Killeen, for their permission to reproduce parts of my article 'Vondel's English Lucifer and Milton's Dutch Satan' (forthcoming). Thanks to the British Library, The Hofwijck Museum, and the Gemäldegalerie der Staatlichen Museen zu Berlin for allowing me to reproduce the images in this book.

I owe an enormous debt to my family on both sides of the channel, the Van Raamsdonken, the Roses, and everyone at Wythall Estate. I am very grateful to Philip and Barbara Rose who gave me a place for eighteen months to finish writing the book undisturbed, except for coffee and cake. Above all, I am thankful to my parents Dinie and Leo, who have lived with this book almost as long as I have, through the agonies and delights of research. They were ever-patient when listening to lengthy Milton monologues, and their support has been incalculable. They gave me Leo Miller's *Milton and the Anglo-Dutch Negotiations*, where it all began. This book is dedicated to Michael Rose. It would not have seen the light without his continuous and patient encouragement, kindness and optimism, proof-reading, and unrelenting appetite for historical facts; and he still married me in the midst of it.

Abbreviations

CPW	*Complete Prose Works of John Milton*, gen. ed. Don M. Wolfe, 8 vols. (New Haven: Yale University Press, 1953–1982).
CPW (OUP) (date)	*Complete Works of John Milton*, gen. ed. Gordon Campbell and Thomas Corns (Oxford: Oxford University Press, 2008–2020).
Institutes	Jean Calvin, *Institutes of the Christian Religion*, transl. and ed. by Henry Beveridge (Edinburgh: Calvin Translation Society, 1845).
ODNB	*Oxford Dictionary of National Biography* (Oxford: Oxford University Press, September 2004; online edition, January 2008).
P&L	*The Poems and Letters of Andrew Marvell*, ed. by H.M. Margoliouth (revised by Pierre Legouis) 2 vols. (Oxford: Clarendon Press, 1971).
PWAM	*Prose Works of Andrew Marvell*, ed. by Annabel Patterson and Martin Dzelzainis, 2 vols. (New Haven: Yale University Press, 2003).
WA	Jacobus Arminius, *The Works of James Arminius*, ed. and transl. by James Nicols, 3 vols. (London: Longman et al, 1825).
Hartlib Papers	All references to Samuel Hartlib's papers are taken from the online database created by the University of Sheffield (www.hrionline.ac.uk/hartlib/).

Introduction

Milton, Marvell, and the Dutch Republic

In 1622, a young Constantijn Huygens set off on his first diplomatic visit to England. His good friend Pieter Corneliszoon Hooft wrote 'Behouden Reis aen Heer Constantijn Huighens naer Engelandt' (Safe journey for Constantijn Huygens to England) to commemorate the occasion. In this erudite sonnet, Neptune's trumpeter orders peace upon the waves until Huygens has crossed. The intrepid sailor himself becomes Arion, the mythical poet whose song could tame the rolling seas: 'His lute calms both sea and storm' (En maecken zeedigh zee en stormen met sijn lujt, l. 14).

It is a typical Dutch seventeenth-century sonnet, packed with classical allusions, with full rhymes and the accentual-syllabic alexandrines pioneered in Dutch by Jan van der Noot in the 1560s and 1570s. The personal and the political cheerfully intertwine.[1] Aside from being an affectionate poetic souvenir of a journey Huygens was to make several more times in his life, the comparison with Arion celebrates Huygens' own skills on the lute. Moreover, the diplomat was set to charm the English court and intellectual society, soothing the waters of international relations. He was sufficiently successful that he was knighted in 1622 by James I; John Evelyn mentions him in his diary (during one of Huygens' later trips) as 'old Monsieur *Zulichem* (Secretary to the *Prince* of *Orange* & an excellent Lat: Poet, & now neere 80 years of age, a rare Lutinist)'.[2]

Clearly the sonnet was treasured; Huygens published it in his own *Otia* in 1625. It is an example of the flourishing Dutch literature of the seventeenth century, and of the confident exchange of culture between the United Provinces and England. For contemporary readers the crossing would have been well-known, and the boon of safe travel over the rough North Sea readily understood. Yet beyond this, the joy with which Huygens is setting out on his diplomatic mission is palpable; perhaps Hooft had in mind that the English were also to be charmed and calmed.

Relations between these two countries could be as temperamental in the early modern period as the waters between them, as mercantile rivals, co-religionists, allies, and enemies. This book sets out to address two lacunae in existing scholarship, both related to crossings such as the ones that Huygens made: first, it contributes to a further understanding of mutual Anglo-Dutch cultural influence in the period, which was a natural consequence of the nations' complex interactions in politics, trade, and knowledge. It places especial emphasis on literature in various forms, though it encompasses many different expressions of culture, and further studies into other cultural production could be equally revealing. Literature plays an important role in national identity and is therefore both my grounding discipline and ripe for re-assessment. The traditional grammar-school narrative of English literature inheriting the classical authors of Rome and Athens, with perhaps some allowance for French or Italian influence along the way, is both outmoded and impoverishing. With a contextualised account of literature and its contributing factors, I explore how ideas, texts, individuals and images crossed back and forth between England and the United Provinces, creating fertile soil for thinkers and writers of all stripes. Second, the canonical English authors John Milton and Andrew Marvell allow me to focus this broader ambition through specific texts and events. Showing previously overlooked Dutch influences in their works – sometimes subtle or disguised, sometimes explicit or stereotypical – enhances our appreciation. Rather than cutting these wonderful writers off from their connections in the name of a nationalist literary project, a transnational approach such as this opens them out to a much wider world, just as they saw it themselves.

The Premise of This Book

Naturally, the choice of Milton and Marvell as my key figures is not arbitrary. Milton, perhaps more powerful a voice than any other in English literature, at times regarded as the very bedrock of its poetry, was nonetheless an international figure. His prose tracts were translated and discussed all over Europe, and he was a key figure in Cromwell's government. While his poetic output seems so self-sufficient as to stand in glorious isolation from quotidian concerns, they are in fact inseparable. In the chapters that follow I will discuss how matters of Dutch religious debate, global trade, kingship, and the publishing industry all left their traces; simultaneously, this presents Milton's own impact on Dutch intellectual life.

Marvell is to some extent the opposite case. A great deal of his political output only makes sense if placed in its proper context. Satirical caricatures and allusions, wry observations on political topics, and attempts to find middle ground between extremes abound. Yet there remains much to do in making this context sufficiently transnational, since so much of his commentary responds to international events and experiences, particularly with the Dutch. As well as his own travels, interest in the fishing trade, and government work during the Anglo-Dutch Wars, Marvell reveals some parallels of literary endeavour, taking up forms and themes also popular among Dutch writers.

Other writers provide additional material for the perspective put forward here. John Dryden's patriotic satires and Edmund Waller's panegyrics are all exploited at times in this book, while numerous Dutch authors, including Constantijn Huygens, Joost van den Vondel, P.C. Hooft, and Tesselschade Roemer, responded to English life and art, sometimes directly. Of course, it is not my argument that Milton and Marvell are unique cases of Dutch influence, nor that they responded only to what was happening in the United Provinces. Rather, they operate as rich exemplars for an ampler treatment of literature and culture in an approach that suggests rewarding new readings of their art; we have much to gain and little to lose. One simple such profit is the provision of some new translations, since several Dutch early modern writers remain largely untranslated into English, making them inaccessible to many international readers. By exhibiting their merits and influence, I hope to stimulate wider interest in Dutch poets and poems of the highest quality.

There could have been many ways to structure this investigation, whether by looking at each author or key text in turn, or through a chronology of Anglo-Dutch relations on the macro scale. Ultimately, however, since the degrees of connection between the countries are so multifarious and fluid, it has proven most effective to treat specific themes or issues as the focus, interweaving points of connection with Milton and Marvell throughout. Each chapter takes as its starting point a certain aspect of the Anglo-Dutch sphere, expanding to discuss the literary ramifications of, for example, religious toleration, propaganda pamphlets, travel diaries, printing culture, Arminianism, cookery books, republicanism, naval law, divine providence, and herring. Milton and Marvell incorporate into their poetry conflicts with the Dutch, the impact of Dutch religious and political tracts, Dutch stereotypes that were continuously recycled throughout the seventeenth century, and their personal encounters with Dutch people or society. Understanding these integrations of their own composite experience may be crucial to a clearer picture of their writing. It may also, as I will argue, make the case for an Anglo-Dutch cultural sphere that was sufficiently intermingled at times to be regarded as a joint entity.

Anglo-Dutch Relations in the Sixteenth and Seventeenth Centuries

Huygens' crossing may have been deemed worthy of commemoration by Hooft, but it was by no means an isolated event. Though his business was unique to himself, he was only part of the dense traffic of merchants, artisans, messengers, travellers, students, refugees, intellectuals, actors, soldiers, and churchmen ploughing this route in one direction or the other.[3]

Great numbers of Dutch people emigrated to England throughout the sixteenth and seventeenth centuries, becoming London's greatest alien population by the early seventeenth century.[4] This was partly the result of the Dutch struggle for independence from Iberian rule. The Dutch Republic was officially founded with the signing of the Union of Utrecht (1579), after which the provinces of Holland, Zeeland, Utrecht, Gelderland, the majority of Friesland, Overijssel and Stad en Ommelanden, agreed to support each other in the war against Spain. From this point onwards, the Low Countries were divided into a free Protestant North – the United Provinces (now called the Netherlands) – and an occupied Roman-Catholic South – the Spanish Netherlands (now Flanders and parts of Northern France). Although perhaps not many people outside the Low Countries understood the politics of this division, it became evident in the 1580s that some sort of separation had taken place.[5] Kingdoms such as France and England acknowledged the Dutch Republic as a separate nation in the years following the Union of Utrecht, but it was not until the Twelve Years' Truce with Spain (1609–1621) that the latter partially acknowledged Dutch independence, followed by full recognition in the Peace Treaty of Münster (1648).[6] Since their greatest rivals and allies in Europe at the time were the old established monarchies – England, France, and Spain – becoming a monarchy appeared the logical model for the new Dutch state to follow.[7] After the assassination of their war-leader William of Orange by the Catholic Balthasar Gerards, rulership was offered to Queen Elizabeth.[8] She declined, however, as the expense of warfare with Spain outweighed the potential advantages of expanding her territories and power. The Dutch constitution consequently remained republican, with the States General as its general body politic, but the provincial states remained the supreme powers.[9]

Though the cautious and impecunious Elizabeth declined the offer of extending her kingdom, she was sympathetic to the Protestant Dutch cause and – somewhat like the Drakean buccaneers at sea – tolerated English adventurers taking part in the war against the Spanish. Some famous names went to the Netherlands, such as John Evelyn, Fynes Moryson, and George Gascoigne.[10] The attitude towards such voluntary service in the Netherlands was varied, and the alliance between the two nations a carefully managed balance of partnership and distance.[11] The image of rebellion that the seven provinces manifested could present a risk to the still-fragile Protestant State in England, so direct support for challenges to authority could not be endorsed. At the same time, however, a significant body of English and Scottish Protestants believed that a nation under the suppression of Catholic Spain should be assisted in their struggle. Well-known aristocrats, such as Philip Sidney and Francis de Vere, lost their lives whilst protecting the Protestant nation of the Dutch Republic, which was regarded as a national sacrifice. In the early seventeenth century, Moryson voiced the not uncommon view that the Dutch were thus in England's debt and – clearly mixing mutual martial pride with uncertainty about the longer-term outcome of this war – that they ought to be accommodating of England's growing trading empire, even where it was in competition with their own: 'if the Dutch with their powerful fleet decided to forget their old league with England [. . .] then such bloody fights at sea [were] like to happen as former ages never knew'.[12] Little did Moryson know that this sentiment would come so vividly to fruition in the second half of the seventeenth century.

Within a couple of decades, the Dutch nation and their powerful fleet had in fact attained world supremacy in terms of trade, an achievement that becomes only more remarkable when considering that the Dutch Republic was fighting a home war, and had virtually no natural resources, little territory, and a small population.[13] The success stemmed from a unique mixture of mercantile opportunism, intellectual and social plasticity, and geography – above all the convenient location of the United Provinces, with sea access, great rivers for transportation, and direct land access to other European nations. In effect, the Dutch became Europe's warehouse and distribution centre for incoming global goods.[14] Fernand Braudel has argued that the Dutch riches and their position as Europe's entrepôt (along with other rising nations in the early Renaissance) emerged through their domination of bulk-carrying trade from the Baltic, which would later develop into rich trades.[15] Jonathan Israel has alternatively suggested that the Dutch world trade primacy could be explained through their involvement in ferrying high-value products from the beginning, especially from the Baltic.[16] However the trajectory towards dominance is described, the Dutch were, within a remarkably few years, sharing and competing in all areas of trade, from essential heavy-duty materials to exotic luxuries. The sudden rise led to admiration, sometimes envy, and often hostility from their neighbours. This mixture of reactions was compounded in the trade relations between England and the United Provinces, which ultimately led to three Anglo-Dutch wars within a period of 30 years.

This book will follow some of the major developments in Anglo-Dutch relations, broadly considered, of the seventeenth century. Pamphlets of stunning invention and vitriol were published by both sides during the Anglo-Dutch Wars, some of which are discussed in Chapter 1. Similarly, poetry and drama included stock characters, or directly satirised both countries. This was greatly assisted by the flourishing exchange of printed texts within and between nations, stimulated by the unusually open attitude to printing and publication taken by the authorities in the United Provinces. This direct influence is clearly present in literature of the period, as studies such as those by Marjorie Rubright and Helmer Helmers have shown.[17] This book will also heed some of the subtler but equally important interactions, and their manifestations in literature.

As mentioned, there were great numbers of Dutch immigrants, often refugees, in England at the time; in its turn, the United Provinces was a haven for royalists during the English Republic, and for republicans during the Restoration, in addition to many who plied their trade between the two nations. Such emigres inevitably brought with them their traditions, politics, and beliefs, affecting their integration and acceptance. On the larger scale, the Arminian controversy shook Northern Europe, and was nowhere more keenly felt than in the United Provinces and England. Fluctuating sympathies for royalism and republicanism were also central to the repeated fracturing and mending of Anglo-Dutch relations. Both countries were striving to achieve political stability and, at times, used the very same arguments to support and condemn challenges to power – in the United Provinces during the Eighty Years' War, and in England during the Civil Wars. These and other factors were re-hashed and replayed during the three Anglo-Dutch Wars, of which trading rivalry was a major cause, but certainly not the only one. These complex developments are all small pieces of an enormous puzzle mapping out Anglo-Dutch relations. It is consequently to some extent necessary to limit ourselves to a coherent stretch of time. Milton was born in 1608, and Marvell died in 1678. These extremities encompass most of the key events discussed in this book, though their roots and causes beyond this will also be addressed. The poets' working years, roughly 1630 to the 1670s, also approximately coincide with the flashpoints of conflict that brought differences into sharp relief: the First Anglo-Dutch War (1652–4) at one end, and the Third (1672–4) at the other.

Imagology

This is a study of connections between the Dutch as a people – their culture, literature, politics, and religion – and the works and lives of Milton and Marvell. In part this will concern the poets' personal experiences, but also the images and ideas that were current in their social and professional orbits, and how they reflected these back in their writing. To a certain degree, it will therefore be an investigation of how a range of images or representations could be adopted, alluded to, or reshaped to the needs of a specific text or audience. Literature, especially when it makes a critique of, or contribution to, public discourse, will naturally draw on images already available to its readers, though whether it exaggerates or undermines the images varies. Though far from exhaustive of the literary qualities of a text (as later discussions will amply illustrate), a concentration on representation can be rewarding in comparative readings. In this case, how the English and the Dutch looked at one another can be equally informative about how they saw themselves, or wanted to. With a complicated shared history, and at a time when both nations were striving to establish their place in a newly expanded world, it is no wonder that they portrayed each other continuously and variously, acting as mirrors, provocations, invitations, and self-justifications.

It has been a useful focus for this book to proceed with what might be called an *imagological method*, complementing a *transnational framework*. Building national identities plays an important part in both Milton and Marvell, as do other aspects of identity. Imagology provides some of the vital theoretical basis for the study of this process of representing the other and oneself at all scales – from the individual to the transnational. Joep Leerssen and Hugo Dyserinck define imagology as the critical study of the use of national characters (ethnotypes) or more general articulations specific to a particular nation or region and its people, as subjective narrative tropes or images.[18] Literature can be seen as just such an expression of culture, in turn driven by community and location. Instances where this relation between literature and community come to the fore in Marvell and Milton provide the skeleton for my analysis.

A good introduction to this method will be to look at the closely connected concepts of image, imagination, character, and stereotype. Chapter 1 goes straight to the most immediately apparent reproduction of stereotyped images, and tours some of the depictions of the Dutch that populated English pamphlets during the seventeenth century. It is important to note, though, that the image as construed in imagology is not limited to physical pictures, which are only one way of conveying an image. Individual depictions may be graphic, textual, performative or linguistic, but 'the image' is the abstraction of many such instances to form 'the mental silhouette of the other, who appears to be determined by the characteristics of family, group, tribe, people, and race'.[19] Any given representation may partake of some part of this silhouette but there is no one quality that all must share, nor a single ur-image from which the others are descended; it is, appropriately enough, what Ludwig Wittgenstein called a 'family-resemblance' concept: not one defining characteristic shared by all, but a range of traits distributed amongst different yet connected examples.[20] This looseness of connection is important for the kind of analysis this book attempts, since the images produced are rarely exact copies, and the point of them – their predictability as well as their creativity – is to work on several different associations, sometimes at once. There is no single essence behind them, but instead a pattern of echoes from many sources. One such example is explored in Chapters 3 and 6, in which Milton and Joost van den Vondel, despite no evidence of direct intertextuality, employ the same biblical narratives and draw on similar highly politicised stereotypes, while nonetheless harnessing them to strongly contrasting polemics.

I have further incorporated a set of related concepts familiar from the later Wittgenstein's work, which stresses both repetition and variation in the creation of significance.[21] Why is repetition important here? Simply because the stereotype is never a one-off – it is the culmination of many uses, each time adapting to a new context or intention. Further, repetition does not presume direct influence or copying. It may be the coming together of several different strands in which ideas are picked up, conflated, and elaborated on, or similar ideas may recur without any obvious connection; sometimes shared associations are sucked into the orbit of a particular stereotype. The supposed origins of the images matter but often less than the effectiveness of their re-application, which comes from their familiarity and portability.[22]

As this illustrates, stereotypes gain their impact by becoming part of a society's verbal currency; individual applications reflect and amplify what is already latent in everyday interactions. In the images we discuss here, it is the interaction both between images and the communities or groups that produce them that reveals their significance. What a particular image means is closely related to the context in which it was made or expressed, as well as its purpose. The 'author' of the image may be consciously creating new associations or biases but may (simultaneously) be simply repeating what has been passed on before, without any intent or awareness of the status or weighting of the image. They may also be repeating images as part of their genre's stock-in-trade, without reference to any other specific text. I argue for such an instance in Chapter 3: Marvell and Constantijn Huygens both wrote a country house poem at the same time, relying on the same images that the genre provided, without any necessary knowledge of each other's poetical endeavours.

Images may therefore be related by their qualities, their application, or both, without necessitating the possibility that all the instances could be reduced to a coherent whole. A silhouette is a shadowy outline; it may shift in different lights, or against different backgrounds.[23] In short, inherent in the use of a stereotype is a perspective, often including a call for the viewer to see things from this same position.[24] This aspect of perspective is important, since for the imagologist studying representations, factual reports are no more than the scaffold on which images can be built. Statements, such as "the Dutch national colour is orange", play no part in the motivation of the imagologist, which is to discern a second skin of moral or characterological representations.[25] There is no neutrality here; the best hope of it may lie in tracing and re-tracing the different outlines of the silhouettes encountered to find their common curvatures – the pressures to which they are responding. An image is usually produced for a specific purpose, but the cause of it being imagined and the purposes behind its repetition may be strikingly different.

It is accordingly always important to retain an awareness of the purpose for which, or context within which, an image has been produced. It cannot be treated as neutral representations of reality, since it will have been informed by cultural bigotry, favouritism, or value judgments, whether this involves exaggeration, occlusion, or simple invention to depict the target in the appropriate light. Anti-Dutch or anti-English pamphlets produced on either side of the channel, inventing demonic creation myths for one another during the first three Anglo-Dutch Wars, are a case in point. To this extent, the study of images is less an examination of the depictions themselves than the subjectivities that prompted and produced them. This innate subjectivity is where the interest lies for imagologists, because it is exactly here that claims about the Other become simultaneously defences of, or ideas about, oneself.[26] The imagologist's task is accordingly a delicate one, aspiring to a relatively neutral and rational treatment of images, without excluding the subjectivity that produced them, or reducing them to a supposedly objective theorisation; a combination of close and contextualised reading seeks to understand the work being done by the images, both inward and outward looking.

Portraying the Other has always been a popular trope in literature. We can find oppositional descriptions of people in the earliest forms of literature.[27] Manfred Beller gives the example of Aeschylus (480 BC) describing the Persians as a barbarous people.[28] The binary that is proposed in these literary representations is a simple one: through negative representations of other people, self-valorisation is achieved. Though straightforward, it is immensely powerful. In Immanuel Kant's *Observation on the Feeling of the Beautiful and Sublime* (translated from *Beobachtungen über das Gefühl des Schönen und Erhabenen*, 1764), the last section, 'Of National Characteristics, so far as they Depend upon the Distinct Feeling of the Beautiful and Sublime', offers a list of characteristics per nation; the Frenchman, the Italian, the Spaniard, the German, the Dutchman, and the Englishman all get a turn. 'The Dutchman is of an orderly and diligent disposition and, as he looks solely to the useful, he has little feeling for what in the finer understanding is beautiful or sublime', whereas the Englishman is 'a bad imitator, cares very little about what others judge, and follows solely his own taste'.[29] This is only one example of a commonplace application of stereotypes from different parts of Europe, with a grand tradition in all kinds of literature. Perhaps *Candide ou l'Optimisme* (1759), Voltaire's riotous tour of all the world's received ideas twisted into cruelties and calamities, is the finest satire in this tradition.[30] And yet Kant, writing almost at the same time, is able to yoke these character types to serious philosophical speculation. It is a curious facet of these enduring stereotypes that we can at the same time ridicule and believe them. They reduce the characteristics of a people to a very small number, so they become instantly recognisable as representative for a particular group, every time they are used. Kant's description of the characteristics per nation, supposedly fixing their relationship to the beautiful and the sublime, continues in the tradition of Julius Caesar Scaliger's *Poetices libri septem* (1561).[31] This work lists the most significant characteristics per people. Scaliger's *Poetics* was hugely influential, and its deep traces can be found in many texts – both erudite and vulgar. Crucially, these always have a moral foundation, which to some degree explains their attraction to Kant: Germans are greedy and the English lazy.[32]

National character (I use this term interchangeably with ethnotype) merits some further development. It should not be confused with nationalism. Nationalism as we now know it is a development of the last four hundred years, and far more mutable than is often assumed. As Leerssen has shown in *National Thought in Europe* (1999), only in the fifteenth and sixteenth centuries was 'Europe [. . .] becoming a modular system of separate states, each with recognizable territory, language and profile'.[33] Complex processes, such as the rise of vernacular language (including through standardised Bible translations), printing presses that made texts more widely available, and the development of cartography, all assisted with this notion of what it meant to be of a certain people or region. When I use the concept of national identity in this book, it is not with the sense of twentieth-century nationalism, but rather as 'national specificity within a European spectrum'.[34] This national identity is constructed, not natural, a consequence of inevitable comparison, rivalry, and shared historical memory.[35] Imagology does not theorise identity as a concept, but focuses instead on a theorising of cultural and national stereotypes. This means it is not a sociological approach; it is not used to understand the workings or opinions of a society at large, but rather look into (often individual) representations, or the processes and repetitions of these representations.

In addition to the embedding function of meaning through repetition mentioned previously, an essential aspect of these ethnotypes is the swift impression they make on a knowing audience. They fix through reassertion a particular combination of traits, however fabulous or contradictory. The English calling the Dutch 'butterboxes' or 'cheeseheads' reveals and invites a whole range of associations with the phlegmatic, dairy-obsessed Netherlanders. The etymology of 'character' as a mark impressed or engraved onto a surface not only recalls how it is something that can be imposed on one (rather than expressed from within) but is particularly apt for this book's discussion of the age of the printing press and the written word.[36]

The connection with theatre is also telling, where the 'characters' for much of the art-form's history were recurring, recognisable types, rather than realistic individuals. In his *Poetics* (c. 335 BC) Aristotle had already proposed that types of characters in drama should always be imminently recognisable.[37] Just as a character in a script (or typeface) must be instantly recognisable for a print to be legible, the character as representative for a group or type of person(s) needs to be recognisable. The idea of sketching fixed characters was taken up by Theophrastus, student of Aristotle, who collected types of satirical characters based on people he witnessed in Athens.[38]

The influence of Aristotle's (and later Scaliger's) *Poetics* was marked in Tudor and Stuart drama. The use of stock characters was an easy way of anticipating plot developments or creating running comic effects in the play.[39] Thomas Dekker's *The Shoemaker's Holiday* (1599), for example, uses the conventions of a stock character by masking the main character as a Dutch shoemaker called Hans, who speaks with a strange accent. Similarly, names of other countries opened up quick possibilities of evoking this package of characteristics. The lowness of the Netherlands (as reflected in the name) also points to the moral character of the Dutch, which must similarly be base. Shakespeare's *The Comedy of Errors* employs the satirical value of the name and geography of the Low Countries:

Antipholus of Syracuse: And where stood Belgia, the Netherlands?
Dromio of Syracuse: Oh, sir, I did not look so low.

(III. ii. 142–143)

Thomas Middleton and Thomas Dekker's comedy *The Roaring Girl* (1611) contains several puns on the Low Countries, such as Mistress Openwork's reference to the Low Countries as the basest part of the body: 'I send you for Hollands, and you're I'th'low countries with a mischief' (II. i. 120). This was based on another pun in Shakespeare's *Henry IV, Part II*, made by Prince Harry to Poins: 'Because the rest of thy low/ countries have made a shift to eat up thy holland' (II. ii. 21–22). The examples here from the late sixteenth and early seventeenth century mock the Dutch character and consequently elevate the English; the reverse would also happen in the later seventeenth and eighteenth centuries, where foreign characters by contrast highlight English inadequacies, such as in Jonathan Swift's *Gulliver's Travels* (1726). As Ton Hoenselaars has shown, although this reversal did take place between the morality of the foreign or the English characters, they still stayed within this strict, limited idea of Aristotle's unity and his characters.[40] As ever, playwrights were quick to recognise comic or tragic value in these ethnic tropes, and making fun of neighbours has never lost its appeal. One only has to think of twentieth-century TV shows such as '*Allo, 'Allo*, the comic books of *Asterix and Obelix*, or indeed the 2013 *Royal Shakespeare Company's* modernising twist on *Candide*.[41]

Of course, there is no definite point when stock characters like these escape their particular narratives and become recognisable as stereotypes – at once less concrete and less anchored, where a byword or single characteristic can contain a whole supposed identity. It may reasonably be said that repetition and reapplication dull the sharper edges of the silhouette to a cruder shape, within which a few choice features are enough. (This is not to argue that stock characters are in any way logically prior to a stereotype, merely to mark a possible direction of travel.) In this combination of relative simplicity and swift identification the cliché, or stereotype, is central to the study of imagology.[42] Its subject is a mass reproduction rather than a one-off sketch. Fittingly, the origins of the word are also linked to printing, and can be read as a mechanised extension of the meaning of 'character' noted previously: '[t]he method or process of printing in which a solid plate of type-metal, cast from a papier-mâché or plaster mould taken from the surface of a forme of type, is used for printing from instead of the forme itself'.[43] The plate reproduces the same print in the same way each time, leading to a series of identical representations. This is the inherent nature of the stereotype: a reproduction of the same image of certain persons, people, nations, and so forth, until it becomes a coherent package of characteristics to be whipped out when a definite audience response is called for. Although stereotypes can appear static, especially when reproduced myriad times within a short space of time, from a more historical perspective they are by no means fixed.

Some stereotypes, especially when they refer to a big group of people, can have a long duration: the connection between temperature and temperament, for example. The hotter the climate in which the people live, the more fiery their temperament, and vice versa. This idea has been around for at least four hundred years, and likely centuries before that. Other stereotypes have fluctuated more rapidly. Images are often recycled, but change over time, or suddenly shift in the face of events. English representations of the Dutch in the seventeenth century are a case in point, marking satan. In the early seventeenth century, the English assisted the Dutch in their struggle against the Spanish, supporting co-religionists against a common foe. After the execution of Charles I in 1649 and over the years culminating in the First Anglo-Dutch War (1652–1654), relations deteriorated, but not into simple antagonism.[44] During this short period, the nations had established a geo-political proximity that encroached on the usual material for war propaganda: two budding maritime trading empires, both anti-Spanish Protestant republics, yet unable to establish a comfortable co-existence. Unlike the old Catholic or monarchical enemy, with ready-made accusations of popish corruption or tyrannical rule, opposition of good and evil had to be established on new grounds. Those differences that could be found were emphasised and exaggerated, as we will see in Chapter 1. Later, during the two subsequent Anglo-Dutch wars in the Restoration period, many of the same images and texts were recycled or updated: elements remained, others became less convenient or effective. A very neat present-day illustration of this agility of the propagandist would be the cartoons in *The Onion's* 'Our Dumb Century' (1999), in which the virtue of the Lady of Liberty is repeatedly assailed by whichever foreign power the US happened to be fighting that year.[45] Ultimately, stereotypes must be studied in their context to be fully understood, including their staying-power and flexibility.[46]

The fluidity of the stereotype is in many ways closely connected to the fluidity of the term given to each group it signifies. In the sixteenth and seventeenth centuries it was, for example, not quite clear what the term 'Dutch' referred to. It could refer to people who inhabited the Low Countries, which would include the Southern Netherlands; or it could also refer only to people in the Northern provinces. Dutch was also used to refer to Low Dutch people, who lived anywhere in the United Provinces, Low Countries, or even in the German Empire. What connected this use? At first glance it ought to be the language of (high or low) Dutch/ Deutsch. But even here the complexities continue, as several languages and dialects have been given this name in different periods. 'Dutch', far from uniquely, could shift its meaning over time, even carrying different and contradictory implications simultaneously. Similarly, the common (derogatory) term for people of other nationalities can shift. The English have used the epithet 'frog' to mean the French, the Dutch or the Spanish at various points in history, though seemingly not simultaneously. The reasons for the transference are largely mysterious, though they do reflect English preoccupations at the time – in other words, the fluidity of the group signified may be as much a factor of the image-builder as the subject of them. Manfred Beller suggests that, '[a]s a result of their concentration on one-sided (and often false) information, stereotypes provide formulaic communication aids; but they obtain their strongest effects in the propagation of cross-national hate figures'.[47] However, these cross-national boundaries may shift in and out of focus as circumstances demand; much like national boundaries to this day the catchment of stereotypes and their language is largely artificial, being as often a feature of administrative agreements as the supposed character of an area's occupants. As we will discuss shortly, the 'one-sided' nature applies only to the explicit aspect of the stereotype, whereas the implicit aspect – that against which we define ourselves – can be a revealing reflection.

Stereotypes are not truthful, but are often treated as such. Our capacity to recognise their exaggerations and conflations, and yet act on them as if regarding them as accurate is the mainstay of their power. The dumb blonde, the fiery redhead, the demure (or evil) brunette: none of us believe in the magical properties of hair dye, yet we have learned to decode what such representations signify; we do it almost without noticing.[48] Partly this comes from the stereotype's resistance to complexity, preferring binaries and generalities. Simplicity is quick and easy, and the repetitions of the types become an obstacle to finer distinctions and reflection.

Leerssen has taken this binary nature as constitutive of ethnotypes: 'they evoke Self-Other oppositions (auto-image vs. hetero-images; ethnocentrism vs. exoticism or xenophobia)'.[49] However, such a strong dichotomy is tied to the Cartesian model of the ego that he uses to illustrate the differentiation – whatever is 'out there' is not me, and I am its opposite. There are limitations to this conception that if left unanswered would be problematic for the imagologist's work. Although a dualist model appears a straight fit for the them/ us form of much stereotyping, it fails to be able to explain how the images change over time; the 'I' must be receptive as well as repelling. Knowledge of oneself is a dialectic with others, a constant play of recognition, difference, rebuff, and reconciliation. In other words, a stereotype may be constructed as 'one-sided' but always carries within it the implicit reflection; the reason (however much repressed or taken for granted) for attributing characteristics to another group is closely connected with one's own self-image, anxiety, or preoccupation.

The changing image of the Dutch, which will be explored in several chapters here, was often a mirror back onto English concerns; the stereotype shifted and self-images shifted with it. It would be simplistic to look for a single causal relation here, which a truly one-sided oppositional view would encourage. Instead, stereotypes, despite their reductive nature, exist only within a complicated web of layered identities, including similarities, tensions, revulsions, hierarchies, and pragmatic goals. Multiple stereotypes may be attributed to the same group simultaneously (the English gentleman and the football hooligan); caricatures can be both positive and negative (German humourlessness yet extreme punctuality); a Dutchman can be viewed as a Westerner, a Northerner, a Germanic, or any number of different types. And the choices of who to tar with which brush, and when, can often be most revealing of the image-maker. Imagology constitutes this step back from the image to see it in context – an interplay of meanings, power and needs – and to trace the shape of the mirror in which it is held.

This provisional and specific attitude towards images is both a tightening of focus and a reduction of scale; it prefers detailed observation and the overlaying of different patterns to broader generalisations. We do not need to perform detailed analysis on the stereotypes – we know what they are – but can gain much from thinking about particular applications. Consequently, this book does not endeavour to measure the English 'public opinion' on the Dutch via the works of Milton and Marvell. The sample is too small for this, nor is the study of imagology intended for such an approach.[50] Instead the interest lies in the rhetorical representation of the image in literary (and quasi-literary) texts. Pamphlets and poetry, political and religious tracts, letters and drama will be used to trace the pathways of imagological rhetoric, as ideas of identity connect, combust or proliferate. To paraphrase the poet Paul Muldoon, history's twisted root can help us to understand art's 'small, translucent fruit'.[51]

Transnationalism

This emphasis on the literary representation of a national image or character has found its most natural place in comparative studies, mostly the result of Hugo Dyserinck's work in Aachen during the 1960s and later, in his Aachen Programme of Comparatism.[52] Over later decades, Leerssen continued the study of imagology in Amsterdam, focusing on the study of literary national images. In recent years, however, imagology has found another fertile ground, namely in the emergence of transnationalism, to which this study belongs.[53]

Transnationalism is a research approach of many strands, insisting on the incorporation of structures and subject matters that traverse or problematise national borders. The conception I employ in this book includes consciousness of the developing contexts of cultural production at different scales, stressing the importance of original-language readings, and recognising how supra-national networks and events, including trade, war, and politics, shape intellectual history and the arts. Early modern transnational research elsewhere has concentrated on networks such as diplomacy, the Republic of Letters, or the development of international law, with gains in mapping European and global interrelations. A significant element of its perspective is the dismantling of romantic or nationalistic stories of isolated groups or individuals, by showing previously invisible connections, influence, and telling echoes. The benefit of my specifically transnational-imagological approach is the possibility of reading texts of many different types as criss-crossing the landscape of a shared but contested Anglo-Dutch sphere. Rather than relying on narrow lines of direct textual reference, such as quotation or imitation, we may place texts within a field of diverse and developing images, relations, concepts, and societal 'moods'. The image is informative through its distortions and mutations as well as its transference.

This means that a transnational approach can be both highly sympathetic to imagology, and yet in tension with it, since the latter focuses on the character of a group or region in opposition to another, where the former might encourage the uncovering of similarity or contact. As the brief discussion earlier has suggested, these two ideas are not mutually exclusive. Antagonism is specific rather than binary, and expresses itself as much through connections as through difference; networks depend on a degree of cooperation but are far from homogenous or symmetrical, and may transmit clashes and stereotypes as easily as factual reports or goods. Understanding the construction of images through boundary crossing and the nature of shared intellectual space through the representations it throws up, facilitates a rounded, contextually alert reading of both specific texts and their generic or cultural position.

Accordingly, the chapters ahead do not seek to provide a linear or exhaustive bibliographical overview of instances in which Dutch influence can be asserted in Milton and Marvell, though these markers can often be important. This would create a no-doubt interesting catalogue, but would be an adjustment of small details, rather than opening the texts to thrilling new readings. Instead, the ambition is to follow a number of important strands or themes to create a background that extends beyond national or linguistic bounds. Against this backdrop can be placed changing politics and attitudes, the development of metaphor and other literary tools, moral and intellectual debates, moments of exchange and collision, travel, and invention. Each of these can be seen to have left its mark on the lives and works of our central poets, caught up in a web of intellectual and material production. Chapter 5, for example, traces the influence of the Arminian debate that gripped Northern European Protestantism throughout the seventeenth century and argues that without seeing the distinct English and Dutch forms that Arminianism took – as well as Milton's access to texts from both strands – our readings of key passages are likely to be skewed.

The unpicking of these marks explains or disarms a number of images – those of the early modern period and our own time – not least the gradually outmoded idea of the 'national' author or poet. Here are texts that speak of, and through, the churning ideas of their time, which passed across geographical and cultural boundaries into a wider European, and indeed global, context.

Chapters of This Book

Milton's and Marvell's biographies as much as their literary work make them useful to the imagological-transnational approach taken, since they were both heavily involved in public and political life during key moments of the seventeenth century. Rather than placing a specific historical event or network at its centre, as some other transnational research has done, I attempt to set out the multifarious nature of Anglo-Dutch relations through two culturally important lives.[54] This is partly a refusal to reduce either the texts or their authors to simply another, differently positioned, characterisation; there is no one opinion or style or influence that defines Milton or

Marvell, any more than there is a simple definition of Anglo-Dutch relations. Trading disagreements with the Dutch, controversial religious doctrines that spread through Europe, the Republic of Letters, the flourishing printing industry and its dissemination of texts, and the contagion of certain political events, were all ingredients in their poetry and prose. The chapter outlines that follow suggest the main topics covered, but there is a lot of interlinking between them, with Dutch writers, interlocutors, or politics making themselves felt in diverse ways. Some chapters will naturally lean more heavily on Milton's works than Marvell's, or vice versa.

Because of this lens, the book predominantly focuses on Dutch presence in English culture where it has previously been unnoticed or undervalued. It would not give due credit to the complexity of Anglo-Dutch relations if the other side of the story, namely the English in the United Provinces, were to be ignored, and several valuable studies have proven the importance of such acknowledgement.[55] Where my discussion allows I have attempted to show both sides of this coin, though it is acknowledged that one face is paid greater attention than the other for reasons of coherence; perhaps the imbalance can be corrected in a subsequent book.

Chapter 1 does a certain quantity of scene-setting on the individual level, by discussing Milton's and Marvell's personal associations with the United Provinces. Both authors travelled on the Continent at various points, though while Marvell spent a considerable time in the Netherlands, Milton restricted his journey to France, Italy, and Geneva. Yet from Milton's prose works, we know that he met with the Dutch intellectual colossus Hugo de Groot (Grotius) in Paris. Currently, we have little evidence of Marvell meeting with known Dutch individuals, though there are clues. In a little-consulted volume of transcribed Dutch foreign correspondence, tantalisingly titled *Secret Correspondence*, a certain Mr Marvell is reported as visiting Ambassador Willem Nieuwpoort in 1659.[56] This can only be our Andrew Marvell and reveals an intriguing area for further research into Marvell's dealings with the Dutch in the late 1650s (and 1660s). More broadly, we have reasons to believe he learned something of the language and culture during his travels. This chapter uses an assessment of the probable Dutch language skills of both authors to establish their connections with the country and its people, examine their engagement with anti-Dutch pamphlets, and look anew at some linguistic ambiguities in selected works.

After political communications and travel, the workings of printing culture form the backbone of Chapter 2. The complicated publication history of Milton's Latin *First Defence* (1651), and responses to it, illustrates a competitive, agile, personal, and sometimes underhand culture of printing and dissemination. Dutch printers and publishers played an important role in the reception of Milton's tracts, allowing him to target a European audience. As Dutch printing houses created a transnational network to produce and market their texts, intellectuals of every stripe and location could contribute to, or comment on, any controversy.

Chapter 3 provides an example of the kind of indirect intertextuality that my imagological-transnational approach allows for. Two apparently parallel but unrelated poems illustrate the ceaseless intellectual exchange between England and the Netherlands, even at times of great tension: Marvell's *Upon Appleton House* (1651) and Huygens' *Hofwyck* (1651). While noting some further kinship with other Dutch authors, such as Joost van den Vondel and Hugo Grotius, the chapter also discusses echoes within Milton's *Paradise Lost* that seem more the result of an overlapping context of production than direct textual influence.

Recent studies, such as those by Freya Sierhuis, have shown the impact of Arminianism on the literary scene of the United Provinces.[57] When the Arminian debate spread to other countries in Northern Europe, it became naturalised and often changed considerably. Chapter 4 disentangles the often-missed differences between English and Dutch Arminianism, and how these were expressed in Milton's and Marvell's prose works. Religious toleration in relation to Arminianism provides the framework for an investigation of Marvell's poetry, *Remarks* (1678), and *Rehearsal Transpros'd*, and *Rehearsal Transpros'd; the Second Part*, (1673) and Milton's tolerationist tracts.

Chapter 5 extends the discussion of Arminianism and its English and Dutch forms, showing the centrality of this pan-European debate to the evolution of Milton's religious thinking. The labyrinthine debates surrounding predestination, free will, and grace are traced in conjunction with Milton's *Samson Agonistes* (1671). The narrative of Samson was a popular source of adaptations in the period, lending itself to contrasting understandings of election, fate, and faith. Discussion of Arminianism is less prominent in Marvell's poetry, but his prose works reveal his characteristically moderate, if perhaps under-defined, responses to nonconformity, toleration, and doctrinal quarrels.

Any extended discussion of English and Dutch culture of the seventeenth century would need to address the pressing issues of kingship and authority that had shaped so much of the political and constitutional landscape of both countries. Chapter 6 again turns to *Samson Agonistes*, but reads it this time as the struggle to define righteous authority and challenges to power. Both the United Provinces and England went through revolts in the seventeenth century, and this inevitably found its way into the literature of the period. *Samson Agonistes* is placed side by side with Vondel's *Samson, of Heilige Wraak* (Samson, or Holy Revenge, 1660). Both texts are to some extent commentaries on possible justifications of revolt, layering the biblical narrative with questions of national identity, divine authority, and representations of moral power.

Anglo-Dutch relations can be characterised by periods of alliance, competition, and open conflict. While Chapter 1 concerns mostly texts written before and during the First Anglo-Dutch War, the two later conflicts also had their impact on Milton and Marvell. The final chapter treats Marvell's quite explicit criticism of the wars – and English naval failures – which can themselves be seen within a broader landscape of globalised trade rivalry. As English and Dutch encounters escaped the limits of Europe and restaged national battles in the race for the spice trade, the vocabulary of imagery and stereotype also changed. I discuss the literary and propaganda resonances of the Massacre of Amboyna for English writers, and Milton's own incorporation of corruption, spices and Dutch stereotyping in even such a transcendent work as *Paradise Lost.*

Notes

1 M.L. Gasparov, 'The Rise of Germanic Syllabo-Tonic Verse', in *A History of European Versification*, ed. by M.L. Gasparov, G.S. Smith, and Leofranc Holford-Strevens (Oxford: Oxford University, 1996): 167–208 (pp. 193–194).
2 Lisa Jardine, *De Reputatie van Constantijn Huygens: Netwerker of Virtuoos* (Amsterdam: Uitgeverij Bert Bakker, 2008), p. 12; A.G.H. Bachrach, *Sir Constantine Huygens and Britain: 1596–1687* (Oxford: Oxford University Press, 1962); John Evelyn, *The Diary of John Evelyn*, ed. by E.S. de Beer, 6 vols. (Oxford: Oxford University Press, 1955), vol. 3 (1650–1672), p. 377 (28 July 1664).
3 John Stoye, *English Travellers Abroad, 1604–1667* (London: Yale University Press, 1989); C.D. van Strien, *British Travellers in Holland during the Stuart Period* (Leiden: E.J. Brill, 1993).
4 Marjorie Rubright, *Doppelganger Dilemmas: Anglo-Dutch Relations in Early Modern English Literature and Culture* (Philadelphia: University of Pennsylvania Press, 2014), p. 2; Marcel Backhouse, 'The Strangers at Work in Sandwich: Native Envy of an Industrious Minority', in *From Revolt to Riches: Culture and History of the Low Countries, 1500–1700*, ed. by Theo Hermans and Reinier Salverda (London: UCL Press, 2017): 61–68; Ole Peter Grell, *Dutch Calvinists in Early Stuart London: The Dutch Church in Austin Friars, 1603–1642* (Leiden: Brill, 1989); Christopher Joby, *Dutch Language in Britain (1550–1702): A Social History of the Use of Dutch in Early Modern Britain* (Leiden: Brill, 2015).
5 Hugh Dunthorne, *Britain and the Dutch Revolt, 1560–1700* (Cambridge: Cambridge University Press, 2014), p. 36; James Tracy, *The Founding of the Dutch Republic: War, Finance, and Politics in Holland, 1572–1588* (Oxford: Oxford University Press, 2008).
6 Jonathan Israel, *The Dutch Republic: Its Rise, Greatness and Fall* (Oxford: Clarendon Press, 1995), pp. 596–597.
7 Martin van Gelderen, *The Political Thought of the Dutch Revolt, 1555–1590* (Cambridge: Cambridge University Press, 1992), p. 168.
8 Van Gelderen, pp. 168–170; Lisa Jardine, *The Awful End of Prince William the Silent: The First Assassination of a Head of State with a Handgun* (London: Harper Perennial, 2006); K.W. Swart, *William the Silent and the Dutch Revolt of the Netherlands* (London: The Historical Association, 1972), p. 25.
9 Dunthorne, pp. 36–37; Wyger R.E. Velema, '"That a Republic is better than a Monarchy": Anti-Monarchism in Early Modern Dutch Republican Thought', in *Republicanism*, ed. by Martin van Gelderen and Quentin Skinner, 2 vols. (Cambridge: Cambridge University Press, 2002), vol. 2: 1–25.
10 Alison Games, 'Anglo-Dutch Connections and Overseas Enterprises: A Global Perspective on Lion Gardiner's World', *Early American Studies*, 9.2 (2011): 435–461 (p. 439).
11 John Guy, *Tudor England* (Oxford: Oxford University Press, 1988), pp. 281–289.
12 Fynes Moryson, qtd. in C.D. van Strien, *British Travellers in Holland during the Stuart Period* (Leiden: Brill, 1993), p. 10.

13 Jan de Vries and Ad van der Woude, *The First Modern Economy: Success, Failure, and Perseverance of the Dutch Economy, 1500–1815* (Cambridge: Cambridge University Press, 1997).

14 G.C. Gibbs, 'The Role of the Dutch Republic as the Intellectual Entrepôt of Europe in the Seventeenth and Eighteenth Centuries', *Bijdragen en Mededelingen Betreffende de Geschiedenis der Nederlanden*, 86.3 (1971): 323–349.

15 Fernand Braudel, *La Méditerranée et le Monde Méditerranéen a l'époque de Philippe II*, 3 vols. (Paris: Livre de Poche, 1993), vol. 1: 572–575.

16 Jonathan Israel, *Dutch Primacy in World Trade, 1585–1740* (Oxford: Clarendon Press, 1989), pp. 10–11.

17 Rubright, *Doppelganger Dilemmas*; Helmer Helmers, *The Royalist Republic: Literature, Politics and Religion in the Anglo-Dutch Sphere: 1639–1660* (Cambridge: Cambridge University Press, 2015).

18 Hugo Dyserinck, *Komparatistik: Eine Einführung* (Bonn: Bouvier, 1977; 3rd ed. 1991); Joep Leerssen, 'Imagology: On Using Ethnicity to Make Sense of the World', *Numéro*, 10 (2016): 13–31; *idem. National Thought in Europe: A Cultural History* (Amsterdam: Amsterdam University Press, 2006).

19 Manfred Beller, 'Perception, Image, Imagology', in *Imagology: The Cultural Construction and Literary Representation of National Characters*, ed. by Manfred Beller and Joep Leerssen (Amsterdam: Amsterdam University Press, 2007): 3–16 (p. 4).

20 Ludwig Wittgenstein, *Philosophical Investigations*, transl. by G.E.M. Anscombe (Oxford: Blackwell Publishers, 1997), §67. For a discussion of the family-resemblance concept as constructed by intertwining uses, rather than devolving from an imagined single origin, see Sonia Sedivy, 'Art from a Wittgensteinian Perspective: Constitutive Norms in Context', *The Journal of Aesthetics and Art Criticism* 72.1 (2014): 67–82. Though this concept is sometimes appropriated from Wittgenstein's writings as if it is simply a theoretical device, Wittgenstein approached the metaphor very practically. Experimenting with photographic techniques in the early twentieth century, he produced composite photos of his own family – layered individual portraits – that illustrated the mixture of resemblance and variation found in family faces; see Michael Nedo, *Ludwig Wittgenstein: Ein Biographisches Album* (Munich: C.H. Beck. 2012), pp. 268–269.

21 Wittgenstein, *Philosophical Investigation*, §139, p. 220e. I am grateful for numerous conversations with Michael D. Rose on Wittgensteinian ways of thinking about language, which have influenced my approach to imagology.

22 Wittgenstein in his discussion of rule-following in *Philosophical Investigations* suggests that it makes little sense to think of a rule that is only ever followed *once*. Ultimately, understanding the meaning of a rule – obeying it – must be part of a practice. See *Philosophical Investigations*, §§199–204. Similarly, stereotypes obtain their purchase on our imagination by being embedded in our social practices – including politics, humour, religion and other deep-level factors.

23 Wittgenstein, *Philosophical Investigations*, §§71–77.

24 Ludwig Wittgenstein, *Culture and Value*, ed. by G.H. von Wright (Oxford: Blackwell Publishing, 1998), p. 23e.

25 Joep Leerssen, 'Image', in *Imagology: The Cultural Construction and Literary Representation of National Characters*, ed. by Manfred Beller and Joep Leerssen (Amsterdam: Amsterdam University Press, 2007): 342–343 (p. 342).

26 In this book I have treated 'self and other' as operating at every level, from the personal to the national. Given the communal view of language and culture that I am insisting on, this distinction is one of degree, not kind.

27 Joep Leerssen, 'Imagology: History and Method', in *Imagology: The Cultural Construction and Literary Representation of National Characters*, ed. by Manfred Beller and Joep Leerssen (Amsterdam: Amsterdam University Press, 2007): 17–32 (p. 17).

28 Beller, 'Perception, Image, Imagology', p. 6.
29 Immanuel Kant, *Observations on the Feeling of the Beautiful and Sublime*, transl. by John T. Goldthwait (Berkeley: University of California Press, 1991), pp. 103, 105.
30 Voltaire, *Candide ou l'Optimisme* (France: Gallimard, 2012).
31 Julius Caesar Scaliger, *Poetices libri septem* (1561).
32 Kant's philosophy is ultimately concerned with ethics and the possibility of rational, free, and moral action. While distinguishing Europeans from 'All these savages [who] have little feeling for the beautiful in moral understanding' (*Observations on the Feeling*, p. 112), the descriptions of the different groups as too preoccupied with their various traits – profit or indolence or self-regard – are signs of their moral lack. Since in his *Third Critique*, true aesthetic judgement is 'disinterested', it is also removed from the grosser characteristics of common life. The refined sensitivity of the genius is at the same time morally good as it steps beyond these borders, even if Kant's schema does not permit that aesthetic contemplation should have 'the Good' as its object: Immanuel Kant, *Critique of Judgement*, transl. by Werner S. Pluhar (Indianapolis: Hackett Publishing Company, 1987), pp. 80–82. See also Paul Daniels, 'Kant on the Beautiful: The Interest in Disinterestedness', *Colloquy*, 16 (2008): 198–209.
33 Joep Leerssen, 'National Character, 1500–2000', in *Imagology: The Cultural Construction and Literary Representation of National Characters*, ed. by Manfred Beller and Joep Leerssen (Amsterdam: Amsterdam University Press, 2007): 63–66 (p. 64); *ibid.*, *National Thought in Europe: A Cultural History* (Amsterdam: Amsterdam University Press, 2006).
34 Joep Leerssen, 'Character (Moral)', in *Imagology: The Cultural Construction and Literary Representation of National Characters*, ed. by Manfred Beller and Joep Leerssen (Amsterdam: Amsterdam University Press, 2007): 284–287 (p. 286).
35 Leerssen, 'History and Method', p. 23.
36 'Character, n', *Oxford English Dictionary*, retrieved 28 February 2019. www.oed.com/view/Entry/30639.
37 Aristoteles, *Poëtica*, transl. by N. van der Ben and J.M. Bremer (Amsterdam: Athenaeum, 1986); Ton Hoenselaars, 'Character: Dramatic', in *Imagology: The Cultural Construction and Literary Representation of National Characters*, ed. by Manfred Beller and Joep Leerssen (Amsterdam: Amsterdam University Press, 2007): 281–284 (p. 281).
38 Leerssen, 'Character (Moral)', p. 285.
39 See also Dorothee Sturkenboom, 'Staging the Merchant: Commercial Vices and the Politics of Stereotyping in Early Modern Dutch Theatre', *Dutch Crossing*, 30.2 (2006): 211–228.
40 Hoenselaars, 'Character: Dramatic', p. 282.
41 This was a performance as part of the RSC's summer programme of 2013. Mark Ravenhill, 'Performance of Voltaire's *Candide*', directed by Lyndsey Turner. www.rsc.org.uk/candide.
42 Manfred Beller, 'Stereotype', in *Imagology: The Cultural Construction and Literary Representation of National Characters*, ed. by Manfred Beller and Joep Leerssen (Amsterdam: Amsterdam University Press, 2007): 429–434.
43 'Stereotype, n. and adj.', *Oxford English Dictionary Online*, retrieved 28 February 2019. www.oed.com/view/Entry/189956.
44 For a more detailed account of the different English and Dutch factions and their connections during the First and Second Anglo-Dutch Wars, see Steven C.A. Pincus, *Protestantism and Patriotism: Ideologies and the Making of English Foreign Policy, 1650–1668* (New York: Cambridge University Press, 1996).
45 Scott Dikkers and Mike Loew, *Our Dumb Century: The Onion Presents 100 Years of Headlines from America's Finest News Source* (Maddison: Three Rivers Press, 1999).

46 Leerssen, 'History and Method', p. 28.

47 Beller, 'Stereotype', p. 430.

48 Roland Barthes, 'Myth Today', in *Mythologies* (London: Vintage Classics, 1993): 109–159.

49 Leerssen, 'Imagology: On Using Ethnicity to Make Sense of the World', p. 17.

50 Joep Leerssen, 'Literature', in *Imagology: The Cultural Construction and Literary Representation of National Characters*, ed. by Manfred Beller and Joep Leerssen (Amsterdam: Amsterdam University Press, 2007): 351–354 (p. 353).

51 Paul Muldoon, '7, Middagh Street', in *Meeting the British* (London: Faber and Faber, 1987).

52 Beller, 'Perception, Image, Imagology', p. 9.

53 Leerssen, 'Imagology: On Using Ethnicity to Make Sense of the World', p. 14.

54 Helmers, *The Royalist Republic*; Freya Sierhuis, *Religion, Politics and the Stage in the Dutch Republic: The Literature of the Arminian Controversy* (Oxford: Oxford University Press, 2015); Margaret C. Jacob and Catherine Secretan (eds.), *In Praise of Ordinary People: Early Modern Britain and the Dutch Republic* (New York: Palgrave Macmillan, 2013).

55 To mention a couple of examples: Keith Sprunger, *Dutch Puritanism: A History of English and Scottish Churches of the Netherlands in the Sixteenth and Seventeenth Centuries* (Leiden: Brill, 1982); Van Strien, *British Travellers in Holland during the Stuart Period*; Alistair Duke, 'The Ambivalent Face of Calvinism in the Netherlands, 1561–1618', in *International Calvinism 1541–1715*, ed. by Menna Prestwich (Oxford: Oxford University Press, 1985): 109–135. There is also one important study on the influence of Milton on the Dutch Republic: Herman Scherpbier, *Milton in Holland: A Study in the Literary Relations of England and Holland before 1730* (Ph.D. thesis 1933, Amsterdam: Folcroft Library Editions, 1978).

56 'Ambassador Nieuwpoort to States General, 28 March 1659', fol. 136v, in MS 1657–1660 Secret Correspondence, 17677 MMM, British Library. This exciting discovery was made in the company of Jack Avery on 31 January 2020, and though we were on the hunt for undiscovered Milton State Papers, it was a thrilling find.

57 Sierhuis, *Religion, Politics and the Stage in the Dutch Republic*.

1 Pamphlets and Propaganda
The Dutch Stereotype

Pamphlet writing provides a powerful barometer for English views of, and concerns about, the United Provinces during the seventeenth century. Production went into overdrive at times of national or international crisis, decrying enemies, misfortunes, or disasters.[1] English pamphlets and similar publications published at the birth of the Dutch Republic still showed support for their Protestant brethren fighting in a good cause; several relate the story of the Dutch Revolt and celebrate English assistance in the campaign for independence, such as Elizabeth I's *A Declaration of the Causes moouing the Queene of England to giue aide to the Defence of the People afflicted and oppressed in the lowe Countries* (1585), or the anonymous pamphlet of 1622 with news from The United Provinces, 'unto such as correspond with friends on the other side'.[2] Good relations were transient, however. The Massacre of Amboyna in 1623 became a marker for a stark change of tone. John Skinner's pamphlets on the subject created an image of the Dutch as a 'cruel and barbarous people' that remained prominent for the remainder of the century and beyond.[3] Yet tellingly, by far the most pamphlets that refer to the massacre were published during and after the First Anglo-Dutch War, thirty years after it had occurred.[4] The incident took on lasting significance as a recurring call to arms.

As might be expected, anti-Dutch propaganda reached new heights during the three Anglo-Dutch wars, with each war producing slightly more pamphlets than its predecessor. Amboyna remained an effective image of the evil-doers across the channel throughout the period. The support that the United Provinces had received from the English in their struggle was now viewed with resentment, and Dutch ingratitude was routinely emphasised.[5] The various stereotypes that such pamphlets relied upon were constantly recycled and reinvented, creating an image of the Dutch and their country that would endure for several centuries.[6] The stereotypes created by these pamphlets would become such a strong force for characterising and caricaturing the Dutch as a nation that the images reappeared in the most unexpected places. In this chapter I will first present some of these images, and English ideas of what constituted a Dutchman, followed by an examination of Milton's and Marvell's personal

acquaintances with the Dutch, with reference to their use of these stereotypes in their poetry and prose.

Anti-Dutch sympathies could take many different forms; there is an assort-
ment of ballads, frequently (and revealingly) set to the tune of a 'Fig for
France', such as *The Dutch damnified: or, The butter-boxes bob'd* (1665?),
A broad-side for the Dutch, with a bounce, a bounce, bounce (1672), and
Englands tryumph, and Hollands downfall (1666). There are poems, satirical verses, short essays, discourses between an Englishman and a Dutchman,
plays, satirical drawings and prose.[7] No matter the genre of the texts, almost
all re-work or re-use the same images, some of them reaching back to medieval times. The anonymous broadsheet *Dr Dorislaw's ghost, presented by
time to unmask the vizards of the Hollanders; and discover the lions paw in
the face of the sun* (1652) (Figure 1.1) nicely incorporates a host of the most
common images. It centres around the assassination of Isaac Dorislaus, a
Dutch representative of Cromwell's Commonwealth, who was murdered in
The Hague in 1649, shortly after Charles I's trial.

Figure 1.1 Anonymous, *Dr Dorislaw's ghost, presented by time to unmask the vizards of the Hollanders*, 1652

Source: Printed by R.I. for T. Hinde, and N. Brooke, in London. Reproduced with kind
permission from the British Library Board, Thomason / 669.f.16 [55–56].

Fourteen 'barbarities' of the Dutch are highlighted, presented roughly clockwise, and listed A to O. Right at the centre of the print (A) the massacre of Amboyna is depicted, which is almost a straight copy from prints in previous pamphlets on the massacre, such as the anonymous *A true relation of the unjust, cruel, and barbarous proceedings against the English at Amboyna* (1632). It would have been instantly recognisable to any early modern reader as a scene from Amboyna, with the same gruesome positions of torturers and tortured, and the clubbing scene just below. The small theatre or courtyard (B, nearly illegible) represents the illicit deals the Dutch made with some of the native inhabitants in the East Indies. The crocodile and hyena on the left (C and D) symbolise ingratitude of the Dutch for the English assistance against the Spanish in their revolt and that the Dutch in the meantime supplied the enemies of the English. The commode chair with eggs beneath (E) uses a well-known image from demonology, and suggests that the Dutch were hatched by brooding devils, a narrative developed in detail in *The Dutch-mens pedigree, or A relation, shewing how they were first bred, and descended from a horse-turd* (1653). In particular, it refers to the match between the Queen of Bohemia (living in The Hague at this point) and Frederick V of the Palatinate, and their offspring. The fox (F), relying on old tales of the crafty fox Reynard, accuses the sly Dutch of stealing English gold, and the chameleon (G) represents the Dutch supporting both sides in the English Civil Wars in order to gain a good profit. In the small scene in the left upper corner (H), we see the treacherous assault on ambassador Dorislaus, with the large figure of Dorislaus himself (I) facing us directly. The masks (K) reflect the dishonesty of the Dutch, who wore a different face during every trading deal they made, which might refer back to the shady deals the Dutch made in B. The current treaty, or the one in the making (L), is described by the pamphlet as a 'Lions paw in the face of the Sun'. The treaty mentioned could be the embassy led by Walter Strickland and Oliver St. John, sent to negotiate with the Dutch in the early 1650s, or Cromwell's offer to incorporate the Dutch Republic in one way or another into the English Commonwealth. Dorislaus is holding the sun, the face of which is marked by the paw of the lion. Egyptian myths relate a story of the god Osiris (the sun) being resurrected with the help of the lion; the English are therefore attempting to return the Dutch back to a true course with their treaty. The mini fleet (M) comments on Van Trump's recent attacks on the English fleet. The figure of Time (N) has called Dorislaus' ghost (O), in the shape of Truth, to tell his tale to his people. In short, the Dutch are not to be trusted.

With this precis of common images in mind, we will now turn to Milton and Marvell. Both met prominent Dutch people, visited the Low Countries (certainly in Marvell's case) and in the second half of the century, were closely involved with diplomatic relations with the United Provinces in various governmental positions. The cases of Milton and Marvell are interesting because they move beyond the 'them and us' dichotomy that stereotypes or cruder forms of imagery typically create. Instead, Milton and Marvell played with the idea of nationality, and blurred the lines of what is Dutch and what is English. As I argue throughout this book, they can be profitably characterised as European, rather than quintessentially English poets, with the influence of Anglo-Dutch relations leaving its mark on their work.

Milton's Continental Journey

Milton's Grand Tour took place a few years before Marvell's, early 1638 to 1639. Milton's earlier biographers write that he chose to travel to Italy in order to 'polish his conversation and learn to know men'.[8] In 1698, John Toland gave a somewhat less noble explanation, namely that Milton's father urged him to go abroad, as '[h]e could not discern the pre-eminence or defects of his own country, than by observing the customs and institutions of others; and that the study of never so many books, without the advantages of conversation, serves only to render a man either a stupid fool, or an insufferable pedant'.[9] In both cases, the pursuit of knowledge would be most effective when visiting a number of countries, but Milton excluded all northern countries. Despite the fact he had 'no small regard for the abilities of the Germans and even of the Danes and the Swedes', he limited his journey to Italy, Geneva in Switzerland, and a brief period in France.[10] It was a rather confined itinerary and did not conform to his own advice that travel should be to 'follow the example of the ancient philosophers [. . .] and aim not merely at the satisfaction of youthful curiosity, but at the acquisition of wider knowledge from every possible source'.[11]

Why did Milton exclude both the Dutch Republic and the Spanish Netherlands from his itinerary? It would have lengthened his journey somewhat. He would have been able to secure recommendation letters from Sir Henry Wotton for the United Provinces, since the latter was a retired ambassador to that country. Wotton advised Milton on his travel (without suggesting he include the United Provinces) in a letter of 1638, and provided him with a recommendation for Paris instead.[12] The only hint of a reason that Milton provides for omitting the United Provinces from his itinerary is found in his *Second Defence*. His sarcastic sally cannot be taken at face value, since he was writing a polemic text in answer to Salmasius, who was a resident of the United Provinces:

> If I had actually been expelled from Cambridge, why should I travel to Italy, rather than to France or Holland, where you, enveloped in so many offenses, a minister of the Gospel, not only live in safety, but preach, and even defile with your unclean hands the sacred offices, to the extreme scandal of your church? But why to Italy, More? Another Saturn, I presume, I fled to Latium that I might find a place to lurk. Yet I knew beforehand that Italy was not, as you think, a refuge or asylum

for criminals, but rather the lodging-place of *humanitas* and of all the arts of civilization, and so I found it.[13]

Naturally this does not form any real argument for Milton's choice of destination, but it does perhaps reveal something about attitudes towards the Low Countries and the Spanish Netherlands, both Milton's own and what he might expect his readers to recognise. By presenting Italy as *the* hospitable domicile of all kinds of scholarship, Milton follows the standard renaissance view of the classical civilisations as the cradles of knowledge, and contemporary Italy as the best place to acquaint oneself with them. This despite the more prosaic reality, of which Milton was fully aware, that the United Provinces had become one of the intellectual entrepôts of early modern Europe, particularly for publishing texts (including his own). He also asked, for example, the young Peter Heimbach to enquire into the price and number of volumes of two Dutch atlases, those of Blaeu and Jansen, when Heimbach was travelling through the Republic. Moreover, he discussed Dutch translations of his *Divorce Tracts* with Lieuwe van Aitzema, a Dutch ambassador for the Hanseatic cities.[14] Rather, Milton's sardonic response to Salmasius makes a comment on the supposed grubbiness of Dutch intellectual life, including excessive tolerance of dubious, self-serving religious views.

Despite this polemical distaste, Milton's journey to the continent was not completely devoid of Dutch culture and its people. In Paris, 1638, he met Hugo Grotius, after expressing the wish to do so.[15] Not a great deal is mentioned about this meeting in the accounts of his life. Perhaps the description of his nephew Edward Philips is the most elaborate:

> My Lord [Scudamore] receiv'd him with wonderful Civility; and understanding he had a desire to make a Visit to the great *Hugo Grotius*, he sent several of his Attendants to wait upon him, and to present him in his Name to that Renowned Doctor and Statesman who was at the time Embassador from *Christina*, Queen of *Sweden*, to the *French* king. *Grotius* took the Visit kindly, and gave him Entertainment suitable to his Worth, and the high Commendations he had heard of him.[16]

John Toland adds to this that 'we may easily imagin that *Milton* was not a little desirous to be known to the first Person then in the World for reading and the latitude of Judgement, to speak nothing of his other meritorious Characters'.[17] We are now unable to determine the content of the meeting, as neither Milton nor Grotius recorded it in letters or diaries. As Gordon Campbell and Thomas Corns argue, '[t]hey had in common Lord Scudamore [. . .] and Dr Theodore Diodati [. . .], and experience of the politics of Arminianism, and Milton's nascent intellectual interests overlapped with those of Grotius'.[18] Grotius does not mention Milton at any point in his printed works or in his letters from around this period. This ought not to be a surprise, despite the clear overlap between their intellectual interests, given that Grotius was then a scholarly authority throughout Europe, whereas Milton was still an unknown young man.[19] Milton, by contrast, mentions Grotius three times in his printed works, and all with admiration, from which can be concluded that the meeting was important for Milton, or at least Grotius' scholarship was for the development of Milton's own works.[20]

Milton's Dutch

Milton, prior to meeting Grotius, had no known personal or professional involvement with the United Provinces and its people. Another significant change came with Milton's appointment as Secretary for Foreign Tongues to Cromwell's government in 1649. This coincided with the build-up to the First Anglo-Dutch War, and Milton's engagement with Dutch documents and delegates was extensive. The key meetings and texts reflecting Milton's involvement will be highlighted throughout this book. But could he read and converse in Dutch himself? The possibility of Milton's Dutch is a question frequently pondered.[21] For instance, a grasp of the tongue would open up a whole array of potential source material for his prose and poetry. Unfortunately, evidence for his fluency is sparse. Roger Williams' letter to John Winthrop (12 July 1654) is the only concrete suggestion we have for Milton's ability to speak Dutch: '[i]t pleased the Lord to call me, for some time and with some persons to practise the Hebrew and Greek, Latin, French and Dutch. The secretary of the council, Mr Milton, for my Dutch I read him, read me many more languages'.[22] The Dutch mentioned in this quotation refers to Low Dutch, since Williams learned his Dutch in New Amsterdam, a dialect that was formed in Holland and spread to the other provinces, and not to High Dutch, which is now called German.[23]

There has been another intriguing suggestion that might point to Milton's acquisition of Dutch. In their biography, Corns and Campbell suggested that Milton made English annotations on an intercepted letter (13 April 1649) in a mixture of Dutch and German by Princess Sophia (Princess Palatine of the Rhine, 1630–1714) to her brother Prince Maurice.[24] As discussed elsewhere, upon studying the letter, I concluded it was in German, and not in seventeenth-century Dutch, and that Milton's annotations were not on the letter itself but on an English translation.[25] This has therefore been excluded as potential evidence for Milton's Dutch.

Perhaps the strongest claim we can make is that Milton had opportunity. In his tenure as Secretary for Foreign Tongues (March 1649 – September 1653), which spanned the First Anglo-Dutch War, there would certainly have been advantages to knowing Dutch, alongside the many other languages in which diplomacy was carried out.[26] He had a potential teacher in the figure of Williams, and he corresponded with native Dutch speakers, such as Lieuwe de Aitzema.[27] The evidence is inconclusive here, although the possibility of Milton's Dutch can likewise not be dismissed. If Milton had Dutch (or at least some knowledge of the language), it would prove direct interaction with the Dutch people and their literature, but it is in any case certain that Milton was immersed in a cross-channel culture through acquaintances and the Anglo-Dutch negotiations, exposing him to Dutch thought and culture.

Marvell's Continental Journey

Marvell's travels on the continent began late 1642 or early 1643, lasting for four years. He took, as Nigel Smith phrases it, 'a gamble with his limited means' and travelled abroad. Although not the main purpose of the journey, Marvell did thereby miss the outbreak of the first Civil War, and any subsequent action in it.[28] Instead, he visited four countries in four years, where he gained knowledge of their customs and languages – excellent expertise to have for work in government upon his return. As mentioned by Samuel Hartlib, Marvell was able to afford the journey as a tutor of noblemen's sons:

> There is one Marvel of 40. *years* of age who hath spent all his time in travelling abroad with Noblemens Sonnes and is skilled in several languages, who is now again to goe with one's Sonne of 8. Thousand a year who is fitter to bee a Secretary of State etc. Hee is advised to make the like contract as Page hath done being thus far in years.[29]

We do not know the exact itinerary nor the time Marvell spent in each individual country, besides what Milton revealed in his recommendation of Marvell for the position of Assistant Latin Secretary:

> I thought my parte to let you know of, that there will be with you tomorrow upon some occasion of busines a Gentleman whose name is Mr: Marvile; a man whom both by report, & the converse I have had with: him, of singular desert for the state to make use of; who alsoe offers himselfe, if there be any imployment for him. His father was the Minister of Hull, & he hath spent foure yeares abroad in Holland, ffrance, Italy and Spaine, to very good purpose, as I believe, & the gaineing of those 4 languages; besides he is a scholler & well read in the Latin and Greeke authors, & noe doubt of an approved conversation.[30]

John Evelyn, who travelled through Europe in the 1640s, writes in his *State of France* (1652) that the best route for the young traveller is to go first to the Netherlands, then Germany, Italy, Spain, and finally to Paris:

> Thus I propose *France* in the last place, [. . .], after which, with a competent tincture of their best conversation (for the over reservednesse of the *Italian*, and the severity of the *Spanyard*, as well as the blunt garb of the *Dutch*, would in an *Englishman* be a little palliated; for fear it

become affected) he may return home, and be justly reputed a most accomplished cavalier.[31]

A journey through these countries would serve as a preparation for public service and knowledge of foreign cultures and languages (including blunt garbs), and could be used to prosper in international trade. The culmination of experience from the four countries befitted a truly rounded cavalier. This post-Elizabethan attitude towards travel, adapting like a chameleon to strange environments, was desired in governmental positions, something that both Marvell and Milton fulfilled after returning from their travel (although not immediately).[32] As with Milton, it is difficult to amass convincing evidence of Marvell's abilities with Dutch, save for Milton's recommendation letter. However, we can safely say that he also had the opportunity and motivation to learn it, and unlike Milton, had experienced the land itself. Undoubtedly, Marvell's poetry shows an interest in English relations with the United Provinces, and perhaps it also tantalisingly suggests a facility with the language.[33]

Marvell's Dutch and His *Character of Holland*

Marvell's itinerary as Milton described it (Netherlands, France, Italy and Spain) does not necessarily give a chronological outline, but it would make sense geographically. It also matches quite closely Evelyn's recommended route through the Continent.[34] Taking the United Provinces as the first country in his itinerary, he could have gone by the most common route, a direct passage from Gravesend to Vlissingen (also called Flushing) or Middelburg. From there, he would have meandered southwards down the continent, before taking a direct journey back from Spain to England by boat. It is generally accepted that Marvell visited the Netherlands first, but the order of travel between Italy and Spain is ambiguous.[35] Alternatively he could have travelled from Hull, his hometown, to Rotterdam. The latter route only took two days, but was renowned for its hazardous weather conditions.[36] As Marvell did not travel through Germany, he entered the United Provinces in the south, either in the Province of Zeeland (Vlissingen or Middelburg) or in Holland (Rotterdam). Travel diaries of English people to the Netherlands show that they mostly confined their tour to the province of Holland, with some trips to Utrecht. There are some exceptions of travellers coming from Germany, or vice versa, but Holland is where travellers spent most of their time. This might reflect why Marvell called his famous poem specifically *The Character of Holland*.

This poem provides the most detailed cultural representation of the Dutch, and especially of Hollanders, in Marvell's works. The poem most likely dates from early 1653, in the middle of the First Anglo-Dutch War (1652–1654), as it mentions sea-admirals Deane, Monck and Blake, who played important roles in the battles early in the year 1653 (before Deane's death, 3 June 1653).[37] The majority of the poem deals with representations or stereotypes of the Dutch that were already widely circulated in popular satires and pamphlets, such as Owen Felltham's *A brief character of the low-countreys under the states being three weeks observation of the vices and vertues of the inhabitants* (1648) and the anonymous pamphlet, *Amsterdam and her other Hollander sisters put out to sea* (1652).[38] Marvell's poem itself has a curious publication history. It was fully published posthumously in Marvell's *Miscellaneous Poems* of 1681, almost thirty years after its first composition.[39] It is difficult to establish to what extent the 1653 manuscript version was circulated among a reading audience, as the poem is no longer extant in manuscript form from before 1665 (we only know that it is entered into the Stationer's Register, 13 June 1665). The *Miscellaneous Poems* of 1681 used the 1653 version.[40]

The original lines 101–152, which refer to the newly established English Republic, were omitted from the 1665 edition of the poem and replaced by eight new lines. This version praises the achievements of the Duke of York, and was published during the Second Anglo-Dutch War when English antipathy towards the Dutch reached new heights. This ending follows the general flow of pamphlets in the period 1664–1666, in which many praise the achievements of the Duke of York, such as Edward Howard's *A pan-egyrick to His Highnesse the Duke of York on his sea-fight with the Dutch* (1666), and William Smith's poem *Ingratitude reveng'd, or, A poem upon the happy victory of His Majesties naval forces against the Dutch* (1665), which was dedicated to the Duke. There is no consensus as to who wrote this new ending to the poem; opinions vary from Marvell having nothing to do with the new version written by an unknown author, to Marvell being aware of the new ending but not knowing of its publication, or merely consenting to the publication of the new poem.[41] However, several scholars have revisited the possibility that Marvell himself could be the author of the 1665 version and may have had a hand in its publication(s).[42] To use Martin Dzelzainis' words, speculation on the authorship of the eight lines in the 1665 version is merely an experimental 'thought process', but an important one, in particular when discussing Marvell's sympathies when it came to Anglo-Dutch relations during the First and the Second Anglo-Dutch Wars.[43] As Member of Parliament, it was important to demonstrate support for the current regime, so it would make sense that Marvell had at least some hand in the updated re-publication of *The Character*. If we indeed adopt the assumption that Marvell is responsible for the different versions, that is to say the 1653 and 1665 variations, the poem could be read as reflections of different historical points. They may not express Marvell's personal opinions on the Dutch per se, but could be a measure of prevalent anti-Dutch sympathies during the different wars.

For now, I will focus on the 1653 version of the poem. At first glance it seems curious that Marvell used so little of his personal experience of the Dutch and the United Provinces in the poem, instead wittily rehashing stock stereotypes. For example, Marvell, similar to the pamphlet *Dr Dorislaw's ghost* makes reference to the Massacre of Amboyna, although more subtly:

> They try, like statuaries, if they can
> Cut out each other's Athos to a man;
> And carve in their large bodies, where they please,
> The arms of the United Provinces.
>
> (ll. 97–100)

English claims of torture and massacre by the Dutch make the carving of the arms of the United Provinces echo the Dutch behaviour in Amboyna. The poem was not written as a personal reminiscence of travel, but rather as a flamboyant covering letter.[44] Through the composition of the poem, Marvell attempted to obtain the position of Assistant Latin Secretary, for which Milton also wrote the recommendation letter mentioned previously. David Norbrook argues that Marvell 'backed up his application' with the poem, showing off his informed and politically palatable writing skills.[45] In that sense it is similar to Milton's publication of *The Tenure of Kings and Magistrates*, which publicly announced his support for the new Republic and the Regicide at the time when he was being considered for the position of Latin Secretary. This makes Marvell's effort more than a mere satire, but a finely-tuned commentary on particular political developments. For decades (particularly in the nineteenth century), Marvell scholars tried to read the poem as a literary piece of work independently from its historical context, but had to conclude that it was a failure on these terms: '[Marvell's] satires in their day were much admired and feared: they are now for the most part unreadable. The subjects of satire as a rule are ephemeral, but a great satirist like Juvenal or Dryden preserves his flies in the amber of his general sentiment. In Marvell's satire there is no amber; they are mere heaps of dead flies'.[46] It is only in the historical context of anti-Dutch satires that Marvell's poem begins to sing.

The poem (that is, the 1653 version with the lines praising the Commonwealth) presents Marvell as a convinced supporter of the relatively new regime, similar to the poem 'In Legationem Domini Oliveri St John ad Provincias Foederatas' (1651), composed only a couple of years before *The Character*.[47] When Marvell returned from his journey, he became acquainted with a circle of literary figures, some of whom were associated with royalist sympathies, such as Richard Lovelace and Thomas Stanley; evidence for Marvell's own royalism relies heavily on three royalist poems published in 1648 and 1649: 'An Elegy Upon the Death of My Lord Francis Villiers', 'Upon the Death of Lord Hastings', and 'To His Noble Friend Mr Richard Lovelace, Upon his Poems'.[48] Marvell's association with Milton might have been an alternative suggestion of republican sympathies, but the poem itself would provide a first-hand testimony of support for the English commonwealth.

In the 1640s and 1650s the Dutch Republic was a refuge for royalists. Supporting the war strategy of the English Commonwealth against the

Dutch during the First Anglo-Dutch war could thus be seen as a critique of the English royalists who had fled to the United Provinces. Although the United Provinces was by institution a republic, there was a strong antipathy towards the English Republic because of the Regicide.[49] There was a general fear that the Dutch Republic could be infected with the English troubles, leading to parallel civil war within the Dutch Republic. Moreover, one of the reasons the proposal of a close alliance between the two countries failed in 1651–1652, culminating in the First Anglo-Dutch War, was that the United Provinces refused to accept the condition that they could no longer offer accommodation to refugees and fugitives from the English Republic, which also meant that the royalists who were already there had to be evicted.[50] Milton's letter mentioned that Marvell had visited the Low Countries, making it widely known among the people in government responsible for the admission of the new secretary that he had experience of a country with potentially royalist sympathies.

Marvell's poem plays with this background knowledge when mentioning The Hague:

> Nor can civility there want for tillage,
> Where wisely for their court they chose a village.
> How fit a title clothes their governors,
> Themselves the hogs as all their subjects boars!
> (ll. 77–80)

This village refers to The Hague, the seat of the Dutch government. The hogs and boars are a pun on the States General situated in The Hague, who called themselves *Hoog-mogenden*, a pun frequently made in pamphlets of the time, such as *The Dutch boare dissected* (1665).[51] More importantly, however, that village also refers to the domicile of the Queen of Bohemia, Elizabeth Stuart, sister of Charles I, who was financially supported by the States General. As we have seen in *Dr Dorislaw's ghost* earlier in the chapter, this was a contentious point in the relations between the United Provinces and the English Republic.[52] It is certainly not inconceivable that the noble sons Marvell had been tutoring were invited by the Queen of Bohemia to an audience, and that he accompanied them. John Evelyn, for example, went to pay his respects in 1641:

> Arrived at The Hague, I went first to the Queen Bohemia's court, where I had the honour to kiss her Majesty's hand, and several of the princesses', her daughters. Prince Maurice was also there, newly come out of Germany; and my Lord Finch, not long before fled out of English from the fury of the Parliament.

There would be no better way of promoting one's (new) republican sympathies than to satirise the United Provinces and their seat of government as a royalist safe haven.

In the poem, Marvell certainly showed knowledge of the current political situation, both in England and the United Provinces, though he largely
recycled existing stereotypes and themes. There are some further instances
within *The Character of Holland* that suggest a deeper engagement is at
play. There are some inventive metaphors and associations that reveal more
than superficial knowledge of the United Provinces and its geopolitics. For
example, the poem focuses mainly on the province or state of Holland, but
without the title being used proverbially for the nation as a whole, as it
is frequently in other pamphlets and even today. As Richard Todd rightly
observes, although some of the lines using the term do refer thereby to
the United Provinces, they are carefully positioned to satirise the idea of
one strong nation that the United Provinces themselves promoted, such as
in their coat of arms (l. 100).[53] The lines 'And now their Hydra of sev'n
provinces' (l. 137) and 'To whom their weather-beaten *province* owes/
Itself' (my italics, ll. 109–110) clearly mock the notion of a coherent Dutch
state.[54]

The geographical imagery of the poem can be split into three parts; it
begins with the creation of land by draining, which was a feature of Holland and Zeeland: 'But who could first discern the rising lands./ Who best
could know to pump an earth so leak' (ll. 44–45). Throughout, the struggle
with water and the process of creating land is mocked – it is the spine of the
poem – similar to many other satires in the period, of which the pamphlet,
*The Dutch-mens pedigree, or, A relation, shewing how they were first bred
and descended from a horse-turd, which was enclosed in a butterbox* (1653),
is perhaps the most outspoken. It relates that the Dutch land was created
by a monstrous horse who drank the shallow waters from the coast of Germany, until the Netherlands were created. The Dutch were consequently
bred from the horse-turd that the horse had left, incubated by Beelzebub's
demons. This was a satirical creation myth that would persevere during all
three wars, such as in the anonymous pamphlet *Lucifer faln, or, Some reflections on the present estate of the low-countries* (1672):

> This State was Dropsical sunk with its weight
> And with ill Humours swell'd too big and great.
> It had too much Sea-Water in't, yet we
> Tap'd the Disease, and brought recovery.
> They were grown great, the wondring World surmis'd
> There some strange birth was in that bulk compris'd
> We shew'd the World the Cheat, and made them see
> All their great Hopes was but a Tympany.
>
> (ll. 9–16)

In many texts the low topographic level of the Netherlands is associated
with the subterranean location of hell, such as in Owen Felltham's *A brief
character of the Low-countreys under the states being three weeks observation of the vices and vertues of the inhabitants*: '[s]ayes one, it affords the

people one commodity beyond all other Regions; if they die in perdition, they are so low, that they have a shorter cut to Hell then the rest of their Neighbours. And for this cause, perhaps all strange Religions throng thither, as naturally inclining towards their Centre'.[55] The commonplace metaphor of up-good, down-bad operates both literally and morally here, with Feltham also yoking together the cussedness of the enemy Dutch and their tolerance for religious variety (and error). In Marvell's poem the position and topography of Hell is more complex, drawing on classical mythology. The Netherlands becomes Pluto's designated region, whereas England is that of Neptune, suggesting a connection with the important contemporary debate on the ownership of the seas between John Selden and Grotius: 'For while our Neptune doth a trident shake,/ Steeled with those piercing heads, Deane, Monck and Blake,/ And while Jove governs in the highest sphere,/ Vainly in Hell let Pluto domineer' (ll. 149–152).

Andrew Fleck has recently discussed this division into three regions – Jove's, Neptune's and Pluto's – in reference to John Selden's *Mare clausum*, who used Homer's lay-out of the universe to support his argument that the seas belong to nations.[56] That classical literature presented the sea as owned by Roman Neptune or Greek Poseidon created an authoritative precedent for Selden for the idea of *mare clausum*. One of the major tussles, but not the only, between the two republics concerned trade, and especially fishing rights off the coast of Great Britain, with neither side willing to compromise.[57] Fishing rights repeatedly feature in anti-Dutch pamphlets, especially in the First Anglo-Dutch War, such as in the anonymous, *The Seas magazine opened: or the Hollander dispossest of his usurped trade of fishing upon the English seas* (1653) and Donald Lupton's *Englands command on the seas, or, The English seas guarded. Wherin is proved that as the Venetians, Portugals, Spaniard, French, [. . .] have dominion on their seas; so the commonwealth of England hath on our seas* (1653). The pamphlet *Amsterdam and her other Hollander sisters put out to sea* (two editions in 1652) opens with a short poem that rather nicely sums up the issues concerning ownership of the seas, and the English attitude:

> Though *Van Trumpe* fight,
> And *Grotius* write
> That the Trade of fishing is free:
> Yet if *Selden* or *Blague*
> Should saile to the Hague,
> The *Hoghens* must beg on their knee.

Trump, the famous Dutch sea-admiral was fighting for what Grotius was arguing, the freedom of the seas, which included trade and free fishing rights. If the English, however, decided to sail to the United Provinces to explain Selden's *Mare clausum*, the States General would beg for mercy. In 1651, Gerard Shaep was sent to London to negotiate matters of trade, and although much was prepared for the first official embassy to the newly established English Republic, no fixed agreement was reached.[58] The States General's unwillingness to cooperate led to Cromwell's decision to remove all ambassadors from the Netherlands in June, but eight months later, Walter Strickland and Oliver St. John were sent back to the Dutch Republic to begin new diplomatic talks. Marvell wrote the poem 'In Legationem Domini Oliveri St John ad Provincias Foederatas' for this occasion. We have no record of the proposal they brought with them, but we do know it was rejected, as was the Dutch counter-proposal by the English. Milton was asked to translate *Intercursus Magnus* during this time, an agreement between Henry VII and the Duke of Burgundy in 1496, on which the Dutch had based their proposal.[59] However, it was to no avail, and escalating tensions ultimately led to open war.[60] The words of St. John upon the failing of the negotiations and the delegation's consequent departure reflect the disappointed and bitter feelings of the English embassy:

> *Alors vous viendrez rechercher pas* [sic] *vos Envoyez ce que nous sommes venus vour offrir si cordialement; mais croyez moi, vous repentirez alors d'avoir rejetté nos offres.*[61]

You will soon send envoys to ask for what we have cordially offered you, but believe me, then you will repent of having rejected our offers thus.

Lieuwe van Aitzema, ambassador to the Hanseatic cities and an acquaintance of Milton, recorded his regret in 1652 when the Dutch rejected the alliance. The quotation shows something of the unnaturalness of the war between the two sister nations, and the natural allies that England and the United Provinces used to be:

> *Onder tussen generaelijck seggen Hollant en wij moeten vrienden sijn ende blijven ende wij moeten elkanderen bijstaen tegen alle monarchen.*[62]

Meanwhile, generals say that Holland and we should be friends and stay friends and we should support each other against all monarchies.

Nevertheless, the violation of the fishing rights was an issue that very much occupied the Rump Parliament, and they were unwilling to compromise; Marchamont Nedham brought out his English translation of Selden's *Mare clausum* in 1652, seventeen years after the original publication, right in the middle of the negotiations. The *dominus maris* position that Selden promotes, reinforced by Nedham's translation, dominated English policy until William of Orange, spokesman for the freedom of the sea, ascended to the throne in 1688.[63]

The connection between Nedham and Marvell in this context is a telling one. Nedham was a public republican, the 'most widely read journalist in puritan England', partly as a result of his *Mercurius Politicus*, of which

Milton was licenser.[64] In *Mercurius Politicus*, Nedham often proposed all kinds of unions between the two nations (in under two years of issues, sixteen entries about the United Provinces can be found), in which the Orangist party would be defeated, consequently weakening the Stuart cause, such as the entry on 3 April 1651:

> Many of the Dutch are as bitter and violent against us as the English, rayle fearfully in our hearing. Others again are well pleased, and over joyed with our coming, and desire with all their hearts that England and Holland may be come as one entire body. These are as much against the Prince of Orange his factions, as we against the Cavaliers.[65]

Perhaps the additions to his translation *Of the Dominion or Ownership of the Sea* are even more telling. The book opens with the poem 'Neptune to the Commonwealth', again representing a collaboration between the sea-god and the English Republic, making England the natural owner of the seas. The preface dedicated to the 'Supreme Authority of the Nation: The Parliament of the Commonwealth of England' is outspoken in its republican convictions (Charles I is frequently referred to as 'the tyrant', for example) and its support of Selden's claim:

> The truth is, too much easiness and indulgence to the Fathers and Grand-fathers of the present Generation was, the first occasion of elevating them to this height of Confidence, in pressing upon the seas of England. For who knows not with what tenderness, and upon what terms, they were first taken into the bosom of Queen *Elizabeth*? [. . .] It was counted Reason of State to permit them to thrive; but they turning that favorable permission into a Licentious Encroaching beyond due Limits, put the King to a world of Trouble and Charge, by ambassies and otherwise, to assert his own interest, and dispute them into a reasonable submission to those Rights which has been received before as indisputable by all the world.[66]

This passage criticises previous monarchs for their leniency towards the Dutch and at the same time thus supports the Commonwealth's recently reinstated strict foreign policy – that war to claim the right of sovereignty over the seas was a better alternative than allowing other nations to dominate the fishing trade.

Grotius' book *Mare liberum* (1609) is mentioned in Marvell's poem (l. 26), as well as another reference to a work on international law by the same author, *De Jus belli et Pacis* (l. 113). *Mare liberum* was the first in a string of publications, and in it Grotius claimed that the seas are an open domain for any nation.[67] Grotius had a difficult position to defend in the tract: on one hand to indict the Portuguese and their monopolistic trade, yet at the same time to avoid undermining the monopolies that the Dutch already maintained (*Mare liberum* contrasts starkly with the Dutch East-Indian policy).[68] As George Downing (1623–1684), English ambassador in The Hague, had noted at the dawn of the Second Anglo-Dutch War, the *mare liberum* principle was promoted by the Dutch in British waters, but in Africa and the East Indies *mare clausum*.[69] By quoting these titles, Marvell gives a testimony of his knowledge of the current debate, and by referring to Selden's work at the end of the poem reaffirms his allegiance to the English Commonwealth. Marvell's decision to rely on Selden's representation of the universe's three regions (Jove's, Neptune's, and Pluto's) means he associates himself indirectly with Nedham, one of the most outspoken republicans of the time, with ties to Milton and other republicans. An endorsement by Nedham, perhaps through a (public) appraisal of *The Character* in *Mercurius Politicus*, might have been even more important for winning the appointment than Milton's recommendation letter. Unfortunately, such a public endorsement never materialised.

The second half of Marvell's poem of 1653 is occupied with descriptions of the competition between the new Commonwealth and the Republic. He briefly invokes the myth of Claudius Civilis, leader of the Batavians:

> Let it suffice to give their country Fame
> That it had one Civilis called by name,
> Some fifteen hundred and more years ago;
> But surely never any that was so.
> (ll. 81–84)

The importance of the myth of Batavia and its leader for the Dutch constitution would be difficult to overstate. Just after the signing of the Twelve Years' Truce, Hugo Grotius proposed in *Liber de antiquitate reipublicae Batavicae* (1610) that the Dutch state and its claim for independence were simply a continuation of the Batavian state centuries before, which had not been ruled by kings but by the best of Batavian citizens (also called the *primores*). The Dutch revolt could therefore not have been a rebellion against a legitimate authority.[70] This meant that the Dutch state had not been newly founded but was one of the oldest in the world (almost 1700 years). The great Batavian hero Civilis and his rebellion against the Roman Empire, mentioned in Tacitus' *Histories*, became the symbol for Dutch protest when liberty was endangered.[71] As early as 1510, humanist writing was concerned with the Batavian inheritance of the Northern Provinces, and its continuing influence is seen in the creation of the Dutch Batavian Republic, which lasted for eleven years from 1795 to 1806.[72] The city council of Amsterdam's commissioning of Rembrandt's painting 'The Conspiracy of Claudius Civilis' (1661–1662) almost one hundred years after the Dutch revolt, P.C. Hooft's play *Baeto* (1617) about the founder of the Batavian nation, and the renaming of Jakarta in Java to Batavia in 1619, are just some examples of its significance to national identity. By brushing away the myth of Batavia, Marvell argues that the English and Dutch republics are almost the same age, and Dutch claims to the authority of antiquity are spurious. *The Character* does not mention the Dutch rebellion directly, but some subtle references can be found: 'Who best could know how to pump an earth so leak,/ Him they their Lord and country's Father speak./ To make a bank was a great plot of state;/ Invent a shovel and be magistrate' (ll. 45–48). This is a nod towards the Union of Utrecht in 1579, through which the Dutch announced themselves an independent nation.[73] The last part of the poem turns to the First Anglo-Dutch War and, with the adapted ending of 1665, also the Second. The English are portrayed as blameless and virtuous, whereas Dutch incivility led to hostilities and eventually war. In the same way that the unnatural behaviour of the Dutch is invoked in terms of their creation of the land, their own announcement as a new state embodies disharmony with nature; consequently the war with England is a disturbance of the same natural equilibrium, as if the Dutch Pluto overstepped the natural boundaries of his hell.[74]

Tellingly, however, Marvell's poem is not a simple rejection and demonisation of an implacable 'Other', despite suggestions of Dutch unnaturalness. Rather, it is an admonition of someone who should know better – a potential peer. One of the ways in which Marvell complicates his criticism is through the inclusion of Dutch words, the recognition of which implicates the reader in an admitted closeness to the supposed enemy. The poem uses five Dutch words in the first 100 lines. The words have several meanings, each enhancing a different caricature of the Dutch, whilst satirising the language itself. If the lines were influenced by pre-existing English satirical sources, in a similar fashion to Marvell's re-use of Dutch stereotypes, those sources would have to have been printed before early 1653.[75] Annabel Patterson argues that the poem is nothing more than 'educated ecphrasis' of already existing satirical images of the Dutch and that the poem thus shows that Marvell himself had not 'yet established personal connections with the United Provinces'.[76] In common with many other Marvell scholars, however, she neglects to provide any analysis of the words chosen. Nicholas von Maltzahn has called it 'incessant wit', while Andrew Fleck even goes as far as to say that the 'poet offers nothing innovative in the poem's first hundred lines'.[77] Such a reading lacks a sustained appreciation of the writing context, as the pamphlets mentioned in this chapter have sought to bring into view: Marvell's Dutch stereotypes are no cruder than those populating the pamphlets of his time, and frequently he treats them with considerable subtlety and erudition, including specific details that show a knowledge of the United Provinces. Naturally, if Marvell composed the poem with a view to arouse the sympathies of potential government employers, he would need to make use of readily available imagery, given a suitably informed twist. His embedding of Dutch words within the poem is one such tweak, suggesting his own valuable skill with the language, properly harnessed to English foreign policy.

Three of these five Dutch words Marvell could have picked up from sources that were around at the time, but two terms are more complicated. First, the term *Heeren* (l. 34), as a polite title for gentlemen, was regularly used in English sources, often discussing Dutch matters; an example of this would be Selden's reference to it in his *Titles of Honor of 1614*: 'We usually stile them *Lords*, as the Dutch their *Heeren*, or *Freeheeren*'.[78] The term is also used in the pamphlet *Amsterdam and her other Hollander sisters put out to sea*, of which traces can be found throughout Marvell's poem. To mention a few examples: the pamphlet describes Amsterdam as having 'as many sects as chambers' (p. 3, see in Marvell lines 71–72); the suggestion that the sneaky Dutch prefer knives to swords (p. 10) is used by Marvell in the poem, where the Dutch cut each other and carve the arms of the United Provinces into their bodies (ll. 97–99). There is a pun on bore and the Dutch *boer* (farmer) (p. 11), which, too, can be found in Marvell's poem (l. 80).

Second, Marvell uses the term *Hans-in-Kelder* (l. 66) as a term for an unborn child, or as a toast to a pregnant woman, which could literally be translated as *Jack-in-the-Cellar*. This expression was not long in use before the publication of the poem; the first recorded Dutch uses were in the early seventeenth century, such as in Constantijn Huygens' poetry. It was then adopted into the English language; in Richard Brome's play, *The Sparagus Garden* (1640), it is used with the correct reference: 'Come here's a health to the Hans in Kelder, and the mother of the boy, if it prove so' (III. iv. 1202–1203); and Brome uses the idiom later on in his play *The New Academy* (1658) (II. i. 936).[79] This suggests that the term was broadly known and used for comical and satirical effect by that time.

Third, the word *dyke-grave* in line 49, denotes the chairman of the council responsible for the maintenance of the dykes. It has to be noted that this word is not printed in italics and thus not highlighted as a foreign word in Nigel Smith's edition of the poem. The *Oxford English Dictionary* notes that this word was also used in English, especially in Lincolnshire, from the sixteenth century onwards, sometimes written as 'dike-reeve', which might explain Smith's reason for not italicising it.[80] It is, however, in italics in the 1665 and 1672 editions of the poem, as well as the *Miscellaneous Poems* edition of 1681. The connection between dyke-grave and the Dutch was made in texts before the publication of *The Character*, such as in James Howell's letter from Amsterdam, written 1 April 1617, published 1650:

> That the chief *Dike-grave* here, is one of the greatest Officers of trust in all the Province, it being in his power, to turn the whole Countrey into a Salt lough when he list, and so to put *Hans* to swim for his life, which makes it to be one of the chiefest part of his Letany, *From the Sea, the Spaniard, and the Devil*, the Lord deliver me.[81]

Generally speaking, if readers at the time were unfamiliar with the meaning of these Dutch words in the poem, the balance in the bilingual chiasmus would explain the content and intention of the pun:

> Whole shoals of *Dutch* served up for *Cabilliau*:
>
> [. . .]
>
> For pickled *herring*, pickled *Heeren* changed.
>
> (Own italics, ll. 32, 34)

In these three instances, Marvell did not need to have any inside knowledge of the United Provinces or of the Dutch language itself.

The two other Dutch words *Cabillau* (l. 32) and *Half-anders* (l. 53) are not as easily traced in early English sources before 1653. The term *Cabillau* means codfish, but also a dish prepared with salted codfish. The term appears in a record in 1608 – Jean Francois' *A Generall Historie of the Netherlands* – but refers to a certain Colonel Cabillau. Marvell could, alternatively, have read it in Anthony Munday's *A briefe chronicle, of the successe of times, from the creation of the world, to this instant* (1611), which mentions 'two intruded factions, called Cabillaux and Hoecks'.[82] This refers to the complex Hook and Cod wars that took place in the Low Countries during the fourteenth and fifteenth centuries, but not directly to the fish (as it is used in the poem).[83] It is also possible that Marvell picked it up during his own journey through Holland. At the time, *cabillau* or as it was later called *kabeljouw* was very much part of the staple diet, in particular in sea-neighbouring provinces.[84] It was widely available, and it is certainly not unimaginable that fishmongers would praise the *cabilliau* on fish-markets, and that it was served at inns at the time. It is only *after* Marvell's poem that *cabillau* becomes associated with the Dutch diet, such as, in William Mountague's *The Delights of Holland* (1669): 'no Fricassee's, Ragou's, or Grilliades, but a good Dish of Cabilliau, Cod-Fish, of which the *Dutch* in general are great Admirers'.[85] An alternative source for the word is that Marvell grew up in Hull, and would become its Member of Parliament at the end of the 1650s (the implications of this during the Second and Third Anglo-Dutch Wars will be discussed later).[86] Since Hull was a port city on the North Sea, very much occupied with fishery, and with a great number of Dutch residing there and with constant trading traffic with the United Provinces, it is likely that words such as *kabeljouw* were in use (at least on the fish markets) in Marvell's home town.[87] This explanation would remove the necessity of Marvell being unusually well-versed in Dutch culture, and would add an element he could reasonably expect an English audience to follow. Nonetheless, it shows his perceptive use of the Dutch language, and may be a further pointer to his understanding of Anglo-Dutch trading tensions.

Finally, the word *Half-anders* presents an intriguing piece of invention of Marvell's own. It does not exist in (early) modern Dutch, nor in German variants, but is clearly styled to resemble a Dutch term. It has never been used anywhere except in Marvell's poem: 'For these *Half-anders*, half wet, and half dry,/ Nor bear strict service, nor pure liberty' (ll. 53–54). The invention of a Dutch word would be another way of demonstrating ability with the language, as claimed in Milton's letter, hence reinforcing the argument that the poem was used for promotional purposes. The word does not exist in Dutch but sounds as if it could feasibly be a Dutch word, even to a native speaker. Various attempts have been made to unlock the origins of the term and Marvell's intended meaning, though none so far quite manage to capture the resonances of its deployment in the poem.

Smith explains the term as a coinage from the two words *half* (half) and *anders* (other or different), or from the word *anderhalf*, meaning one and a half, as defined in Henry Hexham's *Copious English and Netherduytch Dictionarie* (1648).[88] Perhaps Marvell picked it up from George Gascoigne's poem 'Gascoignes voyage into Hollande, An. 1572'.[89] Gascoigne's poem, although in English, has several phrases in Dutch of which one is '*met u*: and *anders niet*' (with you, and not otherwise) (l. 336); no translation is provided in the text. Richard Todd proposes two other readings of the word *half-anders*, namely that the word is a reference to Greek etymology, meaning *half-human*, or a pun on the word half-Flanders.[90] For Steven N. Zwicker, *half-anders* is pressed into service as Marvell's self-description as a poet:

> Here is the 'Half-anders' world of England and the Dutch Republic reimagined by, and as the story of, Andrew Marvell, whom we might think of, by means of a play upon his own name, as half-anders: so, in a fashion, he signed himself in the commendatory verse he wrote for Dr Witty's translation of *Popular Errors*, published in 1651, 'Andrew Marvell. A. F. [Andreae Filiae]': Andrew Marvell, son of Andrew, half-Andrew, half-anders'.[91]

Elegant though this formulation is, it does not withstand close scrutiny. It certainly fits the common image of Marvell as reluctant to be defined by a fixed identity, but lacks sufficient foundation. Zwicker connects the last part of the term to the name Anders, used in 'Dutch, Danish and Norwegian', which would mean the same as Andreas or Andrew in English.[92] This would be an interesting parallel were it not for the fact that this name is not Dutch, but Scandinavian.[93] Nor does this make *The Character of Holland* the 'Character of Andrew', as Zwicker argues, which would perhaps be to treat the poem as much more of a résumé than it is, and not a very good one. This line of thinking, however, does touch on something about the self-reflectiveness of Marvell's poem, just not on the level of introspection.

What might be a more plausible reading is that when an Englishman looks at the Dutch, he sees himself through a distorted mirror. The Netherlands, 'th'off-scouring of the British sand' (l.2), had many commonalities with the English Commonwealth, including their Protestant foundations, republican governments, and anti-Spanish and French policies. How to satirise a sister-nation, so close in geography, religion, and politics? This is where the interpretation of *half-anders* lies. It is a corruption of the existing Dutch expression *heel-anders*, literally translated as 'wholly-different'. 'Whole-anders' would also draw parallels with the word Hollanders. Closely connected to the simple reading of it being a pun on half-landers, which would flow more easily that either Smith's or Zwicker's interpretations, it would fit perfectly with the idea of the Dutch being half wet half dry, and of being the off-scourings of England's sands. This works with the *heel-anders* reading, since they can be half-landers – half-Englanders – if they are half-different, again especially if the claim is that they are geologically and politically dependent on England. There is therefore something of a 'family resemblance' between the two, and just like family, similarities are often unavoidable, even if one would rather disassociate oneself from the other.[94] Reading the Dutch as Marvell does, positions the English as the other self, the *half-anders*, too.

This idea of a distorted image of oneself is certainly one Marvell made conscious use of in an Anglo-Dutch context. In his *Last Instructions to a Painter* De Ruyter looks down 'And his new face looks in the English wave' (l. 534). The mirror distorts the image of the Dutch and the English to unrecognisable people. The reflection of both navies are like 'inveigling colours' (l. 538), blending and mixing in the mirror of the sea, until there are no two sides to the war, but a messy painting of blurred colours that 'want[s] an enemy' (l. 540). In Marvell's poem, the mirror works both ways, as a window looking out on a neighbouring rival, and at the same time as a reflection of England itself, but *half-anders*. Where England exactly stops and the Netherlands begins is muddled because of the fluidity of the boundaries – literally and metaphorically – between the nations.

Marvell's *Character* here demonstrates deep understanding of some of the troublesome relations between the United Provinces and England, as well as eager engagement with the Dutch language. Some of the same differences are seen highlighted earlier in pamphlets, such as locations within the Netherlands, their toleration of religious difference, and their government residing in a village, and their love of drink. But what Marvell also admits is the Dutch proximity to England, that the Netherlands in many ways closely resembled the English Republic. Can one use this poem as an important indication of Marvell's ability in Dutch? At minimum one can say that he understood the country and had good reason and opportunity to know the language; more strongly, this book will argue for the frequent importance of Anglo-Dutch relations and politics to Marvell's life and literature. A similar assertion can be made about Milton.

Milton's political involvement in the English Republic's diplomatic relations with the United Provinces informed his prose writings, especially his *Defences*, as we will see in the next chapter. Marvell's *The Character of Holland*, was written whilst seeking employment in the Commonwealth, and became a political tool to satirize the Dutch during all three Anglo-Dutch Wars. The exchange thus works both ways: Anglo-Dutch relations influencing poetical works, as well as poetical works influencing Anglo-Dutch relations. The European experience of the Dutch that both Milton and Marvell gained on their journeys, their involvement with diplomatic missions, negotiations, and personal acquaintance with Europeans has not only resulted in poetry occupied with constitutional and national issues; their works should be placed firmly on a European (literary) stage. Whereas *The Character of Holland* mocks the Dutch nationality, the word *half-anders* itself stands in tension with the artificiality of absolute national boundaries.

This chapter has sketched the range of associations with the United Provinces that Milton and Marvell experienced throughout their careers. It examined the processes of exchange within their professional careers, as well as noting personal acquaintances. The following chapters will look in more depth at the content of this exchange: the influence of Dutch works in early modern England, and Milton's and Marvell's responses to Dutch literature, religion, and politics.

Notes

1 For a full study on the importance of pamphlets in the early modern period, see Joad Raymond, *Pamphlets and Pamphleteering in Early Modern Britain* (Cambridge: Cambridge University Press, 2003).

2 Elizabeth I, *A Declaration of the causes moouing the Queene of England to giue aide to the Defence of the People afflicted and oppressed in the lowe Countries* (London, 1585); Anonymous, *The 20th of September. The newes which now arrive from diuers parts, translated out of Dutch copies, with some aduertisements sent hither, vnto such as correspond with friends on the other side* (London, 1622); Thomas Scott, *The wicked plots, and perfidious practises of the Spaniards, against the 17. provinces of the Netherlands, before they tooke up arms Being gathered out of severall Dutch writers, by a lover of truth, and an unfained hater of oppression and tyrannie, the bane of commonwealths* (London, 1642).

3 Anonymous, *A true relation of the late cruell and barbarous tortures and execution, done vpon the English at Amboyna in the East Indies, by the Hollanders there residing. As it hath byn lately deliuered to the Kings most Excellent Maiesty* (Saint-Omer, 1624); Anonymous, *A true relation of the vniust, cruell, and barbarous proceedings against the English at Amboyna in the East-Indies, by the Neatherlandish gouernour and councel there* (London, 1624 and re-printed in 1632).

4 One of the latest reference to the Dutch cruelty in Amboyna is in William Seton's, *The interest of Scotland in three essays* (London?, 1700): 'The *Dutch* of all People understands their Interest the best, and stumble least at any thing makes for their Publick Good; otherwise, why would they have attempted the whole Trade of the *East-Indies*, by the Massacre of the *English* at *Amboina?*' (p. 61). Jonathan Swift also famously called a ship with a Dutch captain 'Amboyna' in *Gulliver's Travels* (1726). See also Anthony Milton, 'Marketing a Massacre: Amboyna, the East India Company and the Public Sphere in Early Stuart England', in *The Politics of the Public Sphere in Early Modern England*, ed. by Peter Lake and Steven Pincus (Manchester: Manchester University Press, 2007): 168–190.

5 A few examples: Beaumont, *The Emblem of ingratitude a true relation of the unjust, cruel, and barbarous proceedings against the English at Amboyna in the East-Indies* (London, 1672); J.W., *Brandy-wine, in the Hollanders ingratitude. Being a serious expostulation of an English souldier with the Dutch* (London, 1652); Charles Molloy, *Hollands Ingratitude, or, A serious expostulation with the Dutch shewing their ingratitude to this nation, and their inevitable ruine* (London, 1666).

6 This chapter will only focus on English pamphlets about the Dutch. See for an overview of Dutch pamphlets about the English during the Anglo-Dutch Wars: Elizabeth Staffell, 'The Horrible Tail-Man and the Anglo-Dutch Wars', *Journal of the Warburg and Courtauld Institutes*, 63 (2000): 169–186.

7 Anonymous, *Bellum belgicum secundum, or, A poem attempting something on his majesties Proceedings against the Dutch* (London, 1665); Anonymous, *Two royal achrostichs on the Dutch in a ditch* (London, 1672?); Anonymous, *An Essay upon His Royal Highness the Duke of York his adventure against the Dutch* (London, 1672); Anonymous, *A familiar discourse, between George a true-hearted English gentleman and Hans a Dutch merchant* (London, 1672); John Dryden, *Amboyna* (London, 1673); D.F., *The Dutch-mens pedigree, or A relation, shewing how they were first bred, and descended from a horse-turd* (London, 1653); Anonymous, *Strange newes from Holland, being a true character of the country and people* (London, 1672).

8 John Philips, 'The Life of Mr. John Milton', in *The Early Lives of Milton*, ed. by Helen Darbishire (London: Constable and Co., 1932): 19.

9 John Toland, 'The Life of John Milton, 1698', in *The Early Lives of Milton*, ed. by Helen Darbishire (London: Constable and Co., 1932): 89–90.

10 John Milton, 'Letter to Leonard Philaras', in *Milton's Private Correspondence and Academic Exercises*, transl. by Phyllis B. Tillyard (Cambridge: Cambridge University Press, 1932): 41.

11 John Milton, 'Letter to the Distinguished Mr Henry de Brass', in *Milton's Private Correspondence and Academic Exercises*, transl. by Phyllis B. Tillyard (Cambridge: Cambridge University Press, 1932): 41.

12 John Milton, 'Letter of Wotton to Milton, 1638', qtd. in David Masson, *The Life of John Milton*, 8 vols. (London: Macmillan and Co., 1874), vol. 1, pp. 738–739.

13 *CPW*: IV. 609.

14 John Milton, 'To the accomplished youth Peter Heimbach' and 'To Leo de Aitzema', in *Milton: Private Correspondence and Academic Exercises*, transl. by Phyllis Tillyard (Cambridge: Cambridge University Press, 1932): 38, 32–33; Estelle Haan, *John Milton: Epistolarum Familiarium Liber Unus and Uncollected Letters* (Leuven: Leuven University Press, 2019), pp. 380–381, letter 31; pp. 250–251, letter 16. See also the catalogue of Milton's letters and references on *Early Modern Letters Online*: http://emlo.bodleian.ox.ac.uk/profile/work/1d4dc3ca-04ad-4e36-a10c-a837e70338e2?sort=date-a&rows=50&col_cat=Milton,%20John&baseurl=/forms/advanced&start=35&type=advanced&numFound=55.

15 Gordon Campbell and Thomas Corns, *John Milton: Life, Works and Thought* (Oxford: Oxford University Press, 2008), p. 106.

16 Edward Philips, 'The Life of Mr John Milton', in *The Early Lives of Milton*, ed. by Helen Darbishire (London: Constable and Co., 1923): 56.

17 Toland, p. 90.

18 Campbell and Corns, *John Milton*, p. 106.

19 With thanks to Professor Henk Nellen (ING Huygens Institute) for his assistance on the printed works and Grotius' letters.

20 *Tetrachordon* ('yet living, and one of prime note among learned men'), *Doctrine and Discipline of Divorce* ('A man of these times, one of the best learned') *The Judgement of Martin Bucer* ('able assistant'). Marco Barducci has recently published on Hugo Grotius' influence on English political and religious discourse in the seventeenth century, which also elaborates on the more subtle influences of Grotius' work on Milton: Marco Barducci, *Hugo Grotius and the Century of Revolution, 1613–1718* (Oxford: Oxford University Press, 2017), especially pages 53–55. Some other works that explore the influence of Grotius on Milton: Julie Stone Peters, 'A "Bridge over Chaos": *De Jure Belli, Paradise Lost*, Terror, Sovereignty, Globalism, and the Modern Law of Nations', *Comparative Literature*, 58.4 (2005): 273–293; Philip Dust, 'Milton's *Paradise Lost* and Grotius' *De Jure Belli ac Pacis* (the Law of War and Peace)', *Cithara: Essays in the Judaeo-Christian Tradition*, 33.1 (1993): 17–26; Christopher N. Warren, *Literature and the Law of Nations, 1580–1680* (Oxford: Oxford University Press, 2015).

21 See also Gordon Campbell's, 'Epilogue on the Multilingual and Multicultural Milton', in *Milton in Translation* (Oxford: Oxford University Press, 2017): 493–497 (p. 496).

22 Roger Williams, *The Letters of Roger Williams (1632–1682)*, ed. by John Russel Barlett (Providence: Printed for the Narragansett Club, 1874), pp. 261–262.

23 B. van den Berg, 'Boers en Beschaafd in het Begin der 17ᵉ Eeuw', *De Nieuwe Taalgids*, 37 (1943): 242–246; A. Weijnen, *Zeventiende-Eeuwse Taal* (Zutphen: W.J. Thieme, 1955); Campbell and Corns, *John Milton*, p. 247; J. Huizinga, 'Engelschen en Nederlanders in Shakespeare's Tijd', in *Verspreide Opstellen over de Geschiedenis van Nederland* (Amsterdam: Amsterdam University Press, 1982), p. 124; Francis J. Bremer, 'Williams, Roger (c.1606–1683)', *Oxford Dictionary of National Biography*, retrieved 21 March 2019. www.oxforddnb.com/abstract/10.1093/ref:odnb/9780198614128.001.0001/odnb-9780198614128-e-29544?rskey=wcjG1y.

24 Campbell and Corns, *John Milton*, p. 247; 'English Translation of Letter Sophia to Maurice, 13 April 1649', in the *Stuart State Papers* SP 18/1/55, fol. 142, National Archives, Kew. I will note here that Gordon Campbell in his *A Milton Chronology* (Basingstoke: Palgrave Macmillan, 1997), p. 112, does mention that the annotations are only on the English translation of Sophia's letter.

25 Esther van Raamsdonk, 'Did Milton Know Dutch', *Notes and Queries*, 63.1 (March 2016): 53–56.

26 Robert Fallon, *Milton in Government* (Pennsylvania: Pennsylvania University Press, 1993), pp. 14–18; for a full overview of Milton's responsibilities and his state papers, see Leo Miller, *John Milton's Writings in the Anglo-Dutch Negotiations* (Pittsburgh: Duquesne University Press, 1992).

27 'To Leo de Aitzema', in *Milton: Private Correspondence and Academic Exercises*, transl. by Phyllis Tillyard (Cambridge: Cambridge University Press, 1932), pp. 32–33.

28 Nigel Smith, *Andrew Marvell: The Chameleon* (New Haven: Yale University Press, 2010), p. 45.

29 Samuel Hartlib, *Ephemerides*, 1655, Part 4 [13 August-31 December]. Hartlib Papers: 29/5/43A-58A. Accessed online via the University of Sheffield project (https://hridigital.shef.ac.uk/hrionline/). See also Timothy Raylor, 'Andrew Marvell: Traveling Tutor', *Marvell Studies*, 2.1 (2017).

30 *State Papers*, 18/33 f. 152; *CPW*: IV, part II, 859.

31 John Evelyn, *The Miscellaneous Writings of John Evelyn*, ed. by William Upcott (London: Henry Culborn, 1825), p. 51.

32 Evelyn, *Miscellaneous Writings*, p. 46.

33 See Charles-Édouard Levillain for some general connections between Marvell and the Low Countries as a whole, 'England's "Natural Frontier": Andrew Marvell and the Low Countries', in *The Oxford Handbook to Andrew Marvell*, ed. by Martin Dzelzainis and Edward Holberton (Oxford: Oxford University Press, 2019): 115–127.

34 Evelyn, *Miscellaneous Writings*, p. 51.

35 Smith, *Chameleon*, pp. 45–46.

36 John Stoye, *English Travellers Abroad, 1604–1667* (London: Yale University Press, 1989), p. 68.

37 Nicolas von Maltzahn, *An Andrew Marvell Chronology* (Basingstoke: Palgrave, 2005), p. 89.

38 This is possibly the most printed satire on the Dutch of the seventeenth century. It is re-printed in 1659, 1660, 1662, 1671. Under the title, *Resolves divine, moral, political by Owen Felltham. Brief character of the Low-countries under the states*, it was re-printed three times in 1661, in 1670, twice in 1677, and once in 1696. Under the title, *A true and exact character of the Low-Countreyes; especially Holland or, the Dutchman anatomized, and truly dissected. Being the series of three*

moneths observations of the country, customes, religions, manners, and disposi-tions of the people, it is printed once in 1652. Another edition, entitled *A trip to Holland being a description of the country, people and manners: as also some select observations on Amsterdam,* is printed once in 1699. Under another title, *Batavia: or The Hollander displayed Being three weeks observations of the Low Countries, especially Holland. In brief characters and observations of the people and country, the governement of their state and private families, their virtues and vices,* it is printed in 1672 and 1697. All seventeen editions are printed in London.

39 Nigel Smith (ed.), *The Poems of Andrew Marvell* (London: Longman, 2007), p. 246.

40 Smith, *Poems,* p. 246; John Barnard, 'The 1665 York and London Editions of Marvell's "The Character of Holland"', *The Papers of the Bibliographical Society of America,* 81.4 (1987): 459–464; Von Maltzahn, *An Andrew Marvell Chronology,* p. 89; Stephen Bardle, *The Literary Underground in the 1660s: Andrew Marvell, George Wither, Ralph Wallis, and the World of Restoration Satire and Pamphleteering* (Oxford: Oxford University Press, 2012), pp. 93–94; Martin Dzelzainis, 'Marvell and the Dutch in 1665', in *A Concise Companion to the Study of Manuscripts, Printed Books, and the Production of Early Modern Texts,* ed. Edward Jones (Chichester: Wiley-Blackwell, 2015): 249–265 (p. 250).

> 1653 printed in *Miscellaneous Poems* of 1681 (Wing 872).
> 1665 (A) printed as folio in London for Robert Horn (Wing M867)
> 1665 (B) printed again as folio in York for Stephen Bulkley (Wing M867A).
> 1672 printed as quarto in London for Robert Horn (Wing M868).

I will not look here at the implications of the differences between the two 1665 versions, as Dzelzainis has done that elsewhere, see the article 'Marvell and the Dutch'.

41 *P&L:* I. 309; John Kerrigan, *Archipelagic English: Literature, History and Politics, 1603–1707* (Oxford: Oxford University Press, 2008), p. 241.

42 Dzelzainis, 'Marvell and the Dutch', p. 250; Von Maltzahn, p. 89; Bardle, p. 89.

43 Dzelzainis, 'Marvell and the Dutch', p. 250.

44 Pierre Legouis, *Andrew Marvell: Poet, Puritan and Patriot* (Oxford: Clarendon Press, 1965), pp. 92–93.

45 David Norbrook, *Writing the English Republic: Poetry, Rhetoric and Politics, 1627–1660* (Cambridge: Cambridge University Press, 1999), p. 293.

46 Goldwin Smith, 'Andrew Marvell', in *The English Poets, Vol II: The Seventeenth Century: Ben Jonson to Dryden,* ed. by T.H. Ward (New York: Macmillan and Co, 1880): 383–384.

47 Legouis, p. 92; Edward Holberton, 'Marvell and Diplomacy', *The Oxford Handbook to Andrew Marvell* (Oxford: Oxford University Press, 2019): 97–113 (p. 99).

48 Nicholas McDowell, *Poetry and Allegiance in the English Civil Wars* (Oxford: Oxford University Press, 2008), pp. 1–3.

49 See for the response of the United Provinces to the Regicide, Helmer Helmers, *The Royalist Republic: Literature, Politics and Religion in the Anglo-Dutch Sphere: 1639–1660* (Cambridge: Cambridge University Press, 2015).

50 Samuel Rawson Gardiner, *History of the Commonwealth and Protectorate, 1649–1660* (London: Longmans, 1894), vol. 1: 1649–1660, pp. 362–363.

51 The anonymous pamphlet *Amsterdam and her other Hollander sisters put out to sea, by Van Trump, Van Dunck, & Van Dumpe, Or, A true description of those so called Hoghens Mogens, set out to the life [. . .]* (London, 1652) makes use of the same pun. It also used in the Second Anglo-Dutch War: Anonymous, *The Dutch boare dissected, or a description of hogg-land* (London, 1665); Anonymous, *The Dutch storm: or, it's an ill wind that blows no-body profit. Being a perfect relation of eighteen ships great and small, taken from the Hogen mogen*

stats van Hollandt (London, 1665). And in the Third Anglo-Dutch War: Anonymous, *Hogan-Moganides, or, the Dutch Hudibras* (London, 1674).

52 See my article, co-authored with Alan Moss, on royal tourism in the seventeenth century, including royalist visitors to Queen of Bohemia's court: 'Across the Narrow Sea: A Transnational Approach to Anglo-Dutch Travelogues', *The Seventeenth Century*, 35.1 (2020): 105–124.

53 Richard Todd, 'Equilibrium and National Stereotyping in "The Character of Holland"', in *On the Celebrated and Neglected Poems of Andrew Marvell*, ed. by Claude J. Summer and Ted-Larry Pebworth (London: University of Missouri Press, 1992): 169–191 (fn. 9, p. 172).

54 Presenting the United Provinces as Hydra, with seven individual heads, each able to live independently, as long as one head or province survives, emphasises the (suspect) independent nature of the Provinces, as reflected in the articles of the Union of Utrecht (1579).

55 Felltham, *Three weeks of observations of the low country, especially Holland* (1652), p. 6.

56 Andrew Fleck, 'Marvell's Use of Nedham's Selden', *Notes and Queries*, 55.2 (2007): 422–425 (p. 424).

57 The First Anglo-Dutch War is complex in terms of its causes – they were ideological, religious, political and economic, see Steven C. Pincus, *Protestantism and Patriotism* (Cambridge: Cambridge University Press, 1996); J.R. Jones, *The Anglo-Dutch Wars of the Seventeenth Century* (London: Longmans, 1996); Jonathan Israel, *The Dutch Republic: Its Rise, Greatness, and Fall, 1477–1806* (Oxford: Oxford University Press, 1996).

58 Gardiner, p. 353.

59 Fallon, p. 76.

60 Gardiner, pp. 357–359.

61 Anonymous, *Histoire de la Vie et de la Mort des Deux Illustrer Freres, C et J de Witt* (Utrecht, 1709?), i. 63.

62 Lieuwe van Aitzema, *Pieces associated with legislation*, Nationaal Archief: 1.10.02, 49.

63 W.E. Butler, 'Grotius and the Law of the Sea', in *Hugo Grotius and International Relations*, ed. by Hedley Bull, Benedict Kingsbury, and Adam Roberts (Oxford: Oxford University Press, 1990): 210–221 (p. 212); Willy Maley, "Neptune to the Common-wealth of England" (1652): The "Republican Britannia" and the Continuity of Interests', *The Seventeenth Century*, 33.4 (2018): 463–483.

64 Blair Worden, 'Milton and Merchamont Nedham', in *Milton and Republicanism*, ed. by David Armitage, Armand Himy, and Quentin Skinner (Cambridge: Cambridge University Press, 1995): 156–180 (p. 157).

65 (Only the last date of the issue is named here): 8 Aug 1650 (136–9), 10 Oct 1650 (307), 9 Jan 1651 (512), 16 Jan (529), 23 Jan (542), 20 Feb 1651 (600), 3 April 1651 (quoted earlier) (696–697), 29 May 1651 (816), 5 June 1651 (834), 12 June 1651 (857), 10 July 1651 (908–9, 913), 2 Oct 1651 (1103), 9 Oct 1651 (1110), 20 Nov 1651 (1211), 13 May 1652 (1586–7) and 20 May 1652 (1595).

66 Marchamont Nedham, 'Preface', in *Of the Dominion or Ownership of the Sea* (London, 1652), sig. A.

67 Hugo Grotius, *The Rights of War and Peace*, transl. by A.C. Campbell (London: Walter Dunne Publishers, 1901), p. 104.

68 C.G. Roelofsen, 'Grotius and International Politics of the Seventeenth Century', in *Hugo Grotius and International Relations*, ed. by Hedley Bull, Benedict Kingsbury, and Adam Roberts (Oxford: Oxford University Press, 1990): 96–132 (p. 108).

69 C.R. Boxer, *Zeevarend Nederland en zijn Wereldrijk, 1600–1800* (Leiden: A. W. Slijthoff, 1976), p. 142; David Armitage, *Ideological Origins of the British Empire* (Cambridge: Cambridge University Press, 2000), pp. 109–124.

70 Roelofsen, 'Grotius and International Politics of the Seventeenth Century', p. 104.

71 Tacitus, *The Histories of Tacitus* (Cambridge: Loeb Classics, 1931), vol. 3, pp. 25–71. Tacitus is an important figure in the establishment of the Dutch state. He was one of the few writers of antiquity with a particular interest in the Low Countries and Germany, especially visible in his work *Germania*. As a result, his works, including his detailed account of the Batavian hero Claudius Civilus became staple reading during the Dutch revolt and thereafter.
72 I. Schöffer, 'The Batavian Myth during the Sixteenth and Seventeenth Centuries', in *Britain and the Netherlands: Some Political Mythologies, Papers Delivered to the Fifth Anglo-Dutch Historical Conference* (Den Haag: Martinus Nijhoff, 1975): 78–101 (p. 81).
73 There is a general trend in satirical pamphlets on the Dutch to mention their ingratitude after Britain assisted in the Dutch struggle and helped with the establishment of the Dutch Republic. To give a few examples: J.W., *Brandy-wine, in the Hollanders ingratitude*; Molloy, *Hollands Ingratitude*; Anonymous, *Poor Robins character of a Dutch-man as also his predictions on the affairs of the United Provinces of Holland, together with a brief epitome of the ingratitude of the Dutch [. . .]* (London, 1672).
74 Harold E. Toliver, *Marvell's Ironic Vision* (New Haven: Yale University Press, 1965), p. 198; Warren L. Chernaik, *The Poet's Time: Politics and Religion in the Work of Andrew Marvell* (Cambridge: Cambridge University Press, 1983), p. 165.
75 A few examples of other texts writing in the same tradition besides Owen Felltham's: Anonymous, *A Character of France* (London, 1659); Anonymous, *The Character of Italy* (London, 1660); and John Evelyn's famous version, *The Character of England* (London, 1659).
76 Annabel M. Patterson, *Marvell and the Civic Crown* (Princeton: Princeton University Press, 1978), p. 120.
77 Fleck, p. 423.
78 John Selden, *Titles of Honour* (London, 1614), p. 283. The *Oxford English Dictionary* does not have the term 'Heeren', or 'Heren' in their database.
79 Dryden was especially fond of using this Dutch term; it can be found in *The Wild Gallant* (1663), *Amboyna* (1673), and the *Mistaken Husband* (1674).
80 'dike-grave, n', *OED Online*. Oxford University Press, June 2018. Web. 19 June 2018.
81 James Howell, 'O my Brother, after Dr. Howell, and now Bp. of Bristol, from Amsterdam, 1 April 1617', in *Epistolae Ho-elianae familiar letters domestic and forren divided into sundry sections, partly historicall, politicall, philosophicall, vpon emergent occasions* (London, 1650), p. 9.
82 Anthony Munday, *Briefe Chronologicall Suruay Concerning the Netherlands [. . .]* (London, 1611), p. 404.
83 Sjoerd Levelt, 'Anthony Munday's 'Briefe Chronologicall Suruay Concerning the Netherlands' and the Medieval Chronicle Tradition of Holland in the Early Modern Period: Introduction and Edition', in *The Medieval Chronicle 11*, ed. by Erik Kooper and Sjoerd Levelt (Leiden: Brill, 2018): 258–296 (p. 282).
84 Simon Schama, *The Embarrassment of Riches* (London: Harper Imperial, 2004), pp. 176–177.
85 William Mountague, *The Delights of Holland: or, A three months travel about that and the other provinces with observations and reflections on their trade, wealth, strength, beauty and policy & c. together with a catalogue of the rarities in the anatomical school at Leyden* (London, 1669), p. 36.
86 Paul Seaward, 'Marvell and Parliament', in *The Oxford Handbook of Andrew Marvell*, ed. by Martin Dzelzainis and Edward Holberton (Oxford: Oxford University Press, 2019): 80–95 (p. 81).
87 Edward Holberton, 'Representing the Sea in Andrew Marvell's "Advice to a Painter" Satires', *Review of English Studies* (2014): 71–86 (p. 72).

88 Henry Hexham, *Copious English and Netherduytch Dictionarie* (London, 1648), p. 252; Smith, *Poems*, footnote 53, p. 252.

89 George Gascoigne, 'Gascoigne's voyage into Holland. An 1572', in *A Hundreth Sundrie Flowres* (1573), ed. by G.W. Pigman (Oxford: Oxford University Press, 2000): 319–328.

90 Although inventive explanations of the pun *anders* do hint at the Greek word for half-human μcξόθηρ, Marvell's word would lose some of its hidden meaning when it is no longer concerned with the differences and similarities between the United Provinces and England, see Todd, footnote 35, p. 190.

91 Steven N. Zwicker, 'What's the Problem with the Dutch? Andrew Marvell, the Trade Wars, Toleration, and the Dutch Republic', *Marvell Studies*, 3.1 (2018): 1–12 (p. 8).

92 Zwicker, 'What's the Problem with the Dutch', p. 9.

93 See for example the compilation database of historic dictionaries of Dutch and Frisian for the use of *anders* in the seventeenth century (http://gtb.inl.nl/search/).

94 Ludwig Wittgenstein, *Philosophical Investigations*, transl. by G.E.M. Anscombe (Oxford: Blackwell, 1953), §67.

2   Milton's *Defences* and Dutch Printing Culture

Milton wrote in *Areopagitica* that 'where there is much desire to learn, there of necessity will be much arguing, much writing, many opinions; for opinion in good men is but knowledge in the making'.[1] His polemic concerns liberty of print and publication in England, or within the Republic of Letters, but his discussion is particularly poignant in light of contemporaneous publishing in the United Provinces. Several of the greatest scholarly controversies had their beginnings in Dutch publishing houses, provoking responses from scholars throughout Europe while putting sophisticated argumentation and provocative opinions into the public domain.[2] This pattern can, for example, be seen in the responses to Hugo Grotius' *Mare liberum* (Leiden: 1609), including the Portuguese Serafim de Freitas' *De justo imperio lusitanorum asiatico* (Valladolid: 1625) and John Selden's *Mare clausum* (London: 1635), discussed in the previous chapter.

The Dutch printing and publication scene took a liberal stance, as polemical and progressive texts that sparked fierce debates often converted into considerable profit. Compared to printing controls in several other countries, the Dutch authorities were unusually permissive.[3] This did not mean absolute freedom, however. Some bans were enforced, such as on Baruch Spinoza's texts, but these books tended to be suppressed and the author and publisher not further punished.[4] Jan Rieuwertszoon, for example, who published the works of Spinoza and also a number of other controversial texts, remained, despite the ban, the official printer of the city of Amsterdam.[5] If there was a ban on a certain text, it would be put into place after publication and was often only restricted to one city, a policy quite similar to Milton's proposal in *Areopagitica*. The consequent competition between cities fuelled greater freedom in print, as sometimes 'civic authorities simply refused to exercise censorship', preferring to pursue the wealth or renown that could be accrued through printing.[6] Nonetheless, in those cities that worked in close cooperation with the Dutch Reformed authorities, one could not easily find a Spinoza text.[7]

It is worth briefly elaborating on the role of the universities in the promotion of a liberal printing culture. At the prominent and flourishing universities of Leiden, Franeker, and Utrecht, a cluster of scholars from the

Netherlands and all over Europe were eager to offer their own writings and opinions. These institutions were generally progressive and forcefully stimulated scholarly debates in print; Utrecht was, for example, the first university in Europe at which the ideas of René Descartes were discussed (though it was also the first to ban them). It was the first university to admit a woman, Anna Maria van Schurman, though she did have to sit behind a perforated wall in the lecture theatre so that her male fellow students could still concentrate on the class.[8]

There is a possibility that Andrew Marvell may have seen Dutch universities with his own eyes, and even tasted the learned discourse on offer. Leiden kept daily records of those registering to study, and they are still carefully preserved. If Marvell attended a lecture at the University of Leiden as one of the many international students, or enrolled himself with his tutees at the University for a semester, it would have been recorded, provided he registered under his own name. The accuracy of the records is supported by the visit of John Evelyn, who we know briefly attended the university and mentions it in his diary, including the process of registration.[9] I have searched through the years 1641–1646, but there is no mention of Marvell, including a number of different spellings of his name. Of course, this does not exclude the possibility that his pupils attended the university at some point and immersed themselves in the texts that were available in the university library; it merely proves that Marvell was not registered himself. Perhaps the situation is comparable to the journey Marvell made with his pupil William Dutton to the French Huguenot academy in Saumur, founded in 1591; Dutton would go to the lessons at the academy, whereas Marvell would continue to tutor privately, not attending the academy himself.[10]

Despite Milton being perhaps better-placed to have registered in his own name had he wished, we know that he never visited these Dutch institutions while on his Continental journey, nor did he have direct associations with them. Instead, he was an important contributor to the intellectual jousting facilitated by Dutch printing culture, including debates with their universities' scholars. There was a great array of sources available for any scholar, since many foreigners used Dutch printers and publishers to print texts that were forbidden in their native country, such as works by Galileo and Descartes, which diversified the breadth and depth of intellectual sources available in the cities.[11]

In 1632, William Laud grumpily complained that the Geneva bibles that were sold in England at the time, printed by the Dutch on better quality paper and more legible, were cheaper than the English version by eighteen pence.[12] When William Nicholson visited Amsterdam in the later seventeenth century, he wrote that 'it comes to pass that you may buy books cheaper at Amsterdam, in all languages, than at the places where they are first printed: for here the Copy costs them nothing'.[13] This diversity, partly the result of the cheap prices, would spread to booksellers in other countries. As Milton notes in *Areopagitica*, these international kinds of debates could not always be fully policed within one country, because foreign books that were imported could not be licensed before print, thus granting them a *de facto* right to exist.[14]

Translations of polemical works from other countries were also difficult to regulate, as the grey area between literal and free translation was, and still is, difficult to define.[15] This international milieu, whether in Latin or the vernacular, or communicated through translation, provided the stage for many controversies, as well as facilitating vigorous correspondence between members of the Republic of Letters. Broadly speaking, the literary interaction between nations had two registers: material and imaginative. The former I define in terms of engagement with, use of, and exposure to, the explosion of Dutch printing culture – printing, publishers, and publications. The latter indicates the exchange of intellectual and literary ideas supported by this material architecture. The imaginative exchange between England and the United Provinces is revealed throughout this book, but in particular in Chapter 3. The material exchange forms the central column of this chapter: Milton's encounters – positive and negative – with Dutch printing culture.

By the year 1648, Milton was a 'proven controversialist [. . .] a libertine advocate of divorce reform' in England, but not in Europe.[16] After his Grand Tour, he had some contacts with Italian scholars and poets, but remained virtually unknown in Northern Europe. It is true that his divorce tracts would be later translated into Dutch and published as *Tractaet ofte discours vande echt-scheydinge: waerin verscheyden Schriftuyr plaetsen, ende politycke regulen dese materie aengaende, en der selver lang verborgene meyningen warden ontdect* (Middelburg: 1655), but published nearly ten years after the first edition and anonymously. It is now believed that Lieuwe van Aitzema was involved with these translations.[17] As well as saying something about the potential readership for Milton's tracts in other languages, we might take Milton's own view of this translation as a reminder of the unusual literacy rates in the United Provinces and the position of Dutch scholars, and sometimes merchants, at the heart of international contestation. Responding to Van Aitzema's intended translation, Milton wrote that he would have preferred it not to be translated into Dutch, because he knew from experience how the 'common herd' responds to 'uncommon opinions'.[18] In *Areopagitica*, Milton saw authorship, publication, and printing as a way of influencing a nation (or even nations) and advertising reform, whether this concerned the Church, education, or political institutions, but preferably in the language of the educated. Despite this intellectual elitism, European-wide publication, including in translation, was the ideal medium since 'writing is more publick then preaching; and more easie to refutation'.[19]

The power of the spoken word is ignored in this material account, however, especially given the continuous traffic of diplomats, travellers and merchants between England and the United Provinces. For example, Van Aitzema first heard about *Areopagitica* via a speech of Milton's rather than in print. In his diary he records a sitting of parliament in which Milton made reference to *Areopagitica* and his opinion on licensing:

Onlangs was hier gedrukt Cathechismus Sotinam Racoviams Salex wiert van 't parliament qualijck genoomen; de drucker seijt dat Mr Milton het hadde gelicentieert: Milton gevraegt seijde ja: ende dat hij een boekjen op dat stuck hadde uytgegeve, dat men geen boecken behoorde te verbieden, dat hij van dat boeck niet meer gedaen had als wat zijn opinie was.[20]

Recently, the *Racovian Catechism* was printed here, for which Parliament is blamed; the printer said that Milton had licensed the tract: when Milton was asked he said yes: and that he had published a book that argued that one should not ban books, and that in that book he had not done more than what his opinion was.

The *Racovian Catechism*, a Latin Socinian text, was published in London in 1652. Milton is not introduced in the diary in terms of his function in parliament or his professional title, unlike other officials in the diary, but through his intellectual ideals. This is an important marker of how Van Aitzema regarded Milton and illustrative of the Dutch reception of Milton's tracts: as intellectual rather than political writings.[21]

So far we have only considered Dutch publication and reception of English texts, but there was also a flow in the opposite direction. As well as accommodating the publication and printing of texts that were forbidden in other countries, the Dutch liberal publishing culture led to greater availability of foreign books within England. The Dutch publisher Elzevier exported great numbers of books to foreign nations, including England. Behind the name of Elzevier lies a complex network of publishers within the same family. Lodewijk Elzevier (1546–1617, business established in 1580) was the first to sell books in Leiden. He had seven sons, of which five worked in the business (Matthijs, Lodewijk II, Gilles, Joost, and Bonaventure).[22] This family had an enormous presence in the printing and publishing industry (and still do).[23] Walter Raleigh, Thomas Browne, John Milton, and John Dryden, for example, all possessed Elzevier publications.[24] The Elzeviers, notably, also published the works of Anna Maria van Schurman.[25] Publishing houses in Holland – especially Elzevier, Blaeu and Janszoons or Janssonius – were often commissioned by book sellers in other countries to print certain books, either as the price was significantly lower, or to avoid censorship.

As Stephen Dobranski points out, Milton depended on others both while composing his texts and 'during the practical process of putting his writing into print' (although I would caution that these cannot always be cleanly separated, as the publication process affected later writings, as in the case of his *Defences*); other Miltonists have called this collaboration a 'complex authorial genesis', in which the United Provinces and its printing culture also played a role.[26] A more complete picture of Milton, then, would be as an author operating in a European intellectual sphere: engaging with foreign sources and authors, aiming to influence multiple nations, and continually interacting with Dutch printers and publishers. This perspective naturally invites an assessment of the influence of Anglo-Dutch literary intersection on

Milton's works, whether as inspiration, facilitation, or antagonism; this was a debate fought through and over books by Salmasius, Milton, and others.

It was through Milton's *Defensio pro Populo Anglicano*, 'of which all Europe talks from side to side', that his ambitions of authorship, reform, and international readership really came to fruition.[27] In 1649, Claudius Salmasius or Saumaise (1588–1653) published anonymously his *Defensio Regia pro Carola I. Ad Serenissimum Magnae Britanniae Regem Carolum II. filium natu majorum, Heredem & Successorem legitimum*, printed in the Dutch Republic, possibly by Elzevier, and bearing the inscription 'Sumptibus Regiis' – supported thus by Charles II, who was residing in The Hague at the time. This is similar to the inscription Milton used for his *Eikonoklastes* (1649) as 'published by authority'.[28] Despite initial appearances, it is not strange that Salmasius' pamphlet supporting the English monarchy and condemning the Regicide was published in the republican United Provinces. The Regicide, royal exile, Interregnum, and Restoration were followed with critical attention by Dutch intellectuals, and much depicted in Dutch scholarship and literature. The response to the English Regicide by Dutch royalists, scholars, and the States General was complex, but certainly not positive on the whole.[29] That a scholar at a Dutch University was asked by Sir William Boswell to write a 'manifesto to rouse the continental monarchs against the English Republic' reveals a great deal about the position of the Dutch Republic and its scholarly reputation in early modern Europe, and about its attitude towards the English monarchy and commonwealth.[30] Salmasius' tract was translated from the original Latin into Dutch and French in 1650. There was no English translation in either the United Provinces or the English Commonwealth until several years later. Milton became involved in the debate by invitation of the Council of State and was instructed on the eighth of January 1650 to write a response to Salmasius' tract, leading to the publication of *Joannis Miltonii Angli pro Populo Anglicano Defensio contra Claudii Anonymi, alias Salmasii, Defensionem Regiam* (hereafter called *First Defence*), printed in London, and appearing in February 1651.[31] Milton's *First Defence* became more widely circulated, going through more editions than any other of his works during his lifetime.[32]

This was the start of a vigorous debate in the European scholarly community. As Joad Raymond has argued, Milton set out to write for a European stage in his *First Defence*, but with each new defence his audience shrunk, from his fellow countrymen, to Cromwell alone.[33] This, however, did not affect the wide and varied readership of the tracts, or the diversity of responses.[34] If we look at the most frequently printed works directly answering Milton's in the period 1650–1655 and their places of publication, a pattern emerges. It begins with Salmasius' tract (1649), printed in Holland (there is no exact publication place, but Leiden or The Hague seems likely), followed by Milton's own *First Defence*, printed in London. John Rowland, an English royalist clergyman who lived in the Netherlands, responded with his anonymous tract, *Pro Rege et Populo Anglicano Apologia*, printed in

Antwerp in 1651, thought by Milton to be written by the Irish clergyman John Bramhall.[35] John Philips' tract *Joannis Philippi Angli responsio* was shortly afterwards published in London in December 1651. Pierre du Moulin's tract, at the time thought to be by Alexander More or Morus, popularly known as *Clamor*, was published in The Hague by Adriaen Vlacq in 1652, and Caspar Ziegler and James Schaller's *Caspari Ziegleri Lipsiensis circa Regicidium Anglorum* was published in Leiden in 1653.[36] John Rowland responded again with his *Polemica*, printed twice in Antwerp in 1653. Milton's *Defensio Secundo* came out in London in 1654, with a response by Alexander More, *Ecclesiastae & Sacrarum Litterarum*, printed by Vlacq in The Hague in 1654, with another response by Milton, *Pro se defensio*, in 1655, printed in London.

This list of publications shows that it was a dialogue between the government of the Commonwealth – Milton was assigned to write the first two tracts (as he claims in the *Second Defence*) and it is likely that he assisted with John Philips' defence – and anti-regicides in the United Provinces or printed via the United Provinces, without official consent of the republican States General.[37] Ziegler and Schaller were both German and Du Moulin was a French-born clergyman in the Church of England, yet all these anti-regicide publications were printed in the Netherlands. So the constituency of Milton's European audience and interlocutors was wide and varied, but in some way or another concentrated in the Dutch Republic. Perhaps this adds another dimension to Milton's proud declaration on the front page of his defences that he is *Joannis Miltoni Angli*, staking a claim in this controversy as an Englishman that took place in an Anglo-Dutch printing and publication context. Milton comments on this 'international' character and writes in his *Second Defence* that:

> [T]his circumstance has aroused so much anticipation and notoriety that I do not now feel that I am surrounded in the Forum or on the Rostra, by one people alone, whether Roman or Athenian, but that, with virtually all of Europe attentive, in session, and passing judgment, I have in the *First Defence* spoken out and shall in the *Second* speak again to the entire assembly and council of all the most influential men, cities, and nations everywhere.[38]

Despite Milton's own advertisements, he wrote his tract for an audience in the Low Countries, specifically the United Provinces, illustrated by the fact that the States General are often directly addressed in the preface to the *First Defence*.[39] There are three instances where Milton addresses the 'illustrious council of the Federated Netherlands'; he ends it with a passionate request to the States General to 'cast [Salmasius' tract] from their vaults, for it is no asset, and let it fly abroad on whatever wind it will'.[40] Nonetheless, the States General were not the sole intended audience. Rather it appears as if Milton was paving the way for his tract to be read within the United

Provinces as widely as possible, without a potential licensing by the States General, who might have wanted to protect their fragile relationship with the English Republic.

The majority of the publications in the exchange printed in the United Provinces were anonymous, whereas all publications defending the Regicide were printed with the author's name; even Salmasius' tract was initially published anonymously. It gave Milton a stick with which to hit his opponents, which he took up enthusiastically: '[l]et us then approach this cause so righteous with hearts lifted up by a sure faith that on the other side stands deception, lies, ignorance and savagery, on our side light, truth, reason, and the hopes and teaching of all the greats of mankind'.[41] Milton creates a clear divide here between pro- and anti-regicides, and makes it abundantly clear which side he supports. The reception of the tract in the United Provinces is not so straightforward. Although the list of publications on the Regicide seems to demonstrate that the United Provinces had anti-regicide sympathies and the Commonwealth the opposite, the reception of Salmasius' tract and Milton's responses was complex.

Salmasius had a mixed reputation among Dutch scholars. His work as a philologist was admired by many, and he was invited by universities in several countries, such as France, Sweden and England, to take up positions at their institutions. The freedom he enjoyed in scholarship and publishing in the Netherlands, together with the handsome salary the University of Leiden offered, kept him in the Dutch Republic, however.[42] The somewhat arrogant disposition that this attention seems to have brought out in him lead to conflicts with his host institution – for example, he refused to be called professor, since he was not willing to teach classes – and created plenty of rivals and enemies.[43] The decision to make Salmasius the champion of the royalist cause is a surprising one. He was hardly an expert on contemporary politics given that his specialism was in classics; he was not English but French, living in the Netherlands, and his reputation was far from unblemished. There were rumours that Salmasius had homosexual relationships with certain young admirers, such as Pierre Daniel Huet, while at home he was said to be ruled over by his fierce and dominant wife.[44] These rumours did not only circulate in the Dutch Republic, but also beyond. Milton even used them for personal insults in his *Second Defence*. He constantly hints at Salmasius having a bisexual ('hermaphroditian') nature by referring to him with both the feminine and the masculine form of his Latin name 'Salmasia' and 'Salmasius' – 'for which of the two he was the open domination to his wife, both in public and in private, had made it quite difficult to determine'.[45] In addition, through the use of sexualised Latin language such as *gallus gallinacius* (dunghill cock) and *crumena* (money bag), Milton presents Salmasius as a lusty, seductive and greedy demagogue.[46] It is in these passages that Milton is at his fiercest, deploying linguistic puns and witticisms to create an unforgettable character assassination. This pointed attack was met with merriment by two Dutch families, the Heinssii and Vossii.

These two Dutch humanist families are especially important in the discussion of the Dutch reception of the Regicide debate and the reputation of Milton. Daniel Heinsius (1580–1655) was well-known in the Dutch scholarly community for his classical scholarship, partly through his affiliation with the University of Leiden.[47] He was an outspoken contra-remonstrant, whereas Salmasius supported the remonstrant party, a division that became one of the major factors in their profound disagreements.[48] Heinsius was a powerful enemy, as his reputation in the Republic of Letters was considerable; he was 'made a Councillor of State by Gustav Adolphus, a knight by St Mark of the Republic of Venice and invited to the papal court by Urban VIII'.[49] His son Nicolaas Heinsius (1620–1681) became in turn a renowned classical scholar, working for Queen Kristina of Sweden. This family was in close contact with the Vossii. The father, Gerardus Johannes Vossius (1577–1649), was a linguist, historian and theologian, who also worked at the University of Leiden; his son Isaac Vossius (1618–1689) was a philologist who studied under Salmasius, and became librarian for the Queen of Sweden.[50] The Vossius family had good English connections – they visited England several times and established strong relationships with Laud and Ussher.[51] Isaac's uncle Franciscus Junius (who was acquainted with Milton) resided in England for over twenty years and eventually died there.[52] Initially the Vossii had a close friendship with the Salmasius family; it was Daniel Heinsius, later supported by his son, who began the feud. Through the development of a close friendship with Nicolaas, Isaac Vossius became involved as well.[53] Their personal correspondence provides a rich reflection of how Milton was read and debated by Dutch scholars.

Both Isaac Vossius and Salmasius were at the court of Queen Kristina of Sweden when Milton published the *First Defence*. Vossius had recommended Heinsius and Salmasius to the Queen, who invited both to her court. When Salmasius found out that Vossius had invited his archenemy, too, their friendship broke down irrecoverably. The tract's forthcoming appearance was known, and enemies of Salmasius were already looking forward to the reply. It is worth briefly elaborating on the importance of Sweden in this triangular exchange – England, United Provinces, and Sweden – of Milton's tract. Sweden would play an important role in the duties and responsibilities for Milton as Secretary for Foreign Tongues.[54] The English Republic had a good relationship with Queen Kristina, and when she abdicated and retired to Rome as a Catholic, her cousin Charles X took over, remaining a close ally to Cromwell's government.[55] Vossius and Salmasius knew that three copies of Milton's tract were on their way to Stockholm, as mentioned by Vossius in one of his letters, but only one had arrived. They now had to wait to read Milton's tract until the Queen of Sweden had finished perusing it.[56] It is impossible to say with certainty what happened to these copies, but I will propose a possibility here.

The city library of Norrköping, just under two hours' drive away from Stockholm, has a vast collection of first editions of seventeenth-century

Dutch, French, German, and English texts. It is unusual to say the least for a city library to have such an array of early sources, especially by Dutch and English authors. This library even has some books that had been thought no longer extant. For example, Rutger Wessel van den Boetzelaer's *Meditations Chrestiennes sur trois pseaulmes du Prophete David*, published in 1622 in octavo, had been missing for 200 years.[57] But excitingly, in 2011 a copy was unearthed when librarian Ad Leerintvelt mistyped a search term while browsing the catalogue, and he came across the records of Boetzelaer's *Meditations*. This is a possible source text for John Donne's *Meditations*, and therefore extremely valuable for Anglo-Dutch literary relations.

But how did these books end up where they did? The answer lies in fully appreciating the reach of early modern intellectual society, driven by the material and mercantile structures of the Dutch Republic. The modern Norrköping catalogue incorporated the full library of the nearby Finspång Castle in 1903. The Finspång collection was founded by the De Geers, a Dutch family instrumental in the industrialisation of Sweden in the seventeenth and eighteenth centuries. Louis de Geer I (1587–1652) established an intellectual hub near Norrköping, and began to build a library there, with successive generations extending the collection. From the collection, we can see that the De Geers had a broad interest, ranging from natural history and literature to architecture and theology. Louis de Geer's sons built Finspång Castle in the 1660s, partly to accommodate the growing library. The catalogue and the library's archive contain a wealth of information that can shine light on how texts travelled and were exchanged across Europe in the early modern period, and how Dutch diplomatic relations spread Dutch and other literatures to sometimes rather surprising destinations. The circulation of the Milton-Salmasius-More controversy is a great example of this. This collection happens to have first editions of Milton's first two defences, and Salmasius' tract. They have a first edition of *Clamor*, and most interesting, a Dutch translation of Milton's tract from 1651, and French and Dutch translations of Salmasius' tract from 1650. These texts were probably taken by one of the De Geers to Sweden, which means that they were following the controversy closely. However, it is also not unthinkable that one of the volumes that Vossius was expecting had been diverted en route and ended up in De Geer's collection; perhaps brought to a meeting of intellectuals eager to come to grips with these compelling polemics.[58]

Meanwhile, in Stockholm, the first direct mention of Milton's *First Defence* by Vossius and Heinsius is in a letter from 12 April 1652:[59]

> *Liber Miltoni heri huc est allatus. Exemplar meum petiit a me Regina.*
> *Ipse non nisi cursim dum perlustravi. Nihil tale ab Anglo expectaram,*
> *et certe, nisi me animus fallit, placuit quoque, uno tantum excepto,*

incomparabili nostræ Dominæ. Dicit tamen Salmasius se perditurum auctorem cum toto parlemento.[60]

Milton's book came here yesterday. The Queen asked my copy from me. I have only run through it hastily. I had not expected such a thing by an Englishman; and, unless I am mistaken, it has also pleased, with only a single exception [Salmasius], our incomparable Lady. Salmasius, however, says that he will send the author and his whole parliament to perdition.

The scene alluded to was likewise used by Milton in the *Second Defence*:

[W]hen Salmasius had been courteously summoned by Her Most Serene Majesty, the Queen of the Swedes (whose devotion to the liberal arts and to men of learning has never been surpassed) and had gone thither, there in the very place where he was living as a highly honored guest, he was overtaken by my *Defence*, while he was expecting nothing of the kind.[61]

We know from Vossius' letter that Salmasius was indeed expecting something, but Milton's take did make for a more dramatic story. Shortly after his first letter, Vossius sent another to Heinsius (19 April), in which he revealed in more detail the Queen's admiration for Milton's work: '[s]he highly praised a man of his talents and style of writing'.[62] The compliment is repeated by Milton in the *Second Defence*. Heinsius was back in the United Provinces at the time and his next reply to Vossius (18 May) illustrates something of the great interest that Dutch scholars were taking:

Est hic liber in omnium hic manibus ob argumenti nobilitatem & jam quatuor, præter anglicanam, editiones vidimus: unam in quartâ, ut vocant formâ Goudæ editum, tres in duodecima, quarum primam ludovicus Elzevirius, secundam Johannes Jansonius, tertiam trajentensis nescio quis edidi: quinta in octava forma editis Hagæ sub prælo sudat, ut monet Elzevirius. Belgicam versionem video etiam circumferri, Gallican expectari ferunt.[63]

The book is in everybody's hands here on account of the nobility of the argument and we have seen already four editions, in addition to the English one – one in so-called quarto, published at Gouda; three in duodecimo, of which the first by Lodewijk Elzevier, the second by Johannes Janssonius, and the third by an unknown person at Utrecht: a fifth edition is printed in octavo at a press at the Hague, as Elzevier told me. There is also a Dutch version around, and a French one is expected.

Lodewijk Elzevier was a member of the printing family renowned for the publication of polemical works. That the majority of the tracts were printed in small format is another sign of the text's controversial nature. Printers were quick to recognise profit in the Salmasius-Milton-More controversy, of which the clearest example is Adriaen Vlacq (1600–1667). He is condemned in Milton's *Second Defence* as a corrupt and immoral printer. He first offered to print Milton's forthcoming work, but then printed *Clamor* instead. In the *Second Defence*, Milton burdens the printer with equal responsibility for the content of *Clamor* as its author:[64] 'he is completely indifferent to what he says or does, that he holds nothing more sacred than cash – even a pittance – and that it was not for any public cause'.[65] Vlacq's subsequent publication of Milton's *Second Defence* is therefore a striking example of the flexible nature of Dutch publication in the seventeenth century; the prospect of profit overcoming any scruples or personal affront, to the considerable benefit of free debate.

The Koninklijke Bibliotheek in The Hague has one of these copies of Vlacq's first publication of Milton's *Second Defence* (The Hague, 1654).[66] Vlacq printed it with a separate title page on which Milton's *Defence* is first announced: *Joannis Miltoni Defensio Secunda Pro Populo Anglicano: Contra infamem libellum anonymum cui titulus, Regii Sanguinis Clamor adversus parricidas Anglicanos*; a little lower on the same page the answer by More is printed: *Alexandri Mori, ecclesiastae, sacrarumque litterarum professoris: Fides Publica contra calumnias Joannis Miltoni Scurrae*. Each section within the duodecimo has its own title page (printed as Folio 1, 2, 3 and 4), separating Milton's *Second Defence* from the two responses by More and the introductory notes by Georgius Crantzius and Vlacq himself. It is a miscellany of selected works from the controversy (each printed as if they were the original pamphlets) and the title pages are subsequently not all dated 1654; More's *Supplementum Fidei Publicæ contra calumnias Joannis Miltoni* is dated 1655. All these additions and alterations enhance the sensational atmosphere that Vlacq wanted to create to maximise sales. Throughout the introductory note, Vlacq argues that the printer cannot be made responsible for the content of the books printed, as this would defy the freedom of publication and print.[67] He argues, moreover, that if the printer were indeed responsible, why had Milton's printer not warned him over falsely attributing *Clamor* to More? Throughout, Vlacq appears keen to stoke the controversy, and even his own role within it.

In the *Hollandsche Mercurius* of February 1651, inspired by Nedham's *Mercurius Politicus*, Milton's tract is announced to a Dutch reading audience:

> *Wij sullen Franckrijk nu voor een wijle tijts verlaten, en gaen over zee nae Engelandt: Alwaer tegens Claudius Salmasius sijn vzerdedigingh des Conighs Carolus de I, Aen Carolus de 2 toegewijt, een seer bondinge en dappere latijnsse verantwoordinge voor 't Parlement uyt gekomen is, zijnde in dese tijden niet te vinden, die van politijcke saecken spreeckt: de autheur is geweest eenen Johan Milton, Engelschman, eene der*

Secretarissen van den Raet van Staten binnen London, to wiens tractaet (als zijnde nu in Nederlantsche, Engelse, en Frense Tale overgeset) wy den curieusen leser hier wijzen.[68]

We will leave France now for a while, and go overseas to England: There against Claudius Salmasius' defence for King Charles I, dedicated to Charles II, a succinct and brave Latin defence of parliament has been published, unequalled, which speaks of political issues: the author is a certain John Milton, Englishman, one of the Secretaries of the Council of State within London, to whose tract (which is now translated into Dutch, English and the French language) we would like to refer the curious reader.

These introductory notes, appearing a few years before the publication of Vlacq's little book with the *Second Defence*, are little short of an advertisement for forthcoming attractions. This short piece mentions its publication in multiple languages and, thereby, the interest the Dutch and wider European reading audience had taken in the proceedings.

In the meantime, Salmasius was working on his answer in Stockholm. Heinsius' letter (17 October 1651) to Johann Friedrich Gronovius (1611–1671), a German scholar at Leiden, reveals some anxiety about what he might say:

Salmasius Miltonum suum defricare pergit, in edendo horribili isto scripto graviter desudant operæ typographicæ in sueciâ. Me & patrem immortalitate etiam illa, ut gloriatur, occasione donaturus.[69]

Salmasius continues the debate with Milton, and the printing-presses of Sweden are hard at work to print his horrible book; on that occasion he will, as he boasts, bestow immortality onto me and my father.

With Salmasius having powerful enemies such as the Heinsii and the Vossii, one would have expected a positive reception of Milton's texts, but condemnation of the Regicide and the support of the Stuart cause proved to be resilient, and soon began to influence the debate in early modern Europe. In July 1651, news reached the United Provinces that Milton's book was being burned in Paris and Toulouse, broadcasted by the *Hollandsche Mercurius*:

't Boek van Jan Milton, genaemt Verdediginghe des Volckx van Engelant, geschreven door Claudius Salmasius, wiert op desen tijt te Toulouse en Parijs, met rijpe rade, door den Beul in 't publijck verbrant. De bisschop Londendery in Yerlant schreef oock daer tegens; en om dat de voorz. Milton van een vremt humeur was, soo wiert dit sijn tractaet in Hollant oock met weinigh smaeck gelesen.[70]

The book of John Milton, named the Defence of the People of England, written in response to Claudius Salmasius, is at the moment burned in Toulouse and Paris, with mature deliberation, by the executioner. The bishop of Londonderry in Ireland wrote also against it, and because the aforementioned Milton was of a strange nature [or opinion], his tract is not read with great delight in Holland.

A greater contrast with the advertisement of only five months earlier is difficult to imagine, although the theatre of a condemned text always leads to higher sales. The same news had reached Sweden in August and Vossius reported to Heinsius (5 August) that the news of the burning had greatly delighted Salmasius. What follows in Vossius' letter is a telling echo of *Areopagitica* in defence of the creation of books:

> *Non opus est ut meum de hoc scripto interponam judicium: interim hoc scio, fatum esse bonorum fere librorum, ut hoc modo vel pereant vel periclitentur. Homines plerumque propter scelera & pravitatem manus carnificum subeunt, libri vero virtutis & præstantiæ ergo. Soli fatuorum labores tales non metuunt casus, sed sanè fustrà sunt, qui se hoc modo exstirpare posse existimant Miltoni & aliorum scripta, cum potius flammis istis mirum, quantum clarescant & illustrentur.*[71]

There is no need to intrude my judgment about that book in the meantime; this I know, that it is the fate of many good books to be destroyed or be endangered in this way. Men generally come under the executioner's hands mostly for their crimes and wickedness, but books for their virtue and excellence. Only fools are not afraid of such actions, but they are wrong when they think they can exterminate the writings of Milton and others in this way, since these books will stand out in the flames with a marvellous increase of light and lustre.

The image of regeneration by fire is also used by Milton himself in his *Second Defence*, when he writes: 'You, hastening to put out one fire with another, built a Herculean pyre, whence I might rise to greater fame. We more sensibly decided that the frigidity of the *Royal Defence* should not be kindled into flame'.[72]

There is a difference, nonetheless, between making eloquent arguments with fire and theatre, and convincing people of one's point of view. Notably, neither Vossius nor Heinsius at any point shows direct support for the Regicide, or indeed Milton's arguments. They are impressed with the quality of the Latin and the vigour of the argument, perhaps even its Latin puns, but not with its content. This appears to have been the general consensus, as Van Aitzema's work *Staet van Saeken en Oorlogh* (1662) also reveals:

> *Eenen Milton in Engelandt refuteerd 't selfe boeck van Salmasius; Ende seecker geleert man alhier, schreef dat Salmasius een seer goede saeck, seer qualijck had verdedicht; Milton seer wel een seer quade saeck.*[73]

Milton from England refuted the same book of Salmasius; and a certain learned man from here wrote that Salmasius had defended a very good case very badly; Milton had defended a very bad case very well.

Heinsius (the 'learned man') wrote the same in a letter to Gronovius on 1 July 1651. His careful judgement about the cause and the manner in which the tracts are written reflect the reception that Milton and several other polemical tracts received by the Dutch Humanists; the Dutch recognised its eloquence and scholarship, but did not approve of its general argument.[74] Throughout, what may be taken as a sign of the burgeoning machinery of Dutch printing, and subsequently more sophisticated readership, there is a feeling that printing, publication and, consequently, selling and buying need not amount to endorsement.

The other side of the picture is that the States General, especially after the assassination of the English ambassador Isaac Dorislaus (1649), did not officially endorse tracts by royalists, as it damaged diplomatic relations with the Commonwealth, nor did they officially promote pro-Regicide texts. According to Milton in his *First Defence*, the attitude of the Dutch government was disgracefully chameleon: '[I]t is then with justice that the highest council of Holland, true descendants of the old liberators of their country, have by their edict condemned to oblivion this defence of tyranny, so ruinous to the freedom of all peoples'.[75] Both the *First* and the *Second Defences*, were received, nonetheless, relatively well by the States General. John Toland mentions that Adriaen Pauw, a Dutch anti-royalist ambassador, visited Milton to compliment him on them.[76] They were even used to help relations between the English and the Dutch Republic in 1651: ambassador Gerard Schaep bought 25 copies of the *First Defence* in London in order to distribute them among members of the States General.[77] The States went so far as to forbid Dirk Graswinckel (1600–1666, a Dutch scholar) to write a response to Milton's *First Defence*, and rejected More's request to write an answer to Milton, in which he intended to deny the authorship of *Clamor* after the publication of the *Second Defence*. Vlacq published it in 1655, regardless, but only after the First Anglo-Dutch War had ended.[78]

The Dutch translation, as mentioned earlier, came out in 1651, printed anonymously by Janssonius. The response to the Dutch edition was overwhelmingly hostile. Perhaps Milton's concerns about the Dutch translation of his divorce tract, as mentioned earlier, were based on the negative response to his *First Defence* in Dutch four years earlier. One direct response to Milton's tract, the anonymous pamphlet *De Nederlantsche Nyp-tang* (*The Dutch Pincers*) of 1652, includes a particularly vicious attack on Milton and tells us much about the Dutch reception. The first part of the pamphlet rehashes in rhyme some of the stereotypes that were already around, such as presenting Englishmen with tails, 'staert-man'. It also propounds a new creation myth of the British, assuring readers of their demonic ancestry, and confirming that the island is the devil's natural habitat. It gets strikingly topical when we reach a direct discussion of Milton's role in the defence of the Regicide:

Toen de dolle Honden vielen
Op dien Godts gesalfden knecht.
    Dit wil Milton tegen spreken;
Milton is het Ventjen niet;

Milton blijft los in gebreken;
Milton blaest op 't malle riet;
Milton wil Salmaas beschamen,
Maer den Boy valt veel te swack,
Lastert groote Leeraers namen,
En loopt Staertloos in de sack.[79]

When the mad dogs fell
On that anointed servant of God.
    This Milton wants to speak against;
Milton is not the man;
Milton leaves us wanting;
Milton is going utterly astray;
Milton wants to shame Salmasius,
But the boy is not strong enough,
He defames great Scholars' names,
And walks tail-less in the sack.

The poem goes on to argue that it is no surprise Milton's wife left the marital bed, which may simply be the extension of the common insult in the last line quoted. If so, however, it does seem to be a significant coincidence given the marital problems Milton had in the early 1640s with Mary Powell. At the time there was no Dutch translation of the divorce tracts, so the author of the poem would have required quite detailed personal knowledge about Milton for this to be pointed mockery rather than a general broadside. This could be merely a tit-for-tat response to the insults Milton wrote about Salmasius, but it can also be read as an illustration of the close connections between the countries, even when it takes the form of intellectual gossip.

The rest of its attack on Milton, maintaining the assault for roughly another hundred lines, is not personal, beyond mentioning the *First Defence*. There is a pun on Milton's name: *meel-ton*, meaning flour-barrel. Milton is compared to a flour-barrel that has no straps, a drum without a skin, a brawler without teeth. The barrel is empty, but riddled with cracks, so should be thrown in a nearby pond. The pamphlet refers to Milton's talk about the king being a tyrant, but concludes that empty drums make the greatest noise. The cascade of insults ends with a pointed message that all pious people wish free trade to the North and South, airing an important bone of contention in the First Anglo-Dutch War. Attacks on Milton and his tract were subsumed into Dutch war propaganda. Ultimately, no matter how good Milton's Latin was, his message, especially in translation, could not escape its moorings in the complicated politics of Anglo-Dutch relations.

Having just asked where the author of *De Nederlantsche Nyp-tang* might have heard about Milton's marriage problems, or at least sufficient gossip to inspire part of the poem, we might care to wonder about the channels of information that brought to Milton's ear the disparaging rumours about Salmasius. In this case, the fleet and effective networks of the Republic of Letters are the likeliest source, since it would have required correspondence with someone in the United Provinces at the time. There is a possibility that Marvell had provided some information, recalling things he picked up during his tour of the Netherlands a few years before; it is also probable that Marvell played a role in the editing of the *Second Defence*.[80] Salmasius himself believed that Nicolaas Heinsius and Isaac Vossius were the sources for Milton's *First Defence*. We can read this in Heinsius' concern that Salmasius would take revenge on him and his father Daniel Heinsius in his forthcoming book. We also know, however, that Nicholaas and Isaac had never met Milton, nor corresponded with him; the letters often discuss Milton's background based on what they have heard from others, such as Queen Kristina of Sweden. The rumours surrounding Salmasius and More (his alleged seduction of Mrs Salmasius' lady-in-waiting and the official response to the allegations by the States General to 'Pontia', as Milton called her) were discussed in letters between Vossius and Heinsius before 1653. Lieuwe van Aitzema must have read these letters at some point, as he refers to them in his *Saeken van Staet en Oorlogh*. So it is possible that Van Aitzema, who we know visited Milton in London, passed these titbits on; this must, however, have been after the publication of the *First Defence*. It is unlikely that Milton himself had read the correspondence, as he never mentions either Vossii or Heinsii, but it is likely that he was aware of works by both families.[81] For example, Gerardus Vossius' *De Historicis Graecis libri* (1602) and *Commentariorum Rhetoricorum, sive Oratoriorum institutionum libri sex* (1606) were used at Cambridge when Milton was studying there.[82] Alternatively, other scholars may have discussed Salmasius' problems and the reception of his tract in Europe. Mylius may have heard some snippets of information about Salmasius from the King of Denmark and discussed them with Milton.[83] Another possibility was Willem Nieuwpoort, ambassador for the United Provinces in London, who was in contact with More and had shared acquaintances with Milton. In a letter to More (23 June 1654), in which he assures More that he knows he is not the author of *Clamor*, Nieuwpoort writes:

> [I] asked two gentlemen, friends of mine, who are particularly acquainted with Mr. Milton, to represent to him the reasons for which we desired, in the present juncture of time and affairs, that he should not publish the book we had been assured he had written against another entitled *Clamor Sanguinis Regii*, or at least that he should not do you the wrong of attributing that work to you, and that, if he persisted in refuting that book, he would not insert anything in it that could affect you.[84]

Milton's *Defences* illustrate how communications between the network of European scholars functioned, and how printers and publishers were an important part of the creation of new texts, both materially and in their content. The Dutch Republic operated as an intellectual entrepôt in early modern Europe, so it was only a matter of time before a controversial and ambitious author such as Milton would get involved in one way or other with the Dutch scholarly community and their publishers. The previous responses are only post-publication, but the European network also became involved with works that were still in progress, of which the *Second Defence* is, again, a good example. During the process of its writing, Milton was warned via three different networks that More was not the author of *Clamor*: Vlacq wrote to Milton's friend Hartlib (19 October 1652) in which he emphasised More's innocence, as mentioned in Vlacq's preface to Milton's *Second Defence*; Nieuwpoort sent two gentlemen to Milton, as mentioned earlier, and lastly, John Dury was in Amsterdam in 1654, met with More, and wrote afterwards to Milton warning that More was not the author (14 April 1654).[85] Milton received the information for the *First* and *Second Defence* from this European network, from shared acquaintances or from Englishmen visiting the Netherlands at the time. His tract was subsequently taken throughout Europe to the most unexpected of places, such as Nörrköping, and his person and life eagerly discussed. Gossip travelled fast and far, even in the early modern period.

The examples given previously demonstrate that the Dutch context not only informed European scholarship through the purchase of English copies and re-publication of the works of English authors, but also participated in the creation of its content through correspondence, meetings and naturally the influence of their own (scholarly) publications. Notwithstanding controversy, factions and even war, an Anglo-Dutch community was fully operational.[86]

Notes

1   *CPW*: II, 532.
2   Nigel Smith, '*Areopagitica*: Voicing Contexts, 1643–1645', in *Politics, Poetics and Hermeneutics in Milton's Prose*, ed. by David Loewenstein and James Grantham Turner (Cambridge: Cambridge University Press, 1990): 103–122.
3   Elizabeth L. Eisenstein, *The Printing Revolution in Early Modern Europe* (Cambridge: Cambridge University Press, 2005), *passim*.
4   K.H.D. Haley, *The Dutch in the Seventeenth Century* (London: Thames and Hudson, 1972), p. 124; Marita Mathijsen (ed.), *Boeken onder druk. Censuur en pers-onvrijheid in Nederland sinds de boekdrukkunst* (Amsterdam: Amsterdam University Press, 2011).
5   Maarten Prak, *The Dutch Republic in the Seventeenth Century*, transl. by Diane Webb (Cambridge: Cambridge University Press, 2005), p. 227.
6   J.L. Price, *Holland and the Dutch Republic* (Oxford: Clarendon Press, 1994), pp. 172–182; Prak, p. 227.
7   Steven Nadler, *A Book Forged in Hell* (Princeton: Princeton University Press, 2011), p. 228.
8   Pieta van Beek, *Klein werk: De Opuscula Hebraea Graeca Latina et Gallica, Prosaica et Metrica* (Ph.D. Thesis, University of Stellenbosch, 2004), p. 34. See also

Anne R. Larsen's book on the transnational reception of Van Schurman, *Anna Maria van Schurman, 'The Star of Utrecht': The Educational Vision and Reception of a Savante* (Abingdon: Routledge, 2016); Agnes Sneller, 'Anna Maria van Schurman (1607–1678) als Literair Persoon en Geleerde Vrouw', *Literatuur*, 10 (1993): 321–328; Pieta van Beek, *The First Female University Student: Anna Maria van Schurman (1636)* (Utrecht: Igitur 2010).

9 'The 28, I went to see their Colledg, and Schooles, which are nothing extraordinary; and was Matriculated by the then Magnificus Proffessora who first in Latine demanded of me where my Lod(g)ing in the Towne was; my Name, Age, birth; & to what faculty I addicted my selfe; then recording my Answers in a Booke, he administred an Oath to me, that I should observe the Statutes, & Orders of the University, whiles I stay'd, and then deliver'd me a tickett, by virtue whereof I was made Excise-free; for all which worthy Priveleges, and the paines of Writing, he accepted of a Rix-dollar.' (28 Augustus 1641), in *The Diary of John Evelyn*, ed. by E.S. de Beer, 6 vols. (Oxford: Oxford University Press, 1955), vol. 2, p. 52. The following entry can be found in the record books: 'Rector: professor Otto Heurnius, date 6 August 1641: 'Johannes Evelyn, Anglus generosus, 20 [age], Mat. et Histor. [faculty]'. W.N. Du Rieu (ed.), *Album studiosorum Academiae Lugduno Batavae MDLXXV-MDCCCLXXV: accedunt nomina curatorum et professorum per eadem secula* (Den Haag: Martinus Nijhoff, 1875), p. 326.

10 Nigel Smith, *Andrew Marvell: The Chameleon* (New Haven: Yale University Press, 2012), p. 128.

11 David W. Davies, 'The Geographic Extent of the Dutch Book Trade in the Seventeenth Century', *The Library Quarterly*, 22.3 (1952): 200–207.

12 F. Korsten, 'De Elzeviers en Engeland', in *Boekverkopers van Europa: Het Zeventiende-Eeuwse Nederlandse Uitgevershuis Elzevier*, ed. by Dongelmans, Hoftijzer, and Lankhorst (Zutphen: Walburg Pers, 2000): 195–210 (p. 204).

13 William Nicolson, qtd. in John Stoye, *English Travellers Abroad, 1604–1667* (Cambridge: Cambridge University Press, 2005), pp. 185–186.

14 *CPW*: II. 503; Roeland Harms, Joad Raymond, and Jeroen Salman, 'Chapter 1: The Distribution and Dissemination of Popular Print', in *Not Dead Things: The Dissemination of Popular Print in England and Wales, Italy and the Low Countries, 1500–1820* (Leiden: Brill, 2013): 1–29 (p. 7).

15 The edited volume *Milton in Translation* has many examples of Milton's work in translation: Angelica Duran, Islam Issa, and Jonathan R. Olson (eds.), *Milton in Translation* (Oxford: Oxford University Press, 2017).

16 Gordon Campbell and Thomas Corns, *John Milton: Life, Mind and Work* (Oxford: Oxford University Press, 2010), pp. 228–229.

17 Jacques B.H. Alblas, 'Milton's *The Doctrine and Discipline of Divorce*: The Unknown Dutch Translation (1655) Discovered', *Milton Quarterly*, 28.2 (1994): 35–39; Paul Sellin, 'Lieuwe van Aitzema and John Milton's "The Doctrine and Discipline of Divorce": The Marquette Case', *Dutch Crossing*, 38.3 (November 2014): 235–243.

18 *CPW*: IV. part 2, 872.

19 *CPW*: II. 548.

20 Van Aitzema, 1.10.02, 49.

21 Leo Miller, 'New Milton Texts and Data from the Aitzema Mission, 1652', *Notes and Queries* (1990): 279–288 (p. 281).

22 J. Kingma, 'Uitgaven met Verstrekkende Gevolgen. De Elzeviers als Verspreiders van Nieuwe Denkbeelden', in *Boekverkopers van Europa: Het 17de- Eeuwse Nederlandse Uitgevershuis Elzevier*, ed. by B.P.M. Dongelmans, P.G. Hoftijzer, and O.S. Lankhorst (Zutphen: Walburg Pers, 2000): 107–114 (p. 107).

23 Cornelis W. Schoneveld, *Sea-Changes: Studies in Three Centuries of Anglo-Dutch Cultural Transmission* (Leiden: Brill, 1996), p. 31.

24 Korsten, 'De Elzeviers en Engeland', p. 196; Haley, p. 123.
25 David Norbrook, 'Women, the Republic of Letters, and the Public Sphere in the Mid Seventeenth Century', *Criticism*, 46.2 (2004): 223–240.
26 Stephen B. Dobranski, *Milton, Authorship, and the Book Trade* (Cambridge: Cambridge University Press, 1999), p. 9; John K. Hale, Thomas N. Corns, et al., 'The Provenance of *De doctrina Christiana*', in *Milton Quarterly*, 31.3 (1997): 67–117 (p. 108).
27 John Milton, 'To Mr Cyriack Skinner Upon his Blindness', l. 12.
28 Campbell and Corns, *John Milton*, p. 223.
29 Helmer Helmers, *The Royalist Republic: Literature, Politics, and Religion in the Anglo-Dutch Public Sphere, 1639–1660* (Cambridge: Cambridge University Press, 2015), *passim*.
30 Leo Miller, 'In Defence of Milton's *Pro populo anglicano defensio*', *Renaissance Studies*, 4.3 (1990): 1–12 (p. 2).
31 Campbell and Corns, *John Milton*, p. 229.
32 Leo Miller, *John Milton's Writings in the Anglo-Dutch Negotiations, 1651–1654* (Pittsburgh: Duquesne University Press, 1992), p. 2.
33 Joad Raymond, 'John Milton, European: The Rhetoric of Milton's Defences', in *The Oxford Handbook of Milton*, ed. by Nicholas McDowell and Nigel Smith (Oxford: Oxford University Press, 2011): 273–290.
34 Go Togashi provides a detailed analysis of the readership and reading of the *Second Defence*: 'Contextualizing Milton's *Second Defence of the English People*: Cromwell and the English Republic, 1649–1654', *Milton Quarterly*, 45.4 (2011): 217–244.
35 See for information on John Bramhall, Jack Cunningham, *John Ussher and John Bramhall: The Theology and Politics of Two Irish Ecclesiastics of the Seventeenth Century* (Aldershot: Ashgate Publishing, 2007), *passim*.
36 Martin Dzelzainis, 'Milton, Peter Du Moulin and the Authorship of *Regii Sanguinis Clamor ad Coulum Adversus Parricidas Anglicanos* (1652)', *Notes and Queries*, 60.4 (2013): 537–538.
37 It is difficult to determine the extent of Milton's involvement with John Philips' defence. We know that the latter was living in his uncle's house at the time of the composition, and also that Edward Philips wrote in his biography that Philips showed the manuscript to Milton for 'his examination and polishment' (qtd. in Helen Darbishire, *The Early Lives of John Milton* (New York: Barnes and Noble, 1932), p. 710). For extensive discussion, see Nicholas McDowell, 'Family Politics: Or, How John Philips Read His Uncle's Satirical Sonnets', *Milton Quarterly*, 42.1 (2008): 1–21 (pp. 2–3); Robert Fallon, *Milton in Government* (Pennsylvania: Pennsylvania University Press, 1993), p. 139.
38 *CPW*: IV. part 1, 554.
39 Blair Worden, *Literature and Politics in Cromwellian England: John Milton, Andrew Marvell and Merchamont Nedham* (Oxford: Oxford University Press, 2008), p. 129.
40 *CPW*: IV. part 1, 324.
41 *CPW*: IV. part 1, 307.
42 F.F. Blok, *Isaac Vossius en zijn Kring: Zijn Leven to Zijn Afscheid van Koningin Christina van Zweden, 1618–1655* (Groningen: Egbert Forsten, 1999), p. 30.
43 David Masson, *The Life of Milton*, 8 vols. (Cambridge: Macmillan Press, 1887), vol. 4, p. 174.
44 Blok, pp. 33–34.
45 *CPW*: IV. part 1, 556.
46 Estelle Haan, '*Defensio Prima* and the Latin Poets', in *The Oxford Handbook of Milton*, ed. by Nicholas McDowell and Nigel Smith (Oxford: Oxford University Press, 2011): 292–305 (pp. 297, 301).

47 Edith Kern, *The Influence of Heinsius and Vossius Upon French Dramatic Theory* (Baltimore: John Hopkins Press, 1949), p. 52.

48 Blok, p. 147.

49 Kern, p. 52.

50 Paul Sellin, 'The Last of the Renaissance Monsters: The Poetical Institutions of Gerardus Johannis Vossius, and Some Observations on English Criticism', in *Anglo-Dutch Cross Currents in the Seventeenth and Eighteenth Century* (Los Angeles: University of California Press, 1976): 1–39 (pp. 5–6).

51 See for the cooperation between James Ussher and Isaac Vossius to publish a rediscovered manuscript of *Ignatius*, Leo Miller, 'Milton, Salmasius and Hammond: The History of an Insult', *Renaissance and Reformation*, 9.3 (1973): 108–115.

52 Sophie van Romburgh, 'Junius [Du Jon], Franciscus [Francis] (1591–1677), Philologist and Writer on Art', *Oxford Dictionary of National Biography*, retrieved 4 July 2018. www.oxforddnb.com/view/10.1093/ref:odnb/9780198614128.001.0001/odnb-9780198614128-e-15167.

53 Thomas Seccombe, 'Vossius, Isaac (1618–1689), Philologist and Author', *Oxford Dictionary of National Biography*, retrieved 4 July 2018. www.oxforddnb.com/view/10.1093/ref:odnb/9780198614128.001.0001/odnb-9780198614128-e-28356.

54 Joad Raymond, 'Books as Diplomatic Agents: Milton in Sweden', in *Cultures of Diplomacy and Literary Writing in the Early Modern World*, ed. by Tracey A. Sowerby and Joanna Craigwood (Oxford: Oxford University Press, 2019): 131–145.

55 Robert Fallon, 'Sweden: The War in the North', *Milton in Government* (Pennsylvania: Pennsylvania University Press, 1993): 160–176.

56 Masson, vol. 4, p. 318.

57 Paul R. Sellin, 'P.C. Hooft, Constantijn Huygens, and the *Méditations Chrestiennes* of Rutger Wessel van den Boetzelaer, Baron van Asperen', in *From Revolt to Riches: Culture & History of the Low Countries, 1500–1700*, ed. by Theo Hermans and Reinier Salverda (London: UCL Press, 2017): 167–172.

58 Many thanks to Ola Gustavsson, librarian of Norrköping library, who gave me an 1883 reproduction of the 1747 catalogue when I visited the library.

59 The Vossius-Heinsius correspondence is in the Gregorian Calendar.

60 Petrus Burmannus, *Sylloge Epistolarum a Viris Illustribus Scriptarum*, 3 vols. (Leiden, 1727), vol. 3, p. 595.

61 *CPW*: IV. part 1, 556.

62 'Certe & ingenium istius viri & scribendi genus multus praesentibus collaudavit', Burmannus, vol. 3, p. 596.

63 Burmannus, vol. 3, p. 603.

64 Dobranski, p. 32.

65 *CPW*: IV. part 1, 572–573.

66 *Koninklijke Bibliotheek*, Speciale Collecties, KW. 2203 G 19.

67 Paul W. Blackford, 'Preface to Fides Publica and Supplementum', in *Milton, The Complete Prose Works* (New Haven: Yale University Press, 1964), vol. 4, part II: 1082–1085 (p. 1083).

68 *Hollandsche Mercurius* (Februari 1651), II, p. 16.

69 Burmannus, vol. 3, p. 603.

70 *Hollandsche Mercurius* (July 1651), II, p. 16.

71 Burmannus, vol. 3, p. 621.

72 *CPW*: IV. part 1, 653.

73 Lieuwe van Aitzema, *Saeken van Staet en Oorlogh*, 14 vols. (Amsterdam, 1662), vol. 4, p. 205.

74 Harms, Raymond, and Salman, p. 5.

75 *CPW*: IV. part 1, 311.

76 Campbell and Corns, *John Milton*, p. 237.

77 Leo Miller, 'Milton's *Defensio* ordered wholesale for the States of Holland', *Notes and Queries*, 33.1 (1986): 33.

78 Graswinkel interdictum esse ne pergat in Miltoni confutando ægre fert Salmasius', 'Vossius to Heinsius, 5 Augustus', in Burmannus, vol. 3, p. 621; Masson, vol. 4, pp. 342, 634–635.

79 Anonymous, *Nederlantsche Nyp-Tang* (Amsterdam?, 1652), p. 10.

80 Milton had written to Marvell with the request to give a copy of his *Second Defence* to John Bradshaw (living close to Marvell in Eton) with an introductory letter. He, moreover, sent a copy to Marvell himself, to which Marvell replied that he felt honoured and would learn the *Defensio* by heart. Marvell would later distribute copies of the *Pro Se Defensia* in Saumur, France: Smith, *The Chameleon*, pp. 123, 132.

81 Boswell in his reconstruction of Milton's library includes three books by Daniel Heinsius (*Aristarchus Sacer, De Tragoediae Constitutione* and *First Pythian Ode of Pindar*), as well as a work by Isaac Vossius (*Verses on Rovai*), see Jackson Campbell Boswell, *Milton's Library: A Catalogue of the Remains of John Milton's Library and an Annotated Reconstruction of Milton's Library and Ancillary Readings* (New York: Garland Publishing, 1975).

82 Sellin, 'The Last of the Renaissance Monsters', footnote 83, pp. 34–35. Moreover, when reading Mylius' diary there is a conversation about books mentioned and Christopher Arnold of Nuremburg recommended some titles that are noted down by Mylius in the margins of his diary, among which is a book on the Pelagians by Gerardus Vossius. This small conversation took place when Mylius was in London on business in the early 1650s and illustrates that the works by Vossius were a topic of discussion among intellectuals in 1650s London. Leo Miller, *Milton and the Oldenburg Safeguard* (New York: Loewenthal Press, 1985), pp. 26–27.

83 'Mr. Salmasius, while passing through, was handsomely entertained by the King of Denmark, on account of his *Defensio* for the King of Scotland, whereon people hereabouts have started many tales. I answer that liberality is fitting for kings, and nothing is more suitable to their nature. What his antagonist Mr. Milton informs me, even as I write this, I include in a copy herewith. I have distinguished new intrigues, loose words, and the rest with them, so that I fear the dubious for the certain', Mylius qtd. in Leo Miller and translated by the same, *Milton and the Oldenburg Safeguard*, p. 126.

84 More, *Fides Publica* (transl. Masson, vol. 4, p. 632).

85 Masson, vol. 4, p. 630.

86 Harms, Raymond, and Salman, p. 5.

3 *Paradise Lost, Upon Appleton House*, and the Works of Vondel and Huygens

The lines that follow are taken from 'De Bruiloft van den Teems en Aemstel t'Amsterdam' (The Wedding of the Thames and Amstel in Amsterdam, 1660), a poem by Joost van den Vondel, written to commemorate the wedding in 1641 of Mary Stuart and Willem II of Orange.

> [. . .] *dit roken d'Engelanders,*
> *En de Bataviers, die trou*
> *Nu met onderlinge standers*
> *Gaen gepaert, als man en vrou,*
> *Om de waterstraet te vaegen*
> *Van het ongebonden schuim,*
> *Dat ter helle uit elck quam plaegen.*
> *Tijt is 't dat de zeeplaegh ruim',*
> *En zich weder ga versteecken*
> *In het onverlichte hol,*
> *Met haer grijns en valsche streecken.*
> *Hier staen liefde en eendraght vol.*
> *Amsterdam omhelst nu Londen,*
> *Beide aen een door trou verbonden.*

> [. . .] this rouses the English
> And the Batavians, who true
> With mutual witness
> Are paired, as bride and groom,
> This water-strait to liberate
> From that unbounded froth
> That came from hell to plague.
> It is time to sweep this sea-plague off
> So it will again retreat
> Into the unlit cave
> With her grin and false deceit.
> Here love and unity stand brave

Amsterdam embraces London round,
Both united, in loyalty plighted.

(ll. 83–96)

For Vondel, it was one of the most significant events of the period, marking an alliance between the nations and emphasising their natural kinship
throughout the seventeenth century. It seems strange at first that he waited
nineteen years before publishing the poem, but commemorating this particular wedding during the Restoration provided a reminder that the United
Provinces had supported the English monarchy before and would continue
to do so – arguably culminating in the so-called Glorious Revolution of
1688. This chapter will examine, through Vondel's metaphor of two rivers
flowing together, the Anglo-Dutch bond flowing through the seventeenth
century. In particular, it shows the transnational nature of intellectual and
artistic culture, and the degree to which these countries inhabited a shared
literary space.

The previous chapter looked at material exchange and how the Dutch
printing and publication industry distributed texts, underpinning scholarly debates as well as shaping and promoting some of their content. It
was relatively easy to gain access to Dutch literary sources, whether these
were distributed through Elzevier's cheap duodecimos, spread by diplomats such as Jacob Cats, Lieuwe van Aitzema or Constantijn Huygens in
England, or personally collected by travelling through the United Provinces. We saw how the scholarly community in Europe corresponded in
letters, that books were exchanged and dedicated to foreign scholars, and
that controversies boiled up on a plethora of topics. This chapter will focus
on their imaginative rather than material exchange, and will trace the roots
and nature of specific parallels between the works of Milton, Marvell, and
Dutch writers.

To what extent did Dutch writers read Milton's and Marvell's English
poetry? It is unlikely they had read much, since few Dutch writers and intellectuals had knowledge of the English language, with the significant exception of Constantijn Huygens and a few others. As Cornelis Schoneveld
argues in *Intertraffic of the Mind*, there were no official institutions in the
United Provinces at which one could learn the English language and the
number of personal tutors was relatively small; translations from English
into Dutch were less common than from French into Dutch, for example.[1]
Similarly, John Gallagher's book *Learning Languages in Early Modern
England* argues that 'English in the early modern period was the little-
known and little-regarded language of a small island out on the edge of
Europe'.[2] Moreover, when we read Petrus Rabus (1660–1702), poet, trans-
lator and editor of the *Boekzaal van Europe* (1692–1700) (Library of
Europe), it appears that some individuals were not interested in poetical
writings in English:[3]

Maar 'k voele mijn lust van verder uitschrijven wat gezakt, dewijl onder een deel Engelschen Digters, die ons Hollanders niet veel raken, gelijks als, W. d'Avenant, J. Denham, J. Donne, B. Johnson, J. Milton, J. Oldham, J. Wilmot, Grave van Rochester, W. Shakespear, Ph. Sidney, E. Spencer, J. Lukkling [sic], E. Waller en andere.[4]

But I feel my desire to elaborate somewhat sink, because of a number of English poets, that do not affect us Hollanders much, such as, W. d'Avenant, J. Denham, J. Donne, B. Johnson, J. Milton, J. Oldham, J. Wilmot, Earl of Rochester, W. Shakespear, Ph. Sidney, E. Spencer, J. Sukkling, E. Waller, and others.

Given this limited scope for Dutchmen reading English verse, we must rely on the still-current Latin of the intellectual elite. The discussion in this chapter is related to interaction between English poetry in Latin and a Dutch reading audience, translations of Dutch works into English, and possible engagement with literary sources in Dutch by the English. It has to be noted that translation of English prose works into Dutch was much more firmly established, especially when it came to religious and political texts and natural philosophy. I have earlier discussed the respective possibilities of Marvell's and Milton's acquisition of Dutch, which would have enabled direct interaction with sources in Dutch, whether these could have been read within the United Provinces, in Marvell's case, or distributed through the early modern European network. My purpose here is to discuss some similarities between Dutch writers and Milton and Marvell, not so much in terms of intertextuality (narrowly conceived) or direct engagement, but instead through the notion of a combined Anglo-Dutch literary milieu, a shared 'literary air' that both writers breathed. Two examples here might be considered usefully characteristic of this literary exchange and convergence: first, Marvell's associations with Dutch country house poems, and second, parallels between Milton's *Paradise Lost* and some of the plays by Vondel.

Marvell had the opportunity to experience the Dutch literary environment first-hand when he travelled to the Netherlands in the 1640s and 1660s. He could have gone to Amsterdam's *schouwburg*, the theatre, to see a play by Jan Vos (1610–1667), a much-loved Dutch playwright of the seventeenth century. Casper Barlaeus (1584–1648), Dutch poet and polymath, wrote about Vos' play in a description that would rather have appealed to Marvell:[5]

Ik stae gelijk bedwelmt en overstolpt van geest.
De Schouburg wort verzet, en schoeyt op hooger leest.
Rijst Sophocoles weêr op? Stampt Aeschylus weêr hier?
Of maekt Euripides dit ongewoon getier?

Neen, 't is een Ambachtsman, een ongelettert gast,
Die nu de ganysch rey van Helicon verrast.[6]

I stand both astonished and overwhelmed in spirit.
The theatre shakes and is dedicated to higher wit,
Has Sophocles risen? Does Aeschylus stamp here?
Or is it Euripides we overhear?
No, it is a tradesman, an unlettered man,
Who now all of Helicon surprises.

There is no known correspondence between Marvell and Dutch writers of the so-called *Muiderkring*. This somewhat romanticised name, after the poet and regent P.C. Hooft's castle in Muiden, was given retrospectively in the nineteenth century to a coterie of intellectual friends who exchanged poems and witticisms in the seventeenth century. It was an eclectic group of correspondents, ranging from the political elite (P.C. Hooft, Albert Coenraadszoon Burgh) to shopkeepers (Jan Vos, Joost van den Vondel). Two sisters were often included in the correspondence: Maria Tesselschade Visscher and Anna Roemersdochter Visscher. Vondel and Tesselschade, or 'Tesseltje' converted to Catholicism, whereas others were Protestant. Despite their diversity of standing and conviction, they were all connected through art and literature.

A literary connection between Marvell and one of these correspondents does exist, namely Constantijn Huygens (1596–1687). Huygens was born into a family with good connections and received a high-quality education. He was appointed secretary to stadtholder Frederik Hendrik in 1625, and Willem II in 1647.[7] Besides being a gifted composer and playing several musical instruments, he created an extensive literary oeuvre – over two thousand Latin verses as well as poems in French, English, Spanish and German. For his Dutch poems he is considered one of the most versatile and cosmopolitan poets that the province of Holland has known.[8] Huygens established a broad intellectual network, partly as a result of his diplomatic travels and participation in the Republic of Letters.[9] However, four centuries later, he is curiously unknown to English readers and students. The *Oxford Dictionary of English Biography* has, for example, no entry for him as yet. In 1956, Rosalie Colie wrote about his reputation that 'if he is known at all, it is in the peculiarly frustrating and gratifying fashion, as the father of a famous son, Christiaan Huygens, the physicist. During his own lifetime, however, few Hollanders were better known outside their country than Constantijn Huygens'.[10] During his travels in England – three times during 1618–1623 and twice in the 1660s and 1670s – he became acquainted with Ben Jonson, John Donne, Francis Bacon and Cornelis Drebbel, among others.[11] Huygens was a great admirer of John Donne's poetry, but the index of his library shows he took great interest in English literature as whole; volumes range from a first-folio edition of William Shakespeare, to Geoffrey Chaucer, Edmund Spenser's *Faerie Queene* and Edmund Waller's poetry.[12] Huygens translated more English poems than any other Dutch writer in the seventeenth century, even if the numbers are still remarkably small: poems by John Donne and all of Archibald Armstrong's epigrams.[13]

It is worth briefly elaborating on this connection between Donne and Huygens, since Marvell, too, was heavily influenced by Donne. Huygens and Donne most likely met in London during Donne's visits of 1621 and 1622. He left a deep impression on Huygens with his sermons and poetry, which we can read about in Huygens' letters and verse. In total, Huygens made translations of nineteen of Donne's poems, in two tranches. Authorised versions were first published in his complete works, *Korenbloemen*, of 1658, and republished in 1672. In both editions the translations come complete with the English title directly translated into Dutch, as well as the first line of the English original.[14] Like the rivers Amstel and Thames flowing together, English poetry penetrates Dutch literature and readership, by sharing the same page.

Before publication, Huygens' work was circulated in manuscript form. He sent the first two translations to P.C. Hooft and to another friend, Johan Brosterhuysen.[15] Hooft was deeply impressed by both Donne's poetry and Huygens' translation work. In his return letter he lyrically asserts that this 'English fruit preserved in Dutch sugar makes all Dutch native poetry lose its natural taste'.[16] It is difficult to think of higher praise. The same day that Hooft wrote this letter, he also posted copies of Huygens' translation to his brother-in-law, mentioning that they had already been sent to Laurens Reael, Caspar Barlaeus, Joost van den Vondel, and Tesselschade Roemer. A few days later, Vondel responded to Hooft's letter with a, for him, unusually whimsical poem that mixes praise of, and resistance to, Donne's charms:

De Britse DONN'
Die duistre zon,
Schijnt niet voor ieders oogen,
Seit Huigens, ongeloogen.
Die taelgeleerde Haegenaer
Die watertant naer Kavejaer,
Naer snoftobak, en smooken,
Die raeuwe herssens kooken:
Maer dit is ongemeene kost,
't Is een banketje voor den Drost [.]

The British Donne
That dark sun,
Shines not for everyone's eyes,
Says Huygens, without lie.
That polyglot Haegenaer
Who salivates for caviar,
For snuff, and smoke,

That fires the raw intellect;
Though this is unusual fare,
It is a banquet for Hooft [.]

The poem is stuffed with food metaphors.[17] He compares Donne's poetry to salads later in the poem: no matter how much you eat, you are still hungry in the end. Perhaps the metaphysical aspect of the poetry did not appeal, or it lacked the drama that was Vondel's stock in trade, as we will see in Chapter 6. Vondel is an exception, as those readers who loved *obscuritas* admired Huygens' translations and enjoyed Donne's poems.[18]

What ought we to say about the quality of Huygens' translation? Donne's poetry is renowned for being ambiguous and compact, making it very difficult to translate. Huygens claims in the preface to his translation that Charles I could not believe someone had managed to translate 'a certain English poet', whom he had deemed untranslatable. He adds, with a touch of national pride, that if Charles I had understood Dutch, he would have realised the language was capable of expressing anything with both elegance and clarity. English, he admits, does pose additional problems with its willingness to adopt foreign loan words: 'her language is all languages; and, if it suits her, Greek and Latin become vulgar English'.[19] Huygens' translations consequently rely heavily on Dutch's capacity for double meanings and neologisms. They demonstrate an excellent understanding of passive English. Huygens' grasp is more than merely functional, however, since he shows sophisticated understanding of Donne's text – as well as, history argues, excellent judgement. Of Huygens' nineteen translations, most are still regarded as among Donne's best.[20]

Which is not, however, to say that Huygens' choice of quality ingredients has allowed all readers to enjoy the end product. Koos Daley, for example, is unconvinced by Huygens' translations, and writes that we should ourselves 'judge [. . .] how bland Donne's recipes become when prepared in a Dutch oven'.[21] It is true that the compact grammatical and syntactic structures of Donne's poetry often resist direct translation. This is one of the reasons why Huygens' version of 'Ecstasy' is 30 lines longer than the original. Its generative ambiguity is significantly expunged. However, this is not a mere thinning out of the dough to cover a broader dish, since Huygens' makes delightful additions to the mix. In the 'Triple Fool', which also happens to be Huygens' last translation, we find ambiguities not present in Donne's own version, thereby creating additional layers of meaning. He still uses the occasionally stilted alexandrines of Dutch poetry, and he standardises Donne's often irregular rhyming scheme, but he captures the tone and sentiment of the poem faithfully. He also finds the space to introduce a pun of his own. The line 'was 't dicht in dicht besloten', can be translated as 'my closest pain is trapped in poetry', but also as 'poetry trapped by poetry' (l. 12). Daley has argued that Huygens' work kills the playfulness of some of Donne's poetry, its ambiguity and its vibrancy.[22] This is always a tempting charge when comparing originals to their copies, but in this case the existing studies focus mostly on the earlier translations, in particular Huygens' first, 'On the Sun Rising'. If we instead grant Huygens the favour of reading the translations chronologically, there is a real sense of improvement, as he moves from studied replication to more playful engagement.

The translations are far from being merely or mechanically truthful to the original. While they might lose some of Donne's witty paradoxes and ironies, they compensate through other elements that confirm Huygens' personal investment. He never claimed they were perfect reproductions; in a poem to Tesselschade he calls them mere shadows of the original.[23] Perhaps the perfect translation does not exist, as this current book demonstrates. It seems for me a timely reminder that we might finally leave the obsession with what is *lost* in translation, instead focusing on what is *gained*.[24] Translation has the potential to transmit ideas and motifs across linguistic borders – in this case Huygens' translations contributed to the store of Dutch literature, and Donne influenced Huygens' own writings.

The lasting effect of Donne's metaphysical poetry on Huygens' own work is quite visible. I will focus on one example here. Constantijn Huygens married Suzanne van Baerle in 1627, whom he called Sterre (Dutch for star). Together they had five children, but after ten years of marriage, she died aged 38. Huygens was heartbroken and stopped composing poetry entirely. Tesselschade wrote a sonnet urging him to put down his grief on the page. In it she quotes two lines from Donne's own 'Triple Fool', translated into Dutch: 'Stelt u leed te boeck, soo hoeft ghy't niet t' onthouwen' (place your sorrow in verse, so you do not have to remember it).[25] A year later Huygens began composing some poems on grief and the loss of his Sterre.[26] Perhaps the best of these is 'Cupio Dissolvi: On the Death of Sterre' (1638), in which Donne's influence can be clearly felt:[27]

> Of droom ick, en is 't nacht, of is mijn, Sterr verdwenen?
>   Ick waeck, en 't is hoogh dagh, en sie mijn' Sterre niet.
>   O Hemelen, die mij haer aengesicht verbiedt,
> Spreeckt menschen-tael, en seght, waer is mijn' Sterre henen?
> Den Hemel slaet geluyd, ick hoor hem door mijn stenen,
>   En seght, mijn' Sterre staet in 't heilighe gebied,
>   Daer sij de Godtheid, daer de Godtheid haer besiet,
> En, voeght het lacchen daer, belacht mijn ijdel weenen.
>   Nu, Dood, nu Snick, met-een verschenen en verbij,
>   Nu, doorgang van een' Steen, van een gesteên, ten leven,
> Dunn Schutsel, staet naer bij, 'ksal 't u te danck vergeven;
>   Komt, dood, en maeckt mij korts van deze Cortsen vrij:
> 'Kverlang in 'teeuwigh licht te samen te sien sweven
> Mijn Heil, mijn Lief, mijn Lijf, mijn' God, mijn' Sterr, en mij.

Do I dream it night, or is my Star vanished?
    I wake, it is high day; and cannot see my star.

> O Heavens, who deny me her presence,
> Speak mortal words, say where has my Star gone?
> Heavens beat a sound, I hear it through my sighs,
>   And see my Star stood in the holy place.
> There, see the Godhead, the Godhead beholds her,
> And laughter rings there, laughter at my vain cries.
>   Now, death, now cry, at once appear and flee,
>   Now, through woe, through keening, to live,
> Thin veil, stay near, I will thank you right;
>   Come, Death, make brief this fevered malady.
> I long to float together in heaven's eternal light
> My Grace, my love, my frame, my God, my Star, and me.

One feature of Donne's most iconic sonnets is how they play with the metrical or structural rules of the form. Several of his *Holy Sonnets* break convention in ways significant to their meaning. A famous example would be his 'Death be not Proud', in which the last line rhymes unexpectedly again with the first. The defeat of Death and the idea of eternity are conjured again, since we are invited to re-read the poem by the looping rhyme. In Huygens, we find a similar understanding of such effects. The first 13 lines read as consistent alexandrines, but in the last line the poem slows down to a crawl through the use of monosyllables. There is an urge to stress all words in the last line, an enumeration of grief, partly assisted by the *versus rapportati* (correlative verse or mirroring). Beyond such formal effects, we also hear echoes of the metaphysics of Donne's poetry in the content. Personified Death is portrayed as a coward to be goaded, the joining of souls that features in Donne's 'Ecstasy' resounds in the penultimate line, and poetry that eases as well as emphasises pain is present throughout, recalling the 'Triple Fool'.

With this background to Huygens' poetry and his fascination with English poetry in mind, let us now return to the relationship between Marvell and Huygens. One of the reasons that these poets are often discussed together is that both started writing country house poems in the summer of 1651; the texts have a striking number of similarities. There is an understandable urge to explain this through direct and pertinent links between the two men. Peter Davidson and Adriaan van der Weel, for example, argue that 'the two poets met in the 1640s and that Marvell's memories of Huygens' set speeches on the tour of Hofwijck remained in his memory sufficiently strongly to contribute to the design and form of 'Upon Appleton House'.[28] However, it is not at all clear whether or why Huygens would take Marvell on a tour of his estate. As a matter of fact, this would seem quite unlikely since Marvell, as a tutor of noble sons, would probably not have moved in the same circles of Dutch society Huygens would normally have entertained. Even if Marvell had seen Hofwijck, the time frame (approximately eight years) between the tour and the composition of both poems remains puzzling. Had Marvell indeed received a tour of the property, it would still require both poets to have been inspired, at the same time, to compose on the same subjects, in the same genre, in the summer of 1651. An alternative, which Nigel Smith proposes, is that *Hofwijck* served as a source text for Marvell's poem, and that he thus had seen some manuscript version before 1651 when he began his own poem.[29] However, a substantial draft of Huygens' poem would have been necessary if it is to explain some of the detailed concurrences, as well as the similarities in structure and generic form. Huygens had only finished 252 lines (of 2800) of the poem in the summer of 1650, as we know from the dated manuscript, and started writing again after 14 August 1651.[30] It would have been impossible for Marvell to have seen the whole poem before the beginning of his own composition, since he started his poem in the autumn of 1651.

Ineke Huysman has recently published another article on the potential acquaintance between Marvell and Huygens, based on their country house poem, in which she speculates that Marvell and Huygens met in the train of Queen Henrietta Maria, who travelled to the United Provinces in 1642.[31] It is an interesting proposition, but there is, however, little evidence to suggest that Marvell, travelling to the continent as a tutor, would have been among the unnamed members of the train of the Queen, whether in his own right or in attendance on his tutees; rather, the existence of the two poems is a spur to read the historical possibilities in this light. Unfortunately, even this meeting would not resolve the issue of Huygens and Marvell commencing their poems eight years later at the same time. Huysman's article sets itself a modest remit, stating that it 'is written from an historical, rather than a literary, perspective', and it will therefore 'not provide a detailed comparison of the two poems'.[32] By concentrating on the circumstance and coincidences of the two men, it is hoped to make plausible their parallel compositions. However, it seems to me that a combination of historical and literary analysis yields greater fruit: the poems themselves are exactly where the answers lie. The resemblance cannot be explained in terms of direct or personal influence, but only through a less linear consideration of the context in which both writers were operating, including genre conventions.

In Huygens' *Hofwijck*, the gardens and the house itself are fashioned after The Hague, each in turn representing Eden and Holland. Marvell's poem is divided into three parts (the house, followed by the garden and the wood), whereas Huygens' poem mostly focuses on the estate's lands. Huygens' house is modestly sized, set in extensive grounds, and was finished in the early 1640s. It still stands today, although a nearby railroad track encroaches on the estate, which makes for an interesting view from the train. In Marvell's piece, Nun Appleton and its gardens accommodated the Fairfax family. The main house in Appleton was re-built or extensively renovated, and as Jane Partner has persuasively argued, the house was in the process of being built when Marvell wrote his poem.[33] The house is substantially larger than Huygens', but the latter has the advantage that he can boast about his own house, rather than describing that of a patron.

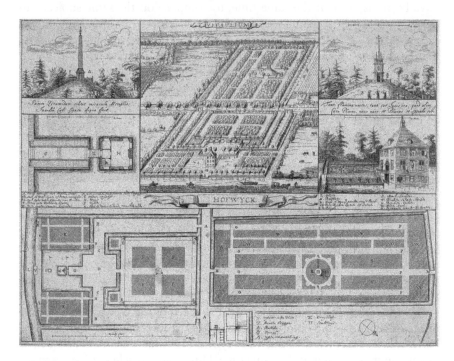

Figure 3.1 Constantijn Huygens', *Hofwijck*, 1653

Source: Reproduced with kind permission from the Museum of Huygens' Hofwijck, Voorburg.

The context in which both poems were written reveals a great deal about the political and religious tensions at play within the works and may explain some of the similarities. In the late 1640s, Marvell's political allegiances were ambiguous; he moved in royalist literary circles and maintained Cavalier friendships with Richard Lovelace and John Hall.[34] In this period, he also composed three lyrical poems with royalist resonances: 'Elegy for Francis Villiers', the commendatory poem for Lovelace's *Lucasta*, and an elegy in *Lachrymae Musarum*. He was working as a tutor in the Presbyterian household of the Fairfaxes.[35] Meanwhile, Huygens was a convinced Royalist and supporter of the Orangist party. We also know that he was a Calvinist member of the Dutch Reformed Church (as illustrated, for example, by his poems on the Lord's Last Supper and satirical poems such as 'Ooghentroost' (1647)) and outspokenly anti-Catholic, despite the fact that he had Catholic friends, such as Vondel and Tesselschade.[36]

The composition of Marvell's poem commenced in the autumn of 1651. Nun Appleton is located in Yorkshire. In the summer of 1651, Charles II planned to invade northern England with his army in Scotland. Fairfax himself was still undecided over which side to support: either to answer the English Government's appeal to return to duty, or to support the Stuart cause.[37] The Fairfax family did not endorse the Regicide, which led to his retirement in 1650 and to him playing an important role in the Restoration of the monarchy nine years later. In 1651, Levellers, under the leadership of Lilburne and Walwyn, camped in Hatfield Chase, only a few miles away from the Fairfax estate. A great number of English army troops were also encamped in Ripon, only twenty miles away.[38] The battle of Worcester was about to begin in September of that year. Milton's 'On the Lord General Fairfax at the Siege of Colchester', although written in 1648, reveals some of the same problems that the Commonwealth was still facing three years later:

> Thy firm unshaken virtue ever brings
>   Victory home, though new rebellions raise
>   Their hydra heads, and the false North displays
>   Her broken league, to imp their serpent wings,
> O yet a nobler task awaits thy hand;
>
> (ll. 5–9)

At this particular moment, Nun Appleton was surrounded by the tumultuous consequences of the English Civil Wars.

Huygens was at this point closely involved with the family Van Oranje. When Willem II died in 1650, the first 'stadhouderloze tijdperk' (era without a stadtholder) commenced, during which the republicans became more influential than the Orangist party. It was a difficult time for Huygens. On the whole, Anglo-Dutch relations became rapidly more hostile during this period, accelerated by the introduction of the Navigation Act (1651). It did not take long for the First Anglo-Dutch War to break out. During these tense times the poems were composed, and by poets who followed political developments in their countries closely; it is thus no wonder that they addressed similar issues, using a genre that accommodated political debate and content.

It is worth briefly highlighting some of the Dutch elements in Marvell's poem, before turning to a close reading. Ann Cotterill has argued that the flooded meadow in Marvell's poem is not unlike the polders of the Netherlands that are constantly at risk of being flooded.[39] De Vere, mentioned in stanza 5, fought under the command of Fairfax in 1629–1632, assisting the Dutch against the Spanish. The emphasis on tulips, in particular, is worth elaborating on. The Fairfax arms are symbolised by tulips, 'pink, and rose' (l. 312) and in line 336, the 'Switzers of our guard' are mentioned. This could, of course, refer to the Swiss guards of the Vatican, as Nigel Smith suggests in his edition. As John Simons has noted, though, it was also a colour variety of tulip in the Netherlands. Many tulips still bear the names of military heroes, and this association would suit the military background of Fairfax and his experience in the Low Countries.[40] Lastly, there is another Dutch word in the poem, used in a similar way to the Dutch in the *Character of Holland*, discussed in the first chapter. The lines 537–538, 'But most the

hewel's wonders are,/ Who here has the holt-fester's care', have the curious word 'holt-fester'. Helen Wilcox and E. Duncan-Jones have persuasively
argued that this is based on the Dutch word *houtvester*, meaning forester.[41]
This Dutch word was already translated into English in Hexham's *Copious
English and Netherduytch Dictionarie* of 1648.

The country house poem has considerable precedent as a vehicle for discussing the establishment, development, and progress of the (e)state, since
the estate functions as a microcosm of the state.[42] Genealogy is one way of
commenting on previous and present political developments. English country houses were often built on the ruins or foundations of medieval manor
houses, enabling the author to use the genealogy of the house to also comment on the genealogy of the family concerned.[43] Nun Appleton House was
built on a former nunnery, and it is through marriage that the house is converted from a house of religion to the present country house:

> A nunnery first gave it birth
> (For virgin buildings oft brought forth),
> And all that neighbour-ruin shows
> The quarries whence this dwelling rose.
>   (ll. 85–88)

This appeal to the authority of a long-established history differs strikingly
from the tone of most Dutch country house poems, as these are often written by the owners of newly built country houses – including Huygens' *Hofwijck* and Jacob Westerbaen's *Ockenburgh* (1654).

Although in both poems the country house and lands are presented as a
retreat from the outside world, they never fail to acknowledge that this ideal
world is still part of a society, including its historical circumstances.[44] Huygens uses a progressively microscopic movement from the state to the small
estate. The narrator takes us from nation to province to area to the village
and on the road to the garden:

> *In Holland, wat een land! Noordholland, wat een landje!*
> *In Delfland, wat een' Kleij; in Voorburgh wat een Sandje!*
> *Aen 't Coets-pad, wat een wegh! Aen 't water, wat een 'Vlied!*[45]
>   (ll. 33–35)

> In Holland, what a country! North-Holland, what a small state!
> In Delfland, what Clay; in Voorburg, what Sand!
> Next to the Coets-pad, what a road! Near the water, what a Flood!

In Marvell's poem, too, the narrator draws attention to the microcosm
within the macrocosm; Appleton is double-guarded within the retreat of
England, itself girded by protective seas:

Oh thou, that dear and happy isle
The garden of the world ere while,
Thou Paradise of foúr seas,
Which heaven planted us to please,
But, to exclude the world, did guard
With wat'ry if not flaming sword;
What luckless apple did we taste,
To make us mortal, and thee waste?
                    (ll. 321–328)

The use of paradise has more connotations than appear at a first reading, besides the echo of *Richard II*'s famous speech by John of Gaunt on 'this sceptred isle'.[46] Katherine Acheson has shown that throughout Marvell's poem the garden is connected to military structures, of which the walled garden is the perfect example of the early modern fortress.[47] It is no great coincidence that the first gardening books were written around the same time as works of military strategy were burgeoning – perhaps reflecting a desire to cultivate sanctuary in times of increasingly systematised conflict – and this contemporaneity is exploited to the full in the poem. The political and religious events occurring outside the estate can in this case be compared to a stone thrown into a pond, causing ripples that reach even the most remote places. Internal and external affairs cannot be excluded, and the watery walls of the channel will ultimately not protect the island.

The pastoral nature of the country house poem, much like Virgil's *Eclogues* that discussed the aftermath of Rome's Civil War, is concerned with the imperfect divide between the peaceful countryside and the troublesome demands of society. The country house attempts to offer a retreat, which is visible in many country house poems of the period, of which Jacob Cats' estate Sorghvliet in his *Ouderdom en Buyten-leven* (Old age, and Rural-life, 1655) is a perfect example. Huygens' pun *Hofwijck* (meaning 'court avoid', 'garden of refuge' or 'the court's neighbourhood') illustrates his consciousness of this tension.[48] In the following lines, Huygens even admits that it adds to the pleasure of his estate:

Hebb ick altoos getelt het dobbele geniet
Van ijet verheughelix op 't kantjen van 't verdriet;
Op 't kantjen sonder schroom; soo dat vast and're smaken
Het ghene mij genaeckt en niet en kan geraken.
                    (ll. 275–278)

I have always counted enjoyment twice
When something pleasurable is close to grief;
Close to grief, without hesitation, so that other experiences
That come near cannot touch me.

Like a church, the woodland estate tries to become a sanctuary from the earth's disequilibrium; a walk through the forest is connected to religious experiences and thoughtful contemplation, a simile used by both poets:

> De Bercken staen om mij als Toortsen, die in Kercken
> Niet half soo dienstigh staen en druijpen op de Sercken,
> Blanck-stammigh is de Boom, gelijck 't wasch vande Bije.
>   (ll. 341–343)

> The birches stand around me like torches, which in churches
> Stand not half as useful, dripping on the tombstones,
> The paleness of the bark like beeswax.

Compare Huygens' candles to the pillars of Marvell's poem:

> The arching boughs unite between
> The columns of the temple green;
> And underneath the wingèd choirs
> Echo about their tunèd fires.
>   (ll. 509–512)

The use of sacred images to describe the estate is a feature of many country house poems, of which Margaret Cavendish's 'Nature's House' (1651–3?), likely composed around the same time as Marvell's and Huygens' poems, is a further example: 'To bear High-roofed Thanks, Ceiled with Praise,/ Windows of Knowledge, Let in Light of Truth,/ Curtains of Joy, are drawn by Pleasant Youth./ Chimneys, of th'Touchstone of affection made' (ll. 8–11).[49] The religious experience induced by the tranquillity of the estate is reinforced by allusions to Eden; its abundant fertility hinting at a Golden Age. This comparison with a voluptuous paradise is a commonplace of estate poems; we find it for example in Edmund Waller's 'On St James Park, As Lately Improved by His Majesty' (1660) (ll. 1–11), Henry Vaughan's 'Upon the Priory Grove, His Usual Retirement' (1645–6) (ll. 30–36), and Richard Lovelace's 'Amyntor's Grove' (1641?) (ll. 67–81).

The reference to Eden, in which mankind is positioned as God's most noble creature, is important for the design of the estate itself. Marvell mentions the perfect and 'holy mathematics' (l. 47) of the human body. Within the first two stanzas, he introduces the horror of 'unproportioned dwellings', empty and vast; one should instead use 'bodies [to] measure out their place' (ll. 10, 16). Huygens, too, designed his estate as a mirror of the human body: 'I saw myself, that is all I had to do/ two windows to see, two for smell, two ears' (l. 980–981). The house is the head, the orchard the trunk, the forest the legs, and the hill the feet. The idea of anthropomorphic homes was not new. Henry Wotton had already argued in 1624 that ideal proportions could be achieved in a building by basing it on the human body. But Wotton did not invent this himself; the roots go back to classical times with Vitruvius *De Architectura* already giving the correct proportions to re-construct the human body in architecture.[50] This was not characteristic of English architectural theory alone, but clearly a feature of the European country house.[51] It is another way of linking the construction of the house to nature. These Edenic resonances lend hope to the project of building a prelapsarian house after the image of God.

Several country house poems emphasise this untainted image of the estate, by, paradoxically, mentioning foreign catastrophes. An example would be Sir Richard Fanshawe's 'An Ode upon Occasion of His Majesty's Proclamation in the Year 1630' (9 Sept 1630), unaware of what troubles England would endure in the next decade:

> Now war is all the world about,
> And everywhere Erynnis reigns,
> Or else, the torch so late put out,
>   The stench remains.
> Holland for many years hath been
> Of Christian tragedies the stage,
> Yet seldom hath she played a scene
>   Of bloodier rage.
>   [. . .]
>   To one blest isle;
> Which in a sea of plenty swam
> And turtles sang on every bough,
> A safe retreat to all that came.[52]
>   (ll. 1–8, 44–47)

The safe retreat allows a calm view on matters occurring outside. Indeed, the dangerous outside world emphasises the utopian vision within; through these visions of foreign warfare, tranquillity and peace emerge by comparison.

This is not the case in Marvell's and Huygens' poems. Marvell's poem is tainted with the memory of the Civil Wars, and in Huygens', too, there is an anxiety about the fragility of the political state. This is visible in the general commentary on tyrannical states – this time biblical ones – for example that of Babel and its king Nimrod (Huygens, ll. 733–792; Marvell, ll. 23–24), recast in terms of estate mismanagement. It is a recollection of the religious controversies and struggles that the poets themselves lived through, re-experienced during the composition of the poems. The speakers cannot escape active participation in events beyond the tranquil estate, as we can see from the personal interferences by the speaker in Huygens' poem and Fairfax in Marvell's, when it comes to religious controversies.

In Marvell's poem, Fairfax makes a ruling based on religious justice, associating his actions with the history of the nunnery on Appleton's estate:

> What should he do? He would respect
> Religion, but not right neglect:
> For first Religion taught him right,
> And dazzled not but cleared his sight.
> Sometimes resolved his sword he draws,
> But reverenceth then the laws:
> For Justice still that Courage led;
> First from a judge, then soldier bred.
> (ll. 225–232)

Marvell's poem is not simply anti-Catholic nonetheless. He does rake over some commonplace myths of the nefarious behaviour of nuns, namely the burial of children (217–224).[53] The nunnery, however, still has something appealing about it, with its exotic perfumes, the lamplight, and its beauty. The fair maiden Thwaites converses with the 'subtle nuns' under the 'summer suns' (ll. 94, 93). From the nuns' eyes flow tears of 'calm pleasure', each a wife, each a queen (ll. 114, 118). This contrasts with the stark severity of the presbyterian manor house. Compare Marvell's poem to the festivity of Ben Jonson's 'Penshurst' and the austerity becomes even more prominent. The nunnery is yet not all that it seems. The subtle conversation of the nuns and their 'smooth tongue[s]' (l. 200) are indirect but clear references to the serpent penetrating paradise.[54] With this realisation the enchantment ends, '[t]he castle vanishes or rends' (l. 270) and the 'wasting cloister with the rest/ Was in one instant dispossessed' (l. 271–272).

More outspoken than Marvell, Huygens, too, makes some references to Catholicism and its rituals. He uses a pun 'misdaad' on the practice of mass:

> *Dat Christelicke vier, in plaets van rad en galgh,*
> *Daer van ick even soo als van uw' misdaed walgh.*
> (ll. 1595–1596)

> That Christian fire, instead of wheel and gallows,
> Of which I am equally disgusted as of your crime.

In this instance, *Mis* means mass, as well as missing a target, with *daad* referring to deed, and combined in the word *misdaad* recalls associations with the word crime (misdeed). The poem, however, is not interested in anti-Catholic propaganda, but instead promotes toleration. All religious violence is barred from Huygens' ideal estate; he consciously remembers the near outbreak of civil war after the controversy between Arminius and Gomarus, discussed further in Chapters 4 and 5. This religious debate between those who believed in free will for salvation (Arminians) and those who followed the more extreme supralapsarian position (Gomarists) culminated in the Synod of Dort, at which followers of Arminius, remonstrants, were deemed heretics. The controversy climaxed in the execution of Johan van Olden-barnevelt, Grand-Pensionary of Holland. Huygens writes that on rare occasions the parliament in The Hague will tolerate such debates as necessary for the state, but they are never allowed at Hofwijck:

> *Ick bann het bits vermaen*
> *Van Kercken-spertelingh: Staet uijt, Arminiaen,*
> *Die op den Gomarist uw' tanden meent te slijpen;*
> *En staet uijt Gomarist; die desen meent te grijpen*
> *En krabben d'oude roof van 't seer van Achtien op.*
> (ll. 1503–1507)

> I outlaw the aggressive stirring
> Of the Church's struggle: Keep away, Arminian,
> Who thought to sharpen your teeth on a Gomarist,
> And keep away, Gomarist, who thought to capture
> And score the old scare of Eighteen.

A revival of the religious struggle of the 1610s and 20s was a real anxiety for Dutch authors of the country house poem. Writing a few years after Huygens, Jacob Westerbaen wrote his country house poem *Ockenburgh* (1654), based on his estate of the same name, built specifically for him. He dedicated his poem to Huygens, and was clearly inspired by *Hofwijck*.[55] Westerbaen's poem lacks the complexity of Huygens', but provides us instead with more direct references to contemporary political events, without the need for the diplomacy and allusion seen in Huygens and Marvell. He, too, makes reference to the Arminius-Gomarus conflict, but similarly to Huygens refuses to let the religious struggle enter his estate:

> *Ick [. . .] wil met u niet twisten*
> *Noch voor d'Arminiaen, noch voor de Gomaristen.*
> *Ick swyge van het jaer van acht-en-negenthien:*[56]

> I [. . .] do not want to wrangle,
> Nor for Arminians, nor for Gomarists,
> I will be silent on the year eighteen-nineteen.

Readers are, however, given some further explanation in a footnote, where the situation of Oldenbarnevelt is explained, something Huygens conspicuously does not do. Westerbaen's glosses reveal that he participated in political discourse, often candidly.

There was a more recent political topic that was heavily debated by the English and the Dutch: the Regicide.[57] Marvell's allusion to the Regicide is more oblique than Huygens'. The reader is first taken through a mowing scene filled with military imagery, echoing the violence of the Civil Wars, after which the world is compared to a blank canvas; the possibility to start anew: 'A new and empty face of things / A levelled space, as smooth and plain' (ll. 442–443). From the meadows, the walk reaches the forest, described in sanctified language, where we find a reference to the Regicide itself, hidden in the forest of the woodcutter:

> Who could have thought the tallest oak
> Should fall by such a feeble stroke!
>
> Nor would it, had the tree not fed
> A traitor-worm, within it bred.
> (As first our flesh corrupt within
> Tempts ignorant and bashful Sin.)
> And yet that worm triumphs not long,
> But serves to feed the hewel's young.
> While the oak seems to fall content,
> Viewing the treason's punishment.
>
> (ll. 551–560)

Besides the more commonplace symbolic use of the oak as a metaphor for Charles I and his execution, this scene also functions as a comment on deforestation. The conflict between man's habitation on the land and the preservation of its natural state was a debate of long standing in poetry, of which Michael Drayton's *Poly Olbion*, might be the longest and most thorough example. As Philip Major has shown, it was powerfully topical for the forest in Nun Appleton, and a discussion that would continue for the remainder of the century.[58] The oak that 'nor ever spoke', but was a 'more certain oracle' in Marvell's 'Upon the Hill and Grove at Bilbrough' has now been felled (l. 73) to fuel the ongoing unrest.

In several places in the Huygens poem, there are also references to the Regicide, often in complex metaphorical settings. One of the first direct references comes halfway through the poem, when the narrator's thoughts wander off during a shooting game:

> *Daer was ick over Zee: afgrijsen doet mij keeren,*
> *Van daer een eenigh Heer gesplitst is in veel 'Heeren,*
> *Van daer een' Croon, een' Croon, en noch een' Croon verrast*
> *Op hoofden is geraeckt daer op sij niet en past.*
>
> There I was overseas: abhorrence made me return,
> From where one Lord was divided into many Lords
> From where a Crown, a Crown, and still another Crown, surprisingly,
> Found its way to heads it does not suit.
>
> (ll. 1241–1244)

The narrator cannot escape the associations of the Regicide within his peaceful estate, leading to powerful feelings of anxiety, of which the following lines become the most explicit allusion to the political developments in England:

> *En staet als kijker bij, of neemt de recht-banck waer,*
> *En oordeelt sittende van 't naeste spelend paer.*
> *En, soo de Kegel valt die Coningh is van achten,*
> *Soo vlieght'er wel een droom door spelende gedachten*
> *Van Coningen ontdaen in 't midden van haer volck,*
> *Dat over einde staet, terwijl de swartste wolck*
> *Die oijt de Sonn besloegh, wolck boven alle wonder,*
> *Drij Croonen zeffens velt met ongehoorden donder.*
> *En soo wordt Bollen ernst, en Kegels parlement;*
> (ll. 2147–2155)

And stands as spectator, or becomes part of the tribunal,
And judges, whilst sitting, the nearest playing pair.
And when the pins falls, hit at the back,
A dream is floating through playing minds,
To dispose of a king in the middle of her people,
That remains standing erect, while the blackest cloud,
That ever hid the sun, a cloud over any thought,
Three crowns fell with outrageous thunder.
    Bowling is no longer a game, and skittles parliament.

The metaphor of the Regicide as a bowling game was not original in literature of the 1640s, of which Salmasius' *Defensio Regia* is perhaps the prime example, though it was later condemned by Milton in his *First Defence* as 'silly rhetoric'.[59] This allusion to Salmasius' tract indicates that Huygens was following the Regicide debate and was familiar with anti- and pro-Regicide propaganda, in common with many other Dutch intellectuals, as discussed in Chapter 2.[60] The fact that the events of the Regicide and Civil Wars in England have reached the tranquil estate of Hofwijck, despite all thoughts of unrest having been summarily banished from this idyllic retreat, reveals the impact it had on the province of Holland; perhaps in this case we should no longer speak of the English political developments as causing ripples, but of perpetually recurring waves within the poem, waves that had the ability to cross the channel.[61] The English political situation is a constant danger to the painfully constructed peace in Huygens' estate, perhaps partly influenced by the imminent Anglo-Dutch war. That there was anxiety about the current diplomatic relations with England is certain.

Both poems offer communion with Creation as the key to preventing the entrance of strife, civil war, and general intolerance. The universal language of nature, the same for every Protestant denomination, is at the core of the country house genre. Marvel turns to the birds and the presence of nature itself, becoming one of them ('Thus I, easy philosopher,/ Among the birds and trees confer', ll. 561–562),[62] whereas Huygens finds solace in the account of Creation as a whole ('*Het Boeck van alle dingh,/ Van alles dat Hij eens in 't groote Rond beving*', The book of all things,/ Of how all things on the great Earth He began, ll. 1599–1600). By listening to the sound of birds and observing the perfection of creation, the inhabitants of the paradisaical estate can regain a prelapsarian universal state and church, in which peace is no longer threatened by political developments from outside.

How can we make sense of the similarities that have been demonstrated so far? Willemien de Vries writes that intertextuality is one of the characteristics of the country house poem.[63] The same themes, vehicles, imagery, and structure return. This does not need to be a direct intertextuality between individual poems, but an intertextuality of genre. The transnationalist approach allows a transcending of 'national' genres. Authors of estate poetry will comment on the lands, the solace that nature can offer, the desire to return to a prelapsarian state, and in various languages. The nightingale will continue to interrupt the narrator with its song and the seasons will pass swiftly by in each estate's year. This is dominantly present in Huygens and Marvell, but in numerous other examples, too. The peaceful estate is always in danger from developments from outside that bring havoc and riot. No wonder that Huygens and Marvell sought escape in the genre of the country house poem in 1651, even if they did not find it. Similar contexts of political and religious turmoil led to the similarities in the poems, which found an expression in the same genre. There is nothing in the poems' parallels that demand we imagine a personal meeting or influence, once we allow that national boundaries are more permeable than often presumed.

Milton and Vondel

In Milton's case, too, we find connecting threads between his literary oeuvre and some Dutch writers. As Milton did not travel through the United Provinces himself, it is unlikely that he directly engaged with many Dutch writers, as John Donne, for example, appears to have done. However, large communities of Dutch speakers resided in London during Milton's life, and their existence has encouraged scholars to contend that Milton had personal connections with the Dutch literary environment.[64] One of the most outspoken advocates for Milton's engagement with Dutch sources was George Edmundson, writing in *Milton and Vondel: A Curiosity of Literature* (1885) that '[n]egotiations with Dutch envoys, controversies with Dutch professors, intercourse with a circle of quasi-Dutch friends, correspondence with Dutch residents, quarrels with Dutch booksellers, all conspired to familiarise Milton with Dutch affairs'.[65] The relations presented here are somewhat more complex than Edmundson suggests. While Salmasius and Vlacq clearly have

Milton's attention in his *Defences*, neither was born in the United Provinces. It is, however, possible that Milton received books that were published in the United Provinces (not necessarily in Dutch) from Lieuwe van Aitzema, or via his intellectual network, which included people with Dutch connections, such as John Dury and Samuel Hartlib.

We know that Milton did meet one grandee of the Dutch literary scene: Jacob Cats (1577–1660). Cats was a well-known poet in his own right. *Sinne- en Minnebeelden* (Images of Sin and Virtue, 1627) was a best-seller in the seventeenth century and beyond. In 1653 Cats went to London to negotiate the peace with Cromwell. It was Milton's responsibility as Secretary of Foreign Tongues to translate the answer to the ambassadors.[66] It is likely that Milton would have encountered Cats during official functions, such as council meetings.[67] Though there is no clear record of a meeting between Cats and Milton, Hermann Mylius records in his diary (20 January 1651) that Milton was visited by an unknown Dutch person: 'And when I had thoroughly informed him of the state of my case, I took my departure. As I was leaving, one of the Dutch came to him'.[68] Who was this? Was it Gerard Schaep who had already met Milton by this point? It clearly was not Van Aitzema, who had not yet arrived in London.

Cats had been sent as Grand-Pensionary of Holland to deliver a Latin oration to Parliament discussing leniency in the Navigation Act.[69] Hartlib commented later that the oration was pedantic and pretentious, though given in eloquent Latin; it was subsequently published in English, Latin, and Dutch in several versions.[70] Van Aitzema, for example, translated and printed the entire oration in Dutch in his *Saeken van Staet en Oorlogh* (Matters of State and War).[71] It is unknown whether Milton was present during the delivery of the speech at Parliament. He was not well at the time after undergoing treatment to stop the failing of his eyesight, and the Dutch envoys often translated papers into English themselves, so his services may not have been required. The oration was also translated by Lodewijk Huygens, the son of Constantijn Huygens.[72] Milton could have encountered a copy, though, given his extensive involvement in the Anglo-Dutch negotiations.

Although it is plausible from this episode that the two writer-intellectuals, Milton and Cats, were acquainted, the relation between Milton and Joost van den Vondel has received much more scholarly attention. This is because of striking resemblances between their poetical works and the intellectual positions taken within them. Edmundson's scholarship sparked an interest in (re)discovering direct Dutch literary influences in the works of John Milton, especially in the relation between Milton and Vondel.[73] It is safe to say that Vondel and Milton never met in person; Vondel never travelled to Britain, or concurrently to any of the countries that Milton visited on his Grand Tour. Vondel's work was also virtually unknown in England in the seventeenth century; there are only sporadic references, such as a second-hand quotation by Hugo Grotius, mentioned by John Dunton in a letter.[74] This did not stop scholars in the late nineteenth and early twentieth century from drawing extensive parallels between the two authors. Edmundson's *Milton and Vondel* proposed that *Paradise Lost* was directly indebted to several of Vondel's plays, among which *Lucifer* (1654) and *Adam in Ballingschap* (1664) foremost.[75] He furthermore argued that *Samson Agonistes* (1671) was derived from *Samson, of Heilige Wraak* (Samson, or Holy Revenge, 1660). This assumption was adopted by other twentieth-century critics, such as Watson Kirkconnell, who thought 'that there are enough close resemblances to make his familiarity with Vondel reasonably assured'.[76]

The similarities in themes between Vondel's trilogy (*Adam in Ballingschap*, *Lucifer*, and *Noach*, 1667), and *Paradise Lost*, as well as *Samson Agonistes* with *Samson, en Heilige Wraak* had already been noticed and evaluated by travellers in the eighteenth and nineteenth centuries, such as John Bowring (1792–1872): '[c]ompare [Vondel] with Milton – for his Lucifer gives the fairest means of comparison – how weak are his highest flights compared with those of the bard of Paradise; and how much does Vondel sink beneath him in his failures! Now and then the same thought may be found in both, but the points of resemblance are not in passages which do Milton's reputation the highest honour'.[77] Despite these similarities of theme and shared context that make comparisons between their writings profitable, the prospect of direct influence between the two authors has now largely been ruled out. Jan Jurien Moolhuizen argued as early as 1892 that it was highly unlikely that Milton had read Vondel's works and adapted them into his own epic; more plausibly, the similarities in their works were the result of similar intellectual resources and contemporary contexts.[78] This is still the generally accepted view, and although in recent years the question of intertextuality between the two authors has received renewed attention, Moolhuizen's work remains central.

Between Milton and Vondel, similarities can be found in the choice of subject, rather than genre; Vondel was foremost a playwright, Milton an epic poet. Jan Frans van Dijkhuizen and Helmer Helmers have introduced new readings of Vondel's plays that substantiate the shared literary milieu that Moolhuizen theorised.[79] Instead of focusing solely on traditional poetic analysis, they set *Paradise Lost* and *Lucifer* within their political context(s). However, the question that has not been asked by others, even when concluding that Vondel and Milton had similar sources available, is how it came to be that they used the same, far from inevitable, biblical narratives for their literary (and politico-religious) purposes when these were practically opposite? Why no Daniel or Abraham or Judith, for example, each as iconic, but Samson, Creation, and the Fall? The differences between the two authors were substantial, after all, and both sustained a complex position within their society: Milton was Puritan and republican, writing from a restored monarchy (in the case of *Paradise Lost*), whereas Vondel was a Catholic convert who was sympathetic to English royalists, writing while residing in a firmly established Protestant republic. The relation between Vondel and Milton is characterised by contrasts. It is true that both Milton and Vondel were intimately familiar with the Bible (however differently they chose to interpret it) and that they were both sufficiently masterful poets to go 'each their own way,' as Moolhuizen argues.[80] The choice to use Genesis, furthermore, was not original in the renaissance, as the Fall of Mankind and Creation were familiar literary topics, and not only in the Anglo-Dutch sphere.[81] One could for example mention Guillaume de Salluste Du Bartas' *Creation du Monde* (1578) and Aemilia Lanyer's *Salve Deus Rex Judæorum* (1611). Moreover, the narrative of the Fall is versatile and eminently suitable for literary purposes, as Grotius explains in the Preface to his own *Adamus Exul* (1601):

> *Historia est prima quae in Sacris occurrit Literis et Catastrophen habet, hominis ex integro felicique statu in hanc miseriam lapsus. Philosophica occurrunt plurima, præsertim Metaphysica, de Deo, Angelis, et animis; physica etiam de rerum creatione; Ethica passim ut apud omnes; Geographica, et Astrologica nonnunquam, quæ Omnia a Scena non essa aliena Euripidis, Epicharmi, et Ennii me docuit exemplum.*[82]

> This history is the first that occurs in the Holy Scripture; it has the catastrophe of the Fall of Man from its blessed position to the miserable status of today. A lot is taken from philosophy, especially metaphysical: about God, the Angels and the Souls; as well as from Physics, the creation of the universe; ethics throughout the work, as with all writers, and in places also Geography and Astrology. All according to the rules of the Stage by the example of Euripides, of Epicharmus and of Ennius.

A narrative describing the creation of the world would naturally be a fitting topic in a period saturated with political and religious beginnings and endings. Although their allegiances were opposed, Milton and Vondel wrote in a century in which national identities were being forged, consciously or otherwise, most strongly in Europe's recently established republics or monarchies (even if these sometimes only survived for a couple of decades). Representing heaven, hell, the garden of Eden and the world after the Fall as independent states was therefore a literary device for opening dialogues about politics and religion, however indirectly. Moreover, the narrative of the revolt of heaven and of mankind was especially topical after the English revolution and Restoration, and the Dutch Revolt at the end of the sixteenth century. Vondel and Milton were both involved in the reshaping of a nation after a revolt, founding, or revolution, and although they worked according to different ideological principles, they asked the same questions within the same topical sphere, namely questions of authority.[83] These questions particularly applied to tyranny, kingship, or divinely appointed rule, whether projected onto Charles I and Cromwell, or the Princes of Orange and King Philip II of Spain. The nature of authority and divine providence, whether religious or political, is at the heart of Milton's and Vondel's plays and poems.

As with Bowring's comparison between *Paradise Lost* and *Lucifer*, the main focus of research on Anglo-Dutch relations in Milton and Vondel has been a comparative analysis of these two particular works. I instead wish to explore connections with Vondel's play *Adam in Ballingschap* and will return to questions of authority and divine intervention. Both writers took the Bible as the starting point of their texts, and had access to what several classical authors had written on the creation of the universe. Perhaps Hugo Grotius' *Adamus Exul* (1601) also served as a common source text, as both writers were familiar with some of his works. That Grotius may have functioned as a bridge between Vondel and Milton has so far been under-explored. The idea that Milton and Vondel used *Adamus Exul* as a source text in this particular instance does have its limitations, however. The play by Grotius was not as accessible as his other neo-Latin plays; it was not reprinted beyond its initial publication in 1601, and there was no translation of it in English.[84] Even though Milton could have read it in Latin, it would have been difficult to get hold of a copy.[85]

We therefore also have to look beyond Grotius' works to others that were more readily available to both Milton and Vondel – the classical authors Lucretius, Empedocles, Democritus, Epicurus, and Ovid, united by their discussion of atomist theories.[86] Each was published in the Dutch Republic throughout the seventeenth century, with the possible exception of Empedocles. As a result of the Epicurean revival, started by Thomas Hobbes (1588–1679) and Robert Boyle (1627–1691), atomist texts were also widely available in England.[87] Galileo, who adopted several Epicurean notions in his work, such as the concept that all things inevitably move, is mentioned directly in Milton's poetry and prose; he is the only contemporary scientist who receives such attention in *Paradise Lost* (I. 288–291).[88] In more general terms, Thomas Stanley's *History of Philosophy* (1655–1662) contains chapters on Empedocles, Democritus, and, particularly extensively, Epicurus, though not on Lucretius. Of course, Ovid was already widely read at this point; Vondel himself translated *Metamorphoses* into Dutch (1671). The manner in which Vondel's play and Milton's poem adopt these classical theories reveals a great deal about the context both texts were written in, and how these authors refined or repositioned them to complement the contemporary religious, literary, and intellectual milieux.

With the contemporary context and classical texts in mind, let us compare the accounts of creation within the two works. In the first ten lines of *Paradise Lost* we receive an impression of the role that chaos is going to play in the epic: '[i]n the beginning how the heavens and earth/Rose out of chaos' (I. 9–10). This eliminates *creatio ex nihilo*, a position Milton also propounded in *De doctrina Christiana*, in which he writes: 'on the whole the moderns are of the opinion that everything was formed out of nothing (which is, I fancy, what their own theory is based on)'.[89] He instead argues for a combination of *creatio ex deo* and *ex materia*: God organised the individual chaotic particles into earth, heaven and hell, and 'afterwards God arranged it and made it beautiful'.[90] Chaos in Milton's epic is presented as a constant battle between the four elements in a Platonically inflected passage, worth quoting in full:

Before their eyes in sudden view appear
The secrets of the hoary deep, a dark
Illimitable ocean without bound,
Without dimension, where length, breadth, and height,
And time and place are lost; where eldest Night
And Chaos, ancestors of Nature, hold
Eternal anarchy, amidst the noise
Of endless wars, and by confusion stand.
For Hot, Cold, Moist, and Dry, four champions fierce
Strive here for mastery, and to battle bring
Their embryon atoms; they around the flag
Of each his faction, in their several clans,
Light-armed or heavy, sharp, smooth, swift or slow,
Swarm populous, unnumbered as the sands
Of Barca or Cyrencë's torrid soil,
Levied to side with warring winds, and poise
Their lighter wings. To whom these most adhere,
He rules a moment; Chaos umpire sits,
And by decision more embroils the fray
By which he reigns: next him high arbiter
Chance governs all. Into this wild abyss,
The womb of nature and perhaps her grave,
Of neither sea, nor shore, nor air, nor fire,
But all these in their pregnant causes mixed
Confusedly, and which thus must ever fight,
Unless the almighty maker them ordain
His dark materials to create more worlds [.]
(II. 890–916)

In Milton's abyss, being the start and the end of creation, elements or atoms on their own can never connect for long enough to become a unity, or a creation.[91] It is not surprising that Satan finds in the anti-creator, Chaos, an unexpected ally.[92] The idea of chaos as a constant rejection of unity was first explored by Empedocles (c. 490–c. 430 BC), who held that unification and separation were performed through the intercessions of love and strife, of which the first connects and the second separates.[93] Empedocles' vision was in theory compatible with Christian doctrine, since the entrance and withdrawal of love and strife into the universal sphere could be divinely ordained. In Milton's epic, the particles would forever remain unbound and chaotic without divine determination; hence the adjective 'embryon' (l. 901), referring to the as yet unformed nature of their future connection. Milton's use of the word 'atom' might bring to mind Democritus (c. 490–c.

370 BC), the first to introduce an atomic model of the universe. Democritus argues that matter is eternal but that the connections between the individual particles are temporary and that these are ordered randomly through connection and disconnection, as a result of the atoms' shapes.[94] This was later adopted by Epicurus (341–270 BC) in his universe without hierarchy.[95] Milton, however, rejects this notion of randomness and makes the constant affirmation of divine interference and authority central to the process of creation in his poem. God's spirit 'satst brooding on the vast abyss/And mad'st it pregnant' and led to the creation of the world (I. 21–22).

Vondel conversely displays a combination of *creatio ex nihilo* and *ex materia* in his play. In the first act, Adam and Eve ruminate about what to sing, after which Adam encourages the angels to follow their song:

> *Wachtenglen, volght ons spoor. heft vrolijck aen: ontvout,*
> *Bij beurte op eene ry, den oirsprong aller dingen.*
> *De galm van 't paradijs schept lust u na te zingen*
> *Hoe dit heelal uit niet zoo heerlijck wiert gebout.*

> Guardian angels, follow our course, reveal and happily sing,
> In single order of the origin of all things.
> The echo of paradise sparks desire to repeat all you sing
> Of how this universe was beautifully built from nothing.
> (ll. 211–214)

These lines state explicitly that the universe was created out of nothing, but at God's command. Vondel therefore frequently refers to God as 'den oirsprong aller dingen' ('the origin of all things'). Throughout the play, a division between God and Nature is emphasised.[96] God creates from nothing, whereas Nature needs God-created matter before it can create in turn. This reinforces the image of God's immutability and immortality, and the temporary character of Nature, arguing that all things are directly or indirectly made by God, yet are not of God:

> *Godt schiep den baiert, woest en duister.*
> *Natuur had maer een aengezicht,*
> *Lagh vormeloos, en zonder luister.*
> *Toen sprack de Hooghste: 't werde licht.*

> God created chaos, bare and dark.
> Nature had only one face,
> Lay shapeless, without beauty.
> Then the Highest spoke: let there be light.
> (ll. 215–218)

It follows Democritus' idea that underlying matter is eternal and could form an infinite number of connections, whereas Nature has but one face, a temporary shape. God first created infinite chaos from nothing, followed by the creation of finite Nature as a shaping of formless matter, adding temporariness as an aspect of this last step. Although the origin of chaos is differently explained, both works describe it as the ante-movement of creation, leading to an eternal battle between the elements, in which the seed of the world, or even different worlds, lies hidden:[97]

> *Rondom den blinden baiert heen,*
> *Daer 's weerelts zaet in lagh gewonden,*
> *En elcke hooftstof ondereen.*

> Around the formless abyss,
> In which the hidden seed of the world lay,
> And order in elements was still amiss.
>   (ll. 224–226)

Vondel's description of earthly seeds awaiting the divine order to sprout reflects the same possibility of multiple worlds that Milton so famously described as 'His dark materials to create more worlds' (II. 916). The aforementioned idea of elemental chaos was taken from Greek classical texts by Empedocles, Epicurus, and Democritus. Both poets, however, also incorporate later works by the Romans Lucretius and Ovid, through the depiction of a fifth element: ether.[98] This substance was posited as weightless and invisible, flying upward to create a sun or several crystalline spheres. In Book 5 of *De Rerum Natura*, for example, Lucretius writes:

> Wherefore earths ponderous bodies did retire
> First to the Center, where declining weight
> Did them i'the lowest region scituate,
> Whose congregation, as 'twas more condense
> Did with more force presse forth those seeds, fro whence
> The greate world's wall, sun, moone, seas, starrs were made
> Who all smoother and rounder elements had,
> And farre lesse seeds then those which did compose,
> The ponderous earth, from whose small chinks first rose,
> In severall parcells, the whole starrie skie
> With which the seeds of fire did upwards flie.
>   (ll. 467–477)

The ponderous elements first congregate at the centre and sink to the bottom, a natural effect of their weight, constituting movement without an external cause. However, ether, being the lightest element in its purest form, is subsequently pushed outward to create the skies encompassing the world. Milton adopts this vision of creation in which different heavenly bodies and the outer wall of the universe are made of ether. In Book 3 he writes:

> And this ethereal quintessence of heaven
> Flew upward, spirited with various forms,
> That rolled orbicular, and turned to stars
> Numberless, as thou seest, and how they move;
> Each had his place appointed, each his course,
> The rest in circuit walls this universe.
>
> (III. 716–721)

This idea also appears in Vondel's play, where crystal, as element, limits and even captures the universe:

> *Een hooftstof, wuft en ongebonden,*
> *Gehoorzaemt hem, die haer beriep*
> *Om hoogh uit grondelooze gronden,*
> *En uit kristal een' hemel schiep,*
> *Om in dien kreits, rondom te vloten.*

> An element, volatile and unbound,
> Obedient to him who commanded her
> Upwards from bottomless grounds,
> And from crystal made a heaven,
> To flow round in its circle.
>
> (ll. 237–241)

Both passages emphasise the active role of the Omnipotent in creation, unlike the self-sustaining determinism present in Lucretius' and Ovid's works.[99] The connection between the atoms is divinely ordained, whereas Lucretius makes the arbitrary movement between *clinamen* (unpredictable swerve of atoms) and the *voluntas* (will), responsible for collisions between the individual particles; as they do not move in straight lines their collisions lead to a movement of creation.[100] Lucretius' universe is random, but as Sarah Ellenzweig has argued, it is also completely self-sufficient, which could explain its appeal.[101] In a less advanced way, Epicurus, too, accepted the idea that humans had no access to *voluntas* since nothing, divine or otherwise, can impart movement; there is only the moving body itself. This separation, I contend, is central to the resemblance between the respective accounts of creation in the play and epic.[102] The similarities between the works of Milton and Vondel emerge in their rejection of specific characteristics of the classical atomist theories and the insertion of divine intervention.[103] The universe obeys natural laws but is rooted in an act of divine creation. Milton's poem also suggests that the divine power that allows the movement of atoms to spark creation can also take this essential motion away. In this case, it works both ways: God creates movement, but also excludes potential future creations. In Book 2, Belial equates thought, the prime consequence of human life, to motion, and thus creation and life:

> The almighty victor to spend all his rage,
> And that must end us, that must be our cure,
> To be no more; sad cure; for who would lose,
> Though full of pain, this intellectual being,
> Those thoughts that wander through eternity,
> To perish rather, swallowed up and lost
> In the wide womb of uncreated night,
> Devoid of sense and motion?
>
> (II. 144–151)

More than any other creature in Milton's universe, the fallen angels embody this incessant aimless motion, constantly wandering: 'In thoughts more elevate, and reasoned high/Of providence, foreknowledge, will, and fate/Fixed fate, free will, foreknowledge absolute/And found no end, in wandering mazes lost' (II. 558–61).[104] Not all motion is therefore divine or benevolent; endless movement without result or consequence can become an eternal punishment. The fallen angels themselves, however, claim that this particular motion is the same that God inspired in the process of creation:

> We know no time when we were not as now;
> Know none before us, self-begot, self-raised
> By our own quickening power, when fatal course
> Had circled his full orb, the birth mature
> Of this our native heaven, ethereal sons.
>
> (V. 859–63)

The angels' 'false philosophy' (II. 565) claims that the force of the swerve, their own 'quickening power' was responsible for their creation, as Lucretius described it, demonstrating that the power came from within, and not through external force. Through the evident delusion of the fallen angels, we receive another confirmation that Lucretius' philosophy on self-conceived creation is to be rejected in Milton's universe. Atomistic philosophy has its limitations and dangers, namely the lie of godless self-creation. The fallen angels are barren movers. In Vondel's play motion is pregnant with possibilities of God's intent; hence the use of the obscure word 'baiert' (l. 222) for universe, meaning abyss of elements; this is similar to Milton's representation of the universe as an egg in the invocation to Book 1. Although Vondel offers no parallel of false creation, the principle that God commands motion would consequently include the power to also take it away, or simply withhold it.

I have already discussed the appropriateness of the Genesis narrative for both writers' various poetical and politico-religious purposes. A further relevant factor is the renaissance ambition to marry classical theories with Christian doctrine; ideas of stoicism and Epicureanism were introduced by figures such as Lipsius and Gassendi.[105] As argued by Philip Hardie, the source to turn to for a classical representative of the 'genre of scientific and philosophical didactic poetry' was Lucretius' poem.[106] It is small wonder then that both Milton and Vondel respond to the scientific creation found in Lucretius and other classical writers. By rejecting Epicurus' and Lucretius' idea that the atoms are arbitrarily connected, preferring instead a purposeful creation of matter through the objective force of the clinamen of the atoms themselves, both authors reinforce the authority of God.[107] This is an important point to make for the Christian, yet classically influenced, writer. Earlier examples of this act of synthesis exist, for example in Dante's *Divine Comedy*, which placed classical atomists who admitted the potential for divine intervention (which includes the idea of an immortal soul) in the first circle of hell, whereas Epicurus suffered in the sixth (Lucretius' text had at this point not been rediscovered). Vondel comments on exactly this disparity between the classical and Christian views of atomic creation in his poem *Bespiegelingen van God en Godsdienst* (Reflections on God and Faith, 1662), a work completely dedicated to a refutation of atheism. In Book 4 of Vondel's longest poem:

> *Lukrees, de schiltknaep en de tolck van Epikuur,*
> *Een' Godt by hem, doortast den boezem van natuur,*
> *Ontvout, uit 's meesters mont, al haer geheimenissen,*
> *Om in 't godtvruchtigh hart der menschen uit te wissen*
> *Het ingedruckte merck van Godts voorzienigheit,*
> *Den Godtsdienst, en 't geloof [. . .]*

> Lucretius, squire and interpreter of Epicurus,
> As a god, touched the heart of nature,
> Reveals, from the master's mouth, all her mysteries,
> To eliminate from man's heart all its pieties,
> The impressed mark of God's providence,
> Of Religion, and of faith [. . .]
>
> (ll. 21–26)

In Vondel's play and Milton's poem the atoms themselves are predestined by God to fulfil a certain function after the Creation, making the process predetermined, though not its outcome. Milton uses this idea in Books 5 and 9 to illustrate the power of free will. Raphael explains to Adam that although the process of creation was ordained, free will and thus a level of autonomy was given to the humans, allowing them to swerve (a little) for themselves:

> As may advise him of his happy state,
> Happiness in his power left free to will,

Left to his own free will, his will though free,
Yet mutable; whence warn him to beware
He swerve not too secure:

(V. 234–38)

Milton and Vondel were politically, religiously, and nationally poles apart, yet they used the same myths and sources. Their similarities are too precise and particular to be overlooked. We can conclude that they were arguing for their own intellectual and artistic positions but from within a shared cultural sphere. However, they also often drew different conclusions from these similarities, points of contrast that result from their opposing views. Lucifer in Vondel's plays, in particular in *Lucifer*, becomes a defence and reaffirmation of divine kingship. In Vondel's universe the hierarchy in heaven is not radically different from that on earth, making prelapsarian and postlapsarian life quite similar. In Milton's work, however, Satan's rebellion is presented as a failed attempt to make the divine political and the political divine. Satan's fall allows him to explore the possibilities of implementing the same monarchic state as heaven both in hell and on earth; without God, however, these states become tyrannical. The state of heaven is significantly different from those on earth and hell; God alone is the rightful ruler of state, and 'no human authority can claim to be anything more than human'.[108] As demonstrated here, parallel studies of Milton and Vondel reveal important similarities in their use of sources and ambition to baptise classical sources, highlighting a shared Anglo-Dutch literary sphere.

In this chapter, we have seen that Milton, Marvell and several Dutch writers discussed similar politico-religious issues that dominated the Anglo-Dutch sphere, such as the Regicide, providence, and civil wars. The close-knit printing and publication culture that the United Provinces and England shared led to a great exchange of scholarly texts and debates, further connecting the intellectual milieu. The same (contemporary and classical) sources were available. The use of the human body in architecture can be traced to the classical authors, as can the creation of the world. It is in these shared sources, the proximity of both countries, politically and religiously speaking, and the use of similar genres and subjects that we can understand the origin of the similarities, rather than in direct intertextuality or acquaintance. They represent in the truest sense a transnationalist dialogue, where the same questions and subjects are employed, but often answered differently.

Notes

1   Cornelis W. Schoneveld, *Intertraffic of the Mind* (Leiden: Brill, 1983), pp. 118, 123–124; Helmer Helmers, 'Unknown Shrews: Thee Transformations of the/a Shrew', in *Gender and Power in Shrew-Taming Narratives, 1500–1700*, ed. by G. Holderness and D. Wootton (Houndmills: Palgrave Macmillan, 2010): 123–144 (p. 125). See for further discussion (and in particular the rise of English in the United Provinces in the eighteenth-century), N.E. Osselton, *The Dumb*

Linguists: A Study of the Earliest English and Dutch Dictionaries (Oxford: Oxford University Press, 1973).

2 John Gallagher, *Learning Languages in Early Modern England* (Oxford: Oxford University Press, 2019), p. 3. See for a study in the use of Dutch in Britain, Christopher Joby, *Dutch Language in Britain (1550–1702): A Social History of the Use of Dutch in Early Modern Britain* (Leiden: Brill, 2015).

3 G.J. van de Bork and P.J. Verkruijse, 'Pieter Rabus', in *De Nederlandse en Vlaamse Auteurs* (Weesp: De Haan, 1985); Peter Rietbergen, 'Pieter Rabus en de Boekzaal van Europe', in *Pieter Rabus en de Boekzaal van Europa, 1692–1702* (Amsterdam: Holland Universiteits Pers, 1974): 1–109.

4 Peter Rabus, *Boekzaal van Europe*, 9 vols. (Rotterdam: Pieter vander Slaart, 1695), vol. 4, p. 442.

5 Nina Geerdink, *Dichters en Verdiensten: de Sociale Verankering van het Dichterschap van Jan Vos (1610–1667)* (Hilversum: Uitgeverij Verloren, 2012), p. 31.

6 Casper Barlaeus, 'To Jan Vos', qtd. in Karel Porteman and Mieke Smits-Veldt, *Een Nieuw Vaderland voor de Muzen: Geschiedenis van de Nederlandse Literatuur, 1560–1700* (Amsterdam: Uitgeverij Bert Bakker, 2009), p. 388.

7 Lisa Jardine, *Gedeelde Weelde*, transl. by Henk Schreuder (Amsterdam: Uitgeverij de Arbeiderspres, 2008), pp. 113–114.

8 Karel Porteman and Mieke Smits-Veldt, *Een Nieuw Vaderland voor de Muzen: Geschiedenis van de Nederlandse Literatuur, 1560–1700* (Amsterdam: Uitgeverij Bert Bakker, 2009), p. 331.

9 See for an extensive discussion of Huygens' relations with England, Thea van Kempen-Stijgers and Peter Rietbergen, 'Constantijn Huygens en Engeland', in *Constantijn Huygens en zijn Plaats in Geleerd Europa* (Amsterdam: University Press of Amsterdam, 1973): 77–141.

10 Rosalie L. Colie, *Some Thankfulness to Constantine: A Study of English Influence Upon the Early Works of Constantijn Huygens* (Den Haag: Martinus Nijhoff, 1956), p. 1.

11 Lisa Jardine, *De Reputatie van Constantijn Huygens: Netwerker of Virtuoos* (Amsterdam: Uitgeverij Bert Bakker, 2008), p. 12; A.G.H. Bachrach, *Sir Constantine Huygens and Britain: 1596–1687* (Oxford: Oxford University Press, 1962), *passim*.

12 Peter Davidson and Adriaan van der Weel, 'Appendix III: Huygens and English Literature', in *A Selection of the Poems of Constantijn Huygens* (Amsterdam: Amsterdam University Press, 1996): 201–217 (p. 201).

13 Schoneveld, *Intertraffic of the Mind*, p. 117; Christopher Joby, 'Huygens and Translation', in *The Multilingualism of Constantijn Huygens (1596–1687)* (Amsterdam: Amsterdam University Press, 2014): 177–220.

14 Jacob Westerbaen's *Minne-dichten* of 1644 has four of the 1630s translations by Huygens, and there are two other anonymous editions of 1644 and 1657. None of these were authorised by Huygens himself, which is evident in some mis-prints in this edition. See Ad Leerintveld, Nan Streekstra, and Richard Todd, 'Seventeenth-Century Versions of Constantijn Huygens' Translations of John Donne in Manuscript and in Print: Authority, Coterie, and Piracy', *Querendo*, 30.1 (2000): 288–310.

15 Leerintveld, Streekstra, and Todd, p. 294.

16 'Het Engelsch ooft, van U Ed. in Hollantsch suiker gezult, heeft my grootelijx verplight, door de maghtighe schaemte, die 't onze boom- of liever aertvruchten aanjoegh, doende verwelken de festoenen', P.C. Hooft, '27 Oktober 1630', in *'t Hoge Huis te Muiden: Teksten uit de Muiderkring*, ed. by M.C.A. van der Heijden, 13 vols. (Utrecht: Uitgeverij Het Spectrum, 1973), vol. 8, pp. 121–122.

17 Joost van den Vondel, 'Op de diepzinnige puntdichten van den engelschen poet John Donne, vertaelt door C. Huigens', in *'t Hoge Huis te Muiden: Teksten uit*

de Muiderkring, ed. by M.C.A. van der Heijden, 13 vols. (Utrecht: Uitgeverij Het Spectrum, 1973), vol. 8, p. 175.

18 M.A. Schenkeveld-van der Dussen, 'Duistere Luister: Aspecten van Obscuritas', in *idem. In de Boeken met de Geest: Vijftien Studies van M.A. Schenkelveld-van der Dussen over Vroegmoderne Nederlandse Literatuur*, ed. by A.J. Gelderblom (Amsterdam: Amsterdam University Press, 2002): 153–173 (p. 165).

19 '[W]ant haer Tale is alle Talen; en, als 't haer belieft, Grieksch and Latijn zijn plat Engelsch', 'Tot Den Leser', *Korenbloemen* (Amsterdam, 1672), pp. 533–534.

20 The poems Huygens translated are as follows (alphabetically): 'The Apparition', 'The Blossom', 'Break of Day', 'The Dream', 'The Ecstasy', 'The Anagram', 'Oh, Let me not serve so', 'The Flea', 'Goodfriday, 1613', 'The Legacy', 'Love's Deity', 'Song', 'The Sun Rising', 'The Triple Fool', 'Twickenham Garden', 'A Valediction Forbidden Mourning', 'A Valediction of Weeping', 'Witchcraft by a Picture', and lastly, 'Woman's Constancy'.

21 Koos Daley, *The Triple Fool: A Critical Evaluation of Constantijn Huygens' Translations of John Donne* (Nieuwkoop: De Graaf Publishers, 1990), p. 138. Daley has written the most extended study of Huygens' translations in English, but has certainly not presented a view that is now generally accepted on the quality of Huygens' translations. See also, Ton van Strien's review of Daley's book, 'Huygens als vertaler van John Donne', *De Nieuwe Taalgids*, 85 (1992): 247.

22 Daley, *The Triple Fool, passim*.

23 'Aen Tesselschade', *Korenbloemen* (1672), pp. 535–536.

24 A more recent example is the book chapter 'Lost and Regained in Translation' by Beverley Sherry in *Milton in Translation* ed. by Angelica Duran, Islam Issa, and Jonathan R. Olson (Oxford: Oxford University Press, 2017), who argues that translation's relevance or success is tied to the light it can shed on the original, which limits the power and merit of translation quite considerably (pp. 33–52).

25 *De Gedichten van Tesselschade* Roemers, ed. by A. Agnes Sneller, Olga van Marion, and Netty van Megen (Hilversum: Uitgeverij Verloren, 1994), pp. 30–33; Tesselschade Roemer, 'Aen myn Heer Hooft, op het ooverlyden van Mevrouw van Sullekom', in *'t Hoge Huis te Muiden: Teksten uit de Muiderkring*, ed. by M.C.A. van der Heijden, 13 vols. (Utrecht: Uitgeverij Het Spectrum, 1973), vol. 8: p. 226. Huygens was deeply moved by this sonnet, since he remembers it fondly in a poem written forty years later, in 1681, 'Tesselschades wijs onderwijs'.

26 See for another poem on the death of his wife: Constantijn Huygens, *Epimikta, Een Rouwklacht in het Latijn op de Dood van zijn Echtgenote (1637–1638)*, ed., transl., and introduced by J.P. Guépin (Voorthuizen: Florivallis, 1996).

27 See Chapter 2 in Jürgen Pieters, *Op Zoek naar Huygens* (Gent: Poëziecentrum, KANTL, 2014).

28 Davidson and Van der Weel, p. 212.

29 Nigel Smith, *Andrew Marvell: The Chameleon* (New Haven: Yale University Press, 2012), p. 49.

30 Ton van Strien, 'Inleiding', in *Constantijn Huygens: Hofwijck*, 2 vols. (Amsterdam: KNAW Press, 2008), vol. 2: 1–65 (p. 17); Helmer Helmers, *The Royalist Republic: Literature, Politics, and Religion in the Anglo-Dutch Sphere (1639–1660)* (Cambridge: Cambridge University Press, 2015), p. 169.

31 Ineke Huysman, 'Andrew Marvell and Constantijn Huygens: Common Grounds and Mutual Contacts', *Marvell Studies*, 3.1 (2018): 1–18.

32 Huysman, 'Andrew Marvell and Constantijn Huygens', p. 5.

33 Jane Partner, 'The Swelling Hall': Andrew Marvell and the Politics of Architecture at Nun Appleton House', *The Seventeenth Century*, 23.2 (2008): 225–243.

34 Nicholas McDowell, *Poetry and Allegiance in the English Civil Wars: Marvell and the Cause of Wit* (Oxford: Oxford University Press, 2008), pp. 1–2.

35 Smith, *The Chameleon*, p. 88.
36 Christopher Joby, '"This is my Body": Huygens' Poetic Response to the Words of Institution', in *Return to Sender: Constantijn Huygens as a Man of Letters*, ed. by Lisa Gosseye et al. (Gent: Academia Press, 2013): 83–104 (p. 83).
37 Derek Hirst and Steven N. Zwicker, *Andrew Marvell: Orphan of the Hurricane* (Oxford: Oxford University Press, 2012), *passim*.
38 Partner, 'The Swelling Hall', p. 227.
39 Ann Cotterill, *Digressive Voices in Early Modern English Literature* (Oxford: Oxford University Press, 2004), pp. 118–119.
40 John Simons, 'Marvell's Tulips', *Notes and Queries*, 36 (1989): 434.
41 E.E. Duncan-Jones and Helen Wilcox, 'Marvel's Holt-Fester', *Notes and Queries*, 4 (2001): 395–397.
42 Robert van Pelt, 'Man and Cosmos in Huygens' *Hofwijck*', *Art History*, 4.2 (June 1981): 150–174 (p. 151).
43 Matthew Dimmock, Andrew Hadfield, and Margaret Healy, 'Introduction', *The Intellectual Culture of the English Country House, 1500–1700* (Manchester: Manchester University Press, 2015): 1–10 (p. 2).
44 Annabel Patterson, *Pastoral and Ideology: Virgil to Valéry* (Berkeley: University of California Press, 1987), pp. 3–5.
45 All quotations from *Hofwijck* are taken from the following edition: Constantijn Huygens, *Hofwijck*, ed. by Ton van Strien, 2 vols. (Amsterdam: Koninklijke Nederlandse Academie van Amsterdam, 2008), vol. 1 (tekst).
46   This royal throne of kings, this sceptred isle,
         This earth of majesty, this seat of Mars,
         This other Eden, demi-paradise,
         This fortress built by nature for herself
         Against infection and the hand of war [.]
                         (II. ii. 40–44)

     William Shakespeare, *Richard II*, ed. by Stanley Wells and Gary Taylor (Oxford: Clarendon Press, 2005): 341–367.
47 Katherine O. Acheson, 'Military Illustration, Garden Design, and Marvell's 'Upon Appleton House', *English Literary Renaissance*, 41.1 (2011): 146–188.
48 Van Strien, *Commentary on* Hofwijck, p. 82; Patterson, *Pastoral and Ideology*, p. 3; Helmers, *Royalist Republic*, p. 154.
49 Margaret Cavendish, 'Nature's House' (1651–3?), in *The Country House Poem: A Cabinet of Seventeenth-Century Estate Poems and Related Items*, ed. by Alistair Fowler (Edinburgh: Edinburgh University Press, 1994): 318–319.
50 Willemien de Vries, *Wandeling en Verhandeling: De Ontwikkeling van het Nederlandse Hofdicht in de Zeventiende Eeuw* (Hilversum: Verloren, 1998), pp. 135–136.
51 Partner, 'The Swelling Hall', p. 230.
52 Sir Richard Fanshawe, 'An Ode upon Occasion of His Majesty's Proclamation in the Year 1630' (9 September 1630), in *The Country House Poem: A Cabinet of Seventeenth-Century Estate Poems and Related Items*, ed. by Alistair Fowler (Edinburgh: Edinburgh University Press, 1994): 123–127.
53 Annotation to the poem by David Ormerod and Christopher Wortham, in *Andrew Marvell: The Pastoral and the Lyric Poetry of 1681* (Nedlands: University of Western Australia Press, 2000).
54 Sarah Monette, 'Speaking and Silent Women in 'Upon Appleton House', *Studies in English Literature*, 42.1 (2002): 155–171 (p. 159).
55 De Vries, *Wandeling en Verhandeling*, pp. 178–186.
56 Jacob Westerbaen, *Arctoa Tempe: Ockenburgh, Woonstede van den Heere van Brandwyck in de Clingen buyten Loosduynen* ('s Gravenhage, 1654), p. 66.

57 Helmers, *Royalist Republic*, pp. 168–171.
58 Philip Major, 'To Wound an Oak': The Poetics of Tree-Felling at Nun Appleton', *The Seventeenth Century*, 25.1 (2010): 143–157.
59 Helmers, *Royalist Republic*, pp. 159–162.
60 From auction catalogues of Huygens' book collection (1688), we can find mention of Latin and Dutch editions of Salmasius' tract, see Ad Leerintveld, 'Constantijn Huygens' Library', in *Crossing Boundaries and Transforming Identities: New Pespectives in Netherlandic Studies*, ed. by Margriet Bruyn Lacy and Christine P. Sellin (Münster: Nodus Publikationen, 2011): 11–18.
61 Helmers, *The Royalist Republic*, p. 157.
62 Ryan Netzley, *Lyric Apocalypse: Milton, Marvell, and the Nature of Events* (New York: Fordham University Press, 2015), p. 157.
63 De Vries, *Wandeling en Verhandeling*, p. 14.
64 See for an example of the Dutch community in London, Hessels' archive of the Dutch Church in London: J.H. Hessels (ed.), *Epistulae et Tractatus cum Reformationis tum Ecclesiae Londino-Batavae Historiam Illustrantes: Ecclesiae Londino-Batavae Archivum* (Cambridge: Cambridge University Press, 1897).
65 George Edmundson, *Milton and Vondel: A Curiosity of Literature* (Toronto: Trubner and Co., 1885), p. 20.
66 Robert Fallon, *Milton in Government* (Pennsylvania: Pennsylvania University Press, 1993), pp. 77–78; Leo Miller, *John Milton's Writings in the Anglo-Dutch Negotiations, 1651–1654* (Pittsburgh: Duquesne University Press, 1992), pp. 9–10; *ibid.*, Miller, *Milton and the Oldenburg Safeguard* (New York: Loewenthal Press, 1985), p. 106.
67 Esther van Raamsdonk, 'Did Milton Know Dutch?', *Notes and Queries*, 63.1 (2016): 53–55 (p. 55).
68 Mylius and Aitzema would become acquainted later in 1652, see for example van Aitzema's diary of the year 1652, *Nationaal Archief*, 1.10.02, 49; Miller, *Milton and the Oldenburg Safeguard*, p. 126.
69 Miller, *John Milton's Writings in the Anglo-Dutch Negotiations*, pp. 10–11.
70 Miller, *Milton and the Oldenburg Safeguard*, p. 116.
71 Lieuwe van Aitzema, *Saeken van Staet en Oorlogh*, 14 vols. (1657–1671), vol. 3 (1669), pp. 699–701.
72 Leo Miller, *John Milton's Writings in the Anglo-Dutch Negotiations*, p. 47. See also Lodewijck Huygens, *The English Journal 1651–162*, ed. and transl. by A.G.H. Bachrach and R.G. Collmer (Leiden: Brill, 1982), pp. 14–19.
73 The list of articles and books is extensive. Just to name a few: A. Mueller, *Milton's Abhaengigkeit von Vondel* (Dissertation, University of Berlin, 1891); Thieme de Vries, *Holland's Influence on English Language and Literature* (Chicago: Grentzebach, 1916); Jehangir Mody, *Vondel and Milton* (Bombay: K and J Cooper, 1942); Gwendolyn Davies, *The 'Samson' Theme in the Works of Rembrandt, Vondel, and Milton: A Comparative Study in the Humanities* (Unpublished Masters Thesis, Wayne State University, Detroit, MI); Hugo Bekker, 'The Religio-Philosophical Orientations of Vondel's *Lucifer*, Milton's *Paradise Lost*, and Grotius' *Adamus Exul*', *Neophilogus*, 44.1 (1960): 234–244.
74 Guillaume van Gemert, 'Between Disregard and Political Mobilization: Vondel as a Playwright in Contemporary European Context: England, France and the German Lands', in *Joost van den Vondel: Dutch Playwright in the Golden Age*, ed. by Jan Bloemendal and Frans-Willem Korsten (Leiden: Brill, 2012): 171–200 (p. 172).
75 Jan Bloemendal, 'New Philology: Variants in *Adam in Ballingschap* (1664)', in *Joost van den Vondel: Dutch Playwright in the Golden Age*, ed. by Jan Bloemendal and Frans-Willem Korsten (Leiden: Brill, 2012): 489–508.

76   Watson Kirkconnell, *The Celestial Cycle* (Toronto: University of Toronto Press, 1952), pp. 627–631.

77   John Bowring, *Sketch of the Language and Literature of Holland* (Amsterdam: Diederich Brothers, 1829), p. 38.

78   Jan Jurien Moolhuizen, *Vondel's Lucifer en Milton's Verloren Paradijs* (Ph.D. Thesis, Utrecht University, 1892), p. 121.

79   Jan Frans van Dijkhuizen and Helmer Helmers, 'Religion and Politics: *Lucifer* (1654) and *Paradise Lost*', in *Joost van den Vondel: Dutch Playwright in the Golden Age*, ed. by Jan Bloemendaal and Frans-Willem Korsten (Leiden: Brill, 2012): 377–405.

80   Moolhuizen, p. 121.

81   A.G. van Hamel, *Zeventiende- Eeuwsche Opvattingen en Theorieen over Literatuur in Nederland* (Utrecht: Hes Publishers, 1973), pp. 60–67.

82   Hugo Grotius, 'Preface', *Adamus Exul* (Den Haag, 1601).

83   Van Dijkhuizen and Helmers, p. 401.

84   Henk Nellen, *Hugo de Groot, Een Leven in Strijd om de Vrede* (Amsterdam: Balans, 2007), p. 393; see for an elaborate discussion on three of Grotius' biblical drama, among which *Adamus Exul*, Arthur Eyffinger, 'The Fourth Man: Stoic Tradition in Grotian Drama', *Grotiana*, 22.1 (2001): 117–156.

85   William Poole, *Milton and the Idea of the Fall* (Cambridge: Cambridge University Press, 2005), pp. 101–106.

86   Stephen Greenblatt, *The Swerve: How the Renaissance Began* (London: Vintage Books, 2012).

87   Rodney Cotterill, *The Material World* (Cambridge: Cambridge University Press, 2008), pp. 25–52.

88   Sarah Ellenzweig, '*Paradise Lost* and the Secret of Lucretian Sufficiency', *Modern Language Quarterly*, 75.3 (2014): 385–409 (p. 388); Angus Fletcher, *Time, Space, and Motion in the Age of Shakespeare* (Cambridge, MA: Harvard University Press, 2007), pp. 130–151.

89   *CWP* (OUP) (2012). VI: 305.

90   *CPW*. VIII: 293.

91   David Quint, *Inside Paradise Lost: Reading the Designs of Milton's Epic* (Princeton: Princeton University Press, 2014), p. 71.

92   I cannot answer here the question fully whether Chaos is evil or good in Milton's epic. I would argue it has the potential for both: in itself it is an objective force, but through the process of creation it can become either evil or good. I find Quint's suggestion persuasive that the dregs of Chaos were used to make hell (Quint, *Inside Paradise Lost*, footnote 14, p. 258), demonstrating that *waste* is not *wasteful*. This contradicts N.K. Sugimura's argument that night is the effect of these dregs ('*Matter of Glorious Trial*': *Spiritual and Material Substance in Paradise Lost* (New Haven: Yale University Press, 2009), pp. 275–276). This would suggest that Chaos is only to some extent 'fertile' for further creation, which seems to defeat the essence of Chaos itself. John Rogers takes a different stance and argues that chaos is a paradox of creation and anti-creation, as Chaos' dregs are 'adverse to life' (VII. 239): *The Matter of Revolution: Science, Poetry and Politics in the Age of Milton* (Ithica: Cornell University Press, 1998), pp. 130–143. We do not know, however, whether these dregs will be rejuvenated through God later, as Chaos on its own is, indeed, adverse to life. There is a wealth of scholarship on these issues of which I will mention a few. Those arguing that chaos is evil: Regina Schwartz, 'Milton's Hostile Chaos ". . . and the Sea was no more"', *ELH*, 52.2 (1985): 337–374; John Leonard, 'Milton, Lucretius and the "Void Profound of Unessential Night"', in *Living Texts: Interpreting Milton* (London: Associates University Presses, 2000): 198–218. Those arguing that Chaos is essentially good: John Rumrich, *Milton Unbound:*

Controversy and Reinterpretation (Cambridge: Cambridge University Press, 1966), pp. 118–133; Quint, *Inside Paradise Lost*, p. 258.

93 Brad Inwood, *The Poem of Empedocles* (Toronto: Toronto University Press, 2001), p. 51; John Burnet, *Greek Philosophy: Thales to Plato* (London: Macmillan, 1928), pp. 72–73.

94 C.C.W. Taylor, *The Atomists: Lucippus and Democritus* (Toronto: Toronto University Press, 1999), pp. 172–174.

95 Ellenzweig, p. 397.

96 F. Korsten, *Sovereignty as Inviolability: Vondel's Theatrical Exploration in the Dutch Republic* (Hilversum: Uitgeverij Verloren, 2009), pp. 45–52.

97 John Rumrich, 'Milton's God and the Matter of Chaos', *Modern Language Association*, 110.5 (1995): 1035–1046 (p. 1038).

98 Katherine Calloway, 'Milton's Lucretian Anxiety Revisited', *Renaissance and Reformation*, 32.3 (2009): 79–97; John Leonard, 'Milton, Lucretius and the "Void Profound of Unessential Night"', in *Living Texts: Interpreting Milton*, ed. Charles W. Durham and Kristin A. Pruitt (London: Associated University Presses, 2000): 198–218. See for Milton's use of Ovid: Richard J. DuRocher, *Milton and Ovid* (Ithaca: Cornell University Press, 1985).

99 Stephen M. Fallon, *Milton among the Philosophers: Poetry and Materialism in Seventeenth-Century England* (Ithaca: Cornell University Press, 1991), pp. 20–21.

100 Don Fowler, *Lucretius on Atomic Motion* (Oxford: Oxford University Press, 2002), p. 415; Fallon, *Milton among the Philosophers*, p. 42; Calloway, p. 83.

101 Van Dijkhuizen and Helmers, p. 404.

102 Ellenzweig, p. 389.

103 Quint, p. 85.

104 William Kerrigan, *The Prophetic Milton* (Charlottesville: University Press of Virginia, 1974), pp. 271–272.

105 Margaret J. Osler, 'Introduction', in *Atoms, Pneuma and Tranquillity: Epicurean and Stoic Themes in European Thought* (Cambridge: Cambridge University Press, 1991): 1–11 (p. 7).

106 Philip Hardie, 'The Presence of Lucretius in *Paradise Lost*', in *Lucretian Receptions: History, the Sublime, Knowledge*, ed. by Philip Hardie (Cambridge: Cambridge University Press, 2009): 264–279.

107 Joan Retallack, *The Poethical Wager* (Los Angeles: University of California Press, 2003), p. 3.

108 Van Dijkhuizen and Helmers, p. 404.

4 Arminian Toleration

In June 1659, nineteen-year-old assistant surgeon Wouter Schouten left the United Provinces aboard the ship *Nieuwpoort* on the long journey to Indonesia and India. There he saw a great variety of different beliefs, ranging from the world religions to small crocodile-worship sects. At every stop he reported in his journal on the striking or exotic details of his encounters, revealing a sense of wonder and consternation, all seen through the values, prejudices and priorities of seventeenth-century Europe. The Muslims he met he often considered brethren, even if their interpretations and practices were deemed misguided, because they believed in the same one God. He befriended a Mohammed and a Hassan on one of his journeys. The Buddhists and Hindus received a more condemnatory response, because of their perceived polytheism and idolatry. None of the believers, however, were regarded without hope; they could be saved if they would only make Protestant Christianity their religion. It is not my intent to argue that Schouten escapes the limitations of his religious and racial perspective, though his openness to what other accounts might reject as simply alien is instructive.

When Schouten travelled to the kingdom of Mrauk-U, in the Bay of Bengal, he observed with consternation the population worshipping at a great Buddha statue called Mahamuni.[1] The local population were in turn baffled by the Dutch celebrating Christmas on a Saturday (did they perhaps think it was Sunday?). Schouten composed some lines about the bewilderment he experienced when seeing the Buddhist 'idol worship':

> *Ellendigh volck, wat troost kan geven*
> *Een beelt van klaij, van hout, van steen?*
> *Eij, waerom 't monster aengebeen*
> *Door menschenhanden t'saemgedreven,*
> *Kont gij de Godt van son en maen,*
> *Dien Opperheerscher dus versaecken,*
> *Kan't levenloos uw dus vermaecken?*
> *Hoe dus verdoolt, verdoolden Indijaen!*[2]
>
> (ll. 89–96)

> Miserable people, what comfort could come
> From a statue of clay, of wood, of stone?
> Aye, why worship a monster
> Built by human hands,
> How could you the God of sun and moon,
> Your lord of lords forsake thus,
> And the lifeless entertain you?
> How lost, those lost Indians!

Schouten's history of religious worship conditioned how he saw and understood these practices. During his journey, he wrote 35 other poems describing his first meetings with some of these religions. The journal is also a detailed first-hand report of how a Dutchman in the mid-seventeenth century understood, practised and expressed toleration when faced with a whole range of different forms of worship. Dutch toleration was far from simple or universal, but in general they were of a more flexible mind than most other European nations at the time – seen for example in their greater accommodation of the Jews in Amsterdam, or their success in building trade relations in the Mediterranean despite vigorous debates on the standing of these religions.

Dutch toleration had a widespread influence on other liberty of conscience movements, including debates on toleration in the England of the 1640s and 1660s, to which both Milton and Marvell contributed. Naturally, religious toleration in the United Provinces and England in this period is a hugely complicated topic and far too large to treat comprehensively in the space of a book chapter. However, as attested to by the ever-expanding literature concerning Milton's and Marvell's religious convictions, it is important to understand the intellectual milieu within which they and their ever-developing outlooks should be situated. With a slightly more modest ambition, then, the first part of this chapter provides some background to key topics, including a brief history of Dutch toleration, the Arminian controversy, and Milton's and Marvell's access to Dutch theological sources. This is followed by some discussion of their direct engagement with Dutch toleration, in particular Arminian toleration, though the issues raised here will also colour the following chapter.

Toleration in the United Provinces

The attitude that Schouten displays in his travel account is, in some ways, liberal for its times. Toleration in the United Provinces was in general more accommodating than most European countries, though the level of specificity varied. In the Thirteenth Act of the Union of Utrecht (1579), liberty of conscience within the provinces is propounded. It argues that religious diversity should be tolerated for the establishment of religious and social peace.[3] After the Union of Utrecht, the Southern Netherlands continued to be governed by Spain, whereas the Northern Provinces adjusted to a more tolerant vision of religion; trials of heresy were abandoned, induced by past experiences of suppression that had fuelled their prolonged war for liberty.[4] Several decades after the Union of Utrecht, Henricus Arnoldi reiterated in his *Vande conscientie-dwangh* (On Compelling Conscience, 1629) that this act in the constitution could and should be interpreted as granting liberty of conscience to the individual, albeit without entailing the liberty of practice or the right to publish one's religious convictions.[5] You were allowed to be, in your heart or in private, a member of marginal denominations such as the anabaptists, but there were statutes in place forbidding public services or attempts to convert other people.

In the early seventeenth century, the majority of the Dutch population was still Roman Catholic, especially in the Eastern and Southern provinces.[6] The seeds of the new Protestant religion had been sown in Erasmus' humanist-Catholic soil, meaning that the religious culture of the Republic never became thoroughly puritan (in the widest definition of the term).[7] *De Belydenisse des Gheloofs* (The Dutch Confession of Faith) by Guy de Brés, published in Dutch as well as in French in 1562, became one of the sources that would organise and establish Calvinism widely in the United Provinces, albeit influenced by Philip Melanchthon, Huldrych Zwingli, Martin Bucer, and Heimrich Bullinger.[8] Catholicism became a suppressed religion after the outbreak of the Great Revolt in 1572, and Catholics were often treated as second-rate citizens, despite their great numbers. They were associated with the Spanish oppression, whereas the Protestants, under the leadership of Willem van Oranje, had become the face of liberation. The Dutch Reformation, however, did not produce a binary opposition.[9] The years 1566–1567 were marked by violent outbursts between denominations but particularly against Catholics, also called the *beeldenstorm* (iconoclasm), despite Van Oranje's attempts to establish full toleration within Dutch Christianity – whether Catholic or Protestant.[10]

The Dutch Republic has sometimes been treated in historical writing in the twentieth century as a paradise of religious toleration.[11] It is commonly held that trade and profit were prioritised above dogma and the control of religious dissent.[12] It is certainly the case that local regents, especially in Amsterdam, inherited an Erasmian attitude to religious nonconformity and strove above all to maintain social order. This is, for example, clearly visible in the treatment of Jews in Amsterdam at the turn of the century.[13] Gary K. Waite's book on Jews and Muslims in the Dutch Republic and England provides an abundance of cases of the treatment of other religions in Amsterdam in the early seventeenth century. He places the first mention of practising Jews in 1603, when Uri ben Jozef Halevi was arrested on the charge of circumcising adults.[14] Despite some cases of individuals expressing anti-Semitic prejudices, it is notably difficult to find responses that demand a full expulsion of Jewish communities from the Dutch Republic; attitudes range from proposed (but rarely forced) conversion, to toleration within restrictions, to turning a blind eye. Hugo Grotius' *Remonstrantie nopende de ordre dije in de landen van Hollandt ende West-vrieslandt dijent gestelt op de Joden*

(Remonstrance as ordered by the States of Holland and West-Friesland on the Jews) distributed in 1615 (though not re-printed and published until 1949), discusses potential attitudes to Jews in Amsterdam, and argues that they should be allowed to enter the Dutch Republic freely and allowed to practise their religion.[15] He repeats the common accusation that the Jews were responsible for murdering Christ, but does concede that at least they did not worship idols, like the Catholics. Some of his proposals – after a Jewish service the congregation had to remain to listen to some further Christian instruction, and they were not allowed to take large collections at their services, for example – were not adopted by the civil authorities, as they were deemed too restrictive.[16] Instead, they relied on evasive ambiguity in their written correspondence and treatment, an attitude they also took with many Christian sects. They allowed a partial freedom of practise, muddling the distinction between liberty of conscience and practice. This attitude proved encouraging to minority groups; by 1639, Amsterdam had more than a 1000 practising Jews, with a synagogue and graveyard. In England, by comparison, such freedom would not be allowed until the late 1650s or early 1660s.[17]

In his tract, Grotius makes the throw-away comment that Dutch society need not fear the contagion of the Jewish religion, since 'the least dangerous are those which differ the most', implying that sibling religions have the fiercest disagreements.[18] His comment turned out to be painfully prophetic, as would be shown in the internal conflicts of the emerging Dutch Reformed Church. It was a national Reformed Church, approved by Willem van Oranje and the States General. It was no state church though, since membership was not mandatory. Although it was protected and financed by the provincial and civic governments, it was not state-run.[19] Its members, mostly zealous Calvinists, actively discouraged other versions of Protestantism, such as the Lutherans, Socinians, Mennonites and Anabaptists, though the majority of the Dutch Protestant population was only 'mildly' Protestant and not as dogmatic as the strict Calvinists, hence supporting toleration to some extent.[20] However, as the Calvinist preachers gathered more support, and confessionalisation in general became more widely implemented in ordinary Dutch society, toleration began to lose ground.[21] A division emerged in which difference of *conscience* was tolerated, but difference in *practice* was not.[22] People were allowed, for example, to have Catholic sympathies privately, but could not hold masses, Catholic processions, or public sermons.[23] A great many *schuilkerken*, or clandestine churches were built in this period. These would range from small church halls in the tops of merchant buildings, to basement churches, and even to great buildings hidden by a façade of a row of houses. Benjamin Kaplan estimates that in the 1620s, Amsterdam alone had twenty Roman-Catholic *schuilkerken*, four Mennonite churches, and several meeting houses for smaller sects.[24] These did not operate in secret, as local regents and councillors knew they existed and the services could be freely, if not openly, attended. This is illustrative of the Dutch *gedoogbeleid*, the choice to allow certain violations of the law in favour of toleration and social order.

Dutch Arminian Toleration

It was during the late sixteenth century and early seventeenth century that doctrinal controversies, especially within the Dutch Reformed Church itself, began to arise. The dispute between theologians Jacobus Arminius (1560–1609) and Franciscus Gomarus (1563–1641), both professors at the University of Leiden, had a profound influence on Dutch society, and ultimately the rest of Europe. The consequences of this debate would be hard to overstate, yet its specifics have seemingly proven harder still for modern scholarship to assimilate.[25] Freya Sierhuis has recently examined the impact of the Arminian controversy on Dutch literature in a detailed and insightful study.[26] More generally however, as Keith D. Stanglin complains, Arminius and Arminianism are still 'grossly misunderstood' in the 'story of Christian theology', and there are plenty of examples available that confirm his conclusion.[27] Brooke Conti, for example, confuses Arminius' doctrine of free will with that of Beza's supralapsarianism.[28] Takashi Yoshinaka proposes that 'Arminians hate the doctrine of grace', which is a contradiction of Arminius' teachings.[29] In the specific case of Milton, John Witte in *The Reformation of Rights* attempts to circumvent discussion of the complex issues at play by calling Milton simply a Calvinist, which he was not.[30] Partly for this reason, Chapter 5 of this book is dedicated to the unpacking of this religious controversy in Milton's and Marvell's poetry and prose.

In this chapter, a more specific focus is taken: Arminianism and its relation to toleration. The doctrinal issues that fired the religious struggle of the 1610s, culminating in the Synod of Dort in 1618, declared Arminianism to be heretical. This gave rise to an explosion of texts on religious toleration, under the leadership of Arminius' student Simon Episcopius. His tract, *Vrye Godedienst* (Free Religion, 1627), and many others, such as Grotius' *Remonstratie*, were first published in Dutch, illustrating how this discussion on religious toleration was – unlike, for example, Milton's Latin *Defences* – not reserved for the clergy or a learned elite, but concerned the whole literate population. Notably, Arminians complained in Amsterdam that they were being treated by society worse than the Jews, a complaint with a specific spine, whatever the hyperbole in the rhetoric.[31] Arminians disagreed with double predestination, but this was shared by the Calvinists and the Jews, although the elect in the latter case were the Jews themselves rather than the invisible elect.

Although Arminian toleration was named after Arminius, it was led by Simon Episcopius and Johannes Wytenbogaert in the 1630s and 1640s. Episcopius' *Vrye Godedienst* argues for freedom of expression, practise, and confession, since all Christian churches (perhaps with the exclusion of Roman Catholicism) agree generally on principles of doctrine. His vision was one of full religious freedom, seen as essential for the stability of the state. Religious freedom would increase patriotism, following an Erastian conviction that the Church and the State could reinforce each other.[32] Equally, the government has a responsibility to maintain peace within the Church, even if they function as two institutions rather than one. In the same year as Episcopius' tract, Grotius published his work on toleration *De Veritate Religionis Christanae*, in Latin. Although by no means as liberal and open as Episcopius, Grotius, too, was in favour of a distilling of the essential doctrines, leading to the inclusion of as many denominations as possible.[33] Throughout the remainder of the century, important names became associated with Arminian toleration, such as Etienne Curcellaeus, the introducer of Descartes' works into the Dutch Republic, Philipp van Limborch, who would play a role in the attempted publication of Milton's *De doctrina Christiana*, and Jean Clericus or Leclerc, an Arminian preacher, later professor of philosophy, in Amsterdam.[34]

Milton, Marvell and Dutch Arminianism

Let us now turn to Milton's and Marvell's ideas on toleration and the impact of Arminian toleration on them. In his 2007 article, 'Milton and the European Contexts of Toleration', Nigel Smith rightly complains that Milton's theology is frequently examined in terms of its final destination, rather than the road that led to these conclusions.[35] This is an especially important point to make when examining Milton's ideas of toleration, since the movements that influenced his thinking were often in flux themselves. That Milton was not of one fixed opinion but developed his thinking throughout his life could similarly be asserted of Marvell, frustrating historians' attempts to establish for him a static religious identity. As John Spurr has argued in his article on Marvell's religion, 'Marvell, possessed of a fluid, subtle mind, was a man of anything but fixed identity. His was an evolving temperament'.[36] Marvell is an especially complicated case to define in concrete religious and political terms. He was – particularly compared to the outspoken and polemical Milton – a diplomatic shape-shifter, carefully manoeuvring through the tumultuous and treacherous politico-religious climate of the seventeenth century. We have already seen this flexibility in the different versions of his *Character of Holland*. Another illustration, partly occasioned by the public office that Marvell kept, is marginalia found in a version of the *Rehearsal Transpros'd*, the first of which reads: 'It is supposed to bee written, by Mr Marvell, A Countrey Gentleman & A Great Republican', to which another reader has replied: 'In saying he is a great Republican you ar very much mistaken for he is one of this parliament and a conformist'.[37] If contemporaries could not reach consensus on Marvell's religious and political convictions, neither have Marvell scholars to this day: Warren Chernaik, Annabel Patterson and John Wallace have all arrived at somewhat different conclusions in their studies.[38]

As briefly mentioned earlier, Dutch toleration of the seventeenth century was heavily influenced by Arminianism and the 1618 ruling of the Synod of Dort in favour of Gomarus and the orthodox Calvinists. In the late 1620s and 1630s, however, Arminianism was introduced in earnest into England, to some degree the consequence of three Arminian Archbishops of York in succession: George Montaigne [Mountain] (1628), Samuel Harsnett (1628–1631) and Richard Neile (1632–1640).[39] The Archbishopric of Canterbury was soon also taken by another Arminian, the previous Bishop of London, William Laud (1573–1645). Laud proved to be a central figure in the aggressive promotion of English Arminianism.[40] It was during these decades that English and Dutch Arminianism diverged; English Arminianism became a polemical term for everything that was not orthodox Calvinist, rather than representative of the teachings of Arminius, hence Nicholas Tyacke's use of the term 'anti-Calvinists' for English Arminians.[41] Dutch Arminianism concerned the individual's responsibility for salvation. This lay at some remove from the emphasis on ritualised communal worship and the role of the clergy (especially in the ecclesiastical vision of Archbishop Laud) that became prominent characteristics of the Arminian movement in England. This love of ceremony was satirised by Marvell in the *Rehearsal Transpros'd*, part 1:

> There was a *Second* Service, the *Table* set *Altar-wise*, and to be called the *Altar*; *Candles, Crucifixes, Paintings, Images, Copes, bowing to the East, bowing to the Altar*, and so many several Cringes & Genuflections, that a man unpractised stood in need to entertain both a Dancing-Master and a Remembrancer.[42]

Moreover, English Arminianism had a monarchical streak to it, since they accused Calvinists of being 'theocrats and in consequence disloyal to the throne', a conversation that did not take place in the United Provinces.[43] Perhaps the pomp and circumstance of the Laudian Church were more suitable to a monarchy than a republic.[44] Grotius' poems and works defending toleration and Arminianism in this period painted the Dutch humanist as a potential ally to those with Laudian sympathies.[45] Later, in the 1650s, as a result of the Civil Wars and the subsequent installation of extreme Calvinists in high positions, such as John Owen (1600–1666) – in the 1650s Vice-Chancellor of Oxford University and chaplain to Oliver Cromwell – the progress of English Arminianism was slowed.[46] Owen believed that Protestantism needed 'strict and relatively narrow parameters', which led to his version of Independency and strict Calvinism, excluding Arminianism, Socinianism and all forms of Anti-Trinitarianism.[47] After the Restoration, Arminianism again flourished, in a manner unprecedented. Having provided a general definition of English and Dutch Arminianism, the term Arminianism in this chapter is used in specific contrast to the Calvinism of Beza and Gomarus – as in Dutch Arminianism – rather than to denote everything non-Calvinist.

Were Milton and Marvell aware of this difference within Arminianism in England and the United Provinces? One way of answering this question is to consider the texts to which Marvell and Milton had access on Dutch theology and toleration. We know that Marvell's own library was small, yet the use of sources in his texts is not. He therefore presumably had access to other collections, such as those of his influential and intellectual friends. The libraries of Arthur Annesley, Earl of Anglesey (1614–1686) and John Owen were most likely used by Marvell while writing his prose tracts, and their catalogues can give some illuminating insights.[48] There is, for example, a wealth of information in these collections on the Dutch predestination debate of the 1610s. Both have some of Arminius' works, such as the three-volume *Opera Varia Theologica* (1635), and Owen also owned a tract dedicated to the controversy between Gomarus and Arminius, *Iacobi Arminii examen thesium D. Francisci Gomari de preadestinatione* (1645). Although the works of Gomarus were not as well distributed or widely published throughout Europe as Arminius', Owen's library had a copy of his *Opera Omnia Theologica dual Partibus uno volumine* (1644).[49] The two collections held texts that discussed the Synod of Dort itself; several different versions of *Acta & Scripta synodalia Dordracena ministrorum remonstrantium in foederato Belgio* (1620) and *Canones Synodi Dordracenae. Cum notis & animadversionibus Dan. Tileni* (1622), but also various responses of European theologians agreeing or disagreeing with Arminius, for example *Lareni Responsio ad Analysin Jac Arminii in 9 Cap. ad Rom* (1616) in Angelsey's collection, and a defence by Episcopius, *Responsio ad Contra-Remonstrantium Contrariam Declarationem* (1658) in Owen's library. Anglesey's and Owen's library records do not give the places of publication. Moreover, none of these texts can yet be found on *Early English Books Online*. It is, therefore, most plausible that they were printed and published in the United Provinces.

The question then remains how Anglesey and Owen acquired their libraries. Edward Millington (1636–1703) is an important figure in the dissemination of Dutch books. He was a bookseller and auctioneer, who, for example, sold the entire library of the Dutch theologian Gisbertus Voetius in England. Like many other booksellers, he imported scholarly books from the continent for sale to English scholars and intellectuals.[50] It is not unlikely that Anglesey and Owen bought at least some of their books from Millington. Of course, Dutch theology dealt with more issues than the predestination debate of the 1610s alone, but the extent to which books on or by Arminius spread across Europe is a good example of how Dutch theological issues were attended to throughout Europe, and that for well-connected people such as Marvell it was relatively easy to get access to Dutch theological texts.[51] It is additionally worth pointing out that Hull was a major trading port with the United Provinces, through which many books were imported to be sold, including those of exiled nonconformists.[52] This could have been another source of Marvell's information.

In Milton's case, we find some direct engagement with Dutch theologians, and with even less widely published works. In the *De doctrina Christiana* manuscript, we find a reference to Gomarus' works on anti-Sabbatarianism: 'Atque in hac ferme sentential doctissimos quosque theologorum, Bucerum, Calvinum, Marturem, Musculum, Ursinum, [Gomarum] aliósque video fuisse'.[53] The name of Gomarus has been added later by Milton himself, and written above the other names. In general, Milton's (religious) works are filled with references to European theologians, of which several are Dutch, such as Franciscus Junius, Gisbertus Voetius and Jacobus Arminius. Milton could have read these works as part of bigger collections, as religious treatises were often bound together. We can conclude that his reading and access to these sources by Dutch theologians was extensive.

There is another person worth mentioning in this context: John Hales (1584–1656), a fellow at Eton until 1649. For both Milton and Marvell he functioned as a learned example of Dutch Arminianism. As chaplain to Sir Dudley Carleton, Hales was present at the Synod of Dort, of which he later famously said, 'there, I bid John Calvin good-night'.[54] His account of the Synod was translated into Dutch *Korte historie van het synode van Dordrecht, vervatende eenige aenmerkelijke en noyt voor-henen ontdekte bysonderheden* (Short history of the Synod of Dort, including some remarkable and previously unknown particularities) and went through six editions in 1671 and 1672. He was a supporter of toleration, following in the footsteps of Erasmus, Richard Hooker and Hugo Grotius, and often accused of Socinianism.[55] After all, in both England and the United Provinces, Calvinists were quick to understand the polemical value of accusing an opponent of being Socinian. Hales was still a fellow at the time that Milton lived in Horton, five miles away. Milton may have had access to the library at Eton; whether this was owned by Hales himself or he was merely closely involved cannot be determined with absolute certainty, but it included many books on Arminianism.[56] Works on the controversy between Arminius and Gomarus during the time of the Synod of Dort were especially well represented (and some were even in Dutch).[57] Access to this particular library in Eton would have exposed Milton to Arminianism in the 1630s, early on in his literary career.

Hales also had some connections with Marvell. As tutor to William Dutton, Marvell was a private servant at Eton.[58] It was at the household of Lady Salter of Richings Lodge that Marvell became acquainted with Hales, though the latter was no longer a fellow of Eton, the consequence of his support for the king. It was an important connection for Marvell, as Arminianism during the 1650s had previously undergone a rapid decline, due to the efforts of high-placed Calvinists in Cromwell's regime.[59] Marvell would later on in his *Rehearsal Transpros'd* remember Hales and their conversations: 'Tis one Mr. Hales of Eaton, a most learned Divine, and one of the Church of England, and most remarkable for his Sufferings in the late times, and his Christian patience under them. [. . .] as I account it no small honour to have grown up into some part of his Acquaintance, and convers'd a while with the living *remains* of one of the clearest heads and best prepared brests in Christendom', and refers to a work by him, *Treatise concerning Schism*, he read many years ago.[60]

English theological texts were also distributed, printed, and published in the Dutch Republic.[61] As explained in the previous chapter, the amount of translation from English into Dutch was relatively small when it came to poetical works, but English religious prose works were readily available in the Netherlands.[62] The tracts were often first printed in the original Latin (or English), but then translated, see for example Wilhelmus Perkins' *Een tractaet van de vrye genaede Gods, ende vrye wille des menschen* (1611) (translated from William Perkins, *A Christian and plaine treatise of the manner and order of predestination: and of the largenes of God's grace,* 1606). Several works of John Dury in Latin (such as *De pace ecclesiastica inter evangelicos procuranda sententiæ quatuor*) can be found in the Dutch archives, as well as works by James Ussher in Latin. John Bunyan's *The Pilgrim's Progress* (1678) was shortly afterwards translated into Dutch (*Eens christens reyse na de eeuwigheyt*, 1683), as were some works by Richard Baxter. These are merely some examples of the commerce in religious texts between the United Provinces and England, but a further illustration of this flow is that religious texts – frequently controversial – were brought to the Dutch Republic in the hope of finding willing printers and publishers that could not be found in England. This was the case with the attempted publication of Milton's *De doctrina Christiana*.

Daniel Skinner recognised the heretical content of Milton's tract and decided to send it, together with some of Milton's State Papers, to the Amsterdam printer Daniel Elzevier, who with his cousin Lodewijk Elzevier was the most controversial publisher of the Elzevier family. Some of Milton's State Papers had already been published by the Dutch publisher Blaeu, without providing details of their printer, bookseller, or place of publication.[63] How Blaeu got hold of the State Papers is as yet unknown.[64] After printing, Skinner intended to distribute the tract and State Papers in England, making use of less censorious Dutch printing culture to feed intellectual debate at home. Skinner's intent is confirmed by an anonymous informant writing to Joseph Williamson, the Secretary of State: 'he is resolved to print [Mr. Milton's writing on the Civil & Ecclesiastical Government of the Kingdom] and to that purpose is gone into Holland and intends to print it at Leyden (and at this present is either there or at Nemeguen) and then to bring and disperse the copys in England'.[65] However, after advice from the remonstrant Philipp van Limborch, the Arianism in Milton's tract led to Daniel Elzevier getting cold feet.[66]

This is only one case study, but some general conclusions about the religious exchange between England and the United Provinces can be drawn. For controversial texts, Dutch printing and publication culture was the place to go. Copies were then often distributed in the country of origin, already evinced in the previous chapter with the publication and distribution of Milton's *Defences*. One further consequence was that a wide array of religious texts from across Europe were available within the United Provinces. In this regard, and considering the public interest in the debates of the Synod of Dort, Dutch society was frequently more intellectually and religiously tolerant than elsewhere in Europe. However, this was not without its tensions and limitations, seen for example in the distinction drawn between freedom of conscience and freedom of practice; not everything was acceptable to pronounce in public. In Milton's *De doctrina Christiana*, this (often shifting) line was crossed: in the end, Daniel Elzevier refused to publish it on the basis of its heretical content.

Dutch Toleration in Milton and Marvell

Milton, during his involvement with the English Commonwealth, and Marvell through his travels and later diplomatic duties, were able to witness different approaches to toleration in Europe. Compared to countries such as the Commonwealth of Poland-Lithuania and the United Provinces, which both had religious toleration written into their constitutions, England was only moderately tolerationist.[67] This is indicated by fluctuating fortunes of Arminianism throughout the seventeenth century. Even though English and Dutch Arminianism drifted further apart during the seventeenth century, after the Restoration English Arminianism again became associated with toleration, a link that had been lost in the 1630s under Laud. As shown earlier, Dutch toleration permitted silent freedom of mind and belief within outward conformity, but this certainly did not extend to free practice or the acceptance of dissent. The Calvinists within the Dutch Reformed Church had concluded that full religious toleration was simply not compatible with political stability, using as their measure the strife between the remonstrants (Arminian sympathisers) and contra-remonstrants (Gomarian sympathisers) of the 1610s. Dutch toleration was, in many ways, very similar to what Charles II envisaged in the 1670s after his Declaration of Indulgence (1672), in which nonconformists were invited to apply for a license that would permit public worship, and Roman Catholics encouraged to worship within their private houses alone.[68] It is not implausible that Charles' idea of toleration was influenced by his time as an exile in the United Provinces.

English Arminian toleration grew out of the Dutch tradition, after which it became a new form of Arminianism, and relatively intolerant in the Laudian Church of the 1630s. The Arminian tradition found fertile soil in England, in particular in the intellectual circles of the Cambridge Platonists and the Tew Group in Oxford, perhaps most clearly in the works of John Hales and William Chillingworth.[69] Both these circles were in contact with Dutch remonstrants at the time, shown by a letter from the Dutch remonstrant Arnold Poelenburg to Isaac Vossius (1664), sending greetings to Thomas Pierce, Master of Magdalen College, Oxford and Henry More, fellow of

Corpus Christi at the University of Cambridge.[70] They also translated and circulated early editions of Grotius' *De Veritate*, as well as texts by Arminius.[71] Through Hales, both Milton and Marvell may have been exposed to this type of Dutch Arminian toleration.

The explosion of texts on toleration after the Synod of Dort was mirrored in England during the tumultuous 1640s and 1660s, especially after the *Blasphemy Ordinances* in 1648 and the *Clarendon Code* in the early half of the 1660s. This was closely connected to radical discussions on freedom of speech, as liberty of religious conscience proved difficult to separate from liberty of expression. Marvell and Milton both participated in these waves of tolerationist writing; Milton with his outspoken *Areopagitica* in 1644 and *Of True Religion, Heresy, Schism, Toleration; and what best means may be used against the Growth of Popery* in 1673, and Marvell's prose works, especially *Rehearsal Transpros'd*, and *The Second Part*, responding to the four acts of the 1660s. As Arminius and Episcopius had argued before, a free intellectual discussion of diverse readings of the Scripture, carried out in print, manuscript, and orally, ought to resolve itself in compatible views of the essential doctrinal issues; this was later to be echoed by Christopher Potter and John Hales in England.[72] In *Part I*, Marvell satirises Mr. Bayes' aversion to the press, joining Milton in favouring freedom of printing and publication.[73] Marvell draws on the example of a '*bulky*' Dutch printer, Laurens Koster, allegedly the inventor of the printing art.[74]

Annabel Patterson writes in the introduction to Marvell's prose that his works discussing toleration can be seen as a bridge between Milton's *Areopagitica* and John Locke's *Letter Concerning Toleration* (1689), 'if one acknowledges that a theory of toleration between Protestants was for all three of these writers quite compatible with politically motivated anti-Catholicism'.[75] The influence of Dutch toleration on English toleration is not always fully appreciated. All three writers had important connections to the United Provinces, and in particular to Dutch toleration. The transition between these three writers can thus not be seen as a chronological English movement alone. Instead we have to acknowledge a shared Dutch influence – with an emphasis on the impact of Dutch Arminian toleration.

Debates around toleration were intense and far-reaching in the United Provinces and England.[76] Milton's *Areopagitica*, besides being written against potential parliamentary censorship, was also a response to the intolerance displayed in the 1630s and 1640s in the English Church, with its Laudian English Arminianism. It asks for full Protestant toleration, though still excludes Catholicism completely. The vision that Milton proposed differs greatly from the hopes of nation-building through toleration, as expressed by Episcopius and Grotius. Milton instead argued that the State and the Church were completely different institutions, with a different foundation, and should therefore not be allowed to regulate one another. The toleration in this case is not based on approval or rejection of the state or the church, but on constant and fearless discussion of Scripture. This testing of multiple interpretations ought to lead to an agreement on the key doctrines of Protestantism:

> Where there is much desire to learn, there of necessity will be much arguing, much writing, many opinions; for opinion in good men is but knowledge in the making. Under these fantastic terrors of sect and schism, we wrong the earnest and zealous thirst after knowledge and understanding which God hath stirr'd up in this City. What some lament of, we rather should rejoyce at, should rather praise this pious forwardnes among men, to reassume the ill deputed care of their Religion into their own hands again.[77]

On this point Milton deviates from those who tried to establish peace within a universal Church, such as Grotius. In Episcopius' Church even Catholicism could be included. In Milton, the power therefore does not lie with the theologians as Arminius would have it, but with the individual, and in learned discussion; State and Church follow this discussion, rather than precede it with ordinances.

Milton's ideas on toleration did not alter a great deal in the thirty years between *Areopagitica* and *Of True Religion, Heresy, Schism and Toleration* (1673). *Areopagitica*'s strong emphasis on free speech in order to mould the strong foundations of truth is re-uttered in *Of Religion*: 'There is no Learned man but will confess he hath much profited by reading Controversies, his Senses awakt, his Judgment sharpn'd, and the truth which he holds more firmly establish't'.[78] There is no mellowing of Milton's attitude towards Catholicism in his tolerationist prose works, as *Of Religion* proves. Unlike Marvell's *Rehearsal Transpros'd*, and *The Second Part*, Milton did not write this tract in favour of Charles II's Act of Indulgence – rather, he argued that it opened the door to Catholicism.[79]

Presbyterians also receive consistent hostile treatment in the majority of Milton's works (with the exception of the anti-episcopal tracts). *Of Religion* does not have any direct reference to either Charles' act or Parliament's response in the Test Act, but the spine of the tract is an attack on Catholicism, to which some core values of Protestant toleration are summarily attached.[80] The Test Act was based on Anglican doctrinal articles, which meant that Anti-Trinitarianism was excluded from the proposed toleration, and the act, moreover, compromised the position of some English Dissenters (which was later compensated for in the bill for the Ease of Protestant Dissenters).[81] Milton similarly refers often to Anglican documents and writers, while showing some sympathy for nonconformists. However, he made use only of those sources that present Socinianism and anti-Trinitarianism as not heretical per se, provided all these Protestant schisms maintain the same principle doctrines:

> The Pharisees and Saduces were two Sects, yet both met together in their common worship of God at Jerusalem. But here the Papist will

angrily demand, what! Are Lutherans, Calvinists, Anabaptists, Socinians, Arminians, no Hereticks? I answer, all these may have some errors, but are no Hereticks. Heresie is in the Will and choice profestly against Scripture; error is against the Will, in misunderstanding the Scripture after all sincere endeavours to understand it rightly: Hence it was said well by one of the Ancients, *Err I may, but a Heretick I will not be.*[82]

Even if Milton did not agree with some or all of their theological interpretations, he still maintained that these authors were not heretical, but 'Learned, Worthy, Zealous, and Religious Men', 'perfect and powerful in the Scriptures, holy and unblameable in their lives'.[83] In Milton's toleration, the revivers of these sects were free to interpret Scripture and arrive at different (if sometimes wrong) conclusions, as long as this all took place within a Protestant framework. They should all be treated 'equally, as being Protestants', which included freedom of practice and the dissemination of their ideas in public print.[84] These ideas were compatible with Arminius', and, indeed, Grotius' ideas on toleration; Hales, too, uses this argument in *A Tract Concerning Schism* (1642).[85] Milton's list of all these schisms does not reveal his preference for any of the sects or any personal allegiance, and each of them receives a certain defence against accusations commonly levelled at them (such as Calvinism making God the author of Sin, and Arminians ignoring the power of God's grace).[86]

Milton's vision of toleration is more limited than Arminian toleration in the United Provinces, or even compared to his contemporary tolerationist writer Roger Williams.[87] Williams argued for full toleration, including Catholics, a version of which he had realised on Rhode Island.[88] Milton's complete toleration by contrast extends only to forms of Protestantism, since 'Popery is the only or the greatest Heresie, [. . .] the obstinate Papist, the only heretick'.[89] The Catholic should not be allowed to practise this religion in public, nor in private.[90] Milton uses the same division between belief and the practice of religion that was current in the Netherlands, but without the acceptance of Catholicism contained within private homes. What Williams and Milton do share, though, and what is absent in Marvell (as we shall see in the following) is a complete division between the Church and the State. Milton argued in *Of Religion* that making religion political leads to usurpation, as among popes in the past.[91] As early as 1644, English tolerationists such as Roger Williams and Thomas Collier had argued for a complete separation of State and Church, almost fifteen years before their Dutch counterparts. This stress on separation means that a national church in which the faiths are united, even within a tolerant environment, is not part of Milton's concept of what toleration should be.[92] Milton had access to sources discussing Dutch toleration, and although his own toleration is more restrictive, both share an emphasis on dialogue and discussion.

When Marvell travelled through the Netherlands in the early 1640s, he would have witnessed the aftermath of the Arminian toleration movement that flourished in the 1620s and 1630s, led by Episcopius. We know from

The Character of Holland that he was aware of it, when he satirises religious freedom in Amsterdam:

> Sure when religion did itself embark,
> And from the east would westward steer its ark,
> It struck, and splitting on this unknown ground,
> Each one thence pillaged the first piece he found:
> Hence Amsterdam, Turk-Christian-Pagan-Jew,
> Staple of sects and mint of schism grew;
> That bank of conscience, where not one so strange
> Opinion but finds credit, and exchange.
> In vain for Catholics ourselves we bear;
> The universal Church is only there.
>
> (ll. 67–76)

This is Marvellian to its core: the tolerationist Marvell attacking the proliferations of Dutch toleration in Amsterdam. He applauds and satirises toleration at the same time.[93] Is he condemning toleration here, or merely the universal church of money by which the United Provinces was supposedly ruled?

Marvell's prose tracts seem to provide a clearer answer to this question than his poetry. The two parts of *The Rehearsal Transpros'd* (1672, 1673) were written in defence of the nonconformists and Charles' policy of religious toleration, and against the radical Episcopalian Samuel Parker. Marvell comments on the position of the Arminians in the Church of England and the Grotian Church, and their toleration. As Martin Dzelzainis and Annabel Patterson note, Marvell saw the rise of Arminianism in the 1630s under the leadership of Laud as one of the main factors leading to the Civil Wars.[94] However, the editors of Marvell's prose do not make a distinction between Dutch and English Arminianism. Marvell himself does make this distinction in the tract, emphasising that Dutch Arminianism was introduced into the English Church with a very different reason, namely to accommodate monarchy and episcopacy: '[i]t was Arminianism, which though it were the *Republican* Opinion there, and so odious to King James that it helped on the death of Barnevelt, yet now undertook to accommodate it to Monarchy and Episcopacy'.[95] From the outset, Dutch Arminianism promoted toleration, in which orthodox Calvinists and Arminians could still be part of the same Dutch Reformed Church. The Arminian tradition has at its heart an acknowledgement of the divine and universal truth in every Christian religion, an openness which could only occur when free debate on these issues was allowed. All other things, such as ceremony, church rituals and liturgy, were pushed to the periphery of Christianity, in which opinion could differ and would not obstruct the universal church. This is quite similar to the attitude of surgeon Wouter Schouten that opened this chapter. It is, however, also radically different from the intolerance that Laud showed with his insistence on conformity to ceremony, and hinted at in his attitude towards the Puritans, as Marvell describes:

> And though there needed nothing more to make them unacceptable to the sober part of the Nation, yet moreover they were so exceeding *pragmatical*, so intolerably ambitious, and so desperately proud, that scarce any Gentleman might come near the Tayle of their Mules. [. . .] For the English have been always very tender of their Religion, their Liberty, their Propriety, and (I was going to say) no less of their Reputation.[96]

Furthermore, in the *Rehearsal Transpros'd*, Marvell uses Hales' *Tract Concerning Schism*, presenting a Dutch-influenced vision of toleration, as a counter-point to Samuel Parker's 'intemperate excess'.[97] Also note that Hales' other tract, on the Synod of Dort, was republished in this same period. It is therefore specifically English Arminianism and its intolerance that Marvell rejects.

Did he then endorse the toleration that the Dutch Arminians in the 1620s and 1630s promoted, under the leadership of Grotius and Episcopius? No. In *The Rehearsal Transpros'd*, he also condemns Grotius as an extreme version of the toleration that Arminius promoted: 'For, in fact, that incomparable Person Grotius did yet make a Bridge for the Enemy to cover over; or at least laid some of our considerable Passes open to them and unguarded'.[98] In Grotius' works of the 1610s and 1620s, especially *Ordinum Hollandiae et Westfrisiae pietas* (1611), *De satisfactione Christi adversus Faustum Socinum* (an explanation of how Arminianism is far removed from Socinianism, 1617) and *De veritate religionis Christianae* (1627) (first published in Dutch as *Bewijs van den Ware Godsdienst*, 1622), he envisaged a united Church that shared essential doctrines, but with individual denominations that could maintain their differing, non-essential, articles of faith. Grotius had corresponded about his ambition to create a united church with Laud and thought that the Church of England was the best option for realising the irenic plan.[99] Grotius' approach to toleration would thus have opened the door to Catholicism in the Church of England – inviting 'the Enemy to cover over'.[100] Marvell, however, was not as outspokenly anti-Catholic as Milton.[101] This is reflected in the response of the Catholic Earl of Castlemaine in his praise of Marvell and hostility towards Milton.[102] It is safe, nonetheless, to say that Marvell also did not support Grotian toleration.

Marvell's famous reflection on the Civil Wars in the *Rehearsal Transpros'd* becomes even more poignant when applying it to the political and religious tumult in the Netherlands in the 1610s and 1620s, and the 1670s, which each led to a debate on toleration, with the threat of political and religious unrest.

> Whether it were a War of Religion, or of Liberty, is not worth the labour to enquire. Which-soever was at the top, the other was at the bottom;

but upon considering all, I think the Cause was too good to have been fought for. Men ought to have trusted God; they ought and might have trusted the King with that whole matter. The *Arms of the church are Prayers and Tears*, the Arms of the Subjects are Patience and Petitions. The King himself being of so accurate and piercing a judgment, would soon have felt where it stuck. For men may spare their pains where Nature is at work, and the world will not go the faster for our driving. Even as his present Majesty's happy Restauration did it self; so all things else happen in their best and proper time, without any need of our officiousness.[103]

Nigel Smith has argued that this passage cannot be read simply as a personal statement of regret about the course of the English conflict. The tract as a whole seems to support the opposite point of the phrase 'the world will not go faster for our driving', namely to implement the King's laws to support toleration as soon as possible.[104] However, at the same time, Marvell does not support complete freedom for either state or religion. Stability is the most important thing, and can only within that freedom, including liberty of conscience, have its place. The emphasis is thus on individual liberty, rather than the liberty of large institutions. Freedom without stability is unsustainable, which goes for both religion and politics. This stability could be established only when there was some sort of regulation, by the court, parliament, or the Church.

In his *Two Treatises of Government* (1689), Locke argued that even if the natural liberty of man is to be free from any power, civil society requires legislative power established by the consent of one commonwealth.[105] This conception of liberty is more limited than that of extreme Dutch Republican tolerationists, such as Baruch Spinoza, the brothers De la Court, and Pierre Bayle (albeit originally French, he lived in Rotterdam), though Locke was heavily influenced by these.[106] It is somewhat closer to Marvell, who was likewise conscious of the positive power of leadership; after all, the *Rehearsal Transpros'd* is written in defence of the court and not in the name of general liberty.[107] Charles II, too, promoted liberty, although he was not supported by the Cavalier parliament and the Church of England. Charles II's suspension of laws against dissenters (March 1662) made a link between Church and State, something that the Anglican Parker, with an Erastian approach to toleration, did not support.[108] Marvell does protest against the tyrannical exercise of state power that Parker promotes, but is not against a moderate Erastian approach to State and Church. Dutch toleration often put freedom before stability, in the hope that the former would lead to the latter; Marvell to some extent the reverse.

Examining traces of principles associated with Dutch toleration in Milton's and Marvell's works demonstrates mutual exchange, and that the different tolerationist movements, whether English or Dutch, escape neat categorisation. Marvell emphasised individual conscience within the haven of state stability. Within toleration, one is allowed to disagree with another, even ignore differences, constructing a society with an emphasis on private practice within a secular state.[109] Unity in Marvell's toleration was always more important than conformity. In contrast, Milton's toleration thrived on dialogue, debate, compromise and disagreement, taking place in a public, uncensored sphere. Pious argument ought to chisel out the truth latent in the marble of men's minds, pecking away the falsehoods of Catholicism. Both are restricted by their anti-Catholicism from the breadth of inclusion that Dutch Arminianism often pointed towards, though they did import some of these ideas through their encounters with Dutch texts and thinkers. To what extent they incorporated Arminius' notion of grace and free will into their texts will be at the centre of the next chapter.

Notes

1 Marijke Barend-van Haeften and Hetty Plekenpol, *Wouter Schouten, Dichter en VOC-Chirurgijn* (Zutphen: Walburg Pers, 2012), pp. 9, 80.
2 Wouter Schouten, 'Op 't tweede boeckx, derde hooftstuck', in Marijke Barend-van Haeften and Hetty Plekenpol, *Wouter Schouten, Dichter en VOC-Chirurgijn* (Zutphen: Walburg Pers, 2012): 80–85.
3 Joke Spaans, 'Religious Policies in the Seventeenth-Century Dutch Republic', in *Calvinism and Religious Toleration in the Dutch Golden Age*, ed. by R. Po-Chia and Henk van Nierop (Cambridge: Cambridge University Press, 2002): 72–86 (p. 77).
4 Gary K. Waite, *Jews and Muslims in Seventeenth-Century Discourse* (Abingdon: Routledge, 2018), pp. 4–5.
5 Henricus Arnoldi, *Vande Conscientie-dwangh, dat is: Klaer ende Grondich Vertoogh, dat de [. . .] Staten Generael in haer Placcaet den 3 Julij 1619 tegen de Conventiculen der Remonstranten ghe-emaneert, gheen Conscientie-dwangh invoeren: Maer allen Ingesetenen der Geunieerde Provincien, van hoedanigen ghelove ofte gevoelen sy zijn, de behoorlicke ende volcomene vryheydt der Conscientie toe-staen ende vergunnen [. . .]* (Amsterdam, 1629), pp. 2–4.
6 Alistair Duke, *Reformation and Revolt in the Low Countries* (London: Hambledon and London, 1990), p. 267.
7 J. Huizinga, *Nederland's Beschaving in de Zeventiende Eeuw* (Groningen: Wolters-Noordhoff, 1926), p. 69.
8 Jonathan Israel, *The Dutch Republic: Its Rise, Greatness and Fall, 1477–1806* (Oxford: Oxford University Press, 1995), p. 104; Gerrit Jan Hoenderdaal, 'The Life and Struggle of Arminius in the Dutch Republic', in *Man's Faith and Freedom: The Theological Influence of Jacobus Arminius* (New York: Abingdon Press, 1962): 11–26.
9 Alistair Duke, 'The Ambivalent Face of Calvinism in the Netherlands, 1561–1618', in *International Calvinism, 1541–1715*, ed. by Menna Prestwich (Oxford: Oxford University Press, 1985): 109–135.
10 H.F.K. van Nierop, *Beeldenstorm en Burgelijk Verzet in Amsterdam, 1566–1567* (Nijmegen: Socialistische Uitgeverij, 1987); Israel, *Dutch Republic*, pp. 361–362.
11 Russell Shorto's popular history book *Amsterdam: A History of the World's Most Liberal City* (New York: Penguin Random House, 2014) is a case in point.
12 Jonathan Israel, 'Religious Toleration and Radical Philosophy', in *Calvinism and Religious Toleration in the Dutch Golden Age*, ed. by R. Po-Chia and Henk van Nierop (Cambridge: Cambridge University Press, 2002): 148–158 (pp. 150–151); Benjamin J. Kaplan, '"Dutch" Religious Tolerance: Celebration

and Revision', in *Calvinism and Religious Toleration in the Dutch Golden Age*, ed. by R. Po-Chia and Henk van Nierop (Cambridge: Cambridge University Press, 2002): 8–26 (p. 8).

13   Peter van Rooden, 'Jews and Religious Toleration in the Dutch Republic', in *Calvinism and Religious Toleration in the Dutch Golden Age*, ed. by R. Po-Chia and Henk van Nierop (Cambridge: Cambridge University Press, 2002): 132–158.

14   Waite, p. 30.

15   Marc de Wilde, 'Offering Hospitality to Strangers: Hugo Grotius' Draft Regulations for the Jews', *Tijdschrift voor Rechtsgeschiedenis*, 85 (2017): 391–433 (p. 392).

16   Hugo Grotius, *Remonstrantie nopende de ordre dije in de landen van Hollandt ende Westvrieslandt dijent gestelt op de Joden*, ed. by Jaap Meijer (Amsterdam, 1949), pp. 107–121; Waite, p. 36.

17   Waite, p. 47.

18   Grotius, *Remonstratie*, p. 113, qtd. in Waite, p. 34.

19   Jonathan Israel, 'Toleration in Seventeenth-Century Dutch and English Thought', in *The Exchange of Ideas: Religion, Scholarship, and Art in the Seventeenth Century* (Zutphen: Walburg Instituut, 1994): 13–41 (p. 14).

20   Gary K. Waite, 'Where Did the Devil Go? Religious Polemic in the Dutch Reformation, 1580–1630', in *Interlinguicity, Internationality and Shakespeare*, ed. by Michael Saenger (Montreal: McGill-Queen's University Press, 2014): 59–73.

21   In 'The Bond of Christian Piety' Judith Pollmann argues that confessionalism only took place in one part of Dutch society, the public part, but that the majority of the Dutch population did not become full members of any congregation — and that these were the supporters of religious toleration: Judith Pollmann, 'The Bond of Christian Piety', in *Calvinism and Religious Toleration in the Dutch Golden Age*, ed. by R. Po-Chia Hsia and Henk van Nierop (Cambridge: Cambridge University Press, 2002): 53–71; Maarten Prak, 'The Politics of Intolerance: Citizenship and Religion in the Dutch Republic (Seventeenth to Eighteenth Centuries)', in *Calvinism and Religious Toleration in the Dutch Golden Age*, ed. by R. Po-Chia Hsia and Henk van Nierop (Cambridge: Cambridge University Press, 2002): 159–175.

22   Judith Pollmann, 'Vondel's Religion', in *Joost van den Vondel: Dutch Playwright in the Golden Age*, ed. by Jan Bloemendal and Frans-Willem Korsten (Leiden: Brill, 2012): 85–100 (p. 87); Israel, *Dutch Republic*, p. 373.

23   See for a more elaborate discussion on how Catholics worshipped in a mainly private sphere, Christine Kooi, 'Strategies of Catholic Toleration in Golden Age Holland', in *Calvinism and Religious Toleration in the Dutch Golden Age*, ed. by R. Po-Chia Hsia and Henk van Nierop (Cambridge: Cambridge University Press, 2002): 87–101.

24   Benjamin J. Kaplan, *Divided by Faith: Religious Conflict and the Practise of Toleration in Early Modern Europe* (Cambridge: Harvard University Press, 2007), p. 174.

25   Carl Bangs, Keith D. Stanglin, and Stephen Fallon are among the exceptions.

26   Freya Sierhuis, *The Literature of the Arminian Controversy*: Religion, Politics, and the Stage in the Dutch Republic (Oxford: Oxford University Press, 2015).

27   Keith D. Stanglin, *Arminius on the Assurance of Salvation: The Context, Roots, and Shape of the Leiden Debate, 1603–1609* (Leiden: Brill, 2007), p. 1.

28   Brooke Conti, *Confessions of Faith in Early Modern England* (Philadelphia: Pennsylvania University Press, 2014), p. 114.

29   Takashi Yoshinaka, *Marvell's Ambivalence: Religion and Politics in the Imagination in Mid-Seventeenth Century England* (Woodbridge: Boydell and Brewer, 2011), pp. 199–200.

30 John Witte, *The Reformation of Rights* (Cambridge: Cambridge University Press, 2010), *passim*.

31 Alexander van der Haven, 'Predestination and Toleration: The Dutch Republic's Single Judicial Persecution of Jews in Theological Context', *Renaissance Quarterly*, 71 (2018): 165–205.

32 Israel, 'Toleration in Seventeenth-Century Dutch and English Thought', p. 21.

33 Marco Barducci, 'Church Government', in *Hugo Grotius and the Century of Revolution, 1613–1718* (Oxford: Oxford University Press, 2017), pp. 116–136.

34 Th. Marius van Leeuwen, 'Introduction', in *Arminius, Arminianism, and Europe* (Leiden: Brill, 2009): IX–XXII (p. XVII).

35 Nigel Smith, 'Milton and the European Contexts of Toleration', in *Milton and Toleration*, ed. by Sharon Achinstein and Elizabeth Sauer (Oxford: Oxford University Press, 2007): 23–44 (p. 42); Mary Ann Radzinowicz attempts something similar in the section on Milton's theology, *Towards Samson Agonistes: The Growth of Milton's Mind* (Princeton: Princeton University Press, 1978), pp. 313–347.

36 John Spurr, 'The Poet's Religion', in *The Cambridge Companion to Andrew Marvell*, ed. by Derek Hirst and Steven N. Zwicker (Cambridge: Cambridge University Press, 2011): 158–173 (p. 159).

37 Qtd. in Annabel Patterson, 'Introduction', in *The Prose Works of Andrew Marvell*, 2 vols. (New Haven: Yale University Press, 2003), vol. 1, xi–liv (xi).

38 Warren Chernaik, *The Poet's Time: Religion and Politics in the Works of Andrew Marvell* (Cambridge: Cambridge University Press, 1983), and the edited volume with Martin Dzelzainis, *Marvell and Liberty* (Basingstoke: Palgrave Macmillan, 1999); Annabel Patterson, *Marvell and the Civic Crown* (Princeton: Princeton University Press, 1978); John Wallace, *Destiny his Choice: The Loyalism of Andrew Marvell* (Cambridge: Cambridge University Press, 1968).

39 Peter White, *Predestination, Policy and Polemic: Conflict and Consensus in the English Church from the Reformation to the Civil War* (Cambridge: Cambridge University Press, 1992), pp. 272–286; Nicholas Tyacke, *Anti-Calvinists: The Rise of English Arminianism* (Oxford: Oxford University Press, 1987), p. 181.

40 As David R. Como has shown, Laud often used informal hearings to 'bully' Calvinist ministers into avoiding the topic of predestination and free will, on threat of imprisonment, 'Predestination and Political Conflict in Laud's London', *The Historical Journal*, 46.2 (2003): 263–294 (p. 283). The rise of Laudanism is a complex development, and there is a great wealth of secondary material on the topic. Just to mention a few: Anthony Milton, *Laudian and Royalist Polemic in Seventeenth-Century England: The Career and Writings of Peter Heylyn* (Manchester: Manchester University Press, 2012) (for an individual case of Laudian conversion); Graham Parry, *The Arts of the Anglican Counter-Reformation: Glory, Laud and Honour* (Woodbridge: Boydell Press, 2006) (for a complete account of the transformation of the Anglican Church under the leadership of Laud); E.C.E Bourne, *The Anglicanism of William Laud* (London: Society for Promoting Christian Knowledge, 1946) (for a (somewhat dated) narrative on the political rise of Laud), Charles Carlton, *Charles I: The Personal Monarch* (London: Routledge, 1983); Julian Davies, *The Caroline Captivity of the Church: Charles I and the Remoulding of Anglicanism, 1625–1641* (Oxford: Clarendon Press, 1992) (for overviews of Charles I's role in the assistance of Laud); and Kevin Sharpe, *Image Wars: Promoting Kings and Commonwealths in England, 1603–1660* (New Haven: Yale University Press, 2010) (for the ideological aspect of Laud's rise).

41 Tyacke, *Anti-Calvinists, passim*.

42 *PWAM*: I. 188–189; Mortimer argues that English Calvinism was much less strict than its Dutch sister, and that English Socinianism was not the same

as Dutch Socinianism. The boundaries between different Protestant religions appear to have been more fluid in England: Sarah Mortimer, *Reason and Religion in the English Revolution: The Challenge of Socinianism* (Cambridge: Cambridge University Press, 2010), pp. 42–43.

43 Tyacke, *Anti-Calvinists*, p. 246.

44 J. van den Berg, 'Dutch Calvinism and the Church of England in the Period of the Glorious Revolution', in *The Exchange of Ideas: Religion, Scholarship, and Art in the Seventeenth Century* (Zutphen: Walburg Instituut, 1994): 84–99 (p. 87).

45 Christopher N. Warren, *Literature and the Law of Nations, 1580–1680* (Oxford: Oxford University Press, 2015), pp. 185–186.

46 In the 1640s, there was a rise in sectarian manifestations of Antinomianism, a more extreme version of Calvinism that claimed that the Law of Moses is no longer necessary for the elect, further pushing Arminianism into the background (Nicholas Tyacke, 'Arminianism and the Theology of the Restoration Church', in *The Exchange of Ideas: Religion, Scholarship and Art in the Seventeenth Century* (Zutphen: Walburg Instituut, 1994): 68–83 (p. 69)).

47 Nigel Smith, 'Best, Biddle and Anti-Trinitarian Heresy', in *Heresy, Literature and Politics in Early Modern English Culture*, ed. by David Loewenstein and John Marshall (Cambridge: Cambridge University Press, 2006): 160–184 (p. 163).

48 *Bibliotheca Angleseiana, sive catalogus variorum librorum* (1686) and *Bibliotheca Oweniana* (1684). See for the discovery of Marvell's links to the Earl of Anglesey: Annabel Patterson and Martin Dzelzainis, 'Marvell and the Earl of Anglesey: A Chapter in the History of Reading', *The Historical Journal*, 44.3 (2001): 703–726.

49 A search of *Early English Books Online* (in August 2018) reveals that there are no records of Gomarus (or Gomari, Gomarii, Gomarius) as an author of books printed in Britain, although he is mentioned in 226 records. Arminius (Armini, Arminii or Hermanszoon) is the author of two records printed in London, and mentioned in 917 records.

50 Brian Cowan, 'Millington, Edward (*c.*1636–1703)', *Oxford Dictionary National Biography*, retrieved 23 March 2019. www.oxforddnb.com/view/10.1093/ref:odnb/9780198614128.001.0001/odnb-9780198614128-e-52142.

51 See for the religious exchange between England and the United Provinces, Keith Sprunger, *Dutch Puritanism: A History of English and Scottish Churches of the Netherlands in the Sixteenth and Seventeenth Centuries* (Leiden: Brill, 1982), pp. 3–12.

52 N.H. Keeble and Johanna Harris, 'Marvell and Nonconformity', in *The Oxford Handbook of Marvell*, ed. by Martin Dzelzainis and Edward Holberton (Oxford: Oxford University Press, 2019): 145–163 (pp. 146–147).

53 *CPW* (OUP) (2012): VIII (part 2). 1052–1054.

54 John Hales, *Golden Remains* (London, 1659), sig. A4*v*.

55 'Best, Biddle and Anti-Trinitarian Heresy', p. 163; Mortimer, pp. 81–83; Basil Greenslade, 'Hales, John (1584–1656)', *Oxford Dictionary of National Biography*, retrieved 23 March 2019. www.oxforddnb.com/view/10.1093/ref:odnb/9780198614128.001.0001/odnb-9780198614128-e-11914.

56 Gordon Campbell and Thomas N. Corns, *John Milton: Life, Work and Thought* (Oxford: Oxford University Press, 2008), pp. 88, 104.

57 William Poole, 'Analysing a Private Library, with a Shelf List Attributable to John Hales of Eton, c. 1624', in *A Concise Companion to the Study of Manuscripts, Printed Books and the Production of Early Modern Texts*, ed. by Edward Jones (Chichester: Wiley-Blackwell, 2015): 41–65 (pp. 52–59).

58 Nigel Smith, *Andrew Marvell: The Chameleon* (New Haven: Yale University Press, 2010), pp. 110–111.

59 Tyacke, 'Arminianism and the Theology of the Restoration Church', p. 69.

60 *PWAM*: I. 130.
61 Keith Sprunger's book, *Dutch Puritanism*, examines the immense influence of English and Scottish immigrants in the Netherlands up until the Glorious Revolution. His study looks at churches in the major cities, as well as discussing the effects English synods had on the Dutch religious milieu. Another book examining the international character of Calvinism is by Ole Peter Grell, *Brethren in Christ: A Calvinist Network in Reformation Europe* (Cambridge: Cambridge University Press, 2011), which focusses in particular on identifying the spread of Calvinism and the fluidity of the early modern religious culture.
62 Cornelis W. Schoneveld, *Intertraffic of the Mind* (Leiden: Brill, 1983), pp. 118–124; E. Osselton, *The Dumb Linguists: A Study of the Early English and Dutch Dictionaries* (Oxford: Oxford University Press, 1973).
63 Gordon Campbell, Thomas Corns, John K. Hale, and Fiona J. Tweedie, *Milton and the Manuscript of De doctrina Christiana* (Oxford: Oxford University Press, 2007), p. 14.
64 We do know after Kelley's work that this edition was published in Amsterdam, and that Blaeu was responsible for publishing it: Maurice Kelley, 'Letter in Times Literary Supplement', (29 April 1960), p. 273.
65 Anonymous, 'Letter to Joseph Williamson', qtd. in Campbell, Corns, Hale, and Tweedie, p. 13.
66 Kęstutis Daugirdas, 'The Biblical Hermeneutics of Philip van Limborch (1633–1712) and Its Intellectual Challenges', in *Scriptural Authority and Biblical Criticism in the Dutch Golden Age: God's Word Questioned* (Oxford: Oxford University Press, 2017): 220–258; Campbell, Corns, Hale and Tweedie, p. 7.
67 Smith, 'Milton and the European Contexts of Religion', p. 24.
68 Keith W.F. Stavely, 'Preface to Of True Religion, Heresie, Schism, Toleration', in *Complete Prose Works of John Milton*, 8 vols. (New Haven: Yale University Press, 1982), vol. 8: 408–415 (p. 408).
69 Mortimer, p. 64; H. Trevor-Roper, *Catholics, Anglicans and Puritans: Seventeenth-Century Essays* (Chicago: Chicago University Press, 1988), pp. 166–230.
70 'Arnoldus Poelenburgh to Isaac Vossius' (1664), Bodleian Library, University of Oxford, shelf mark MS. D'Orville 470 p. 50 (*Early Modern Letters Online* link: http://emlo.bodleian.ox.ac.uk/profile/work/9ea893f8-b2f6-4831-9e4c-7da194cc49d7?sort=date-a&rows=50&rec=isaac,%20vossius&aut=poelenburgh&baseurl=/forms/advanced&start=4&type=advanced&numFound=8). See also Tyacke, 'Arminianism and the Restoration Church', p. 72.
71 Barducci, *Hugo Grotius*, p. 127.
72 Christopher Potter (1590?-1646) was Dean of Worcester when he was accused of Arminianism and Pelagianism as a result of his ties with Bishop Laud: J. Hegarty, 'Potter, Christopher (1590/91–1646)', *Oxford Dictionary National Biography*, retrieved 23 March 2019. www.oxforddnb.com/view/10.1093/ref:odnb/9780198614128.001.0001/odnb-9780198614128-e-22607.
73 *PWAM*: I. 44–46.
74 *PWAM*: I. 46.
75 Patterson, 'Introduction', xxxiv.
76 Perez Zagorin, *How the Idea of Toleration Came to the West* (Princeton: Princeton University Press, 2003), p. 147.
77 *CPW*: II: 554.
78 *CPW*: VIII: 437–438.
79 Reuben Marquez Sanchez, '"The Worst of Superstitions": Milton's *Of True Religion* and the Issue of Religious Tolerance', *Prose Studies*, 9 (1986): 21–38.
80 Stavely's persuasive argument that Milton's tract was written after the Test Act had been passed by Parliament is based on Milton's confidence in the magistrates and the fact that he does not make his own recommendations for what should be done (*CPW*: VIII. 430, note 55).

81 Stavely, 'Preface to *Of True Religion, Heresie, Schism, Toleration*', p. 413; Michael Lieb, *The Theological Milton: Deity, Discourse and Heresy in the Miltonic Canon* (Pittsburgh: Duquesne University Press, 2006), p. 236.

82 *CPW*: VIII: 422–423.

83 *CPW*: VIII: 426.

84 *CPW*: VIII: 426.

85 John Hales, *A Tract Concerning Schism* (London, 1642), pp. 23–24.

86 Lieb, p. 241.

87 In the middle of the seventeenth century Roger Williams in his *The Bloudy Tenent of Persecution, for cause of Conscience, discussed in a Conference betweene Truth and Peace* (London, 1644) had written that heathen and Judaic sects should be allowed to 'live without molestation' and state persecution: Alexandra Walsham, *Charitable Hatred: Tolerance and Intolerance in England, 1500–1700* (Manchester: Manchester University Press, 2006), p. 235.

88 Thomas N. Corns, 'Milton, Roger Williams, and Limits of Toleration', in *Milton and Toleration*, ed. by Sharon Achinstein and Elizabeth Sauer (Oxford: Oxford University Press, 2007): 72–85 (p. 76). See Jeremy Dupertuis Bangs, 'Dutch Contribution to Religious Toleration', *Church History*, 79.3 (2010): 585–613, for an overview of the impact of Dutch toleration on American toleration.

89 Smith, 'Milton and the European Contexts of Toleration', p. 30; *CPW*: VIII. 421.

90 *CPW*: VIII. 430.

91 *CPW*: VIII. 429–431.

92 Nicholas von Maltzahn, 'Milton, Marvell and Toleration', in *Milton and Toleration*, ed. by Sharon Achinstein and Elizabeth Sauer (Oxford: Oxford University Press, 2007): 86–104 (p. 98).

93 S.N. Zwicker, 'What's the Problem with the Dutch? Andrew Marvell, the Trade Wars, Toleration, and the Dutch Republic', *Marvell Studies*, 3.1 (2018): 1–12 (p. 10).

94 Arminianism was rapidly introduced into the English Church in the 1630s under the leadership of Laud; in return the English Arminians swore absolute loyalty to the Crown. When some of Laud's liturgy was forced upon the Presbyterian Scots, a rebellion broke out, ending Charles I's personal rule, leading to the Civil Wars: Patterson, 'Introduction', pp. xvi–xviii. Although some historians still follow a version of this theory on the Civil Wars, such as Tyacke (*Anti-Calvinists*), others such as Peter White (*Predestination, Policy and Polemic*) have written against it.

95 *PWAM*: I. 189.

96 *Rehearsal Transpros'd*, *PWAM*: I. 190.

97 N.H. Keeble, 'Why Transpose the Rehearsal?', in *Marvell and Liberty*, ed. by Warren Chernaik and Martin Dzelzainis (London: Palgrave Macmillan, 1999): 249–268 (p. 264).

98 *PWAM*: I. 63.

99 Hugh Trevor-Roper, 'Hugo Grotius and England', in *The Exchange of Ideas: Religion, Scholarship, and Art in the Seventeenth-Century* (Zutphen: Walburg Instituut, 1994): 42–67 (pp. 52–61).

100 *PWAM*: I. 63.

101 Marvell's *An Account of the Growth of Popery and Arbitrary Government* can be used for making a stronger case that Marvell was anti-Catholic, but as Von Maltzahn has argued, this tract is more an attack on the state of Rome rather than the Church, and is concerned with France as well: Von Maltzahn, 'Milton, Marvell and Toleration', p. 90.

102 Martin Dzelzainis, 'Marvell and the Earl of Castlemaine', in *Marvell and Liberty*, ed. by Warren Chernaik and Martin Dzelzainis (Basingstoke: Palgrave Macmillan, 1999): 290–312 (p. 203).
103 *PWAM*: I. 192.
104 Nigel Smith, 'The Boomerang Theology of Andrew Marvell', *Renaissance and Reformation*, 25.4 (2001): 139–155 (p. 151).
105 John Locke, *Two Treatises of Government* (London: Everyman's Library, 1978), p. 127.
106 Philip Milton, 'Religious Toleration', in *The Oxford Handbook of Philosophy in Early Modern Europe*, ed. by Desmond M. Clarke and Catherine Wilson (Oxford: Oxford University Press, 2011): 571–590.
107 Keeble, 'Why Transpose the Rehearsal?', p. 252.
108 Jon Parkin, 'Liberty Transpos'd: Andrew Marvell and Samuel Parker', in *Marvell and Liberty*, ed. by Warren Chernaik and Martin Dzelzainis (London: Palgrave Macmillan, 1999): 269–289 (p. 270).
109 Von Maltzahn, 'Milton, Marvell and Toleration', p. 86.

5 Predestination and Grace in Milton's *Samson Agonistes* and Marvell's *Remarks*

In *Paradise Lost*, the fallen angels have lost the ability to penetrate the Scripture. They have no scriptural authority and become endlessly lost in theological debate:

> [. . .] In discourse more sweet
> (For eloquence the soul, song charms the sense)
> Others apart sat on a hill retired,
> In thoughts more elevate, and reasoned high
> Of providence, foreknowledge, will, and fate,
> Fixed fate, free will, foreknowledge absolute,
> And found no end, in wandering mazes lost.
> (II. 555–561)

It is difficult when reading Arminius' and Gomarus' texts on predestination not to sympathise, and feel we, too, have been in wandering mazes lost. In an age of both crucial religious contestation and flourishing scholarship, theological distinctions could be monstrously subtle, yet of enormous consequence. Understanding this complexity has become no easier at a historical distance, and there remains a frequent lack of clarity, particularly about Dutch Arminianism, in current studies of English literature.[1] Milton's and Marvell's Arminianism is consequently often misrepresented. It is therefore worthwhile to return in this chapter to the nitty-gritty of the Arminian debate, allowing a refining of how aspects of Dutch Arminianism can be traced in Milton and Marvell, and the implications of their presence.

As explained in the previous chapter, the Arminian controversy had many strands, and was not about a single issue such as predestination; it encompassed republicanism, sovereignty, State and Church, and toleration. Its multiplicity of factors were in play in the rise and fall of Arminianism in both England and in the United Provinces. Anthony Milton has said that more recent studies see predestination as a mere side notion in the rise and fall of Laudians – or as Peter Lake called them 'avant-garde conformists' – and that the doctrine of grace was far removed from the key issues at play in the Anglican church in this period.[2] Similarly, Keith D. Stanglin has suggested that Arminius would have objected strongly to the notion that his theology could be reduced to the idea of predestination, as Peter White, for example, does in his *Predestination, Policy, and Polemic*. However, it would be wrong to deny that predestination and its theological consequences should be either ignored or simplified. Arminius' ideas of salvation are important for a full understanding of Milton and Marvell, as this chapter will argue. It presents a basic outline of soteriological differences between Arminius and Gomarus. A full understanding of the theological differences between the two would, as Theodore Beza wrote in a letter to Johannes Wtenbogaert, 'require books big enough to fill a house'.[3] Without an appropriate lens we might, like the fallen angels, sink into an eternal dialogue, discussing it until the end of times. Let us hope that limiting this discussion to literary responses to Anglo-Dutch models of salvation in Milton and Marvell will ensure a manageable finitude. As I will argue, Milton's conception of predestination plays a key role in his presentation of Samson, and it is strongly (Dutch) Arminian. While Marvell is characteristically less definite in his use of the concept, the framework through which he views predestination is at odds with a more Bezaean or contra-remonstrant understanding.

Much of the conflict and confusion around predestination between Christian movements flows from interpretations of Romans, in particular verses 7:13–23.[4] Unlike the Church Father Augustine, who counselled that predestination is shaded in ambiguity and should remain so, Gomarus, Perkins, Beza, Calvin, Arminius and many other early modern reformers attempted to resolve the inexhaustible complexities of the Apostle Paul's letter.[5] In this, Arminius had more common ground with his adversaries than many modern commentaries would like to admit. He shared, for example, the same ideas on original sin, traditional obedience and repentance, or the division of the soul into *intellectus* and *voluntas*.[6] Both Gomarus' and Arminius' ideas on predestination were based on Calvin's explanation of Romans (7 and 9). Gomarus, though, followed a more extreme version, similar to that of Theodore Beza and William Perkins, which became known as the High Calvinist or supralapsarian convention. From this difference springs the interpretation of Arminianism as largely a response to Beza's explanation of predestination in *Tabula praedestinationis* of 1555.[7] According to the distinctions that emerged within this field, Beza – and indirectly Gomarus – were therefore arguing for both supralapsarianism and creabilitarianism (predestination in the first degree, followed by creation, followed by a divine authorisation of the Fall). Calvin by contrast held a comparatively moderate lapsarian view, implying infralapsarianism (creation in the second degree, which means predestination after the Fall), although it was not a term ever used in his works.[8]

An important text in the predestination debate is Arminius' response to Perkins' *De praedestinationis mode et ordine et de amplitudine gratiae divinae* (1598).[9] Perkins (1558–1602) was a renowned professor of theology at Cambridge University and followed the supralapsarian point of view in soteriology. Although Arminius' tract was an answer, he was unable to send it to Perkins before the latter passed away. Arminius' animadversion is helpful, as both sides of the argument, including its supposed errors, are presented, even though his *Declaratio sententiae* (1608) is often thought the key text for a full understanding of his body of thought. Arminius' outspoken response to supralapsarianism was not only against the supralaparianism of Beza in Geneva or Perkins in Cambridge, but against its dominance in his own circles in Leiden.[10]

Before diving into the particulars of Arminianism in Milton and Marvell, I will provide a very broad definition of some of the key terms in predestination. The studies of Stanglin, *Arminius on the Assurance of Salvation*, and with Thomas H.M. Call, *Arminius: Theologian of Grace*, William den Boer, *Duplex Amor Dei*, and Evan Dekker, *Rijker dan Midas*, constitute insightful and detailed studies on the complexities of Arminius' theology and historical context. I will concentrate here only on some aspects of Arminianism that are required for the discussion of Milton and Marvell.[11]

(Ir)resistible Grace

Gomarus and Perkins divided the concept of grace into two categories, common grace (*gratia generalis*) and peculiar or special grace (*gratia specialis*).[12] Common grace applies to all people, whether they are elect or non-elect, whereas the latter is only for those predestined to receive it. Common grace together with peculiar grace permits ultimate salvation. Following this logic, Christ did not die for all of mankind, but only for a select few.[13] The actualisation of predestination for the individual will take place as the temporal life transmutes to the eternal, but the outcome of the salvation process has already been determined since before the creation of human beings and the Fall, which itself was divinely authorised. This in effect means a form of two-fold predestination, encompassing the elect as well as the reprobate.[14]

Arminius, however, divides grace into two aspects of the internal persuasion instigated by the Holy Spirit, namely 'salvation sufficient' and 'salvation efficacious'.[15] He argues that salvation is a universal phenomenon allotted to every rational being, but that this exists in potential rather than as an application. Salvation efficacious is the blood of Christ, for those – the faithful – who choose to accept it: salvation sufficient combined with faith will lead to salvation efficacious. This emphasis on the active choice of faith is one of the points of Arminius' doctrine that led to accusations of Pelagianism (which denies the doctrine of original sin, arguing that mankind can establish its own salvation by following the good example of Christ, and does not require divine aid).[16] If the human acceptance of faith is the determining factor, is this in effect claiming we could force God's hand? Arminius defended himself by insisting that faith is only given by divine grace and cannot be established by mankind itself. To be faithful thus includes the condition of being elect, but as a gift made by the love of God.[17] This argument is similar to Beza's claim that faith is a sign of election, but in Arminius' theology individuals are not pre-selected, as it is up to each individual to accept the hand proffered by the divine.[18]

Arminius in turn accused Gomarus (and Beza) of making God the author of sin. In the dramatic ending to his *Examen thesium Gomari*, he concludes of Gomarus' theses on predestination that they imply that 'God is the Author of sin that God really sins; that God alone sins; and that sin is not sin'.[19] If the Fall was not an act of human free will, its authorisation cannot be anything but the will of God, hence creating sin.[20] Both Perkins and Gomarus counter this logical chain by dividing God's authority into his will on the one hand and his permission on the other, taking care not to offend his omnipotence in the process. He did not will the Fall but permitted it to take place.[21] Mediate power illustrates his permission, whereas immediate power represents his will.[22] This underpins the (High) Calvinist statement that God foresees all events, because he has decreed them in the past, though this may be through either mediate or immediate power.[23]

Alongside the problem that God might be the author of sin, Arminius' charge also implies a lack of free will, since God has discerned in advance of all events how every being will act. Gomarus denies that there is no free will in his theology, insisting that no decisions are made according to a forced determinism.[24] Adam, in his prelapsarian state, did have the will to choose whether to eat the fruit or not. It is in a postlapsarian universe that humans can still choose to do good works because of common grace, but cannot choose our own salvation. Arminius, however, attributes free will to every rational being, which is flexible to either side by the aid of grace, maintaining the potential for reprobation as well as salvation.[25] He nevertheless retains the concept of original sin (which explains the universal presence of sin), with the understanding that man is 'addicted' to evil. In this state we find ourselves unable to choose faith without divine grace – a belief shared by Calvin and his reading of Augustine.[26] This grace is, however, resistible; it may be offered by God, but needs to be accepted by mankind individually, whereas Perkins and Beza argue that divine grace is irresistible.

In Arminius' doctrine, there is therefore a distinction between believing and the ability to believe.[27] The latter is universal, whereas coming to believe is the outcome of a process of faith, grace and human acceptance. As Deni Kasa has recently pointed out, the concept of co-operation is crucial here, since despite their infinite inferiority, humankind must be in a participatory relationship with God to attain salvation. This avoids the charge of Pelagian self-reliance in favour of an essential degree of reciprocity.[28] It is thus also possible to fall from grace, to break from the co-operation.[29] Arminius writes that the seeds that are planted in men's heart are not immortal and that lost sheep can be seized by Satan; perseverance in faith demands continued striving, of which not all are capable.[30] This does not argue that God willingly permits sin, but allows mankind several genuine moments of choice. It is to God's glory when individuals commit voluntarily, with the help of divine grace; faith follows, and the believer becomes a regenerate man.[31] Gomarus and Perkins on the other hand follow the doctrine of eternal security: once saved, one is forever saved.[32] God's omnipotence is thereby preserved and demonstrated. Arminius' response was that God's love is *Duplex Amor Dei*, two-fold: love for each poor sinner, and yet love for what is right and just.[33] The doctrine of eternal security risks one being drawn into believing that salvation has already been secured (or denied) irrespective of one's own efforts.

Election

Though there remain almost unlimited further refinements and outgrowths to the concept of predestination, there is a final great link in the logical chain that will be discussed here. This is the not inconsiderable problem of determining the extent of the salvation applied or offered to mankind. As already mentioned, Gomarus, Calvin and Perkins believed that predestination was only for a select few, those for whom Christ had sacrificed himself.[34] The exact number of the elect was unknown. Arminius is on this point closer to Calvin than one might expect given the usual narrative of his holding an opposing stance to the Gomarian camp. Despite his condemnation of the election defined by Gomarus and others lapsarians, one may find something akin to it in his reading of Romans. He says: 'For He has honoured some of His creatures with supernatural gifts, as angels and men, and others, indeed all others, he has made without supernatural gifts'.[35] This apparent contradiction and what Arminius means by supernatural gifts will later be discussed in greater detail, through Milton's specific deployment of Dutch Arminianism, which also still allowed special treatment of certain individuals. Arminius, however, argues that men are not saved because they have a desire to be saved, but because God allows them to be. This does not mean universal salvation and universal reprobation: all of mankind receives their share of opportunities, but salvation and reprobation occur at the individual level.[36] Arminius tried to find a balance between the extremes of High Calvinism's lapsarian positions, and Pelagian necessitarianism.[37] Stanglin sums up the essence of the difference succinctly: 'Do you believe because you are elect (Gomarus), or are you elect because you believe (Arminius)?'.[38]

Milton's Arminianism

Arminius' model of predestination and free will features prominently in several of Milton's works. In Chapter 3, I briefly mentioned some Arminian resonances in Milton's account of Creation in *Paradise Lost*, and in the previous chapter I argued that Milton's theological convictions altered throughout his life – including a deeply considered Arminianism. It is likely that Milton's family attended a Laudian chapel in the 1630s, when Laudian Arminianism was at its height.[39] Traces of this sympathy can perhaps be found in *Comus* (1634); in Campbell's and Corns' words: 'the most complex and thorough expression of Laudian Arminianism and Laudian style within the Milton oeuvre, and, indeed, the high-water mark of his indulgence of such beliefs and values'.[40] This relates not only to elevated ceremony and sacrament within the masque, but also to Arminian ideas of salvation: throughout, providence is presented as undetermined and un-fixed, even in the character of Comus himself:

> [. . .]   in a place
> Less warranted than this, or less secure
> I cannot be, that I should fear to change it,
> Eye me blest Providence, and square my trial
> To my proportioned strength. Shepherd lead on . . .
>   (ll. 325–329)

Yet Nicholas McDowell has argued that Milton did not feel comfortable in the baroque Laudian style of poetry in fashion at Cambridge in the 1620s and 1630s, and that 'Lycidas' (1637) shows a rejection of Laudian clericalism, as well as the ornate poetic style connected with Laud.[41] If it is granted that Milton and his family had some earlier Laudian leanings, it is safe to say that after 1637 Milton was no longer of that persuasion. Nonetheless, his early prose works of the 1640s show curiously little criticism of Laud's soteriological ideas.[42] The fact that Arminianism was not a fashionable topic at that particular moment could serve as an explanation, or that Milton was already too Arminian at this point to 'centre his critique of episcopalianism in doctrine'; or perhaps the fact that his adversary, Joseph Hall, was not an Arminian made the issue inconsequential.[43] He was, nonetheless, highly critical of Laudian High Church elements in *Of Reformation* (1641). As will be discussed shortly, the mature Milton presented clear and outspoken ideas on Arminianism in his works, meaning there was a progression from (Laudian) Anglican Arminianism to Dutch Arminianism sometime in the 1630s and 1640s.

Perhaps the answer to Milton's silence can be found in his ambiguous ideas on salvation and grace. A change from sacramental Arminianism to Dutch Arminianism would require intimate knowledge of Arminius' *Opera* and his complicated arguments on salvation. In the two works of the 1640s in which Arminius is mentioned, *Doctrine and Discipline of Divorce* (1643) and *Areopagitica* (1644), Milton's conceptions of Calvinism and Arminianism become convoluted. First, in the *Doctrine and Discipline of Divorce*, Milton associates 'the sect of *Arminius*' with Jesuits who 'are wont to charge us of making God the author of sinne in two degrees especially, not to speak of his permissions', in which the 'us' refers to Calvinists.[44] This follows the common polemic of accusing English Arminians of Catholicism.[45] Even Perkins accused Arminius of this.[46] The lines between Catholicism and Protestantism are not as clear cut as they might seem, at least in soteriological terms. It would, however, be following the same crude reading of Arminianism as some contemporary Calvinists to call them 'more Catholic than the pope', as Raymond Waddington also does in his otherwise insightful book.[47] Even in such heightened debates authors might have recourse to the tools of stereotyping imagery. Second in *Areopagitica*, Arminius is presented as being 'perverted' from the Calvinist doctrine by a book – most likely an anonymous tract by Dirck Coornhert (1522–1590), a famous Dutch tolerationist – that he at first desired to prove wrong: 'It is not forgot, since the acute and distinct *Arminius* was perverted meerly by the perusing of a namelesse discours writt'n at *Delf*, which at first he took in hand to confute'.[48] At the same time, *Areopagitica* shows a passionate defence of free will and toleration, the latter being strongly associated with Arminianism in the seventeenth century as discussed in the previous chapter.[49] It appears that during the 1640s, Milton worked to find his path through the theological maze that Arminius, Calvin, and armies of other theologians had created with their doctrines of grace and salvation; he arrived at a coherent presentation of Arminianism in his mature poetical and prose works. Milton's *Of True Religion* has an interesting passage that contradicts what he earlier said about Arminianism and Catholicism in *Doctrine and Discipline of Divorce*: 'The *Arminian* lastly is condemn'd for setting up free will against free grace; but that Imputation he disclaims in all his writings, and grounds himself largly upon the Scripture only'.[50]

This brings us to the influence of (Dutch) Arminianism seen in his later works, and in particular *Samson Agonistes*, which will be discussed with reference to *De doctrina* and *Paradise Lost*, as further elaborations on ideas of predestination and determinism. Milton's tendency towards Arminianism in his mature religious convictions is generally accepted by a majority of Milton scholars.[51] In the main, Milton agreed with Arminius on three points: that grace is offered to all and not limited to an elect few, that grace is resistible, and that one's salvation depends on individual free will rather than on divine predestination.[52]

The theological similarities (and disparities) between *De doctrina* and *Paradise Lost* have been extensively discussed as evidence in favour of Milton's Arminianism by Maurice Kelly in the early half of the twentieth century, afterwards supported by scholars such as Dennis Danielson and Stephen Fallon.[53] Milton's ideas on predestination, and the seeming inconsistency between the theories of salvation – potential supralapsarianism in *Paradise Lost* (Book 3) and Arminianism in *De doctrina* – are sometimes used as arguments to deny Milton's authorship of the latter.[54] This at first sight seems natural, as the ideas on predestination of Arminius and Gomarus (as well as Beza and Perkins) are completely incompatible; otherwise the Synod of Dort would never have been necessary.[55] However, since the early 2000s, some have begun to argue that the passage in *Paradise Lost*, Book 3 and predestination in *De doctrina Christiana* can both be read as Arminian.[56] In this Chapter I pursue a similar strategy, but via a reading of *Samson Agonistes* as an Arminian narrative. This will then allow us to place the seemingly Calvinistic passage in *Paradise Lost* in the same Arminian framework, and by extension reject claims that Milton could not possibly be the author of *De doctrina* on the basis of theological inconsistency.[57]

Samson Agonistes is a particularly interesting example of Milton's agreement with three Arminian points (that grace is universal, grace is resistible, and free will is necessary for salvation). As Fallon has noted before, the biblical Samson presents a more complex view on predestination, namely 'the freedom of even those specially chosen by God to fall'.[58] Samson's story is therefore usefully problematic for discussions of salvation and divine intervention. This sparked Russ Leo's examination of the influence of Calvin's 1559 *Institutio* on the representation of predestination in Milton's dramatic poem.[59] Leo concludes that Milton strays markedly from Calvin's and Ames' ideas on election and the Trinity.[60] However, apart from touching on Arminius and the influence of the Synod of Dort on early modern European theology, he does not discuss Arminian doctrine within Milton's poems (although he does compare Arminius' reply to Perkins with *De doctrina Christiana*).[61] Milton's strong rejection of Perkins' theory (and thus also Gomarus' ideas) on reprobation and election is noted, as well as Arminius' rejection of Perkins, but the crucial similarities contained in these two rejections are left unexamined.[62] Leo goes on to state that 'Milton is no Arminian; on the contrary, he adapts and exaggerates Arminius' fourfold division of decrees by introducing the additional Ramist distinction general/special'.[63] Although it may be granted that Milton does not follow Arminius' theories on reprobation, I will argue against the notion that this adaptation amounts to a rejection. If Milton was undeniably unorthodox, he was yet of an Arminian persuasion.

Samson's narrative concerns an elect individual within an elected group of people – a man chosen by God to liberate the people of Israel from the Philistines. It is a difficult story to fit into Arminian doctrine because of its direct engagement with election and predestined purpose, which the biblical narrative relates explicitly. The opening lines of *Samson Agonistes* – 'A little onward lend thy guiding hand/ To these dark steps, a little further on' (ll. 1–2) – continue the line of providence with which *Paradise Lost* had ended:

> The world was all before them, where to choose
> Their place of rest, and providence their guide:
> They hand in hand with wandering steps and slow,
> Through Eden took their solitary way.
>
> (XII. 646–649)

In Book 3 of *Paradise Lost* this line of providence also appears when God describes his plan for the salvation of humankind before the Fall has occurred. He begins his speech with a puzzling view on election, which appears to be orthodox Calvinism:

> Some I have chosen of peculiar grace
> Elect above the rest; so is my will:

> The rest shall hear me call, and oft be warned
> Their sinful state, and to appease betimes
> The incensèd Deity, while offered grace
> Invites; for I will clear their senses dark,
> What may suffice, and soften stony hearts
> To pray, repent, and bring obedience due.
> To prayer, repentance, and obedience due,
> Though but endeavoured with sincere intent,
> Mine ear shall not be slow, mine eye not shut.
> And I will place within them as a guide
> My umpire conscience, whom if they will hear,
> Light after light well used they shall attain,
> And to the end persisting, safe arrive.
> This my long sufferance and my day of grace
> They who neglect and scorn, shall never taste;
> But hard be hardened, blind be blinded more,
> That they may stumble on, and deeper fall;
> (III. 183–201)

God seemingly refers here to *peculiar* grace, a term often associated with Calvin's theories on predestination in the *Institutes* (later reiterated by Perkins and Gomarus): only a select few will receive grace, which is irresistible, separating mankind into a small group of elect and the rest, the reprobate.[64] Arminius rejected this view and insisted that *common* grace is available to all. Together with personal faith, it will lead to salvation efficacious, creating a division between those who accepted God's grace and the damned who chose to reject it.[65] Arminius does admit that there are a number of people with the potential for a greater bond of love between God and the individual, but such people still have to come via faith to accept this grace in order to be saved. Waddington accordingly claims that because the same principles of salvation apply to all people, the existence of a group of people with a greater love of God simply 'does not matter' for the greater argument of salvation.[66] This would, however, be an oversimplification, since it matters to Arminius in the same way it matters to Milton. It is true, nonetheless, that Milton argues for grace available to all in *De doctrina*: 'There seems, then, to be no particular – but only general – predestination and election, that is, of all those who believe from the heart and persist in believing; no one is predestined or chosen inasmuch as he is Peter or John, but insofar as he believes and perseveres in believing; and then at last the general decree of election is applied to each believer individually and confirmed for those persevering'.[67] Grace is therefore closely connected to mercy.[68]

We find a seemingly similar difference between election and common grace in *Samson Agonistes*, in which Samson is introduced as one of the chosen few, with an elected life. He is described as both Israelite and as Nazarite, the meaning of the latter name already illustrating a separation from the rest of mankind: 'I was his nursling once and choice delight,/ His destined from the womb,/ Promised by heavenly message twice descending' (ll. 633–635). It is difficult to overlook the certainty of election in this story or many others in the Bible – Abraham, Daniel, and several prophets all being chosen for a particular role, elected above the rest. (There are also examples of individuals with a special vocation in the New Testament – Timothy 1:9.) Arminius could not deny this, either. His position accordingly allows for some election, the favouring of certain persons with a great (-er) share of God's love:

> You will say that, if he has apprehended the offered grace by the aid of peculiar grace, it is, then, evident that God has manifested greater love towards him than towards another to whom He has applied only common grace, and has denied peculiar grace. I admit it, and perhaps the theory, which you oppose, will not deny it. But it will assert that peculiar grace is to be so explained as to be consistent with free-will, and that common grace is to be so described, that a man may be held worthy of condemnation by its rejection, and that God may be shown to be free from injustice.[69]

How does this greater love manifest itself? We have already established that some biblical personages receive a special calling from God; they are elected to serve. This call by God is a manifestation of his greater love. This means there is a possibility that some people are elected for a particular role during their life, but the same rules of salvation will still apply to all: salvation through faith, rather than through right. This means there is equality in salvation, but not in the potential or purpose of each individual; election can thus co-exist with free will, as this election of purpose can, just like faith, be refused or lost.

There are three instances in *De doctrina* (in particular chapter 1.17 'On Renewal, and also on Calling') in which this idea of the 'elections of individuals as instruments of God' is discussed.[70] God's speech in *Paradise Lost* does connect these few elect to his 'day of grace', which is open to all. Salvation is offered, conditionally, to all – including those chosen few (III. 198).[71] Milton's ideas on salvation are more explicit in Book 12, in which the process of salvation from the Fall onwards is further illustrated:

> So law appears imperfect, and but given
> With purpose to resign them in full time
> Up to a better covenant, disciplined
> From shadowy types to truth, from flesh to spirit,
> From imposition of strict laws, to free
> Acceptance of large grace, from servile fear
> To filial, works of law to works of faith.
> (XII. 300–306)

The superseding of the law through faith (*sola fide, sola scriptura*, and *sola gratia*) (leading to a change from legal theology to evangelical theology) is a general agreement of all Protestant denominations. However, Arminius' specific interpretation of this aspect can be found in Milton's work. Arminius writes in an undated letter to his friend Wtenbogaert that salvation shifts from obedience to the law to faith in Christ, also called the law of faith (*'Jam vero duplex est lex Dei, una operum, altera fidei'*), which is echoed in the last line of the *Paradise Lost* quotation.[72] No one is excluded from this 'better covenant' (XII. 303) since people were endowed with the ability to receive grace, another point of incompatibility with Calvin's concept of limited atonement. This change from one path of salvation to the other was universal: the law applied to all until Christ became the new law, which then became the only route to salvation for all. Arminius condemns Perkins' idea that for some the law still applied while for others the law of faith was additionally necessary for salvation. This inequality would imply that God is stricter towards humankind than towards the angels, despite the fact that the latter sinned, too, and not through the persuasion of a third party.[73] In the quotation from Book 12, there is also a clear distinction between the two paths of salvation, which will ultimately lead to 'large grace' (XII. 305) as the only means of salvation, and open to all, which can be seen as a further clarification of the passage in Book 3. Samson is a clear example from the time before Christ functioned as the law. In *Samson Agonistes*, there are several instances in which he refers to his reliance on the Judaic law for his salvation: 'I with this messenger will go along,/ Nothing to do, be sure, that may dishonour/ Our Law, or stain my vow of Nazarite' (ll. 1384–1386) and 'Yet this be sure, in nothing to comply/ Scandalous or forbidden in our Law' (ll. 1408–1409). This law, however, should not be perceived as a constraint, but as a process or path that can be followed to reach salvation.[74]

Returning to the quotation in Book 3 of *Paradise Lost*, we read that those who 'neglect and scorn shall never taste;/ But hard be hardened, blind be blinded more,/ That they may stumble on, and deeper fall' (III. 199–201).[75] On this particular idea Arminius and Calvin, and Milton, too, agree, sharing ideas of original sin – '[t]heir sinful state' (III. 186) – and eternal damnation for those who willingly and freely reject faith -'and deeper fall' (III. 201) – both present in God's speech. In *Samson Agonistes* we see an individual case of this reprobation.[76] Calvin links absence of God's grace to the punishment of greater blindness, even if the individual demonstrates repentance:

> To some it seems harsh, and at variance with the divine mercy, utterly to deny forgiveness to any who retake themselves to it. This is easily disposed of. It is not said that pardon will be refused if they turn to the Lord, but it is altogether denied that they can turn to repentance, inasmuch as for their ingratitude they are struck by the just judgment of God with even greater blindness.[77]

Calvin argues that those who are destined for reprobation will remain reprobate without any capacity for repentance. In Milton and Arminius we also find the hardening of hearts after the choice for reprobation, but only after the individual has exercised their free will.[78] Although Samson's lamentation begins with a description of the loss of his mortal eyes, Milton continues the digression by connecting it to a blindness of the light within the soul, similar to Calvin's explanation of God's induced greater blindness: '[. . .] if it be true/ That light is in the soul,/ She all in every part; why was the sight/ To such a tender ball as the eye confined?' (ll. 91–94).[79] This follows Augustine's reasoning that the multi-partite nature of the body is at odds with the form of the soul, which 'is not diffused in bulk through extension of place, but in each body, it is both whole in the whole, and whole in each several part of it'.[80] As a result, each thing that affects a particular part of the body will affect the soul in its entirety, which Calvin's and Arminius' notions of individual reprobation accord with ('sometimes he also causes those whom he illumines only for a time to partake of it; then he justly forsakes them on account of their ungratefulness and strikes them with even greater blindness'[81]). Bodily and spiritual blindness are unified not only through the extended metaphor but also the mirroring nature of the physical and the soul:

> O that torment should not be confined
> To the body's wounds and sores
> With maladies innumerable
> In heart, head, breast, and reins;
> But must secret passage find
> To the inmost mind,
> There exercise all his fierce accidents,
> And on her purest spirits prey,
> As on entrails, joints, and limbs,
> With answerable pains, but more intense,
> Though void of corporal sense.
> (ll. 606–616)

Calvin's use of blindness is a metaphorical one, Samson's a literal and spiritual one, which makes Samson's punishment of blindness more potent, signifying both reprobation and the physical darkness itself. Despite this similarity between the doctrines on reprobation in Arminius and Calvin, Milton has a somewhat different version of the double reprobation illustrated here.[82] This type of reprobation could be seen as double predestination of damnation: human will has nothing to do with God's reprobation in this case:

> Election, therefore, is not part of predestination, and much less so is reprobation. For since predestination properly includes within it the idea

of an aim – the salvation of at least believers, which is indeed essentially desirable – whereas reprobation involves the extinction of unbelievers, which is essentially unpleasant and hateful, then surely God in no way purposed reprobation as an aim for himself or predestined it. [. . .] If God wanted neither sin nor the death of a sinner, that is, neither the cause nor the effect of reprobation, then surely he did not want the thing itself. Reprobation, therefore, is no part of divine predestination.[83]

Election is thus the whole of predestination, and not a mere part of it. Reprobation is no part of either, and only the consequence of the choice not to believe. There is no rejection *by* God only *of* God. This echoes Arminius' own problems with the artificial distinction between election and reprobation. If humans have the free will to choose then neither can be separated, or even seen as different things: 'Reprobation and election are spoken of as things separate and opposite; one is not without the other. Hence no act can be attributed to one of them, the opposite of which, either affirmative or negative, may not be attributed to the other'.[84] This contrasts with Calvin's comment, which also implies that those who reject faith were never predestined to receive it in the first place, nor will they ever receive it in the future; they were damned with the Fall. In Calvin, faith is therefore a consequence solely of election, and not of an individual acceptance of grace. Arminius, by contrast, argues that mankind is allowed to reject faith, and will be punished (even doubly punished by God's reprobation), but retains the possibility of a return to God's grace with the return to faith. In this case, those who accepted grace can resist it later and vice versa, as a direct result of free will – something we see clearly in the character of Samson.[85]

Milton had already emphasised the necessity of free will in *Areopagitica* and his belief in free will's role in salvation remained unchanged throughout his life. In *Paradise Lost*, too, it features prominently: 'freely they stood who stood, and fell who fell' (III. 103).[86] In *Samson Agonistes*, Samson repeatedly focuses on his own birth, destined by God for a fixed purpose, foretold by angels; Milton explicitly denies that God was the author of Samson's sin. The same argument was often used by Arminius and other remonstrants against Gomarus' and Perkins' ideas of supralapsarianism and other High Calvinists' conceptions of predestination. Why God made his vulnerability reside in his hair, Samson does not know, but he 'must not quarrel with the will/ Of highest dispensation, which herein/ Haply had ends above my reach to know' (ll. 60–62).[87]

Moreover, Arminius' doctrine that God is all-knowing but has not decreed events in advance (or even before Creation and the Fall, as the supralapsarians believed) is reiterated by Samson when he speaks about the divine promise that he was charged to fulfil, the delivering of Israel from the yoke of the Philistines:

> Yet stay, let me not rashly call in doubt
> Divine prediction; what if all foretold

Had been fulfilled but through mine own default,
Whom have I to complain of but myself?

(ll. 43–46)

Arminius' insistence on free will, available to every rational being, allows the risk that God's divine grace could be rejected by humans.[88] Samson rejected God's grace as a chosen Nazarite, and slipped from that same grace: he has a 'sense of heaven's desertion' (l. 632). Calvin, Perkins and Gomarus had by contrast argued that divine grace was irresistible and that the predestined seeds of faith were immortal. Samson, though, having first been granted the highest state, fell to the dungeon in which he now resides – a descent that is echoed by the chorus, such as in lines 168–172:[89]

> Strongest of mortal men,
> To lowest pitch of abject fortune thou art fallen.
> For him I reckon not in high estate
> Whom long descent of birth
> Or the sphere of fortune raises;

Arminius' idea of free will also permit the individual the possibility of redeeming themselves after a fall from grace. Divine election can only be determined in the final reckoning. Since all are offered opportunities to accept or spurn grace, redemption is always personal and provisional. There may even be multiple moments of redemption within one's lifetime.[90] Samson made a last leap of faith, since he was blind to whether or not he would regain God's favour with his final act. With Samson's renewed acceptance of God's grace through his faith, his strength returned, leading to the fulfilment of his birth promise, as well as his own ending. Manoa reflects upon this two-fold nature of salvation after Samson's death when he says: 'To himself and father's house eternal fame;/ And which is best and happiest yet, all this/ With God not parted from him, as was feared,/ But favouring and assisting to the end' (ll. 1717–1720). The salvation as sufficient, present as God's *Duplex Amor Dei* (love for men as sinners and also for what is just), was always with Samson. When he chose to accept it as a result of his restored faith, the salvation was applied.

I will take the whole of Samson's narrative a step further in terms of its Arminian nature, in order to demonstrate why this particular biblical narrative with its antinomian emphasis was especially suitable for the discussion of predestination, grace, and free will. John Rogers has insightfully discussed the Socinian (sometimes called Unitarian) tendencies in Milton's work and its rejection of (High) Calvinist orthodoxy.[91] As explained in his article, Milton denies the theory of ransom, also called the idea of penal substitution, which is inherently Calvinist: if there is a debt between two parties (God and mankind) and a third pays the ransom (Christ's voluntary crucifixion), mankind can refuse to believe that this debt has been paid or that there was a debt at all, but yet it would still have been paid. Christ's sacrifice for our own salvation does not require our assent. The narrative of Milton's dramatic poem is constructed against the idea that a third party could pay the ransom for someone else, especially visible in the narrative of Manoa in the poem – Milton's device, for which there is no biblical precedence.[92] Rogers links the rejection of any kind of ransom to Socinianism and their alternative interpretation of salvation, but I argue that this rejection could as easily lead to Arminianism, albeit that the latter accepted the Atonement and the Socinians did not.[93]

Socinianism was more extreme in its vision of the person's role in their own salvation, rejecting the necessity of Christ's sacrifice, since individual faith is sufficient. There remain, however, a number of similarities with Arminianism, mostly in the rejection of Calvinist ideas on election and irresistibility of grace.[94] Socinians did not deem God and Christ (and the Holy Spirit) functioning in a Trinity to be necessary for the process. Arminius by contrast wrote, 'Christ is the foundation for that blessing, not as God, but as θεάνθρωπος [God-man], Mediator, Saviour and Head of the Church'.[95] In Arminius' view, Christ was the salvation that applied to all. Socinian theology rejected this idea and made mankind solely responsible for its own redemption, without interference from any divine being, in effect denying that original sin could possibly exist. In this schema of human-divine binary, Christ becomes merely one example of a saviour's deliverance of freedom, of which there are several others in the Bible. This rejection of the Trinity and denial of Christ's divinity fits conveniently with Milton's adoption of elements of Arianism (pre-existence of the Son before the Fall) and Socinianism (denying the Trinity).[96] His difficulties with presenting Christ's Passion in any of his poetical and prose works suggest that Milton did not necessarily see the Crucifixion as the centre of Christianity. 'The Passion', although one of his earlier works, is the most obvious example. Milton argues that it was not the crucifixion but Christ's having offered himself that fulfilled the new covenant, which goes against both Calvin and Arminius.[97] Milton additionally does not accept the Socinian idea that Christ is merely an example, as is shown in the quotation from *Paradise Lost* Book 12 discussed earlier, but believes that Christ's acceptance of his own offering redeemed us, not his moral teachings.[98] Granted, in *Paradise Regained*, Milton creates a narrative in which the Son defeats Satan through reason, and not through the act of Atonement, but the Son remains necessary for salvation, even if he functions as a potentially Socinian example in the epic.[99]

Rationalism was consistently associated with Arminianism and Socinianism. Arminians were accused by Calvinists of focussing too much on reason and applying that to the Scripture, when faith should be the central concern. It is not difficult to see that both Marvell and Milton must have felt attracted to Arminianism on these grounds alone. From a doctrinal point of view, it can be concluded that Milton was not a Socinian even if he adopted some unconventional readings of the Bible that could be said to align with those of the Socinians (and often the Arminians, too). He disagreed on the most important foundations of the Socinians: the role of the Son in salvation, original sin, and mankind's reliance on God's grace, as argued by Michael Lieb.[100] In his chapter 'The Socinian Imperative', however, he does not allow that some of the similarities between Milton's reading of Scripture and the Socinians find common ground in the Arminians; I argue that this is essential for a complete understanding of the rest of his theology.

In *Samson Agonistes*, we find an analogy (but not equal) of Christ's role as sole redeemer of mankind (contradicting Socinianism) and not necessarily in terms of ransom (contradicting Calvinism) within the character of Samson. Milton's dramatic poem is especially interesting in this regard as it has two redeemers: Samson as the deliverer of Israel from the Philistines and Manoa as deliverer of Samson. The first succeeds, but the latter does not, and there is a reason why Milton invented this particular additional story line as a counterpart to Samson's success. The difference between these two is that one pays the debt himself, whereas Manoa functions as a mediator. The first of these follows ideas of Arminianism about one's own responsibility for salvation. When we read the lines near the end of the poem, in which Manoa exclaims: 'no time for lamentation now,/ Nor much more cause, Samson hath quit himself/ Like Samson' (ll. 1708–1710), it is clear that Samson established his own salvation through God's grace. This is by no mean a Pelagian reference, as Samson accepts God's grace, but he does not earn it. He is, however, himself responsible for this acceptance. Manoa, on the other hand, functions as an answer to the idea of Calvinist predestination. He tries to negotiate Samson's freedom by paying the ransom and functioning as the third party, but finally comes to see that liberty and salvation cannot occur through mediation alone.[101]

In this reading of *Samson Agonistes* as an Arminian narrative, it is clear that Milton deviates from the High Calvinist doctrine on predestination. Samson as a character demonstrates that grace is resistible, even when elected for a special vocation, that this grace is universal, and that personal faith as a result of free will is necessary for redemption, leading to salvation. Although Milton differs from Arminius (and Calvin) on the question of whether election can work both ways – election for salvation and election for reprobation – since for Milton reprobation can never be part of predestination and election, he is clearly writing from within an Arminian paradigm, in which the life and choices of the individual are as integral to salvation as God's grace.

Marvell and Arminianism

As we have seen, Milton's concern with theological issues such as predestination is direct and often explicit in his poetry. This contrasts sharply with Marvell, whose allusions to free will and divine providence are remarkably subtle, even elusive. Through these contradictions, there are, however, tantalising hints that would suggest that Dutch Arminianism with its toleration

would be a natural context for Marvell's ideas on religion. Notions of predestination associated with different doctrines spring up, seeming to contradict each other, in what Nigel Smith has called his boomerang theology.[102]
Scattered throughout his poetry are small suggestions that refer to divine
providence and free will. These allusions are especially prominent in the
poems discussing Cromwell, where they may be a reflection of Cromwell's
explicit Calvinism. 'A Poem upon the Death of his Late Highness the Lord
Protector' (1658–1659) opens with:

> That Providence which had so long the care
> Of Cromwell's head, and numbered ev'ry hair,
> Now in itself (the glass where all appears)
> Had seen the period of his golden years:
> And thenceforth only did attend to trace
> What death might least so fair a life deface.
>
> (ll. 1–6)

These lines can be interpreted variously, and typical of Marvell, in contradicting ways. Cromwell can be seen here as an agent of providence, who
worked God's plan. Alternatively, we might read that providence blessed
Cromwell, ushering in his golden years, and now has returned to bring his
life to a close.[103] Moreover, in the poem 'The First Anniversary of the Government under his Highness the Lord Protector' (1654/1655) reference is
made to the elected and the reprobate, though Marvell is silent on how
these are divided or determined upon: 'The world by sin, does by the same
extend./ Hence that blest day still counterpoisèd wastes,/ The ill delaying,
what th'elected hastes' (ll. 154–156). A similar ambiguity inhabits Marvell's
'An Horatian Ode upon Cromwell's Return from Ireland' (1650):

> 'Tis madness to resist or blame
> The force of angry heaven's flame;
> And, if we would speak true,
> Much to the man is due:
>
> (ll. 25–28)

Is it madness to resist God's grace, hinting to Calvin's irresistible grace, or to
blame God for the existence of evil? This would underpin a Calvinist interpretation of the poem. Or is it merely madness to attempt to understand the
motion of heaven's flame? The last line, at the same time, suggests free will
and choice.

   As Takashi Yoshinaka has argued, the majority of Marvell's poems seem
to function without divine agency, with epicurean references to neither a hell
nor a heaven, excluding discussions of predestination and its implications.[104]
Some poems, meanwhile, still reveal a sense of earthly reprobation and even
original sin. In 'Upon Appleton House' images of the Royal Oak are likened
to men tainted with sin after the Fall, making their flesh corrupt:

That for his building he designs,
And through the tainted side he mines.
Who could have thought the tallest oak
Should fall by such a feeble stroke!

Nor would it, had the tree not fed
A traitor-worm, within it bred.
(As first our flesh corrupt within
Tempts ignorant and bashful Sin).
                    (ll. 549–556)

It is only within the 'holy leisure' of Appleton House that a state of innocence could be preserved (l. 97), although the danger of sin and the world itself is always looming on the boundary of the estate, as discussed in Chapter 3.

If we take the word 'fortune' to be an occasional synonym for 'providence' whether divine or not, and therefore an antonym of chance, there are several instances in Marvell's poetry in which we see that the lives of individuals are ruled by the decisions of some higher power.[105] Milton, too, adopts this use of the word fortune in the *Art of Logic* (1672), in which he writes 'fortune should be placed in heaven, but should be called by the different name of divine providence'.[106] In 'An Horatian Ode', Marvell salutes Cromwell with: 'But thou the War's and Fortune's son/ March indefatigably on;' (ll. 113–114). Providence is assisting Cromwell in his endeavours.

However, in other poems, contrasting images of determinism can be found, such as in 'Upon Appleton House', in which the phrase 'destiny their choice' leads to a highly ambiguous reference to providence: 'Whence, for some universal good,/ The priest shall cut the sacred bud;/ While her glad parents most rejoice,/ And make their destiny their choice' (ll. 741–744). These contradictory images cannot be explained as a result of chronology, or evolution of Marvell's views over his lifetime, since all of the poems mentioned here were written in the late 1640s and 1650s.[107] It is safe to say that it would be fruitless to search Marvell's poetical works with hopes of a coherent and consistent theology on divine providence and free will; in Marvell's own words, such a thing might only be glimpsed in passing: '[t]hat 'tis is the most which we determine can' ('The First Anniversary of the Government', l. 143).[108]

We have to turn to his prose for any prolonged discussion of Arminianism and Calvinism. *Remarks Upon a Late Disingenuous Discourse* (1678) most outspokenly discusses the disparity between doctrines of predestination. Marvell's *Remarks* were published as a response to John Howe's (Presbyterian minister, 1630–1705) letter to Robert Boyle (natural philosopher, 1627–1691), entitled *The Reconcileableness of God's Prescience of the Sins of Men, with the Wisdom and Sincerity of his Counsels, Exhortations, and Whatsoever Other Means He uses to Prevent Them* (1677), and to congregationalist Thomas Danson's response to Howe, entitled *De Causa Dei: or, A Vindication of the Common Doctrine of Protestant Divines, concerning Predetermination (i.e. the Interest of God as the first Cause in all the Actions, as such, of all Rational Creatures:) From the Invidious Consequences with which it is burdened by Mr. John Howe in a late Letter and Postscript, of God's Prescience* (1678).[109] Some critics, such as Yoshinaka, present Marvell as taking a middle path (accepting a number of Calvinist points, as well as Arminianism) when it comes to the issue of predestination, partly based on his *Remarks* and the variable theology in his poems.[110] Such a notion would be supported by *A Short Historical Essay on General Councils* (1676), which constantly emphasises the search for compromise, toleration and middle ways. In the case of Arminianism and the middle way this would imply that Marvell followed the school of thought of Amyraldism (also called Moderate Calvinism), which still adopted the Calvinist theology on predestination, except that Christ's Atonement was not only for the elect, but universal. Moïse Amyraut (1596–1664) was the principal of the academy of Saumur from 1641–1664. We know that Marvell visited this academy sometime in 1655.[111] Even if he did not adopt Amyraut's theology completely at this point (or ever), he was immersed for some time in a tolerant and moderate environment, which quite possibly influenced his later works. Other contemporary followers of this doctrine were Richard Baxter and John Howe.[112]

Although the *Remarks* deals with issues of predestination that Howe and Danson quarrelled about, it does not directly engage with the main points that the two were disputing. Marvell's choice to write the tract as remarks rather than an animadversion confirms the view that the author himself did not want to comment directly on the controversy and its immediate content.[113] The fact that the front page is anonymous, but signed '[b]y a protestant', highlights Marvell's ambition to concentrate on writing style and ethics, rather than theological ambiguity, disdaining to conform to any particular Protestant division. Within the first few pages, he provides an explanation for why he does not comment on the content of the debate:

> [A]rguing upon such points [God's Prescience and Predetermination] as no man, unless he were *Prior* and precedent to the First Cause, can have the Understanding to comprehend and judge of: and most of them do but say and unsay; and while in words they all deny God to be the Author of sin, yet in effect, and by manner of their reasoning, they affirm it; I, therefore, being both apprehensive of the danger in such Arguments, and more particularly conscious of mine own weakness, shall not presume to interpose my Opinion in the differences about this matter.[114]

This stance is maintained throughout the tract and constantly reinforced: 'I that intermeddle not as an Opinionist either way, but endeavour only to comprehend as far as I can *Its* meaning, shall for that purpose put a Case in *Its* own terms'.[115] The tract was written in support of Howe's letter, and as such a number of the statements from Howe's work are quoted. They can, nonetheless, be read by both Arminians and Calvinists as truthful, for example '*That God doth not by an Efficacious Influence universally move and determine Men to all their Actions, even those Actions which are most wicked*'.[116] The only opinion claimed as Marvell's own occurs relatively early in the tract, in which he describes the history of evil and good, and that this is sufficient for every Christian:

> [T]hat second Chapter of Genesis contains the plain History of Good and Evil, and (not to mention so many attestations to it of the Old and New Testament,) what other Comment needs there, for what belongs to Good, than that, Jam. 1.17. that it is from God only, *That every Good Giving, and every Perfect Gift descendeth?* And, as to Evil that also of St. James, is sufficient conviction, *cap.* I. *v.* 13, 14. *Let no man say, when he is tempted, I was tempted of God; God cannot be tempted with Evil, neither tempteth he any man: But every man is tempted, when he is drawn aside by his own lusts and enticed.* Or that of the same Apostle, *cap.* 4. *v.* I. *From whence come Wars and Fightings among you?* (and even that *Logomachia,* I fear, with which this question is vexed,) *Come they not hence? even from your lusts that fight in your members.* And there is no examining Christian but must find both these Truths evidently witnessed by his own Conscience.[117]

This conviction is reaffirmed towards the end, when Marvell quite bluntly states that 'this Predetermination is not the stated Doctrine of Protestants'.[118] The purpose of this tract was thus only to 'hinder one Divine from offering violence to another'.[119] It is interesting to see that even in a defence of his own tract, he does not seek support of any particular Christian denomination, but maintains the same overarching Protestant affiliation that the front page also displayed, italicised in print for emphasis: 'And, if I should be molested on that account, I doubt not but some of the *Protestant* Clergy will be ready therefore to give me the like Assistance'.[120]

Where does this leave us in a discussion of Marvell's theology? Prominent Marvell critics remain divided: Pierre Legouis calls him a rationalist, a thinker of a later time.[121] Warren Chernaik has called him sympathetic to nonconformists or even an occasional nonconformist himself, but this runs counter to assertions (if highly ironic) from the prose, such as '[a]nd I must confess, when I have sometimes considered with my self the dullness of the Non-Conformists, and the acuteness on the contrary of the Episcopalians' (*A Short Historical Essay*),[122] or in the *Rehearsal Transpros'd*: 'I might, if it appeared so, decline the dangerous acquaintance of the Nonconformists, some of whom I had taken for honest men, nor therefore avoided their Company. But I took care nevertheless, not to receive Impressions from any of their party; but to gather my lights from the most impartial Authorities that I could meet with'.[123] Yet, at the same time, he is sympathetic to the non-conformists in general in *The Rehearsal Transpros'd*, and *The Second Part*. Annabel Patterson has called Marvell '[i]n religion indecisive'. Yet, in the introduction to his prose works, she argues that 'the *Remarks* is, however, necessary reading to get a full picture of Marvell and confirm that on this central issue in theology Marvell and Milton were both left-wing Arminians, however self-contradictory those terms might seem'.[124] Some also think of him as an Arminian, due to his links to Howe and his visit to Saumur, yet he fervently disliked Laudian Arminians and blamed them for the Civil Wars.[125] All agree that he was anti-Catholic.[126]

In this chapter, I have tried to uncover clues that would point to Arminian sympathies, but using the content of the *Remarks* as evidence of Marvell's Arminianism is problematic, as it does not comment on the arguments of pre-destination itself, but is a discussion of the *way* Howe and Danson presented their arguments. That it was written in support of Howe, who adopted some Arminian principles, would perhaps be a sounder statement. It is notable that Marvell does not applaud Howe in terms of these principles, but instead praises his attempt to find compromises between two bickering doctrines on the basis of Scripture. This in itself is not an argument for Marvell's Armin-ianism, and on the evidence we have, assigning him fully to a particular sect of Protestantism is hardly possible. We can conclude, as N.H. Keeble has argued, which individuals he defended and on whose behalf he was writing, but not that he was one of them.[127] If oblique in other matters, Marvell was outspokenly in favour of religious toleration. This is demonstrated by the acquaintances and friendships he maintained throughout his life: heretical and opinionated Milton; the conservative Puritans, the Earl of Anglesey and Harley, with whom he corresponded; more libertine circles such as that of the Duke of Buckingham; the moderate Calvinist John Howe; and John Hales, an outspoken Arminian. Even Catholics do not always feature in negative terms in his works, such as Douglas in the 'Loyal Scot', and their treatment in the *Rehearsal Transpros'd* is mild.[128] The tolerant approach to religion is a more comfortable fit with an Arminian environment than an orthodox Calvinist one, as seen in the previous chapter. This was supported by important points in his life: his moderate clergy father, his exposure to tolerant and moderate forms of doctrine at Saumur and in the Netherlands, associations with all denominations, and being an eye-witness to the ravages that anti-tolerant religionists could cause.[129]

A beautiful demonstration of the toleration that both Milton and Marvell promoted is that Marvell defended his old friend, 'a man of great Learning and Sharpness of Wit as any man' in the *Rehearsal Transpros'd, The Second Part*.[130] Despite their divergent visions of toleration, Arminianism, and other theological differences, our readings of both often come together.[131] In his book *Milton and the English Revolution*, Christopher Hill concludes, after trying to fit Milton as a follower of several heretical sects, that he was 'an eclectic, the disciple of no individual thinker'.[132] Perhaps the same could be said about Marvell. Both were deeply learned men, and although Marvell was not as outspoken in his personal opinions as Milton, they do share some facets of the same theology: an interest in Dutch Arminianism, a rejection of Laudian Arminianism, an interesting mixture of different ideas on toleration, and an antipathy to Catholicism. As we have seen in previous chapters, the close and varied exchange between the United Provinces and England led to a continuous influx of texts, of which many were religious tracts. Neither Milton nor Marvell adopted any Dutch tradition completely, or blindly for that matter; they reformed them to fit into their own theology and doctrine, hence contributing to the hybridisation of religious communities between the United Provinces and England. In the next chapter we will see how the Samson narrative also provided the stage for discussions of authority and rulership fundamental to English and Dutch self-fashioning.

Notes

1 Of course, there are notable exceptions to this such as Stephen M. Fallon, *Milton's Peculiar Grace: Self-Representation and Authority* (Ithaca: Cornell University Press, 2007) and Larisa Kocic, 'Predestination in Milton's *Paradise Lost* and *De doctrina Christiana*', *The Anachronist* (2003): 65–84.

2 Anthony Milton, 'Arminianism, Laudians, Anglicans, and Revisionists: Back to which Drawing Board?', *Huntington Library Quarterly*, 78.4 (2015): 723–742; Peter Lake, 'Lancelot Andrewes, John Buckeridge, and Avant-Garde Conformity at the Court of James I', in *The Mental World of the Jacobean Court*, ed. by Linda Levy Peck (Cambridge: Cambridge University Press, 1991): 113–153.

3 Theodore Beza, 'Letter to Wtenbogaert, 29 July 1593', qtd. in Carl Bangs, *Arminius: A Study in the Dutch Reformation* (New York: Abingdon Press, 1971), p. 194.

4 All quotations and references from the Bible are from the unmodernised King James version.

5 As Nicholas Tyacke also points out, Augustine changed his mind about predestination during his lifetime, which made it possible to use his own texts to contradict themselves, hence reinforcing the image of ambiguity: Nicholas Tyacke, 'The Rise of Arminianism Reconsidered', *Past and Present*, 115 (1987): 201–216 (p. 204); Brian Cummings, *The Literary Culture of the Reformation: Grammar and Grace* (Oxford: Oxford University Press, 2002), p. 412; Aza Goudriaan, '"Augustine Asleep" or "Augustine Awake"? Jacobus Arminius's Reception of Augustine', in *Arminius, Arminianism, and Europe*, ed. by Th. Marius van Leeuwen, Keith D. Stanglin, and Marijke Tolsma (Leiden: Brill, 2009): 51–72.

6 Keith D. Stanglin, *Arminius on the Assurance of Salvation: The Context, Roots and Shape of the Leiden Debate, 1603–1609* (Leiden: Brill, 2007), pp. 73–114.

7 Peter White, *Predestination, Policy and Polemic: Conflict and Consensus in the English Church from the Reformation to the Civil War* (Cambridge: Cambridge University Press, 1992), p. 13.

8 As Peter White points out in his book, the prefixes to the term predestination infra-, sub-, and supra-, did not occur until after the synod, meaning that Arminius, Beza and Calvin could not possibly have used this terminology, but the concepts behind these were already very much present, p. 16.

9 Arminius' later publications were more cautious in their arguments on predestination and for reasons of clear contrast, I have chosen to use this work in order to discuss the doctrine of Arminianism.

10 Stanglin, *Arminius on the Assurance of Salvation*, p. 92.

11 Stanglin, *Arminius on the Assurance of Salvation*; William den Boer, *Duplex Amor Dei: Contextuele Karakteristiek van de Theologie van Jacobus Arminius, 1559–1609* (Apeldoorn: Instituut voor Reformatie Onderzoek, 2008); Evert Dekker, *Rijker dan Midas: Vrijheid, Genade en Predestinatie in de Theologie van Jacobus Arminius, 1559–1609* (Zoetermeer: Boekencentrum, 1993).

12 *WA*: III. 479–481.

13 *WA*: III. 349, 473, 483–484.

14 Th. Marius van Leeuwen, 'Introduction: Arminius, Arminianism, and Europe', in *Arminius, Arminianism, and Europe*, ed. by Th. Marius van Leeuwen, Keith D. Stanglin, and Marijke Tolsma (Leiden: Brill, 2009): IX–XXII (p. XIII).

15 *WA*: III. 335–336, 512.

16 *WA*: III. 522; Bangs, *Arminius*, p. 215.

17 White, p. 35.

18 White, p. 20.

19 *WA*: III. 383; William den Boer, 'Jacobus Arminius: Theologian of God's Two-fold Love', in *Arminius, Arminianism, and Europe*, ed. by Th. Marius van Leeuwen, Keith D. Stanglin, and Marijke Tolsma (Leiden: Brill, 2009): 25–50 (p. 32).

20 *WA*: III. 383.

21 White, p. 25.

22 *WA*: III. 391–394.

23 This is a highly complex issue that was debated and complicated after Arminius and Gomarus' death (as were many other aspects of predestination), see Richard A. Muller, *Post-Reformation Reformed Dogmatics: The Rise and Development of Reformed Orthodoxy, ca. 1520–1725*, 4 vols. (Michigan: Baker Academic, 2003–6), vol. 3: *The Divine Essence and Attributes*, pp. 412–413.

24 Stanglin, *Arminius on the Assurance of Salvation*, p. 77.

25 *WA*: III. 510.

26 Arminius based this idea mainly on Romans 5:12: 'Wherefore, as one man's sin entered into the world, and death by sin; and so death passed upon all men, for that all have sinned', as well as Genesis 8:21, 1 Kings 8:46, Psalms 80:3, and Job 25:4; *WA*: III. 469–471; E.J. Bicknell, *The Christian Idea of Sin and Original Sin, in the Light of Modern Knowledge* (London: Longmans, 1923), pp. 17, 27.

27 *WA*: III. 481–482.

28 Deni Kasa, 'Arminian Theology, Machiavellian Republicanism, and Cooperative Virtue in Milton's *Paradise Lost*', *Milton Quarterly*, 50.4 (2016): 260–276.

29 *WA*: III. 456–458.

30 *WA*: III. 507; Cummings, p. 407.

31 *WA*: III. 507–509.

32 *WA*: III. 507–508.

33 Boer, 'Jacobus Arminius', pp. 25–50.

34 *Institutes*, 3.23.6; Bangs, p. 213.

35 *WA*: III. 370.

36 *WA*: III. 349.

37 Bangs, p. 212.

38 Stanglin, *Arminius on the Assurance of Salvation*, p. 112.

39 Edward Jones, 'Milton's Life, 1608–1640', in *The Oxford Handbook of John Milton*, ed. by Nicholas McDowell and Nigel Smith (Oxford: Oxford University Press, 2009): 3–25 (p. 14); Gordon Campbell, Thomas Corns, John K. Hale, and Fiona J. Tweedie, *Milton and the Manuscript of De doctrina Christiana* (Oxford: Oxford University Press, 2007), p. 114.

40 Gordon Campbell and Thomas Corns, *John Milton: Life, Works and Thought* (Oxford: Oxford University Press, 2008), p. 84. See for a different reading of *Comus*, Cedric C. Brown, *John Milton's Aristocratic Entertainments* (Cambridge: Cambridge University Press, 1985), pp. 57–77, who interprets the Ludlow Masque as a reformation (almost Calvinist) text with an emphasis on morality and providence.

41 Nicholas McDowell, 'How Laudian was the Young Milton?', *Milton Studies*, 52 (2011): 3–22.

42 Thomas N. Corns, 'Milton's Antiprelatical Tracts and the Marginality of Doctrine', in *Milton and Heresy*, ed. by Stephen B. Dobranski and John P. Rumrich (Cambridge: Cambridge University Press, 1998): 39–48 (p. 42).

43 Corns, 'Milton's Antiprelatical Tracts', pp. 43–44.

44 *CPW*: II. 293.

45 Stephen N. Dobranski, *Milton's Visual Imagination: Imagery in Paradise Lost* (Cambridge: Cambridge University Press, 2015), p. 48.

46 *WA*: III. 523.

47 Raymond B. Waddington, *Looking into Providences: Designs and Trials in Paradise Lost* (Toronto: University of Toronto Press, 2012), p. 22.

48 *CPW*: II. 519–520.

49 Kevin Sharpe, *The Personal Rule of Charles I* (New Haven: Yale University Press, 1992), p. 301.

50 *CPW*: VIII. 425–426.

51 Maurice Kelley, *This Great Argument: A Study of Milton's De doctrina Christiana as a Gloss upon Paradise Lost* (Princeton: Princeton University Press, 1941); Dennis Danielson, *Milton's Good God: A Study in Literary Theodicy* (Cambridge: Cambridge University Press, 1982), p. 59; Stephen Fallon, 'Milton's Arminianism and the Authorship of *De doctrina Christiana*', *Texas Studies in Literature and Language*, 41.2 (1999): 103–127. A few examples of scholars who argued that Milton perhaps shared some ideas with Arminius, but cannot be called an Arminian, are John Shawcross, *John Milton: The Self and the World* (Lexington: University Press of Kentucky, 1993), pp. 139–140; Paul Sellin, 'John Milton's *Paradise Lost* and *De doctrina Christiana* on Predestination', *Milton Studies*, 34 (1996): 45–60.

52 Fallon, 'Milton's Arminianism and the Authorship of *De doctrina Christiana*', p. 103.

53 Maurice Kelley, *This Great Argument, passim*; Danielson, *Milton's Good God, passim*; and Stephen Fallon, '"Elect above the rest": Theology as Self-Representation in Milton', in *Milton and Heresy*, ed. by Stephen B. Dobranksi and John Rumrich (Cambridge: Cambridge University Press, 1998): 93–116.

54 Look for example to Paul Sellin's article, 'John Milton's *Paradise Lost* and *De doctrina Christiana* on Predestination', pp. 45–60; William B. Hunter, 'The Provenance of the Christian Doctrine', *The English Renaissance*, 32.1 (1992): 129–142.

55 Danielson in *Milton's Good God* does try to find a middle ground in which he uses both ideas on predestination in order to complement each other within Milton's epic. However, there is no real middle ground between Beza and Arminius in their reading of predestination; more, they often arrive at opposite conclusions. Tyacke also described a middle way, in which a minority is absolutely elected, and the rest receive the possibility to save themselves as long as they accept God's grace (Tyacke, 'Arminianism and the Theology of the Restoration Church', p. 72).

56 See, for example, Larisa Kocic, 'Predestination in Milton's *Paradise Lost* and *De Doctrina Christiana*', *The Anachronist* (2003): 65–84.

57 Some critics have used the passage (Book III, 183–201) from *Paradise Lost* as a sign of Amyraldism (which is further explained in the following text): see

N.H. Keeble, 'Introduction', in *The Complete Prose Works of Andrew Marvell*, ed. by Annabel Patterson, 2 vols. (New Haven: University of Yale Press, 2003): 381–411 (p. 388) and Nigel Smith, *Andrew Marvell: The Chameleon* (New Haven: Yale University Press, 2010), p. 129. Amyraldism was still loyal to three of Calvin's five points.

58 Stephen Fallon, *Milton's Peculiar Grace: Self-Representation and Authority* (Ithaca: Cornell University Press, 2007), p. 250.

59 Russ Leo, *Affect before Spinoza: Reformed Faith, Affectus, and Experience, in Jean Calvin, John Donne, John Milton and Baruch Spinoza* (Ph.D. Thesis, Duke University, 2009).

60 See Leo's Chapter 4 'The sense of Heav'ns desertion": *Lustratio, Affectus* and God's Special Decree in John Milton's *Samson Agonistes* (1671)', pp. 329–383.

61 Several works that deal primarily with Milton's theological doctrine completely ignore Arminianism within his work, such as Michael Lieb, *Theological Milton: Deity, Discourse and Heresy in the Miltonic Canon* (Pittsburgh: Duquesne University Press, 2006).

62 Leo, pp. 380–383.

63 Leo, p. 376.

64 Bangs, pp. 212–213.

65 Fallon, '"Elect above the rest"', p. 95.

66 Waddington, pp. 21–22.

67 *CPW* (OUP) (2012): VIII (part 1). 79; Benjamin Myers, 'Prevenient Grace and Conversion in *Paradise Lost*', *Milton Quarterly*, 40.1 (2006): 20–36 (p. 25).

68 Paul Hammond, *Milton's Complex Words: Essays on the Conceptual Structure of Paradise Lost* (Oxford: Oxford University Press, 2017), p. 236.

69 *WA*: III. 481–482.

70 *CPW* (OUP) (2012): VIII (Part 1). 95: 1.4 ('On Predestination') 'he saw in whatever way wishing or else running (it is probable that they are here called 'ordained'), to them he gave the ability to wish and run more fully, that is, to believe'.

   CPW (OUP) (2012): VIII (Part 1). 265: 1.6 ('On the Holy Spirit) 'But in 1 Cor. 12:11 he is said *to distribute gifts to each individual just as he wishes*; and himself, I say, to be distributed to each individual according to the will of God the father, Heb. 2:4; and in John 3:8, too: *the wind blows where it wishes*'.

   CPW (OUP) (2012): VIII (Part 1). 545: 1.17 ('On Renewal, and also on Calling') 'Special calling is that by which God whensoever he wishes invites these rather than those, whether they are so-called 'chosen ones' or 'reprobates', [and does so] more clearly and more often'.

71 Fallon, "Elect above the rest", p. 96.

72 'Letter Arminius to Wtenbogaerd (1599?)', qtd. in William den Boer, *Duplex Amor Dei: Contextuele Karakteristiek van de Theologie van Jacobus Arminius (1559–1609)* (Apeldoorn: Instituut voor Reformatie Onderzoek, 2008), p. 120.

73 'Letter Arminius to Wtenbogaerd (13 January 1605)', qtd. in den Boer, p. 123.

74 See also Christopher N. Warren, 'Samson and the Chorus of Dissent', in *Uncircumscribed Mind: Reading Milton Deeply*, ed. by Charles W. Durham and Kristin A. Pruitt (Selinsgrove: Susquehanna University Press, 2008): 276–291, and Jason Rosenblatt, *Renaissance England's Chief Rabbi: John Selden* (Oxford: Oxford University Press, 2006).

75 Radzinowicz argued that Milton '*rejected the view that God damns unbelievers or reprobates them or hardens their hearts; unbelievers damn, reprobate*, and *harden themselves*', Mary Ann Radzinowicz, *Towards Samson Agonistes: The Growth of Milton's Mind* (Princeton: Princeton University Press, 1978), p. 340. This view is simplistic, however, as these lines in *PL* already contradict this

statement. It is true that in Milton's theology, and visible in his version of the Samson narrative, the individual is free to fall, but the punishment can become more severe as a result of God's withdrawal.

76 Anthony Low, *The Blaze of Noon: A Reading of Samson Agonistes* (New York: Colombia University Press, 1974), pp. 93–95.

77 *Institutes*, 3: 24.8.

78 *WA*: III. 368.

79 Albert R. Cirillo, 'Time, Light, and the Phoenix: The Design of *Samson Agonistes*', in *Calm of Mind: Tercentenary Essays on Paradise Regained and Samson Agonistes*, ed. by Joseph Wittreich (London: Western Reserve University, 1971): 209–234 (p. 219).

80 Augustine of Hippo, 'St Augustine: On the Holy Trinity, Doctrinal Treatises, Moral Treatises', in *Nicene and Post-Nicene Fathers*, ed. by Philip Schaff (New York: Cosimo, 2007), p. 101.

81 *Institutes*, 3: 24.8; Bangs, p. 213.

82 There are hints of Socinianism here and its ideas about the mortality of both body and soul. As the soul is accountable for sin, it will be punished by perishing together with the body. For a more elaborate explanation of this idea within Milton's works, see John Rogers, 'Delivering Redemption in *Samson Agonistes*', in *Altering Eyes: New Perspectives on Samson Agonistes*, ed. by Mark R. Kelley and Joseph Wittreich (Newark: University of Delaware Press, 2002): 72–97 (especially p. 75).

83 *CPW* (OUP) (2012): VIII (part 1). 75.

84 *WA*: III. 364.

85 Fallon, '"Elect above the rest"', p. 102.

86 William Poole, 'Theology', in *Milton in Context*, ed. by Stephen Dobranski (Cambridge: Cambridge University Press, 2010): 475–486 (p. 477).

87 David Loewenstein, *Representing Revolution in Milton and his Contemporaries: Religion, Politics, and Polemics in Radical Puritanism* (Cambridge: Cambridge University Press, 2001), p. 272.

88 *WA*: III. 510.

89 John T. Shawcross, 'Irony as Tragic Effect: *Samson Agonistes* and the Tragedy of Hope', in *Calm of Mind: Tercentenary Essays on Paradise Regained and Samson Agonistes* (London: Western Reserve University, 1971): 289–306 (pp. 289–299).

90 Bangs, p. 73.

91 Rogers, 'Delivering Redemption in *Samson Agonistes*', pp. 72–97.

92 See Wittreich's book, especially chapters 2 and 3, on which parts of the Judges narrative Milton omits, which he adopts, and which he adds himself: Joseph Wittreich, *Interpreting Samson Agonites* (Princeton: Princeton University Press, 1986).

93 This chapter does not discuss the impact of Socinianism on Dutch theological thought, but see Mortimer, especially 'Chapter 2: Socinianism in England and Europe', pp. 39–62.

94 Milton's own sympathy for the Socinians is shown in the fact that he licensed the *Cathesis Ecclesiarum quae in Regno Poloniae* (1652) (translated in English as *The Racovian Catechism*), which was a full introduction to the theology of the heretical Socinians.

95 'Nam Christus Fundamentum istius benedictionis est, non qua Deus, sed qua θεάνθρωπος, mediator, salvator et caput Ecclesiae', William den Boer, *God's Twofold Love: The Theology of Jacob Arminius (1599–1609)* (Göttingen: Vandenhoeck & Ruprecht, 2010), pp. 114–115. Thanks to Paul Martin for suggestions on the Greek.

96 For works by critics on Milton's Arianism see: Michael Bauman, *Milton's Arianism* (Frankfurt: Lang, 1987); John P. Rumrich, 'Milton's Arianism: Why It Matters', in *Milton and Heresy*, ed. Stephen B. Dobranski and John P. Rumrich (Cambridge: Cambridge University Press, 1998): 75–92; C.A. Patrides, 'Milton

and Arianism', *Journal of the History of Ideas*, 25.3 (July 1964): 423–429; William Hunter, 'Milton's Arianism Considered', *Harvard Theological Review*, 52 (1959): 9–35; Maurice Kelley, 'Milton's Arianism Again Considered', *The Harvard Theological Review*, 54.3 (July 1961): 195–205.

97   John Rogers, 'Milton and the Heretical Priesthood of Christ', in *Heresy, Literature and Politics in Early Modern English Culture*, ed. by David Loewenstein and John Marshall (Cambridge: Cambridge University Press, 2006): 203–220 (p. 212).

98   Poole, 'Theology', p. 479.

99   Nigel Smith, 'Best, Biddle and Anti-Trinitarian Heresy', in *Heresy, Literature and Politics in Early Modern English Culture*, ed. by David Loewenstein and John Marshall (Cambridge: Cambridge University Press, 2006): 160–184 (pp. 176–178). See for another narrative on anti-Trinitarianism Radzinowicz, pp. 324–336. See for the role of Christ in *Paradise Regained*: Barbara Lewalski, *Milton's Brief Epic: The Genre, Meaning, and Art of Paradise Regained* (Providence: Brown University Press, 1966), pp. 182–192.

100   Lieb, *Theological Milton*, pp. 213–260.

101   Rogers, 'Delivering Redemption', p. 91.

102   Nigel Smith, 'The Boomerang Theology of Andrew Marvell', *Renaissance and Reformation*, 25.4 (2001): 139–155.

103   Waddington, p. 28.

104   Takashi Yoshinaka, *Marvell's Ambivalence: Religion and Politics of Imagination in Mid-Seventeenth Century England* (Cambridge: Cambridge University Press, 2012), p. 138.

105   Margarita Stocker, *Apocalyptic Marvell: The Second Coming in Seventeenth-Century Poetry* (Brighton: Harvaster, 1985) pp. 72, 327, n. 84.

106   CPW: VII.14; see for the importance of providence in the early modern period: Alexandra Walsham, *Providence in Early Modern England* (Oxford: Oxford University Press, 1999).

107   Some argue that some of these poems such as 'A Dialogue between the Soul and the Body' were composed in the late 60s and 70s. See for example, John Spurr's essay that claims that after 1667, Marvell took a more religious stance, of which 'A Dialogue between the Soul and the Body' is a feature: John Spurr, 'The Poet's Religion', in *The Cambridge Companion to Andrew Marvell*, ed. by Derek Hirst and Steven N. Zwicker (Cambridge: Cambridge University Press, 2011): 158–173 (pp. 160–161). I, however, follow Smith's dating in the *Poems of Andrew Marvell*.

108   Christine Rees reads 'A Dialogue between the Resolved Soul and Created Pleasure' as a poem in the Catholic tradition with a Protestant purpose, which in itself highlights the complex intertwining of Marvell's use of religion. Her reading of 'The Coronet' and 'Bermudas' as representing 'three points on a spectrum of Puritan thinking about the possibility of spiritual choice', namely 'innate depravity and arbitrary grace' is highly problematic, as these notions of arbitrariness and Calvinism do not easily go together, nor are they a feature of puritanism per se: *The Judgment of Marvell* (London: Pinter Publishers, 1989), pp. 8–9.

109   See N.H. Keeble's persuasive arguments for the attribution of the *Remarks* to Marvell, 'Introduction', *The Prose Works of Andrew Marvell*, 2 vols. (New Haven: Yale University Press, 2003), vol. 2: pp. 381–411 (pp. 399–408).

110   Yoshinaka, pp. 9, 174–175.

111   Smith, *Chameleon*, pp. 128–129.

112   Keeble, 'Introduction', pp. 389–390. See for Richard Baxter's defence of Amyraldus, *Certain Disputations of Right to Sacraments* (London, 1657).

113 Keeble, 'Introduction', p. 402.
114 *PWAM*: II. 417.
115 *PWAM*: II. 433.
116 *PWAM*: II. 421.
117 *PWAM*: II. 416.
118 *PWAM*: II. 479.
119 *PWAM*: II. 482.
120 *PWAM*: II. 482.
121 Pierre Legouis, *Andrew Marvell: Poet, Puritan and Patriot* (Oxford: Clarendon Press, 1965), p. 233.
122 *PWAM*: II. 145.
123 *PWAM*: I. 181; Warren Chernaik, *The Poet's Time: Politics and Religion in the Work of Andrew Marvell* (Cambridge: Cambridge University Press, 1983), p. 123.
124 Annabel Patterson, *Andrew Marvell* (Plymouth: Northcote House, 1994), p. 66, and 'Introduction', in *The Prose Works of Andrew Marvell*, 2 vols. (New Haven: Yale University Press, 2003), vol. 1: xi–xli (p. xxi). I have traced these contradictory affiliations, which are in several ways problematic. Christopher Hill was the first to make the distinction between left-wing Arminians (supporting the oppressed) and right-wing Arminians (believing in divine right of the monarch and magistrate) in *Milton and the English Revolution* (London: Faber and Faber, 1977), pp. 268–278, reiterated in his essay 'From Lollards to Levellers', in *Rebels and Their Causes*, ed. by Maurice Cornforth (London: Lawrence and Wishart, 1978), pp. 58–59. This idea of Milton as a left-wing Arminian has spread through scholarship and is visible in, for example, Brian Manning, 'The Levellers and Religion', in *Radical Religion in the English Revolution* (Oxford: Oxford University Press, 1984): 65–90 (p. 69); Catherine Gimelli Martin, *Milton Amongst the Puritans: The Case for Historical Revisionism* (Farnham: Ashgate Publishing, 2010), p. 49, and more recently, Stephen Dobranski, who used this explanation in *Milton's Visual Imagination: Imagery in Paradise Lost* (Cambridge: Cambridge University Press, 2015), p. 48.
125 N.H. Keeble, *The Literary Culture of Non-Conformity in Later Seventeenth-Century England* (Athens: University of Georgia Press, 1987), p. 327.
126 Martin Dzelzainis, 'Marvell and the Earl of Castlemaine', in *Marvell and Liberty*, ed. by Warren Chernaik and Martin Dzelzainis (Basingstoke: Palgrave Macmillan, 1999): 290–312 (p. 291).
127 Keeble, *The Literary Culture of Nonconformity*, n. 10, p. 327. I am grateful to N.H. Keeble and Johanna Harris for sharing their chapter before publication that concludes: 'He was a tolerationist and, in Annabel Patterson's terminology, a liberal, a defender of moderate, reasonable dealings in the religious sphere against partisanship and extremist churchmanship, whether among nonconformists or conformists' (p. 28). 'Marvell and Nonconformity', in *The Oxford Handbook of Andrew Marvell*, ed. by Martin Dzelzainis and Edward Holberton (Oxford: Oxford University Press, 2019): 145–163 (p. 163).
128 See for Marvell's sometimes unexpectedly lenient position towards Catholicism: Dzelzainis, 'Marvell and the Earl of Castlemaine', pp. 290–312.
129 Andrew Marvell senior is an interesting case. His sermons were not particularly Calvinist, or Laudian. But most intriguing of all, he possibly had a copy of the *Racovian Catechism* in his possession, which was considered heretical all over Europe. Whether he was an anti-Trinitarian or not, this does provide evidence for an open mind in terms of biblical scholarship, creating a tolerant environment for Andrew Marvell junior to grow up in (Smith, *Chameleon*, pp. 20–22).

130 *PWAM*: I. 417.
131 John Rogers, 'Ruin the Sacred Truths: Prophecy, Form, and Nonconformity in Marvell and Milton', in *The Oxford Handbook of Andrew Marvell*, ed. by Martin Dzelzainis and Edward Holberton (Oxford: Oxford University Press, 2019): 672–686 (p. 679). Another example of how Milton and Marvell are often drawn together yet divided, is Phillip Connell's article: 'Marvell, Milton and the Protectoral Church Settlement', *Review of English Studies*, 62.256 (2011): 562–593. Connell explores the literary friendship between the two poets, as well as their opposing views on the Protector's religious reform in the Interregnum, through an examination of their prose works and their poetry.
132 Hill, *Milton and the English Revolution*, p. 285.

6 Samson's Revolution

A retelling of history is never neutral – from the choice of which story to tell and to whom, down to the details of characterisation and description. Whether overtly or unconsciously, the teller brings their own emphases and expectations to bear. In seventeenth-century writing, the invocation of history as authority incorporated not only recent history and the glories of antiquity, but the precedents of biblical, or sacred history. In the following quotation, Grotius in the 'Prolegomena' to *De jure belli ac pacis* (1631 edition) relies on both Roman antecedents and Genesis as literal history to support his argument that war must be a breach of our natural kinship:

> Sacred history, besides that part which consists of precepts, greatly excites our social feeling, since it teaches us that all men are sprung from the same first parents; so that in this sense too we can truthfully say what Florentinus said in another sense, that there is a kinship established among us by nature: and as a consequence that it is wrong for one man to plot against another.[1]

The reference to Scripture *prima facia* gives any argument strength, since its riches were considered divinely inspired, and its moral landscape direct instructions to humankind. Nonetheless, if handled skilfully its narratives could be bent into unexpected shapes to suit a purpose. Grotius is perhaps leaning on biblical authority for his point rather than retelling the story of man's beginnings, but his use is instructive of its power to comment on contemporary events and issues. A full-scale restaging of such a narrative could, if less directly, carry equal weight – perhaps inescapably; '[f]or while [a biblical] story purported to dramatize ancient events in the history of (usually) Israel, the narrative had been chosen and shaped in accordance with the author's own experiences, needs, and desires, which is to say his or her interpenetrating narratives about self, community, and nation at the time of composition'.[2]

In the previous chapter, a theological reading of *Samson Agonistes* revealed an Arminian framework of salvation and predestination. Understanding authorial choices through this doxal lens must, of course, also be related to the further contexts of a text's composition. This chapter develops a comparative reading of *Samson Agonistes* (1671) and Joost van den Vondel's *Samson, of Heilige Wraak* (Samson, or Holy Revenge, 1660), bringing into view the political stakes behind the diverse treatments of the Samson narrative in the period. Revolt, personal sacrifice, and the justification of violence all resound in the story of the Israelite warrior-judge. It is therefore instructive to read both Vondel's and Milton's adaptation against understandings of the English Restoration, and to study the images available to them, regarded with an imagological eye.[3] Although the two authors write with opposing objectives, the tools they use are often remarkably similar.

Little comparative scholarship has been made of these two treatments of this biblical narrative, though there are sufficient exceptions to indicate their parallels and contrasts.[4] Perhaps the most interesting is by the Dutch poet Albert Verwey (1865–1937).[5] In his *Inleiding tot Vondel* (Introduction to Vondel, 1892–1893), an immense work of nearly 1500 pages, Verwey presents quotations that illustrate both similarities and differences:[6]

> See Milton's and Vondel's Samson. The first is a Samson, deviated from what is written in the Bible; he through all kinds of imagined incidents comes to his death. The second one, from deed to deed shaped meticulously according to the biblical, for Vondel the reality. The first is a Unity, on its own, as the body of Milton's own passion. The second is a Unity, as a result of the art with which Vondel carefully compiled hundred studies of the biblical and lived reality. The first has its boldness as an advantage, but the second its precious reality.[7]

Verwey treats authentic poetic licence as Milton's greatest quality, whereas Vondel preserved the ring of truth. This is an immediately problematic distinction, since both Milton and Vondel changed a short biblical narrative into a full play; the invention of new material was unavoidable. In neither case are the extensions fully original creations, nor yet fully grounded in received versions of the story. It is a combination of a kind with Christopher Hill's quip that in history we know how it ends, yet in art it is what we make of it.[8] As Tobias Gregory argues, '[i]n making long poems out of brief bible stories, Milton adds a great deal of extrabiblical matter: description, explanation, digression, backstory, some of which is his own invention, some adapted from prior tradition'.[9] The same could be argued of Vondel's play, where Samson's birth angel Fadael has an extensive role, even after Samson's death, or the framing insertion of the Queen and King of Gaza staging a play. Importantly, what neither does is contradict the source text; both authors were re-adapting what they considered a divinely inspired narrative that was extremely well-known to their spectators or reading audience. Both writers retain the crucial impact and authority of their source, but inevitably introduce their own understanding of its events, including those complexities and ambiguities that still render them fascinating today. It is with an awareness of this balanced process of adaptation that a comparison between the texts ought to begin.

Milton's *Samson Agonistes* has elsewhere been compared to other contemporary Dutch biblical adaptations alongside reflections on their political context. In *Literature and the Law of Nations, 1580–1680*, Christopher Warren excavates a poetics of international law by comparing different types of law with certain literary genres. The renaissance term 'law of nations' or 'national law' – used by Milton in *Areopagitica* – is not concerned with the laws of one particular nation, but rather the laws between nations, so *international* in the vocabulary of today.[10] In this study's transnational approach the Dutch dimension in the English judicial system could not be overlooked. In his chapter 'From Biblical Tragedy to Human Rights', Warren brilliantly examines the law of nations within biblical tragedy through the comparison of Milton's *Samson Agonistes* and Grotius' *Sophompaneas* (1635) (printed in England in 1639, and translated into English in 1652 under the same title).[11] Comparing the Samson narrative to that of Joseph in Grotius' works, which both deal with nationhood and international law in different ways, is effective. Reading these narratives as set within an international scene reveals a sphere in which law, jurisprudence, and politics cross national boundaries and find a place within a multi-cultural literature.

Vondel's play on Samson was similarly indebted to this work by Grotius.[12] Vondel had translated Grotius' play into Dutch, entitled *Huigh de Groots Josef of Sofompaneas* (Hugo Grotius' Josef of Sofompaneas, 1635), and *Samson* deals with the same questions of nation that Grotius raised: it draws direct connections with the law.[13] It is accordingly fair to say that in both Milton's and Vondel's work, the biblical narrative is significantly flavoured with contemporary political concerns.

Christopher Kendrick's comparative article on Milton and Vondel's work, 'Typological Impulses in *Samson Agonistes*', is also worth mentioning here. He argues that Milton's exegesis of Judges ultimately leads to the 'loss of the political', and that Vondel and Milton consciously (he follows Edmundson's now marginalised claim of direct textual exchange between the two authors) decided to interpret the Samson narrative in opposing ways, although both far removed from the political.[14] By contrast, I will highlight some of the similarities to be found in both dramatic works, concluding that the authors were writing in different political contexts and with different aims, but these nonetheless led to striking parallels that are most certainly political.

Vondel's Samson

Samson was never regarded as one of Vondel's masterpieces, and was only performed three times in his lifetime.[15] Perhaps relatedly, there is not a great deal of literary scholarship about it, a lack recently mourned by Yasco Horsman in his psycho-analytic reading of the play.[16] Its first performance was in

1660, significantly in the midst of the English Restoration. Frequently, the narrative of David's banishment and reinstallation had been used in both English and Dutch contexts to dramatise the Stuart cause, yet here the story of Samson, too, becomes a vehicle for staging the Restoration.[17] Vondel was a strong supporter of the Stuarts, which means that he was writing his Samson from the doubly opposite situation to Milton's: the former writing in a republic but as a supporter of English royalism, the latter a republican writing under a rehabilitated monarchy.

To my knowledge, Vondel does not use the character of Samson in his other works, which might have offered direct contrasts between his appearances and their responsiveness to political contexts. However, in the early modern Low Countries more generally Samson was called upon sufficiently to be highly illuminating. The Northern Netherlands had struggled through the Eighty Years' War, seeking the independence from Spain finally concluded in 1648. Republicanism in the new Dutch nation was not unnaturally concerned with justification for their initial revolt, an interest that recurred through at least the first five decades of its existence. Samson's scriptural rebellion against Philistine rule was a natural vehicle for such self-reflection, or vindication, which involved questions of both moral right and legal precedence.

After the signing of the Twelve Years' Truce, Hugo Grotius proposed in *Liber de antiquitate reipublicae Batavicae* (1610) that the Dutch state and its claim for independence were merely a continuation of the Batavian state of centuries earlier; the current revolt could therefore not be a rebellion against a legitimate authority. Instead the monarchical institution imposed by the King of Spain could only be a tyrannical state, illegitimately ruling one of the oldest republics in the world.[18] The Samson narrative deals with the same problems that were present in discussions of the Dutch revolt: rebellion and its divine authorisation, tyranny, and (national) self-sacrifice. Parallels between the Israelites and the Dutch, and between the Philistines and the Spanish were easy to make, and could be richly exploited.

The demonstration of an independent Dutch nation took place in part through production of a vernacular Bible, the *Statenvertaling* (State's Translation, 1637); the original edition was tellingly printed with annotations and introductions by the translators and editors.[19] The annotation to verse 16:28 of Judges, for example, favours a reading in which Samson's prayer is answered by God, and that his revenge was in the name of God, thereby justifying Samson's revolt:

> *Dit badt hy uyt geloove, ende wert van Godt verhoort, die hem, door het uytgraven sijner oogen van de Philistijnen tot uytvoeringe sijns beroeps [. . .] onduchtich gemaeckt zijnde, dese occasie, dit voornemen, ende extraordinare sterckte gegeven, dit gebet ingegeven, ende hem in sijnen doot wonderbaerlijcke victorie verleent heeft, als in sijn leven: tot sijns H. Naems eere, bespottinge der Afgoden, ende beschaminge sijner vyanden.*

This he prayed from belief, and was fulfilled by God, who gave him, via the loss of his eyes by the Philistines through the execution of his profession [. . .] was made powerless, this occasion, this intention, and was given extraordinary power, this prayer was inspired, and has given him in death miraculous victory, as in his life: to the honour of God, dishonour of false gods, and the humiliation of his enemies.

This implies that God gave Samson this particular opportunity to stage one final revenge to God's glory before his death. This annotation of the narrative clearly offers an authoritative reading of Samson that could easily be transposed to a justification of the Dutch people's own revolt. The impact of this would be difficult to overestimate, consecrated as it was within the most frequently used translation by the majority of Dutch people, just as the King James Bible influenced English society's language and narrative understanding of Scripture in unparalleled ways.[20] In fact, if we compare the *Statenvertaling* and its annotations to the King James Bible, the role of God in Samson's final act received much less emphasis in the latter. The influence of the volatile climate of production can be felt: James I would be anxious not to encourage revolt against authority, whether lawful or unlawful. This distinction will be further explored in this chapter, including to what extent revolt meant something different in a Dutch context or an English one.

Rembrandt van Rijn's (1606–1669) representation of the Samson story exemplifies how this understanding of the narrative carried contemporary political resonances. Between 1628 and 1641, he produced five Samson paintings.[21] *Simson Bedreigt zijn Schoonvader* (Samson threatening his father-in-law, c. 1635), perhaps not as instantly recognisable as *De Blind-making van Samson* (The Blinding of Samson, 1636), suggests how the Samson narrative was imagined and experienced in the Dutch Republic.[22] A burly, farmer-handed Samson is the central figure, shaking his fist at an enemy raised up within his solid house, dressed in the red of Catholic Spain. Rembrandt's famous dark-light technique has the light spilling directly onto Samson and then reflecting on his father-in-law. The light shining on Samson and his long locks draws attention to his sacred position as a Nazarite of God. It is not difficult to see parallels between the Dutch standing up against a foreign enemy and this depiction of Samson demanding his rights from the Philistines. Rembrandt painted it well after the Twelve Years' Truce had ended, and the Dutch Republic was again at war with Spain. Sharon Achinstein has argued that in republican times Judges was a 'favourite of those authors thinking about virtuous self-rule without kings', since it tells of repeated conflicts with foreign enemies, and the valiant struggles of the Israelites against the great powers of their time.[23] Samson could 'serve as a model for the Republic's stadtholder', who generally argued in favour of war with Spain.[24] As John Durham has noted, Samson's father-in-law has his hand firmly on the metal latch to the window, ready to retreat to safety in the face of this mighty man's demand of the entry that is due to him.[25]

Figure 6.1 Rembrandt van Rijn, *Simson Bedreigt zijn Schoonvader*, 1635? Oil on
        Canvas. 158.5 cm × 130.5 cm

Source: Reproduced with kind permission from the Gemäldegalerie der Staatlichen Museen zu
Berlin. Photograph by Christoph Schmidt.

Watson Kirkconnell's collection provides a corpus of European adaptations
of Samson.[26] Although far from an exhaustive account, of the texts he lists
for the period 1500–1700, the majority were written and performed in Germany, the Swiss Confederation, and the Low Countries (26 texts), compared to five works being produced in England and ten in Spain, Italy and

Portugal.[27] It was clearly a popular subject in Germanic literature. Could there be a link between republics and an interest in the Samson narrative? The case of Rembrandt certainly suggests a happy correlation between Samson's bold resistance and the defensive concerns of republics surrounded by large monarchies. The six adaptations in the successfully republican Swiss Confederation between 1543 and 1600 would support such a view. It served as a republican example in Europe until the mid-sixteenth century, when the Myth of Venice took over.[28] Several of the Germanic adaptations turn the traditional medieval representation of Samson as a love-struck hero into one of a fierce agent of God who executes divine revenge on foreign heathens, such as Marcus Andreas Wunstius' *Simson, Tragoedia Sacra* (c. 1600), a full play in Latin. Similar shifts in emphasis occur in Dutch adaptations, of which Rembrandt's paintings and the annotations in the *Statenvertaling* are related phenomena. Vondel's play is also set firmly within this Dutch republican context, reacting to recent political events in the United Provinces – and in Vondel's case, in England, too.

The Politics of *Samson Agonistes*

The (political) ambiguity of *Samson Agonistes* has not gone unnoticed in Milton scholarship.[29] This has led some to conclude that it ought not be read as a political allegory at all.[30] We do know, however, that the 1660s and the Restoration of the monarchy were the 'work's natural home'; ignoring their significance to the text would scrub away many of its most substantial features. Others have constructed two distinct political readings of the play.[31] The first is that the poem can be seen as a signal of reassurance, even hope, for the nonconformists or the passive republicans: oppression can and will be broken.[32] The second is a more violent, negative view, in which the oppression by the heathen Philistines is a reflection of Milton's disappointment with the Restoration and failure of the English Commonwealth.[33] Samson is a glorified terrorist and Milton is writing in praise of religious violence. Recently, Tobias Gregory has convincingly argued that these attitudes to the play are not mutually exclusive, and I take this assumption as my starting point: the play and its context allow for both drivers' presence in the text.[34]

Unlike Vondel, Milton had employed the figure of Samson several times in earlier works, suggesting his usefulness to political arguments. The first appearance of the Nazarite is in *Reason of Church Government* (1642). At the climax of the pamphlet, a state appears stripped of its locks of justice, shaven off by the prelates in the figure of Delilah:

> But laying down his head among the strumpet flatteries of Prelats, while he sleeps and thinks no harme, they wickedly shaving off all those bright and waighty tresses of his laws, and just prerogatives which were his ornament and strength, deliver him over to indirect and violent

councels, which as those Philistims put out the fair, and farre-sighted eyes of his natural discerning, and make him grinde in the prison house of their sinister ends and practices upon him. Till he knowing this prelatical rasor to have bereft him of his wonted might, nourish again his puissant hair, the golden beames of Law and Right; and they sternly shook, thunder with ruin upon the heads of those his evil counsellors, but not without great affliction to himselfe.[35]

Soon after, a reference in *Areopagitica* (1644) makes a direct comparison with the English state: '[m]ethinks I see in my mind a noble and puissant Nation rousing herself like a strong man after sleep, and shaking her invincible locks'.[36] By using a female pronoun, Milton explicitly excludes the association between Samson and the king, and focuses instead on the state and its parliament, often addressed at the time by female pronouns.[37] Andrew Marvell, for example, refers to the English nation as 'Lady State' in the first line of *Last Instructions to a Painter*.

The connection between the king (and state) and Samson seen in *Reason of Church Government* is made more explicit in *Eikonoklastes*, in his response to the use of Samson in *Eikon Basilike*. Milton writes: '[a]nd if the Parlament so thought not, but desir'd him to follow their advice and deliberation in things of public concernment, he accounts it the same proposition, as if *Sampson* had bin mov'd *to the putting out his eyes, that the Philistims might abuse him*'.[38] This point is reiterated later in the same prose tract: '[t]he words of a King, as they are full of power, in the authority and strength of Law, so like Sampson, without the strength of that Nazarites lock, they have no more power in them then the words of another man'.[39] Milton argues that Charles, without the support of a state or other form of legality, is shorn of any special power.[40] A final reference to Samson in his prose works is in the *First Defence* (1651).

> With equal justice, I maintain, none but a country's foes think a tyrant is her king. It matters not whether Eglon was a foreigner and our man a native, since they were both enemies and tyrants. If it was right for Ehud to slay the one, it was right for us to punish the other. Even the heroic Samson, though his countrymen reproached him saying, Judges 15 'Knowest thou not that the Philistines are rulers over us?', still made wax single-handed on his matters, and whether prompted by God or by his own valor, slew at one stroke not one but a host of his country's tyrants, having first made prayer to God for his aid. Samson therefore thought it not impious but pious to kill those masters who were tyrants over his country, even though most of her citizens did not balk at slavery.[41]

What underlies all of these examples? Most notably, Samson is not always explicitly God-inspired, in the manner stressed by the *Statenvertaling*. In the last example it is Samson who thought it not impious but pious to kill those Philistine tyrants; there is no mention that God communicated this view to him. This need not preclude the possibility of divine inspiration, but it does allow the ambiguity of an act of faith – an expression of autonomy – in Samson's final act. Perhaps Milton's Samson thereby speaks of the vulnerability of the mighty without God's guidance, or even good council. It asks to what extent violence can be virtuous. These questions are at the heart of *Samson Agonistes*.

The Theatrical Philistines

Similarities can be found in the way both narratives present the monarchy of the Philistines. They are rare within the Samson tradition in the theatricality of the Philistine state presented – reinforced by the dramatic genre in which they are written.[42] Wunstius' *Simson: Tragoedia Sacra*, mentioned earlier, and the Dutch adaptation by Abraham de Koning, *Simson's Treurspel* (Samson's Tragedy) (1618), for example, did not introduce the Philistine monarchy. This has been noted by David Loewenstein, too, who briefly comments that 'only Vondel's *Samson or Holy Revenge* approaches Milton's self-conscious theatricalism [in their staging of the monarchy] [. . .] Both Milton and Vondel exploit the ironies inherent in the competition between the dramas of Dagon and God'.[43] In a similar way to Milton's *First Defence*, the monarchical institution in *Samson Agonistes* and in *Samson, or Holy Revenge* becomes associated with the Philistines, and Dagon in particular: Dagon, the idol, becomes the restored monarchy.[44] The dramatic characteristics of the play, the pomp and circumstance of Dagon, draw connections with the Restoration, especially the event itself in 1660 and the coronation spectacle of 1661.[45]

The excess displayed both in the Netherlands and England became characteristic of the rule of Charles II. Samuel Pepys described it is as a '[g]reat joy all yesterday in London, and at night bonfires than ever and ringing of bells and drinking of the king's health upon their knees in the streets, methinks is a little too much'.[46] John Evelyn's diary entry is almost identical: 'for joy wheroff, were many thousands of rumps, roasted publiquely in the Streetes at the Bonfires this night, with ringing of bells, & universal jubilee: this was the first good omen'.[47] In Abraham de Wicquefort's diary, entitled *Verhael in forme van Journael* (1660), translated by William Lower as *A Relation in the form of Journal* (1660?), the public's interest in the new king and the great efforts of the Dutch States General to celebrate the English Restoration are the central concern. This short extract reveals some of the general expressions of ecstatic feeling for the King's presence in the United Provinces:

> And to the end, to prevent the disorder among the people, which were come there in crowds from the neighbour towns [to see the king], the

company which had the guard, was commanded to seise themselves of the avenues of the Chappel, and particularly to possess the dore, which leads into a little Partition, where the Princes of Orange heretofore caused a bench to be made cloathed with black velvet, and covered with a canopy of the same stuff for themselves, and for persons of quality, that were ordinarily of their train.[48]

The self-creation of Charles II as the king of a new monarchy was all about 'the dramaturgy of royal power'.[49] Staging extravagance and expense became core values of power, hence links were often made between the theatre and the monarch: '[t]he government staged Charles II's English coronation. 'Staged' is the appropriate verb, as historical precedent was studied and developed to produce royal pageantry of breath-taking splendour'.[50]

The fact that Milton changed the house of the Philistines, as it is described in Judges, into a theatre is thus significant:

> The building was a spacious theatre
> Half round on two main pillars vaulted high
> With seats where all the lords and each degree
> Of sort, might sit in order to behold,
> The other side was open, where the throng
> On banks and scaffolds under sky might stand;
> (ll. 1605–1610)

Dagon's monarchy plans to stage Samson's downfall in a Philistine version of the Globe or a classical amphitheatre.[51] In addition to the decadent description of the theatre, the 'national' day of Dagon with '[s]acrifices, Triumph, Pomp and Games' belies an antipathy to the excesses of imperial ceremony or royalism – a shadow to the peacocking of the Restoration itself.[52] Such a comparison of the Stuart monarchy and actors had, of course, already been made before by Marvell, who famously described Charles I as the 'royal actor' ('An Horatian Ode', l. 53), an idea that was similarly condemned by Milton in *Eikonoklastes* as 'stage-work'.[53] This aversion to spectacle may extend to Milton's decision to write a closet-drama, or a dramatic poem, that in its own form contrasts with the theatricality of the (Philistine) monarchy. Milton's play becomes an internal and individual experience, allowing long speeches, which are at the heart of this text.

Vondel's play presses on in a different direction, embellishing by multiple means its inherent theatricality (although Vondel is still fond of long speeches). The staging is dramatic, and its Philistine monarchy revels in displays of excess and emotion. The play opens with an introduction to the pagan sovereign of the Philistines, Dagon. He is dressed as a stereotypical devil, with batwings and a long staff, without reference to his origin as a sea-god. In many ways, Dagon is presented more as a Lucifer than the Philistine deity.[54]

In a graveyard setting, Dagon enters with a long soliloquy, explaining his hunger for the rituals of pomp and circumstance that will dominate the rest of the play:

> *Daer Dagons priesterdom, eerbiedigh ten altaere*
> *Getreên, ter eere van mijn godtheit stieren slaght,*
> *Spijsoffers inwijt, en den grootvorst van den nacht*
> *Met juichen en triomf verwelkomt, en gezangen,*
> *En offerspelen, daer wy spoocken naer verlangen.*
> (ll. 14–18)

> There Dagon's priesthood, towards the altar respectfully
> He treads, in honour of my godhead bulls slaughtered,
> Sacrifices dedicated, and monarch of the night
> With cries and triumph is welcomed, and songs,
> And games of offering, we, idols, most desire.

Note that Dagon in this passage announces himself as a royal, the 'monarch of the night', hence establishing his rule over the Philistines. In the same speech Dagon announces the real advantage of Samson's fall, namely that it might fuel the imposition of religious and political authority over the rebellious Israelites, including a new law that the Israelites must obey. Although Milton, too, argued in his *Tenure of Kings and Magistrates*, that the king (or any man) is always subject to the law: 'he that bids a man reigne over him above Law, may bid as well a savage Beast': Dagon's new law is illegitimate.[55] The Jewish nation would be ruled not through a legitimate monarchy but through Dagon's unlicensed manipulation of the law, executed through the king and queen of the Philistines. The rituals and festivities are thus a celebration of a renewal of the Philistine dominance. Soon after, he hides in a statue of himself that is present on stage throughout the play, inserting a twisting irony into the notion of the heathen monarchy worshiping, and being ruled by, a false idol.

Dagon's foreshadowing of the theatrical pomp and circumstance to be staged in honour of Samson's defeat is also demanded by the Queen in *Bedryf* (act) 3, and later supported by the King:

> *Vorstin:*   *Het Godtsbancket verheuge, en op een kercktooneel*
> *Zijn kunst vertoone, voor 's lants vorsten, en vorstinnen.*
> *Zoo kuntge Dagons gunst, en 't hart der heeren winnen*
>
> [. . .]
>
> *Vorst:*   *Tooneelspel heeft voorheene ons meer dan eens bedrogen*
> *Met schijn van waerheit, en niet ongeluckigh: want*
> *Zoo wort de deughd met vreught den vorsten ingeplant,*

Al 't weereltlijck beloop naer 't leven afgeschildert,
Door spreeckende schildry. Men ziet een hof verwildert,
Verwart, en overendt, geverft met prinssenmoort.

(ll. 662–664, 668–673)

Queen: God's banquet is excited, and on a church-stage
                Will see [Samson's] art, before the nation's kings and queens.
                So Dagon's favour and the heart of lords can be won.

                [. . .]

King: In the past, theatre has fooled us more than once,
                With the appearance of truth, but not unhappily, since
                Virtue with pleasure is so planted within each king,
                The world is painted as it is in life,
                Through speaking paintings; one sees a garden wild,
                Confused and standing, painted with regicide.

Vondel's play within a play argues the exact opposite of Milton's closet drama. As Elizabeth Sauer has pointed out, closet drama overcomes the criticism of antitheatricalists such as William Perkins and Philip Stubbes, that 'playwrights and actors transfixed and corrupted spectators': by removing the staged elements, corruption is removed.[56] Vondel's play instead presents itself as having the power of a cautionary example. Plays, like mirrors, prompt self-reflection; this makes sense of the sudden and surprising mention of regicide quoted earlier. It appears there to continue the process of self-reflection. The representation might not be perfect, but the moral will shine through. The reference to regicide on the stage seems to be a direct comment on the anti-theatrical policies of the English Republic, as Helmer Helmers has argued.[57]

Of course, Vondel had not written a simple morality play, and the commentary is complicated by the means of its delivery. How effective might such a stance against antitheatricality be when uttered by the Philistines? Vondel creates a different route of signification, however, through his emphasis on location – with similar but inverse effects to Milton's theatre. Instead of the house in Judges, we are taken to a 'kerktoneel' (church-stage). It highlights the hypocrisy of the Puritans by suggesting that their anti-theatre piety is in many ways just as much a hollow performance as the thing they attack. It sketches further parallels with the antitheatricality of the Puritans government, associating the false shows of the Philistines with the false religion of the Protestant regicides.

The two interpretations of Samson's house of the Philistines in Judges is of crucial importance for an understanding of the Philistine monarchy in both texts. In Milton's poem it becomes an attack on the theatricality of the Stuart monarchy, whereas Vondel plays up that same theatricality to comment on the antitheatricality of the Puritans. Both authors made a conscious effort to portray the Philistines in a way that would comment on their contemporary context. Closely related to this is their representation of violence. How to portray violence in a sacred narrative?

Violence and the Samson Narrative

It would be difficult to recount the story of Samson without some degree of violence – even leaving aside lion-wrestling, brawling, arson, maiming, and hairdressing, the denouement of self-entombment calls for the brutal killing of a congregation of hundreds. Throughout his story, Samson is less a wise leader of the people than a super-powered vigilante. This poses the question of how to treat such violent acts in a narrative that aims to be righteous and morally improving. Several critics have addressed this aspect of the Samson narrative (especially Milton's version), such as Michael Lieb and Feisal G. Mohamed.[58] Kendrick concludes that the violence of Samson's triumph in Vondel's work 'receives an equal stress to that in Milton's play'.[59] It is true that Milton's poem is the fiercest in his oeuvre; Tobias Gregory sums it up rather nicely by saying it is 'politically unrepentant, morally uncompromising, and equivocally homocidal'.[60] Undeniably, Milton fails to explicitly condemn religious violence in the poem.

Placing *Samson Agonistes* in parallel with Vondel's play, however, ought to reveal some of the moderate choices Milton made. These should be taken into account when assessing violence in the text. Most obviously, the reader does not see the horrific final scenes at all, with Samson's demolition and demise only reported upon – very different to Vondel's detailing of gore and dismemberment. At a distance Manoa describes a 'hideous noise' (l. 1509) and it is only through a messenger that we hear of the devastation, indirectly, although a 'horrid spectacle' (l. 1542). At no point do we see the aftermath of Samson's act. The description stops immediately after the collapse of the temple. As Christopher Hill noted, Milton 'indeed went out of his way to save the people from destruction'.[61] Unlike the original narrative where the Philistine people stand on the roof of the building that is destroyed by Samson, Milton places the 3000 common Philistines outside of the building, and they survive; it is the Philistine leadership that suffer. This is of crucial importance. So restrained is this strange climax that a staged performance would lack any of the drama and spectacle required. Tellingly, George Frideric Handel's adaptation of Milton's play into an oratorio entitled *Samson* (1741, performed 18th February 1743) included a remedy to this reticence. Newburgh Hamilton (1691–1761), the librettist, replaced the Chorus with a single person.[62] The most striking change, however, is the ending. After the messenger has delivered the tragic news, Manoa orders that Samson's body should be retrieved, cueing a morbid funeral march in which Samson's body is actually carried on to the stage. However difficult it may be to parse Milton's attitude to righteous violence from the episode, it is clear that he stopped short of expected levels of representing it for the contemporary stage.

In this area Vondel was less likely to leave audiences wanting, and *Samson* climaxes in a loud, bright and violent scene, in which the bloody aftermath of Samson's destruction is presented in gross detail:

> [. . .] *Schenckels, darmen,*
> *En hooft, en ingewant, een misselijck beslagh,*
> *Door een gemengt, en vleesch, en been, en brein den dagh*
> *Bezwalcken met een lucht, die haest een pest zal baeren.*
> [ll. 1621–1624]

> [. . .] Shanks, intestines
> And head, and organ, a sickening mixture
> Joined together, and meat, and bone, and brain
> Will infuse the air with a stench birthing a plague.

The horrific vision far exceeds in visceral and sensory impact Milton's reportage. Vondel describes how the survivors go through mountains of dust and debris to find their family; the dead are now unrecognisable and they identify bodies through old scars (ll. 1613–1634). The reader (or spectator) is even informed about the specifics of Samson's own death: a heavy stone that fell directly on the heart.

In Milton's poem, the closest we receive to an image of Samson's body is that it might be 'Soaked in his enemies' blood, and from the stream/ With lavers pure, and cleansing herbs wash off/ The clotted gore' (ll. 1726–1728). It is an indirect representation, even a prediction, as Manoa is yet to find the body. The traumatising events that Vondel describes only distantly relate to Milton's poetic and purified representation of Samson's death, of which we only hear that 'unwounded of his enemies he fell' and 'by his own hands' (ll. 1582, 1584).

Of course, part of this difference can be explained by their genre. Vondel's Senecan play uses violence to make it work on the stage. He may have employed some of the stage machinery that he had already used in other biblical spectacles, such as *Lucifer*. He responds to antitheatricality with heightened theatricality. People were, after all, paying to see the spectacle; simply put, Vondel's play does not work on text alone. Milton's closet drama has no need for the same devices; its language is more complex, the argument more layered. Paradoxically, it is a play that reacts against theatricality without creating a spectacle. This distinction becomes even more apparent when we look at the divine authorisation of Samson's violence in the final act.

Now we have established that in both cases the monarchy and its restoration are described through heathen rituals and an unlawful yielding of the nation's judicial system, it is important to understand whether Samson's act in both dramas is divinely authorised or not.[63] This is closely connected to the level of violence; if God sanctioned Samson's final deed in the two texts, the violence that followed would be divinely authorised. In Milton's case, this could provide an emblem of hope for those in equal disappointment about the failure of the ideal republican state, which might still be redeemed by God's help. It would, moreover, continue the line of defence of the Regicide and English Revolution that Milton began in his prose works in the 1640s. In Vondel's narrative, this would mean a justification of the Dutch revolt (so eagerly sought by Dutch republicans) and a divine blessing for the independent Dutch State. The question of divine endorsement inherent in the Samson narrative was not new in these poetical reinventions of the narrative, as these were already part of exegeses of Judges throughout the centuries.[64] In Milton's poem, whether Samson's 'rousing motions' are divinely inspired or not remains something of an ambiguity.[65]

The sanctification of Samson's revenge is an important problem. Are we viewing a private act of vigilantism that should be condemned, or the symbolic struggle for liberation from an oppressor?[66] There is something comforting in Lieb's proposal that Samson's revenge is not his own but a 'theomachic' confrontation between God and Dagon, and that Samson is merely God's agent.[67] Loewenstein's argument that Milton's poem emphasises Samson's impulse to defeat the Philistines through a spectacular action is another way to make sense of the violent narrative; violence is paid with violence, an eye for an eye.[68] Wittreich has argued that the violence in Milton's narrative undermines Samson's heroism, but this seems to place an inappropriate moral constraint on a narrative unavoidably dealing with violent acts. Comparison with Vondel's goriness and revelling in destruction's aftermath suggest Milton was deliberately moderate in his use of violent imagery and language.[69] It is not the bloody revenge that matters in Milton's poem (unlike Vondel's exhibition), but the holy reckoning of the one God, the attack on Dagon, and the promise of the coming freedom of the Chosen People.[70]

Samson's Three Justifications

Three justifications have been proposed that might illuminate divine endorsement, inspiration, or explanation of Samson's final act. Samson could be acting as a magistrate, which would allow him to rise up against the unlawfulness of Dagon's proposed rule. Another would be if Samson and his people rise up against a tyrannous regime, and this tyranny is proven. Lastly, he may have been divinely inspired to execute God's wish. I will come back to Vondel later, but first let us see how Milton's Samson grapples with these three potential justifications of violence.

Judges tells us that Samson had acted as a judge for twenty years, yet both Vondel's and Milton's narratives concern only the final day of his life. His years as a judge are, however, crucial, because it makes him not only a Nazarite rebelling against Philistine oppression but also a representative of the law acting on behalf of the entire nation. Theologians in the United

Provinces as well as in England were understandably keen to establish this powerful connection between God's individual agent and the nobility of his people's cause.[71] Despite its seeming appropriateness, this legitimatisation of Samson's act is never mentioned in Milton's poem.[72] Serjeantson suggests that this could be the result of Samson's association with dissenters, which would draw direct parallels with the English situation.[73] It would give non-conformists magisterial power after the Clarendon Code (1661–5), which would be a dangerous step to take. Moreover, Herapha accuses Samson of acting as a private person in rebellion, and not as a representative of the entire nation:

> Is not thy nation subject to our lords?
> Their magistrates confessed it, when they took thee
> As a league-breaker and delivered bound
> Into our hands: for hadst thou not committed
> Notorious murder on those thirty men
> At Ascalon, who never did thee harm,
> Then like a robber stripp'dst them of their robes?
> The Philistines, when thou hadst broke the league,
> Went up with armed powers thee only seeking,
> To others did no violence nor spoil.
> (ll. 1182–1191)

This eliminates the option that Samson operates as symbol of the public through his wielding of the law.

Perhaps some answer to Samson's justification without being a magistrate can be found in Grotius' line of thought in *De jure praedae commentarius* (1603) (English translation *Commentary on the Law and Prize of Booty* (1950)): '[t]o be sure, the fact that Samson was moved by the Spirit of God [to seek an occasion for conflict with the Philistines exonerates him], in that he had no need of public authorization'.[74] Samson's magistrature is rendered moot. Grotius suggests that Samson cannot escape from the state, as both are inherently connected through God, yet Samson is at the same time not subservient to the state; God authorises him, rather than the people.[75] This point occurs repeatedly in Milton's poem. First Samson is described as the 'mirror of our fickle state' (l. 164), then in the next line, the resemblance is denied, as he is a 'man on earth unparalleled' (l. 165). The same rejection of unity can be found with Israel's governors, who refuse to acknowledge Samson's deeds in delivering Israel from the Philistines:

> That fault I take not on me, but transfer
> On Israel's governors, and heads of tribes
> Who seeing those great acts which God had done
> Singly by me against their conquerors

Acknowledged not, or not at all considered
Deliverance offered:

(ll. 241–246)

Samson cannot be a deliverer or magistrate of the people when the people (or their chosen representatives) have withdrawn their support. Milton had already argued this in the *Tenure of Kings and Magistrates*.[76]

Second, Milton had previously asserted the sovereign right of the people to rise up against the monarchy, or any elected authority displaying tyranny in his prose works, published and unpublished, 1644–1648.[77] His arguments would have equal resonance for the Dutch situation. *Tenure of King and Magistrates*, however, further complicates this view. There are lawful actions that can be taken against tyranny. The front page of the first edition of the tract boldly claims that it is 'proving, That it is Lawfull, and hath been held so through all Ages for any, who have the Power, to call to account a Tyrant, or wicked king, and after due conviction, to dispose, and put him to death; if the ordinary Magistrate have neglected, or deny'd to doe it'.[78] In the second edition Milton added the following phrase: 'to doe justice on a lawless King, is to a privat man unlawful, to an inferior Magistrate lawfull', making his tract less radical (and perhaps more persuasive to open-minded Presbyterians).[79] The inferior magistrate referred to here includes all authorities inferior to the king, such as Parliament standing against the king in the English Revolution.[80] However, when the magistrates fail in their duty, 'the people are as it were without Magistrates, yea worse, and then God giveth the sword into the peoples hand, and he himself is become immediately thir head'.[81] The problem in Samson's case (in Milton's poem) is that he is *neither* legitimated nor supported by his own people, meaning he cannot be acting even as their *ad hoc* leader in this sense. George Buchanan (1506–1582), a Scottish humanist, provided a possible solution in his *De iure regni apud Scotos* (1579). Buchanan writes that 'it shall be lawfull for any man to kill a Tyrant', as long as his tyranny is firmly established.[82] Milton follows this position in his *Tenure*, in which he, too, argues that 'the right of choosing, yea of changing thir own Government is by the grant of God himself in the People'.[83]

This means that Milton has rejected several rationales for sanctifying Samson's revolt: first, in the poem, Samson is not acting as magistrate, which would place the law above the king, justifying his actions. Second, Samson and his people are not rising up in union against the tyranny of the Philistines, but Samson acts privately. Third, his private revolt may be directly divinely endorsed, though only when it is against tyranny. Whether it is tyranny or not can only be determined when the individual is 'govern'd by reason'.[84] There is enough biblical evidence to support such a notion: Ehud, Moses and Deborah are just three examples. It is, after all, through the 'rousing motions' that Samson felt that he would be able to achieve 'something extraordinary' (ll. 1382–1383), which very clearly implies a divine injection of power beyond that of a mere human, but it is only *after* his decision to rise up that he feels this divine endorsement.[85] As shown in Chapter 5, Samson was elected by God for the purpose of defeating the Philistines, and it is not until Samson returns to this vocation – his faith – that his strength returns, resulting in a continuation, or resuming, of Samson's destined purpose. This means God did not inspire but endorse. This is a reading that agrees with Giovanni Diodati's interpretation of the Judges passage, whom Milton met in Geneva (and who was the uncle of Milton's friend Charles Diodati), cited repeatedly throughout his works.[86] That God's authorisation of Samson's act is veiled in ambivalence, as critics have noted, may be linked to its dangerous political implications; it would not only defend, in the Restoration, the position of the republicans in the Civil Wars, but it would also sanctify the Dutch revolt, and many other uprisings (such as the French Huguenots).[87]

Vondel's Legitimatisation of Samson's Act

The same issues that Milton grapples with in his poem – sanctification of Samson's revolt, a justification of his chosen death, and the presence of God within this violent narrative – affect Vondel's narrative, but they are boldly and unambiguously addressed. The different arguments for sanctifying Samson's act are considered but ultimately rejected in Milton's poem; they are all present in Vondel's play, too. It is immediately clear that it is not Samson's vengeance, but God's, which is visible in the title *Samson, of Heilige Wraak* (Samson, or Holy Revenge).[88] Marvell, too, reads Samson as chiefly an avenger, as shown in the poem 'On Paradise Lost': 'So Samson groped the temple's posts in spite/ The world o'erwhelming to revenge his sight' (ll. 9–10). This is supported by recurring analogies between Samson and Christ, already emphasised in the preface to Vondel's play, 'because he is made from God's wisdom to depict a greater deliverer through his birth, life, and death' ('*want hy is van Godts wijsheit geschickt om eenen grooten Verlosser door zijn geboorte leven en sterven uit te beelden*').[89] In stark contrast to Milton, Samson is frequently referred to as the 'Joodsche Rechter' (Jewish Judge), indicating that he also acts as a legal representative of all Hebrews. Samson, therefore, does not act as a private person. This is clear right from the start of the play; the viewers are not left questioning Samson's motivations.

Moreover, at the end Vondel's audience receives reassurances that we do not get from Milton. Samson's birth angel Fadael descends from Heaven to record that Samson is saved:

> [. . .] *nu heeft de helt Godts wraeck*
> *Stantvastigh uitgevoert, uit yver voor Godts zaeck.*
> *Zijn doodt bedroeve u niet. De geest, bevrijt van kommer*
> *En 's lichaems blintheit, waert gerust in koele en zoete lommer*
> *By d'oude helden, hem grootdaedigh voorgetrêen.*
> (ll. 1666–1670)

[. . .] Now God's revenge is through the hero
Steadfast executed, out of piety for God's plan.
His death should not sadden you. The spirit, freed from pain
And its body's blindness, rest now in cool and sweet shade,
With those old heroes, who nobly preceded him.

We can thereby be certain that Samson's violence and consequent death are endorsed and supported by God, and that his revolt was divinely sanctified. Vondel maintains the same arguments used in early Dutch republicanism that justify the Dutch revolt and the Dutch State's independence, whilst writing as a convinced supporter of the Stuart Restoration; Samson is supported by God to rise against the Philistines, in the same way that the Dutch as a people were divinely endorsed to stand up against Spanish tyranny.

Dutch Samson and English Samson

After noting the similarities in the theatricality of monarchy and the differences in the divine authorisation of Samson's rebellion, the question remains how these narratives can be read in opposing contexts. The settings in which Samson's defeat was staged – in Milton's case a theatre not unlike Theatre Royale at Drury Lane (built in 1660) or Dorset Garden Theatre (built in 1671), and in Vondel's play a church – is where the answer perhaps lies. Milton was writing in the aftermath of the collapse of the English Commonwealth. Vondel had a very different agenda, visible through his other examples of Restoration literature, such as his poem 'Opgang van Karel Stuart den Tweeden' (Return of Charles II), mentioned in the Epilogue. His play attacks the antitheatricalism of the Puritans, hence the Philistines staged their 'play', or as Vondel has it, their religion, in the church. In Vondel's 'Samsons Grafschrift' (Samson's Elegy), a short commemorative poem that would be read at the end of the performance of the play, he does not refer to the house in Judges but again the 'kercke', the church of Dagon. The Restoration was thus for Vondel not only a restoration of the lawful king, but also of the theatre. The Samson of Milton's poem redeems himself by destroying the same theatre that Vondel hoped to be restored. Milton criticises monarchy and its associated theatricality, whereas Vondel attacks religion and antitheatricality. The tense relation between war, justice and truth in Milton's poetical works, as we have seen in the difficulties of representing Samson's revenge, are quite opposite to Vondel's glorification of divine violence.

As Miltonists have been arguing for decades, Milton was opposed to military discord, or only permitted it when it could be controlled and kept within certain (juristic) boundaries.[90] We have seen in *Samson Agonistes* that, for Milton, warfare could be justified when justice was prioritised over peace; Samson's integrity is preserved only and because he opposed oppression. Bound together with this moral, there is Milton's much gentler *Paradise Regained*, in which the Son rejects temptation after temptation.[91] These poems can thus be seen, as Knoppers argues, as 'fostering hope and fortifying resistance in dissenters and political radicals'.[92] Vondel, however, was born in the early stages of the Eighty Years' War, which means that for the first 61 years of his life he was at war. After the Peace of Westphalia, only five years elapsed until the United Provinces were at war again, this time with England. War was unavoidable in the state's account of itself.

Biblical narratives get shaped to their political context, including an author's own view, imagology, historical perspective, and genre. The two plays that have been discussed in this chapter differ in various ways; these discrepancies can be tied to the religious, artistic, and political concerns of their authors. Vondel arguably seeks a clearer moral than Milton. He creates a narrative that can co-exist with a legal or moral justification of Dutch resistance but still keep a lid on law and order. By choosing to portray Samson in a sensory and sensational play, he is able to critique the antitheatricality of the English Puritans, and celebrate Charles II's restoration of the throne and the theatre. Milton's discussion of these topics is not as straightforward. Naturally, this is partly the result of the two different genres. Perhaps Milton is less interested in the representation of dramatic events than in the different ways in which the exercise of power could, or should, be authorised. Samson's final act cannot be justified only through his title of judge, since its value and legitimacy are dependent on those who approve the office (and its limits). Milton also avoids making divine instruction the underwriter of the act, since that would deprive Samson of his human agency and dissolve the difficult moral choice of the individual to resist tyranny. Instead Samson must decide for himself a righteous path, of which he is never certain in advance; he performs an act of faith. Both authors tease out the difficulties of this strange, Old Testament life, signalling through their revitalising of history an acute awareness in both English and Dutch circles of the precarity of peace and the sometimes terrifying proximity of violence.

Notes

1 Transl. and qtd. in Richard Tuck, *The Rights of War and Peace: Political Thought and the International Order from Grotius to Kant* (Oxford: Oxford University Press, 2001), p. 101.

2 Christopher Warren, *Literature and the Law of Nations, 1580–1680* (Oxford: Oxford University Press, 2015), p. 166.

3 Helmer Helmers also proposed a reading of these two texts in a Restoration context in *The Royalist Republic* (Cambridge: Cambridge University Press, 2015), pp. 237–258.

4 Helmers, *The Royalist Republic*, pp. 237–258; Watson Kirkconnell, *That Invincible Samson: The Theme of Samson Agonistes in World Literature with Translations of the Major Analogues* (Toronto: Toronto University Press, 1964), pp. 179–181; J.N. van Hall, 'Nederlands Tooneel: *Samson of Heilige Wraak*, Treurspel van Vondel', *De Gids*, 70 (1906): 166–174; George Edmundson, *Milton and Vondel: A Curiosity of Literature* (London: Trubner and Co, 1885); Nigel Smith, 'The Politics of Tragedy in the Dutch Republic: Joachim Oudaen's Martyr Drama in Context', in *Dramatic Experience: The Poetics of Drama and*

the Early Modern Public Sphere(s), ed. by Katja Gvozdeva, Kirill Ospovat, and Tatiana Korneeva (Leiden: Brill, 2017): 220–249.

5 Mea Nijland, 'Albert Verwey en John Milton', in *Europen Context: Studies in the History and Literature of the Netherlands, presented to Theodoor Weevers*, ed. by P.K. King and P.F. Vincent (Cambridge: Modern Humanities Research Association, 1971): 248–267 (p. 250).

6 Verwey's book was published in serial instalments between 1892 and 1893.

7 'Ziet den Samson van Milton en die van Vondel. De eerste is een Samson, met afwijking van wat in den bijbel staat, door allerlei verbeelde voorvallen komend tot de daad van zijn dood. De tweede een, van daad tot daad angstvallig gevormd naar den bijbelschen, voor Vondel's werklijken. De eerste is een Eenheid, vanzelf, als het lichaam van Miltons hartstocht. De tweede is een Eenheid, dank zij de kunst waarmee Vondel de hundred studies naar bijbelsche en doorleefde werklijkheid zorgzaam heeft saamgesteld. De eerste heeft de stoutheid voor, maar de tweede zijn kostelijke werkelijkheid', qtd. in Nijland, p. 254.

8 Christopher Hill, *The Experience of Defeat: Milton and Some Contemporaries* (London: Verso, 1984), p. 313.

9 Tobias Gregory, 'The Political Messages of *Samson Agonistes*', *Studies in English Literature 1500–1900*, 50.1 (2010): 175–203 (p. 180).

10 *CPW*: II. 513.

11 The text in Latin was printed by Richard Hodgkinson in London in 1639, which was an unauthorised volume of Grotius' poetical works.

12 Grotius' work as translated by Vondel as *Somfompanes* (1635) is the first in Vondel's Joseph trilogy, followed by *Jozef in Egypte* (1640) and *Jozef in Dothan* (1644). Vondel's translation of Grotius' play saw over sixty performances between 1638 and 1665. In Latin, Grotius' play was only performed once, in 1660. For more information on Vondel's translation, see Freya Sierhuis, 'Therapeutic Tragedy: Compassion, Remorse, and Reconciliation in the Joseph Plays of Joost van den Vondel (1635–1640)', *European Review of History*, 17.1 (2010): 27–51; Madeleine Kasten, 'Translation Studies: Vondel's Appropriation of Grotius' *Sophompaneas*', in *Joost van den Vondel: Dutch Playwright in the Golden Age*, ed. by Jan Bloemendal and Frans-Willem Korsten (Leiden: Brill, 2012): 249–271; Warren, *Literature and Law of Nations*, p. 184.

13 See Russ Leo's article for a more extensive comparison between Grotius' works and Vondel's play: 'Grotius among the Dagonists: Joost van den Vondel's *Samson, of Heilige Wraeck*, Revenge and the *Ius Gentium*', in *Politics and Aesthetics in European Baroque and Classicist Tragedy*, ed. by Jan Bloemendal and Nigel Smith (Leiden: Brill, 2016): 75–102.

14 Christopher Kendrick, 'Typological Impulses in *Samson Agonistes*', *University of Toronto Quarterly*, 84.2 (2015): 1–30 (pp. 9, 11). Perhaps some of Kendrick's readings can be explained by the fact that he read Vondel's play in Kirkconnell's translation, which at times deviates considerably from the original.

15 Yasco Horsman, 'Psychoananalysis-Law, Theatre, and Violence in *Samson* (1660)', in *Joost van den Vondel: Dutch Playwright in the Golden Age*, ed. by Jan Bloemendal and Frans-Willem Korsten (Leiden: Brill, 2012): 445–459 (p. 445).

16 Horsman, pp. 445–446.

17 An example would be another play by Vondel: *Koning David in Ballingschap* (King David in Exile), which was published and performed in 1660. There were, however, also literary works that presented Cromwell as David. See Marvell's 'Horatian Ode'. Annabel Patterson, '*Bermudas* and the *Coronet*: Marvell's Protestant Poetics', *ELH*, 44.3 (1977): 478–499 (pp. 478–479); and see for a full discussion of the David narrative, Mary Ann Radzinowicz, 'Forced Allusions: Avatars of King David in the Seventeenth Century', in *The Literary Milton: Text,*

Pretext and Context, ed. by Diana Trevino Benet and Michael Lieb (Pittsburgh: Duquesne University Press, 1994): 45–66.

18 C.G. Roelofsen, 'Grotius and International Politics of the Seventeenth Century', in *Hugo Grotius and International Relations*, ed. by Hedley Bull, Benedict Kingsbury, and Adam Roberts (Oxford: Oxford University Press, 1990): 96–132 (p. 104).

19 C.C. de Bruin, *De Statenbijbel en zijn Voorgangers* (Haarlem: Nederlands Bijbelgenootschap, 1993).

20 *The Oxford Handbook of the Bible in Early Modern England, c. 1530–1700*, ed. by Kevin Killeen, Helen Smith, and Rachel Willie (Oxford: Oxford University Press, 2015), *passim*.

21 Shelley Perlove and Larry Silver, *Rembrandt's Faith: Church and Temple in the Dutch Golden Age* (Pennsylvania: Pennsylvania University Press, 2009), p. 107.

22 Rembrandt's painting is just one example. Others include the Samson and Delilah paintings by the Dutch and Flemish painters Peter Paul Rubens (1609–1610), Gerrit van Honthorst (1615), Matthias Storm (1630), Christiaen van Couwenberg (1630) and Jan Steen (1667).

23 Sharon Achinstein, '*Samson Agonistes* and the Drama of Dissent', *Milton Studies*, 33 (1997): 133–158 (p. 136).

24 Perlove and Silver, p. 112.

25 John I. Durham, *The Biblical Rembrandt: Human Painter in a Landscape of Faith* (Macon: Mercer University Press, 2004), p. 235.

26 Watson Kirkconnell, *That Invincible Samson: The Theme of Samson Agonistes in World Literature* (Toronto: Toronto University Press, 1964).

27 A play by Edward Jubye and Samuel Rowley (1602) (now lost); Francis Quarles' heroic poem, *The Historie of Sampson* (1631); the anonymous poem *Sampsons Foxes agreed to fire a Kingdom: Or, the Jesuit, and the Puritan, met in a round to put a kingdom out of Square* (1644), and Milton's poem. See Eco Haitsma Mulier, 'The Language of Seventeenth-Century Republicanism in the United Provinces: Dutch or European', in *The Languages of Political Theory in Early Modern Europe*, ed. by Anthony Pagden (Cambridge: Cambridge University Press, 1987), 179–195 (p. 186); Kirkconnell, *That Invincible Samson*, pp. 145–215.

28 Eco Haitsma Mulier, *The Myth of Venice and Dutch Republican Thought in the Seventeenth Century* (Assen: Van Gorcum, 1980); Salvo Mastellone, 'Holland as a Political Model in Italy in the Seventeenth Century', *Low Countries Historical Review*, 98.4 (1983): 568–582.

29 The dating of Milton's poem has led to some disagreements between Miltonists. It is now generally assumed that it was written after the Restoration due to the many references to Restoration politics, see Mary Ann Radzinowicz, *Towards Samson Agonistes: The Growth of Milton's Mind* (Princeton: Princeton University Press, 1978), Appendix E.

30 See for example, E.M. Krouse, *Milton's Samson and the Christian Tradition* (Princeton: Princeton University Press, 1949); Barbara Lewalski, 'Milton's *Samson Agonistes* and the "Tragedy" of the Apocalypse', *Proceedings of the Modern Language Association of America*, 85 (1970): 1050–1062.

31 Elizabeth Sauer, 'Pious Fraud: Extralegal heroism in *Samson Agonistes*', *Studies in English Literature, 1500–1900*, 53.1. (2013): 180–196; Nicholas Jose, '*Samson Agonistes*: The Play Turned Upside Down', *Essays in Criticism*, 30.2 (1980): 124–150. I am indebted here to R.W. Serjeantson's helpful distinction in Samson scholarship: '*Samson Agonistes* and "Single Rebellion"', in *The Oxford Handbook of John Milton*, ed. by Nicholas McDowell and Nigel Smith (Oxford: Oxford University Press, 2011): 614–631 (p. 614).

32 Sharon Achinstein, '*Samson Agonistes* and the Politics of Memory', in *Altering Eyes: New Perspectives on 'Samson Agonistes'*, ed. by Joseph Wittreich and

Mark Kelley Wittreich (Newark: University of Delaware Press, 2002): 168–191 (pp. 179–83); Radzinowicz, *Towards Samson Agonistes*; Appendix E; Blair Worden, 'Milton, *Samson Agonistes*, and the Restoration', in *Culture and Society in the Stuart Restoration*, ed. by Gerald MacLean (Cambridge: Cambridge University Press, 1995): 111–136; Laura Lunga Knoppers, *Historicizing Milton: Spectacle, Power, and Poetry* (Athens: University of Georgia Press, 1995), pp. 42–66; Laura Lunga Knoppers, '"England's Case": Contexts of the 1671 Poems', in *The Oxford Handbook of Milton*, ed. by Nicholas McDowell and Nigel Smith (Oxford: Oxford University Press, 2011): 572–588 (p. 588); Jane Mueller, 'The Figure and the Ground: Samson as a Hero of London Nonconformity, 1662–1667', in *Milton and the Terms of Liberty*, ed. by Graham Parry and Joad Raymond (Cambridge: Cambridge University Press, 2002): 137–162; William Riley Parker, *Milton: A Biography*, 2 vols. (Oxford: Clarendon Press, 1986), vol. 2, pp. 903–917, is an example of arguing that the poem was written in the 1640s.

33 Irene Samuel, '*Samson Agonistes* as Tragedy', in *Calm of Mind: Tercentenary Essays on Paradise Regained and Samson Agonistes*, ed. by Joseph Wittreich (London: Western Reserve University, 1971): 235–257; Joseph Wittreich, *Interpreting Samson Agonistes* (Princeton: Princeton University Press, 1986).

34 Tobias Gregory, 'The Political Messages of *Samson Agonistes*', *Studies in English Literature 1500–1900*, 50.1 (2010): 175–203.

35 *CPW*: I. 859.

36 *CPW*: II. 557–558.

37 Warren, *Literature and the Law of Nations*, p. 171.

38 *CPW* (OUP) (2013): VI. 347.

39 *CPW* (OUP) (2013): IV. 393.

40 Warren, *Literature and the Law of Nations*, p. 171.

41 *CPW*: IV. part 1.402.

42 Christopher N. Warren, 'Samson and the Chorus of Dissent', in *Uncircumscribed Mind: Reading Milton Deeply*, ed. by Charles W. Durham and Kristin A. Pruitt (Selinsgrove: Susquehanna University Press, 2008): 276–291 (p. 286). See also Russ Leo, *Tragedy as Philosophy in the Reformation World* (Oxford: Oxford University Press, 2019), pp. 210–240.

43 David Loewenstein, *Milton and the Drama of History: Historical Vision, Iconoclasm, and the Literary Imagination* (Cambridge: Cambridge University Press, 2006), p. 140.

44 Worden, 'Milton, *Samson Agonistes*, and the Restoration', p. 118.

45 Steven N. Zwicker, *Lines of Authority: Politics and English Literary Culture, 1649–1689* (Ithaca: Cornell University Press, 1993), pp. 90–91.

46 Samuel Pepys, *The Diary of Samuel Pepys*, ed. by Robert Latham William Matthews, 11 vols. (Berkeley: University of California Press, 1971), vol. 1 (1660), p. 122.

47 John Evelyn, *The Diary of John Evelyn*, ed. by E.S. de Beer, 6 vols. (Oxford: Oxford University Press, 1955), vol. 3 (1650–1672), p. 242.

48 Abraham de Wicquefort, *A Relation in the form of Journal*, transl. by William Lower (London, 1660), p. 73.

49 Knoppers, *Historicizing Milton*, p. 72.

50 Ronald Hutton, qtd. in Thomas Corns, *Regaining Paradise Lost* (London: Longmans, 1994), p. 138.

51 Walter S.H. Lim, *The Arts of Empire: The Poetics of Colonialism from Raleigh to Milton* (Newark: University of Delaware Press, 1998), p. 234.

52 Achinstein, 'Drama of Dissent', p. 139.

53 *CPW* (OUP) (2013): VI. 385.

54 Helmers, *Royalist Republic*, p. 238.

55 *CPW* (OUP) (2013): VI. 158.

56 Elizabeth Sauer, 'The Politics of Performance in the Inner Theater: *Samson Agonistes* as a Closet Drama', in *Milton and Heresy*, ed. by Stephen B. Dobranski

and John P. Rumrich (Cambridge: Cambridge University Press, 1998): 199–216 (p. 203).

57 Helmers, *Royalist Republic*, p. 240.

58 Michael Lieb, '"A Thousand Fore-Skins": Circumcision, Violence, and Selfhood in Milton', *Milton Studies*, 38 (2000): 198–219; Feisal G. Mohamed, 'Confronting Religious Violence: Milton's *Samson Agonistes*', *Proceedings of the Modern Language Association of America*, 120.2 (2005): 327–340.

59 Kendrick, p. 7.

60 Gregory, 'The Political Messages of *Samson Agonistes*', p. 193.

61 Hill, *The Experience of Defeat*, p. 314.

62 Kees Wisse, 'Samson in Music', in *Samson: Hero or Fool? The Many Faces of Samson* ed. by E. Eynikel and T. Nicklas (Leiden: Brill, 2014): 161–176 (pp. 167–169).

63 As John Roger has noted in his article, it is the question of divine authority within the play 'that has most consistently provoked Milton's critics', John Rogers, 'The Secret of *Samson Agonistes*', *Milton Studies*, 33 (1997): 111–132 (p. 111).

64 Serjeantson, pp. 616–617.

65 John T. Shawcross, *The Uncertain World of Samson Agonistes* (Cambridge: Cambridge University Press, 2001); John Rogers, 'The Secret of *Samson Agonistes*', pp. 111–112.

66 Regina M. Schwartz, '*Samson Agonistes*: The Force of Justice and the Violence of Idolatry', in *The Oxford Handbook of John Milton*, ed. by Nicholas McDowell and Nigel Smith (Oxford: Oxford University Press, 2011): 633–648 (p. 634).

67 Lieb, *Theological Milton*, p. 186.

68 David Loewenstein, *Representing Revolution in Milton and his Contemporaries: Religion, Politics, and Polemics in Radical Puritanism* (Cambridge: Cambridge University Press, 2001), pp. 269–295.

69 Wittreich, *Interpreting Samson Agonistes, passim.*

70 Loewenstein, *Representing Revolution in Milton*, p. 289.

71 Guilelmus Estius, *Annotationes a Ureae in praecipua ac difficiliora Sacrae Scripturae loca* (Cologne, 1622), p. 169. We know Milton read Martin Bucer from his divorce tracts and Bucer, too, performed a similar reading of Samson in *Psalmorum libri quinque ad Hebraicam veritatem traducti, et . . . enarrati. . . . Commentarii in librum Iudicium, & in Sophoniam Prophetam* (Olewig, 1554); as Serjeantson has shown, the English annotator of Judges makes a similar point in *Westminster Annotations*, sig. Iii4r (on Judg. 14:19), p. 621.

72 Camille Wells Slights, 'A Hero of Conscience: *Samson Agonistes* and Casuistry', *Proceedings of the Modern Language Association of America*, 90 (1975): 395–413 (p. 404).

73 Serjeantson, p. 620.

74 Hugo Grotius, *Commentary on the Law of Prize and Booty*, ed. by Martine van Ittersum (Indiapolis: Library Fund, 2006), p. 84.

75 Warren, *Literature and the Law of Nations*, p. 177.

76 'Since the King or Magistrate holds his authoritie of the people, both originaly and naturally for their good in the first place, and not his own, then may the people as oft as they shall judge it for the best, either choose him or reject him, retaine him or depose him though no Tyrant, meerly by the liberty and right of free born Men, to be govern'd as seems to them best', *CPW* (OUP) (2013): VI. 158–159.

77 N.H. Keeble and Nicholas McDowell, 'Introduction', in *The Complete Works of John Milton: Volume VI, Vernacular Regicide and Republican Writings* (Oxford: Oxford University Press, 2013): 1–125 (p. 12). This is a principle dating back to the Italian states of Northern Italy in the fourteenth century, see Ursula Goldenbaum, 'Sovereignty and Obedience', in *The Oxford Handbook of Philosophy in Early Modern Europe* (Oxford: Oxford University Press, 2011): 500–521 (pp. 501–503).

78 *CPW*: III: 189.
79 *CPW*: III: 257; Martin Dzelzainis, 'Milton's Politics', in *The Cambridge Companion to Milton*, ed. by Dennis Danielson (Cambridge: Cambridge University Press, 1999): 71–83 (pp. 79–81).
80 Keeble and McDowell, p. 38.
81 *CPW* (OUP) (2013): VI. 181.
82 George Buchanan, *De jure regni apud Scotos* (London, 1680), p. 130.
83 *CPW* (OUP) (2013): VI. 159; Dzelzainis, 'Milton and Politics', p. 79.
84 *CPW* (OUP) (2013): VI. 151.
85 Rogers, 'The Secret of *Samson Agonistes*', pp. 111–132; Serjeantson, p. 627.
86 Giovanni Diodati, *Pious and Learned Annotations upon the Holy Bible* (London, 1651), sig. 2B3ᵛ.
87 See for example, Shawcross, *The Uncertain World of 'Samson Agonistes'*, passim; Rogers, 'The Secret of *Samson Agonistes*', pp. 111–132.
88 This is in direct contrast with Marvell's reading of Samson, as shown in the poem 'On Paradise Lost', in which Marvell presents Samson as a human revenger: '(So Samson groped the temple's posts in spite)/ The world o'erwhelming to revenge his sight', ll. 9–10.
89 Joost van den Vondel, 'Preface', to *Samson, of Heilige Wraak*; Philip Connell, *Secular Chains: Poetry and the Politics of Religion from Milton to Pope* (Oxford: Oxford University Press, 2016), p. 91.
90 Stella Revard, *The War in Heaven: Paradise Lost and the Tradition of Satan's Rebellion* (Ithaca: Cornell University Press, 1980); James Freeman, *Milton and the Martial Muse: Paradise Lost and European Traditions of War* (Princeton: Princeton University Press, 1980); Elizabeth Oldman, 'Milton, Grotius, and the Law of War', *Studies in Philology*, 104.3 (2007): 340–375 (pp. 341–342); Hill, *The Experience of Defeat*, p. 314.
91 Oldman, p. 366.
92 Knoppers, 'England's Case', p. 587.

7   The Anglo-Dutch Wars, Empire, and Anxiety

Sir William Temple (1628–1699), ambassador to the United Provinces during the Second Anglo-Dutch War, described like a true Dutchophile in his *Observations upon the United Provinces of the Netherlands* the miraculous rise of that small republic of such uncertain beginnings:[1]

> Having lately seen the State of the *United Provinces*, after a prodigious growth in Riches, Beauty, extent of Commerce, and number of Inhabitants, arrived at length to such a height (by the strength of their Navies, their fortified Towns and standing-Forces, with a constant Revenue, proportion'd to the support of all this Greatness,) As made them the Envy of some, the Fear of others, and the Wonder of all their Neighbours.

Besides emphasising his own role in this account, he illustrated the culture he encountered in the Low Countries with colourful (sometimes near-fictional) anecdotes. Such admiration stood in contrast to those who accused the Dutch Republic of not showing enough gratitude to the English nation that helped them defeat the Spanish, or saw them as dangerous and feared trading rivals. Those same anxieties spawned the fantastical pamphlet images of Chapter 1. It is significant, however, that Temple's description explicitly links commercial success to the fortification and martial strength of the country; this is not just a celebration of mercantile ingenuity. It logically follows that a striving, forceful state will be the envy or enemy of its rivals and neighbours. No doubt Temple had thoughts of his audience at home in this quotation, for whom displays of Dutch strength would naturally lead to comparison and self-evaluation. Diplomacy and travel frequently allowed such 'a series of reflections on one's own identity and culture' as much as reacting to the foreign lands encountered.[2] Both Milton and Marvell travelled through Europe during their tours, and similarly to Temple, they were able to compare and contrast what it meant to be English, European, or 'the Other'. It is a trend visible in many travelogues from the period.[3] Through travel and trade, we also come to understand that Anglo-Dutch relations moved beyond the borders of Europe to the Far East and West, reflecting the increasing geographical awareness of early modern culture.[4]

Milton's and Marvell's works, too, travel over the globe – not only in translations of their works, as the recent *Milton in Translation* abundantly shows; their poetry and prose takes the reader on sometimes vast journeys.[5] Milton's *Paradise Lost* brings us frequently 'to fresh woods, pastures new' ('Lycidas', l. 193), and Marvell's 'Bermudas' (1653–1654) 'reveal[s] a deep-seated cartographic awareness'.[6] As Milton wrote in the Preface to *Brief History of Moscovia*, the 'study of Geography is both profitable and delightful'.[7]

In the previous chapter, we surveyed the ultimately diverging ambitions and motifs of a Dutch and English author, writing within the same narrative framework in a shared literary culture; Vondel's avenging Samson is a strikingly different man to Milton's tragic character. With the adaptations of Samson, we already entered the Restoration period. This chapter continues the chronological push into the later stages of Milton's and Marvell's lives. Having treated Marvell's *Character of Holland* in Chapter 1, coincident with the First Anglo-Dutch War, we can now turn the spotlight onto his *Painter Poems*, against the backdrop of the Second and Third wars. The remainder of the chapter follows Satan's journey in *Paradise Lost* as a merchant, connecting it with the politics and cultural anxiety of Anglo-Dutch relations in a seventeenth-century of ever-growing empires.

The *Advice-to-a-Painter* Poems

In 1665, Edmund Waller's poem *Instructions to a Painter* was published, praising the achievements of the Duke of York in the battle against the Dutch at Lowestoft in June 1665. Waller (1606–1687) had sat as Member of Parliament for several different constituencies, and at the time of his *Instructions* was MP for Hastings.[8] The poem follows the panegyric tradition of the early 1660s, through which the restored monarchy was so often praised (such as Dryden's *Astræa Redux* (1660) and *Annus Mirabilis*, the latter also celebrating English successes in 1666). Waller modelled his poem on Giovanni Francesco Busenello's 'Prospettiva del nauale ripotato dall Republica Serenissima contra il Turco' (1656) addressed to the painter Pietro Liberi, which gave English satirists a new and very suitable literary device: *Ut pictura poesis*, in which ironic directions were given to the painter.[9] Within this dialogue the poet could indirectly criticise what occurred on the canvas, though Waller rather reversed the political polarities of the original.[10] Busenello's poem describes the defeat at sea of the Turks by the Republic of Venice.[11] *Instructions to a Painter* instead praises the English monarchy in its battle with the Dutch Republic. Nonetheless, the association of England with the maritime power of Venice could be harnessed successfully. During the Restoration, many poems, including Waller's and Dryden's, connected maritime power to royalty: the maritime supremacy of Venice became that of England. In these English adaptions, Charles learns navigational tactics, which can only lead to a 'natural' domination of the seas and an increase in trade and wealth.

In the seminal *The Poetry of Limitation: A Study of Edmund Waller*, Chernaik writes that '[p]anegyric and satire, the poetry of praise and the poetry of blame, are sister forms. [. . .] The boundary between them is not absolute'.[12] Noelle Gallagher has also insightfully shown this in her article on the panegyric and the satire as '"partial" varieties of historical writing'.[13] The series of poems with their advice to a painter shows this extremely well. Waller's first advice invited a number of satirical and critical responses, of which Marvell's *Second Advice to a Painter* (April 1666) was one of the first.[14] Mary Tom Osborne has identified a staggering 32 painter poems between the Restoration and the Glorious Revolution.[15] It can therefore be regarded a significantly popular genre, quickly taken up to remark, often anonymously, on contemporary political events. It is not surprising then that the authorship of the *Advice-to-a-Painter Poems* has been problematic since their composing. The *Second* (April, 1666) and *Third Advice* (Late-1666–1667) and *Last Instructions* (September, 1667) are now generally attributed to Marvell, despite fluctuations in their verse and form quality.[16] Perhaps there were several authors responsible per advice, of which Marvell was one. Readers at the time, such as Roger L'Estrange, nevertheless, spotted similarities in style between the *Rehearsal Transpros'd* (and the *Second Part*) and the *Second* and *Third Advice*.[17] The *Fourth* and *Fifth Advice* are still regarded unattributable by all editors, similarly *Further Advice*.

Marvell's Painter Poems were initiated by the Second Anglo-Dutch War, a conflict that greatly contrasted with its predecessor. Trading disagreements were again part of the dispute, but ideologies between the two nations were now also radically different. The First was fought between two Protestant republics, both expanding their trading empire, fuelling commercial rivalry and ultimately hostility. Politically and ideologically the states had never resembled each other so closely before, nor would they again in the seventeenth century.[18] Lieuwe van Aitzema wrote in his diary of his homeland: '*Dat dese landen haer mochten spiegelen [. . .] aen de nabuyrighe in Englandt* (that these lands could mirror [. . .] their neighbours in England).[19] Such reflective sentiment was much less prominent during the later wars. The Second War pitted a relatively unstable, recently restored monarchy against a surprisingly successful republic; in the mid-1660s, there was uncertainty about the best way of governing the English state, and the Dutch War was presented by Charles as 'necessary to the country's economic survival'.[20] The fact that both were Protestant countries did not avert warfare, despite the common narrative of Protestant brotherhood, usually a defensive formation against Catholic powers: 'For others' sport, two nations fight a prize:/ Between them both religion wounded dies' (*Third Advice*, ll. 425–426). After the First Anglo-Dutch War, during the Commonwealth and earlier part of the Restoration, the English fleet – source and signal of English power – was expanded exponentially.[21] Similar increase was granted the Dutch navy over the same time-span, making the Second Anglo-Dutch War the 'hardest-fought battle of the three'.[22] The outcomes were also very different. The First was won by the English, the Second by the Dutch. This bitter reversal heavily influenced the atmosphere in England.

Charles II's pragmatic and opportunistic approach to European politics had done little to improve England's international relations.[23] In the 1660s, the United Provinces reached what was arguably the zenith of its republicanism, under the leadership of Johan de Witt.[24] He was adamantly against any restoration of the Prince van Oranje as stadtholder – who was also the nephew of the English king – pushing relations between the nations even further apart.[25] As ever, it would be difficult to separate the political from the personal, economic, ideological or expedient in characterising how the countries related to each other, and simple opposition would be reductive. Marvell, typically highly informed about the Dutch political situation, recognised the complexity of Anglo-Dutch relations in the mid-1660s in the *Advices*, peppering them with topical bite – as shown in these lines from the *Second Advice*:

> Or if as just, Orange to reinstate:
> Instead of that he is regenerate.
> And with four millions vainly giv'n, as spent;
> And with five millions more of detriment;
> Our sum amounts yet only to have won
> A bastard Orange, for pimp Arlington.
>
> (ll. 329–334)

There is sympathy for neither the Dutch republicans nor the Orangists in these lines.

The greatest difference between the First and Second Anglo-Dutch Wars for Marvell personally was his own involvement in the war administration during the latter. In 1659, he became Member of Parliament for Hull. As Edward Holberton has shown, the city was greatly affected by the Second War, being an important port. The navy were heavily involved with local politics, since they were assisted by Trinity House, an organisation established to support seamen (irrespective of nationality, including the Netherlands); it also had jurisdiction over laws concerning the sea.[26] Marvell had plentiful first-hand experience of the War's influence on England through his service, not least that during 1666 and 1667 Hull's trade came to a near standstill.[27] Before that, in 1665, Marvell was appointed to a committee that would manage goods taken from the Dutch and inquire into claims of embezzlement. Later, in 1667, Marvell became a member of another parliamentary committee, this time occupied with investigating some of England's failures, especially the disaster that was Chatham. Edmund Waller was a fellow member of the committee.[28] Furthermore, Marvell's personal acquaintances included men involved in the maritime trade and with connections to Hull Trinity House, such as his nephew William Popple.[29] Marvell's political background and personal involvement with the war found expression in the Painter Poems, mingling specific frustrations and pre-occupations with wider judgements about the enterprise. *The Character of Holland* can be read as a self-promoting riff on popular stereotypes, whereas the Painter Poems perform a personal critique of the war policy of England, or, as Warren Chernaik has argued, a direct critique of Charles II.[30]

As noted earlier, the Painter Poems celebrated the maritime prowess of England (often through comparison with Venice), and has many references to geography and navigational skills. This aspect of the panegyric Painter Poems was continuously played up and satirised by Marvell. In his *Last Instructions* he mocks, for example, Baptist May and Henry Bennet, First Earl of Arlington's capital mistake of confusing Canvey Island with Crete, as the science of 'Modern Geographers' (l. 401). In his *Second Advice to a Painter*, the scale decreases rapidly from addressing a fleet, to a ship, to one man – overturning Waller's ever-expanding geographical stage, as noted by Gallagher.[31] The English fleet is here not quite ready to explore the globe, while Marvell's narrator zooms in on the individual (the microscope is mentioned in *Last Instructions*, l. 16). Moreover, Neptune often sides with England in the panegyric poems, recalling Merchamont Nedham's translation of Selden's *Mare clausum*, discussed in Chapter 1.[32] Waller's poetry fixates on English ownership and mastery of the seas, which the poem 'Of a War with Spain, and a Fight at Sea' illustrates quite straightforwardly, in the somewhat clunky lines: 'Others may use the ocean as their road,/ Only the English make it their abode' (ll. 25–26).[33] Dryden mentions in his Preface to *Annus Mirabilis* that 'Providence has cast upon [Charles] a want of Trade, that you might appear bountiful to your Country's necessities', and in the poem itself, there is a reference to a 'British Neptune' (l. 733). Marvell, too, refers to the king as an 'Imperial Prince' in the *Second Advice* (l. 345), though this turns out to be a much less straightforward epithet than one might expect within the panegyric tradition.

As David Armitage has shown, ownership of the seas remained a hot topic throughout the seventeenth century, and the Anglo-Dutch Wars only fanned the flames.[34] In *Last Instructions*, Marvell presents a Neptune who once invested the English nation with his empire, as in *Mare clausum*, but whose trust now seems misplaced, and lost:

> When agèd Thames was bound with fetters base,
> And Medway chaste ravished before his face,
> And their dear offspring murdered in their sight,
> Thou and thy fellows held'st the odious light.
> Sad change since first that happy pair was wed,
> When all the rivers graced their nuptial bed,
> And Father Neptune promised to resign
> His empire old to their immortal line!
>
> (ll. 743–750)

This marriage of the Thames and Medway, and its violation by the Dutch, strikes an entirely different tone to the stately betrothal of the Amstel and Thames described by Vondel, discussed in Chapter 3. Gone are decorum, prosperity, and hope. And yet, the efficacy of allegorising national politics through rivers remains, as does the capacity for mirroring relations with neighbouring countries, as Van Aitzema proved. The trope of personified rivers flowed abundantly in Drayton's *Poly Olbion*, for example, but was also used in diverse literary forms later in the seventeenth century. In Thomas D'Urfey's opera *Cinthia and Endimonion* (1695), rebellious Thames is chided for not worshipping Cinthia, and compared to the national and pious rivers of Tamar, Sabrin [Severn], and Ooze [Ouse], and internationally, the Ganges and the Tiber.[35] Marvell's poems reverse the trope of presenting the English nation as a maritime empire, owner of the seas, enjoying unceasing increase of national wealth. Instead private (often corrupt) gain holds the spotlight, interrogated through 'a complicated scheme of approval and disapproval'.[36] Marvell's inside knowledge of the failures and successes of the War leads to very precise references to events and individuals, where neither the Dutch nor the English are praised. Rivers may work as mirrors, but like the weather, politics can discompose the surface, creating fractured or disturbing images; in the play between the true and the distorted, Marvell can criticise failure and hypocrisy, while inviting a hubristic nation to take a good look at itself.

As might be expected, neither calls for self-reflection nor hydrological imagery were confined to English shores. In Constantijn Huygens' poetry of the 1660s, the sea similarly operates as a call to introspection. Roughly contemporary to the Painter Poems, his long poem, 'Zee-straet' (Sea-road, 1665), commemorates the paved road from The Hague to the sea that he designed. It is not a directly political poem in the way Marvell's Painter Poems are. His design for the road is the central concern, and his 1000-line poem describes the process of construction. However, in sections of the poem the implacable sea comes to the fore, functioning as a mirror to humanity's transience. Huygens invites youth from The Hague to travel down the new road to the sea-front, where the endless movement of the tides remind Huygens that denominations, countries, and wars are temporary – all while a war was being fought in that same patch of sea:

> *In all het Wereltsche gaet even sulcken Vloed,*
> *En sulcken Ebb te rugg: siet Menschen, Huysen, Staten*
> *En Koninghrijcken aen; daer is geen toeverlaten*
> *Op evenstandigheit; die schael moet op en neer.*
> *[. . .]*
> *De Rijcken waggelen, de Konincklicke Steden,*
> *En die men gisteren sagh staen, waer zijn sy heden?*
> (ll. 578–581, 587–588)

> In the world, each same flood flows,
> And each Ebb returns: see Man, Genealogy, State
> And Kingdoms; there is no depending
> On a stable balance; the scales rise and fall.
> [. . .]
> The rich stumble, those royal Cities,
> One once saw standing, where are they now?

The war is not mentioned directly in the poem, which is curious, as some of its maritime engagements could likely be seen from the dunes of Scheveningen. The narrator instead presents himself as an old man, reminiscing about his travels abroad, the different countries he has seen, and how the relentless flow of time spares none, in the end. That the war is not mentioned, yet the futility of argument and human ambition is constantly emphasised, seems to linger on, or hope for, the temporality of the Second Anglo-Dutch War; whatever victories or glories it may claim, from the narrators' perspective its achievements were fleeting, its passing inevitable.

At no point does Huygens, or Marvell for that matter, position the sea as the site of panegyric praise-singing. This becomes abundantly clear if set against Dryden's rhapsodic *Annus Mirabilis*, where war is tinted with classical glory, the inevitable lot of a proud, watchful nation:

> Thus mighty in her Ships, stood *Carthage* long,
>   And swept the riches of the world from far;
> Yet stoop'd to *Rome*, less wealthy, but more strong:
>   And this may prove our second Punick War.
>
> What peace can be where both to one pretend?
>   (But they more diligent, and we more strong)
> Or if a peace, it soon must have an end
>   For they would grow too pow'rful were it long.
>   (ll. 17–24)

Zwicker even proposes that Dryden's *Annus Mirabilis* was composed as a counter-response to the critiques in the *Second Advice* in order to divert damaging attention away from James Stuart, Duke of York and Anne Hyde, Duchess of York (and perhaps also composed with an eye on the position of Poet Laureate).[37] In Dryden's paean, the fleet swells to such an enormity that the surface of the sea is as good as obscured, defeating any attempt to gaze into its waters and reflect. Whatever Dryden's exact motivation, his writing forms part of an extended net of lyrical exchange, containing conspicuously detailed notice of individual and particular events. This may be explained by the readership of the material, certainly on the English side of the channel. Harold Love and Nigel Smith have argued that the Painter Poems were written for Members of Parliaments and other governmental officials.[38] The parallels between the official parliamentary enquiry into the miscarriages of the War during the 1667–1668 session and Marvell's *Last Instructions* would support the supposition of a parliamentary readership.[39] The detailing of the Painter Poems, on which the satire is built, assumes the reader is highly informed about the individual performances of the people mentioned and the complex war administration. The English nobility are satirised both generally and specifically, such as in the scene in the *Second Advice* that describes Edward Montagu, Duke of Sandwich looting a Dutch ship filled with commodities from the East Indies, which he distributed amongst his own generals rather than handing it over to the Crown (ll. 295–306). Individual Dutch admirals are depicted, sometimes relying on common satires on the Dutch, such as the ridiculing of Jacob van Wassenaer, Lord Opdam in the line: 'Then, in kind visit unto Opdam's gout' (II. l. 45). The connection between the Dutch and gout – associated in turn with gluttonous indulgence – was already well-established, such as in *Bellum Belgium Secundum, Or, A poem, Attempting something on his majesties proceedings against the Dutch* (1665).[40] At the same time, there is approval for some (English) individuals, such as in the *Second Advice*, where Captain Jeremy Smith receives praise for his prevention of an attack on the Duke of York: 'Smith took the giant, and is since made knight' (ll. 214). This seemingly arbitrary patterning of praise and contempt only makes sense given an understanding of the complex English politics behind the poems; in this case, Smith is praised as a naval war veteran, an experienced seaman; he is a stout foil against the court-appointed sailor with no experience, often blinded by self-promotion and profit. The result is a deliberately ambiguous and irregular depiction of the war as a whole, and of the two parties involved. Not even mighty Neptune can decide upon a preferred outcome: 'Draw pensive Neptune, biting of his thumbs,/ To think himself a slave whos'e'er o'ercomes (*Second Advice*, ll. 157–158).

One constant in the Painter Poems is that they undermine the delusion of war with the Dutch as a heroic enterprise. In the *Second Advice* the battle of courageous Hercules with the Hydra in *The Character* is replaced with noisome, morally undifferentiated bedlam:

> They stab their ships with one another's guns;
> They fight so near it seems to be on ground,
> And ev'n the bullets meeting, bullets wound.
> The noise, the smoke, the sweat, the fire, the blood,
> Are not to be expressed nor understood.
>
> (ll. 204–208)

The Advices became more pointedly satirical as the war progresses – and as Marvell became more deeply involved with the administration. *Last Instructions* presents an England defeated after the raid on the Medway, a decisive point in the conflict, when the fleet was burned and its two prime ships stolen.⁴¹ Marvell loads the retelling with images of rape and shame, changing the image of England as a nation:

> Ruyter the while, that had our ocean curbed,
> Sailed now among our rivers undisturbed,
> Surveyed their crystal streams and banks so green
> And beauties ere this never naked seen.
> Through the vain sedge, the bashful nymphs he eyed:
> Bosoms, and all which from themselves they hide.
> The sun much brighter, and the skies more clear,
> He finds the air and all things sweeter here.
> The sudden change, and such a tempting sight
> Swells his old veins with fresh blood, fresh delight.
> Like am'rous victors he begins to shave,
> And his new face looks in the English wave.
> His sporting navy all about him swim
> And witness their complacence in their trim.
> Their streaming silks play through the weather fair
> And with inveigling colours court the air,
> While the red flags breathe on their topmasts high
> Terror and war, but want an enemy.
>
> (ll. 523–540)

Michiel de Ruyter (1607–1676) sails up the English rivers, looking at their clarity, and while he looks into the English waves, it is not the English looking back but his own crew. In Waller's poem, the Dutch look into the 'raging sea' but there the 'Prince's look appears' (ll. 205–208).⁴² The changed mood from heroic to pastoral in Marvell's scene does not present gallant love, but reinforces the horror of the raid within a tranquil environment: the contrast makes the admiral seem grossly out of place.⁴³ The appearance of Admiral de Ruyter changes when he looks into the sea as into a mirror – the potential violent events at sea form his reflection.⁴⁴ As George deF Lord argues, 'the pictures that [Restoration satires] paint are always, to some extent, distorted. The mirror they hold up to flawed human nature is often flawed itself'.⁴⁵ A literal reflection in the poem (De Ruyter's) can at the same time be a different reflection for the reader, who sees in the Dutch success English failings. Marvell emphasises De Ruyter's untroubled progress, made possible by corruption within the English admiralty, and especially the courtly officers, which led to the disaster at Chatham.⁴⁶ In the *Second* and *Third Advice*, as well as *Last Instructions*, it is personal gain placed over public good that is condemned, and the people responsible for this kind of behaviour, such as Edward Hyde, Earl of Clarendon, are presented as greed personified.⁴⁷

The same events received a noble appraisal of the court in *Annus Mirabilis*:⁴⁸

> He, first, survey'd the charge with careful eyes,
> Which none but mighty Monarchs could maintain;

Yet judg'd, like vapours that from Limbecks rise,
  It would in richer showers descend again.
                                (ll. 49–52)

The praise of the monarch in this quotation – his careful examination of the war – stands in stark contrast to Marvell's address to the king at the end of each *Painter Poem*. Marvell opines on the war policy, administration, and the conflict's futility but remains equivocal about his sympathies. In *The Last Instructions*, his advice becomes more outspoken, hoping that king and country can be restored to peaceful cooperation: '(But Ceres corn, and Flora is the spring,/ Bacchus is Wine, the Country is the King)' (ll. 973–74).[49] The clear-cut opposition of the Dutch as the enemy, and the English as Neptune's empire has been muddied; instead, blurred images of sea battles predominate, emphasising the inglorious consequences of war.

Milton, Marvell and Empire

In this last sketch of Anglo-Dutch relations, the rivalry that Marvell and Milton witnessed is taken beyond European territory to the Far East. Neptune's contested empire extended its tendrils through naval supremacy, dominion over the trade of exotic goods, and the foundations of early colonial power. Despite their supposed marginality to core national narratives – a key tenet of imperial self-representation – these territories supplied, paralleled, and sometimes contradicted their European centres' self-image.[50] At the time of the Second Anglo-Dutch War, for example, the English (alongside the Kingdom of Makassar) were also fighting the Dutch in Eastern Indonesia.[51] Dryden's *Annus Mirabilis* opens with a description of the Dutch trade in the East, revealing an English desire for superiority, and the conviction that England *should* be the centre of the world:[52]

Trade, which like bloud should circularly flow,
  Stop'd in their Channels, found its freedom lost:
Thither the wealth of all the world did go,
  And seem'd but shipwrack'd on so base a Coast.

For them alone the Heav'ns had kindly heat,
  In Eastern Quarries ripening precious Dew:
For them the *Indumæan* Balm did sweat,
  And in hot *Ceilon* Spicy Forrests grew.

The Sun but seem'd the lab'rer of their Year;
  Each wexing Moon suppli'd her watry store,
To swell those Tides, which from the Line did bear
  Their brim-full Vessels to the *Belg'an* shore.
                                (ll. 5–16)

The struggle for imperial dominance in the East thus played an important role in the Anglo-Dutch Wars, both stoking the rivalry and paying for its machinery. Marvell briefly hints at exotic trade and colonial ambitions in his Painter Poems. As mentioned, the Duke of Sandwich divides up captured Dutch cargo from the East Indies among his officers in the *Second Advice*: 'Two Indian ships, pregnant with eastern pearl/ And diamonds, sate the officers and Earl' (ll. 305–306). Moreover, *Last Instructions* acknowledges that the loss of Chatham's harbour also hit English global trade:

> The houses were demolished near the Tower.
> Those ships that yearly from their teeming howl
> Unloaded here the birth of either pole -
> Furs from the north and silver from the west,
> Wines from the south, and spices from the east;
> From Gambo gold, and from the Ganges gems -
> Take a short voyage underneath the Thames:
> Once a deep river, now with timber floored,
> And shrunk, lest navigable, to a ford.
>
> (ll. 714–722)

The Thames, England's fighting spirit, is so diminished that it no longer carries the spoils of the world to the city. The circulation of blood as a metaphor for trade was still a fresh image then, and enables the imperial power to connect its trading profits not with endeavour and partnerships with others, but with a natural necessity for its own survival. Dryden's claim that the Dutch were clogging channels is not just rivalry: they were wickedly harming the English. Marvell's stretching of the influx of goods to every corner of the world – though less grasping – still connects national well-being with international trade. The following discussion covers the inevitable imagological accompaniment to the growth of global trade. Specifically, the much fought-over spice trade, on which great fortunes were built, is connected to Anglo-Dutch relations and their mutual representation.[53]

Spice Trade

Food is political. What we prepare, share, eat, and trade provides a strong signal – often self-consciously – of social identity. The notion of a 'national cuisine' has innumerable associated images, both reflected inward and imposed from outside. It is, however, a developing rather than fixed identity, connected to commerce, politics, class, and production.[54] The early modern period illustrates the intertwined impact of these factors, as ever more varied comestibles reached European markets in the rush towards globalised trade networks. For maritime nations such as Portugal, England

and the United Provinces, these commercial webs – especially the lucrative spice trade – became not only a means of profitable enterprise, but essential to the whole economy. Consequently, what was imported, bought, and eaten, transcended novelty or exotic luxury; it defined aspects of national identity, with links to taxation, foreign policy, migration, and fiscal planning. By extension, national ideology and the sense of the nation's place in the world became bound up with the spice trade, as did that of trading partners and rivals.[55]

As early as the fifteenth century, capitalism and European colonial expansion changed the diets of Europeans.[56] The medieval tradition of food as 'symbols of material comfort and social prominence' was replaced by signifiers of much more: economics, politics, sociability and, even more important, national identity.[57] Travellers visiting European countries brought back new cuisines to England, or gossiped about the strange behaviours they had seen. Those in England unable to travel could, after about 1600, find recipe books with dishes attributed to specific countries: a satirical cookbook published in 1664, claiming to be by the late Cromwell's wife, Joan, has a recipe for boiling pigeons the 'Dutch way'.[58] Throughout the late sixteenth and seventeenth centuries, books and pamphlets were published that reveal the apparently incidental political dimensions to the internationalisation of the English diet. Gervase Markham's *Countrey Contentments or The English Huswife* (1623) warns readers against indulging in foreign food. Likewise, Robert Herrick's celebration of a simpler existence in his poem 'The Country Life' rejects the use of foreign spice:

> Thou never plough'st the ocean's foam
> To seek and bring rough pepper home;
> Nor to the Eastern Ind dost rove
> To bring from thence the scorched clove;
> Nor, with the loss of thy lov'd rest,
> Bring'st home the ingot from the West.
>
> (ll. 5–10)

Clearly the influx of foreign flavours and ingredients would have to have been well established for such warnings to be felt necessary, and this was felt nowhere more necessary than in the lucrative trade in spices. Even after the so-called Glorious Revolution, John Houghton attacked the Dutch domination of clove imports, counselling his readers to rather support "English" commodities such as cardamom and grains of paradise.[59] Milton and Marvell were writing in this time of rapid change and would have been well aware of contemporary dialogues on foreign foodstuff and their place in the wider network of politics and commerce. The politics of spice accordingly form an appropriate final stop in this book's journey – specifically as their traces can be found in *Paradise Lost* and some individual poems by Marvell – with reference to the Massacre of Amboyna.

Generally speaking, there were two types of imported spice in England during the seventeenth century: those from the New World (vanilla and chilli) and those from the East (cinnamon, cloves, etcetera). The spices from America were relatively new, whereas those from the East had already been mentioned in works as early as 1400.[60] For comparison, a search on *Early English Books Online* reveals that vanilla is mentioned 5 times in 2 records, while cloves appear 10827 times in 1095 records.[61] Some Eastern spices, such as cinnamon, also featured in the Bible and therefore carried religious connotations. The symbolic and cultural possibilities of spice were multifarious – one only has to think of Joseph who was taken to Egypt by a spice caravan transporting aromatic gum, balm, and myrrh, each associated with kingship (Genesis 37:25). Eastern spices had a wealth of associations, uses, and prejudices that had not yet developed around spices from the Americas.[62] One of the most significant was the connection between spice and Paradise.[63] It was widely thought in medieval times that Paradise was physically located on Earth, in the Far East near India, yet still inaccessible; the literalness of this conception is visible on the Mappa Mundi of Hereford, which places Paradise near India.[64] While the early modern view of the world had broadened considerably since the 1300s, it is important not to imagine that the world was yet tamed by cartographers; much was still unknown – and equally much still possible.

It appears that Marvell plays with this belief in an earthly Paradise in his poem 'Bermudas', in which the coloniser does not sail East, but West, presenting a 'quest for a colonial Eden as misguided'.[65] The references in the poem suggest that on this new world the oldest habitat of all can be found, Eden, with an 'eternal spring/ Which here enamels ev'rything' (ll. 13–14).[66] The remoteness of the Island, both in location and nature itself, is constantly emphasised, not necessarily to make it unreachable, but merely to show the vastness of the globe.[67] This echoes other accounts of Bermuda, such as Edmund Waller's 'The Battle of the Summer Islands' (1645) that presents an ideal garden – in this case not an Eden, but 'Th'Hesperian Garden' – filled with crude inhabitants.[68] It is, however, difficult to read Marvell's account of the landscape as anything other than satirical when aware of the excesses of other contemporary accounts of Bermuda, such as John Smith's *Generall Historie of Virginia* (1624) and William Strachey's *A True Reportory of the Wreck and Redemption of Sir Thomas Gates, Knight, upon and from the Islands of the Bermudas* (1609), which both present a caricature post-lapsarian island, with tempests, vermin, poor soil and gloomy winters.[69]

Of course, the English were not alone in exploring the globe, nor Marvell in yoking the thrill of new-found lands to literary aims. Luís Vaz de Camões' (c. 1524/5–1580) epic Portuguese poem *The Luciads* (1572) describes Vasco da Gama's (c. 1460–1524) travel to the East, including the exploration of the very valuable Spice Islands. Whether Milton had read Luis de Camões' (c.

1524–1580) poem before writing *Paradise Lost* is unknown, but Satan's flight has often been compared to Da Gama's voyage.[70] There are, indeed, several similarities, including in the descriptions of the hazardous journey and the Spice Islands. However, by the time Milton was composing his epic, the spice monopoly of the Portuguese had been taken over by the English and the Dutch. They were greatly assisted by a single book: Jan Huygen van Linschoten's, *Itinerario: Voyage ofte Schipvaert van Jan Huygen van Linschoten near Oost ofte portugaels Indien* (1596), translated into English as *John Huighen van Linschoten: his discourse into ye Easte and West Indies: devided into foure books* (1598). This text describes the vulnerabilities of the Portuguese in the East through several maps, commercial manuals, and suggestions for navigation.[71] Not long after, the spice trade was in the hands of the English and the Dutch: pushing Anglo-Dutch relations and tensions beyond the boundaries of Europe into the Far East.

Milton's Spiced Satan

Unlike some of the more common devilish representations of the Dutch, Milton's image draws in a whole range of senses. Rather than relying on horns and tails and wild debauchery, his Satan reveals his cross-channel affiliations through markers of smell and taste, which I will explore in more detail later. In tandem with this broader range of qualities, Milton's text incorporates details and themes that are by their nature transnational. The full richness of Satan's ventures only becomes available through a contextualised reading that notes the politics that shadow them, as well as resonances with Milton's other writing.

There is a thread of suspicion running through many of Milton's works, connecting spicy odours with bodily or moral corruption. Indulgence in 'pompous delicacies' is one of the temptations presented to the Son in *Paradise Regained* (1671), Satan's serving up spiced foods, emblematic of over-reaching and vain greed. In *Samson Agonistes* (1671), in an even closer personification, Delila becomes the very vessel that carries spices around the world, a merchant ship plying the waves:[72]

> Comes this way sailing
> Like a stately ship
> Of Tarsus, bound for th'isles
> Of Javan or Gadire
> With all her bravery on, and tackle trim,
> Sails filled, and streamers waving,
> Courted by all the winds that hold them play,
> An amber scent of odorous perfume
> Her harbinger, a damsel train behind;
> (ll. 713–721)

Nowhere, perhaps, does the global trade in spices achieve such direct relevance as in *Paradise Lost*, however. From Satan's very entry into this world, as he prepares for his journey to earth, he is clothed in the language and associations of a spice merchant:

> As when far off at sea a fleet descried
> Hangs in the clouds, by equinoctial winds
> Close sailing from Bengala, or the isles
> Of Ternate and Tidore, whence merchants bring
> Their spicy drugs: they on the trading flood
> Through the wide Ethiopian to the Cape
> Ply stemming nightly towards the pole. So seemed
> Far off the flying fiend:
>
> (II. 636–643)

The sea-voyage character of Satan's crossing of Chaos towards Eden is one of 'dark/ Illimitable Ocean without bound' (II. 891–92), as previously noted by Su Fang Ng.[73] Following the path of the locations quoted previously additionally takes the reader from east to west, mimicking the arrival of spices into Christian Europe. This impression of a network of traders is further enforced in Book 4 (ll. 157–165) when the reverse journey is narrated.

The Moluccas, or Spice Islands, are a natural reference in this description, and Milton's identification of two of them – Ternate and Tidore – ties Satan's route to that taken by merchant ships bound for Africa, and thence Europe. The Dutch monopoly on clove production was centred on these islands, with tight controls maintained on other sites in order to maintain scarcity value. This included destroying rival nations' operations and charging heavy tariffs on others making use of associated harbours or goods, allowing the Dutch to maintain supremacy throughout the seventeenth century.[74] The monopoly had been established by expelling the previously dominant Portuguese (1604) and Spanish (1609), with the takeover justified by a convenient narrative of gratitude: for delivering them from the brutal Iberians, the inhabitants of the Moluccas were apparently moved to offer the Dutch all their cloves at a very reasonable price.[75]

Less straightforward but equally revealing is Milton's listing of Bengala (Bengal) in the itinerary. From the 1630s onwards the Bay of Bengal was a successful trading hub for the Dutch, this time with an emphasis on textiles.[76] The majority of the silk imports to the Dutch Republic arrived from the Bay by the late 1640s.[77] Commodity trades are rarely a simple direct exchange, however, instead functioning as inter-linked operations. The spice trade depended in its turn on textiles from Bengal being taken to the Moluccas; Hendrik Brouwer, a future governor-general of the East Indies had in 1621 called the Coromandel Coast, of which Bengal is part, the 'left arm of the Moluccas and the surrounding islands because without textiles that come from there [...] the trade in the Moluccas will be dead'.[78] Milton's description therefore picks out not only a route of travel or a particular commodity, but reveals a complex intercontinental system – indicating considerable understanding of the processes and dependencies regulating trade. It is accordingly the merchants undertaking trading journeys – not the inhabitants of each place – that provide the associations with Satan in Milton's description. Even when not on the move, Satan is characterised as a flamboyant, wealthy merchant showing off his exotic gains, when he decorates Pandemonium with 'sparkling, orient gems' (III. 507).[79]

This same merchant network controlled the journeys of Wouter Schouten (1638–1704), introduced in Chapter 4. As a surgeon with the VOC (Verenigde Oost-Indische Companie, or United East-Indian Company) he followed the various stations of the trade routes, including the spice islands of Ternate, Tidore, and Ambon, keeping journals and composing poems about what he saw.[80] Memorable sights included bountiful clove groves and the abundance of fabrics being sold in the Bengal markets:

> *De winckelen vol schooner stof*
> *Van al wat Asija kon geven.*
> *Tapitserijen schoon geweven,*
> *Sij, pelang, en lijwaten fijn en grof'*
> (ll. 37–40)

The markets full with the finest fabric
Of all that Asia could give,
Tapestries beautifully woven,
Silk, damask, and linen, fine and coarse.[81]

At every harbour, other VOC ships, their crews, suppliers and traders were encountered, ferrying goods between points along the great mercantile chain. From Schouten's vivid, albeit subjective, descriptions we get a sense of well-established and flourishing Dutch trading dominance.

Within Milton's poem lies a palpable unease with colonialisation in the East, which can be read as a general anxiety about the corrupting nature of trading expansion and competition.[82] There are also specific references to African locations associated with Portuguese voyages (ll. 399–401). It is not, therefore, my claim that Satan can only or fully be understood as an anti-Dutch caricature. It remains evident nonetheless that the prominence of Anglo-Dutch relations in the East – and Dutch success – influenced the poem. Many places mentioned in the East Indies were solely in Dutch hands, and Satan's extended voyage was essentially following a Dutch trade route. Furthermore, the anti-Dutch sentiments locate Milton within an existing body of English writing, not least Dryden's *Annus Mirabilis* (1666). Though stopping well short of Dryden's propaganda, there are connections between his selection of details and the sense of a natural order disrupted by Dutch impertinence in *Annus Mirabilis*:

> Already we have conquer'd half the War,
>   And the less dang'rous part is left behind:
> Our trouble now is but to make them dare,
>   And not so great to vanquish as to find.
>
> Thus to the Eastern wealth through storms we go;
>   But now, the Cape once doubled, fear no more:
> A constant Trade-wind will securely blow,
>   And gently lay us on the Spicy shore.
>
> (ll. 1209–1216)

It would have been entirely convenient for my argument if Satan's final destination had been the United Provinces, bringing with him a cargo of cloves and silk. Instead he lands in Eden, though (in subtler guise) he has brought with him some remnants of the spice trade. Imbued with the aromas of his travels, his arrival creates a striking conflict between two "scentscapes" or "aromaramas". Eden is a very English garden, and in it flourish a host of aromas and herbs with strong biblical connections. Rafael walks its forests, releasing all manner of delicious smells:[83]

> Into the blissful field, through groves of myrrh,
> And flowering odours, cassia, nard, and balm;
> A wilderness of sweets; for nature here
> Wantoned as in her prime, and played at will
> Her virgin fancies, pouring forth more sweet,
> Wild above rule or art; enormous bliss.
> Him through the spice forest onward come
> Adam discerned [.]
>
> (V. 292–299)

This is an explosion of biblical spices, gesturing towards, for example, Solomon 4:14: 'Spikenard and saffron; calamus and cinnamon, with all trees of frankincense; myrrh and aloes, with all the chief spices'. The symbolic value of each can therefore not be discounted from Milton's vision; as mentioned earlier, the connotations of each biblical ingredient would have been familiar to his reading audience. In particular, myrrh's value as a 'prophylactic against devils', might allow us to imagine a ring of protective, aromatic defences around Paradise, raised to ward off Satan and his competing VOC odours.[84]

The poem repeatedly connects heavenly or angelic scents with native or natural spices, and by contrast associates exotic imports with a fallen and sinful world. God's angels circle the world, exuding their own perfumes, which are reminiscent of the scents of the Holy Land, rather than the Spice Islands:

Fanning their odoriferous wings dispense
Native perfumes, and whisper whence they stole
Those balmy spoils. As when to them who sail
Beyond the Cape of Hope, and now are past
Mozambic, off at sea north-east winds blow
Sabean odours from the spicy shore
Of Arabie the blest, with such delay
Well pleased they slack their course, and many a league
Cheered with the grateful smell old Ocean smiles.

(IV. 157–165)

A consistent geo-aromatic contrast is thus developed that in part is a feature of Milton's multi-sensory rhetorical arsenal, though it is also goes beyond this moral binary to indicate a pervasive English anxiety about Dutch monopolising of the East India trade.[85]

The region had been contested between the two maritime powers (alongside other players) since the first decades of the seventeenth century, leading to sometimes violent and co-ordinated clashes, ranging from localised skirmishes to full international treaties and their contestations.[86] Milton was no outsider to these fraught relations. Through his parliamentary employment, he handled correspondence and information on traded goods, quantities, and values, as well as documentation of the disputes and settlements they generated. As part of Cromwell's eastward-looking government, Milton would have been relied upon to understand the key sites and products underpinning the trade.[87] He was doubtless aware of what could be at stake in these merchant endeavours, and the lengths those involved could be pushed to in search of profit.

The grimmest flashpoint was perhaps the Massacre of Amboyna, which Milton invokes through his inclusion of Ternate and Tidore (II. 639). Ambon, the other clove island of the Muluccas, is hereby called to mind.[88] As discussed in Chapter 1, the 1623 torture and murder of English merchants by the Dutch became a touchstone of English propaganda, especially during the later Anglo-Dutch wars. Pamphlets abounded showing the despicable actions of the Dutch, often in gruesome specificity.[89] Milton was only fifteen when these events took place, but he was surely aware of the general narrative, which was repeated as a staple of anti-Dutch imagery throughout the century. He may also have known about the massacre from more personal sources: among his father's acquaintances was pastor Thomas Myriell, who had published his own letter to Maurice Abbott, Governor of the English East India Company. In *The Stripping of Josepf [. . .] With a Consolatorie Epistle, to the English-East-India Companie, for Their Unsufferable Wrongs Sustayned in Amboyna, by the Dutch There* (1625), he recalls and condemns the frightful cruelty of the perpetrators.[90]

Milton's government work also ensured that he was informed of the particulars of Amboyna and similar incidents, well beyond the propaganda of pamphleteers. His State Papers from the Anglo-Dutch negotiations have been collated by Leo Miller.[91] They include the *Papers of Demands* finished in March 1652, printed in *Literæ Pseudo-Senatûs Anglicani*, with an attribution to Milton.[92] The 16 pages in Latin are divided into four sections: a cover letter, followed by two sets of claims (A), 15 additional articles with claims (B), and the reproduction of a 1645 catalogue of claims (C). The central concern is Anglo-Dutch exchanges in the East Indies, including frequent references to Amboyna. According to Miller's analysis, the cover letter was translated by Lewis Rosin, but Milton was responsible for editing the catalogue's Latin. The other sections are considered sufficiently close to Milton's classical style for the attribution to be sustained.[93]

From the papers it is clear that Amboyna was only the most infamous of several collisions between English and Dutch interests. Compensation is demanded in section A for some fruits destroyed on the island of Polloroone when it was captured by the Dutch.[94] Section B mostly concerns recompenses demanded for losses on the Moluccas, Banda and Ambon, including in the clove trade (articles 3 and 4). The injustice of the Dutch monopoly – imposing steep customs duty on cloves on Ambon – is complained of, with the Amboyna massacre referred to twice. For the period between 1621 and 1652, when the papers were written, the English demand compensation for the way they have been excluded from the trade through violent attacks on Ambon and Polloroone, calculating the staggering sum of 36,000 pounds owed (article 4).[95]

Milton's involvement in these unhappy affairs seems coated in the smell of cloves and other spices, with petitions, demands, and pleas flooding from the East towards his office in London. Little surprise, then, that he mirrored this in a 'Dutch' Satanic passage to earth. *Paradise Lost* reflects a raft of personal and national anxieties concerning trade, colonialisation and maritime competition, though in its own fashion. It eschews the chest-thumping patriotism of much of Dryden's writing, but remains steeped in an atmosphere of suspicion and uncertainty created by Anglo-Dutch rivalry – and its manifestation on England's marketplaces and dinner tables.

To some extent Milton's *Paradise Lost* adopts a similar stance to Marvell's *Second* and *Third Advice to a Painter*, and his *Last Instructions*. These invert the sentiment of panegyric poems published during the second Anglo-Dutch war that present England as a maritime empire, owner of the seas.[96] Milton and Marvell instead meditate on the temptations and corruptions of profit – usually private and sometimes clandestine.[97] Where we might look for simplistic reductions of the 'other' to an opposing evil, the imagery has the capacity to trouble the reader through its invitation to reflect. Perfidy and greed are condemned, yet the differences between an English and a Dutch merchant are contingent, not absolute.

In Dryden's *State of Innocence* (1674), written during the Third Anglo-Dutch War, it is striking that in a debate Lucifer proposes an organisation of a States General with direct reference to the United Provinces:

Most high and mighty Lords, who better fell
From Heav'n, to rise States-General of Hell,
Nor yet repent, though ruin'd and undone,
Our upper Provinces already won,
(Such pride there is in Souls created free,
Such hate of Universal Monarchy;)
Speak, (for we therefore meet) – –
If Peace you chuse, your Suffrages declare;
Or means propound, to carry on the War.
(Scene 1, ll. 85–93)

Not only does this support my 'Dutch' reading, since it suggests that the contemporary audience would have made the same connection, it also underlines Milton's comparative restraint in the epic. The 'Dutchness' of the imagery is a route towards thinking of the spice trade in troubling terms, but Milton's representation invites self-reflection not simply rejection. The route favoured by the Devil is an open sea, which anyone might choose to sail.

Marvell's *The Character of Holland* was composed in the same period as Milton's state papers dealing with the Dutch after the Massacre. English claims of torture and massacre by the Dutch, repeated with fresh outrage on many occasions, such as in the anonymous pamphlet *A true relation of the unjust and cruel proceedings against the English at Amboyna* (1624), make the carving of the Arms of the United Provinces in the poem ring with echoes of Dutch behaviour in Ambon. The Massacre became a symbol for Anglo-Dutch competition and rivalry in the East and a great propaganda tool, of which Dryden's play *Amboyna* (1673) is perhaps the grandest example. The play was performed during the Third Anglo-Dutch War, demonstrating the continuing potency of Amboyna to induce anti-Dutch sympathies. *The Character of Holland* was similarly recycled and adapted during all three Anglo-Dutch Wars. It is unlikely that Milton will have seen Dryden's play, but not improbable that Marvell did. Its prologue encourages English warfare with the Dutch, and is worth quoting it here in full, as it can be read as a summary (however skewed) of tangled Anglo-Dutch relations during the seventeenth century.

The dotage of some *Englishmen* is such
To fawn on those who ruine them; the *Dutch*.
They shall have all rather then make a War
With those who of the same Religion are.
The *Streights*, the *Guiney* Trade, the Herrings too,
Nay, to keep friendship, they shall pickle you:
Some are resolv'd not to find out the Cheat,
But Cuckold like, love him who does the Feat:
What injuries soe'r upon us fall,
Yet still the same Religion answers all:

Religion wheedled you to Civil War,
Drew *English* Blood, And *Dutchmens* now wou'd spare:
Be gull'd no longer, for you'l find it true,
They have no more religion, faith – – – then you;
Interest's the God they worship in their State,
And you, I take it, have not much of that.
Well Monarchys may own Religions name.
But States are Atheists in their very frame.
They share a sin, and such proportions fall
That like a stink, 'tis nothing to 'em all.
How they love *England*, you shall see this day:
No map shews *Holland* truer than our Play:
Their Pictures and Inscription well we know;
We may be bold one Medal sure to show.
View then their Falshoods, Rapine, Cruelty;
And think what once they were, they still would be:
But hope not either Language, Plot, or Art,
'Twas writ in haste, but with an *English* Heart:
And lest Hope, Wit, in *Dutchmen* that would be
As much improper as would Honesty.

(ll. 5–34)

The religious accusations in this prologue reveal a great deal about the souring of Anglo-Dutch relations in the 1670s. Charles II's second attempt at war was regarded by the opposition in Parliament as endangering the European Protestant cause, hence the reference in the prologue to the Protestant religion they both share.[98] In order to justify the war, Charles II employed two writers of propaganda: John Dryden and Henry Stubbe (1632–1676).[99] They would argue in the following months that the Dutch were not quite Protestant, as they attacked their Protestant brethren in the East, of which Amboyna was the most obvious and effective example.[100] Stubbe attacked the Dutch mostly in prose tracts, published in journals such as the *London Gazette*. In the Third Anglo-Dutch War, he wrote two tracts: *A Justification of the Present War Against the United Netherlands* (1672) and *A Further Justification of the Present War Against the United Netherlands* (1673).[101] Dryden created his play *Amboyna*.[102] Unsurprisingly, neither Marvell nor Milton directly contributed to this rhetorical movement in and around the Third Anglo-Dutch War. Nonetheless, these examples show that the East Indies had extended the theatre of complicated Anglo-Dutch relations, in which conflicts and rivalry were 'shaped, mediated, and muted by a common faith and an ongoing history of military alliance in Europe'.[103] Given this milieu, it is no surprise to find traces of a realisation that the scene of Anglo-Dutch relations had become global rather than European in *The Character of Holland*, the Painter Poems, and *Paradise Lost*.

In a way, it is fitting to end this final chapter with Dryden's *Amboyna*, as embodying many of the topics discussed in this book. The prologue drags into dubious service many stereotypes that Milton and Marvell, too, encountered (and sometimes used in their own poetry), such as the Dutch love for pickling and herring, or Felltham's remark that profit or interest is the Dutch universal church. It nods to the Protestant bond between England and the United Provinces, though this is suggested to be superficial, due to the revealed Atheism of the States (i.e. the States General). The Dutch have shown their true faces of 'falshood, Rapine and Cruelty', making explicit exactly Amboyna's aim and effect as a propaganda tool, and global trade's centrality to the diplomacy between the two nations. Even in this attack however, where one might regret the collapse of alliance and mutual recognition that seemed possible only a few decades earlier, the enemy is familiar, the conflict knotty. Literature partook of this same tension between neighbours. Whether this emerged as inflammatory rhetoric, demons with spices on their wings, melancholy, or self-reflection, English and Dutch authors understood themselves – and should be understood – as writing about or against an Other who was at times dangerously different, at time, troublingly close.

Notes

1　William Temple, 'Preface', in *Observations upon the United Provinces of the Netherlands* (London, 1673), p. A3; J. Davies. 'Temple, Sir William, Baronet (1628–1699), Diplomat and Author', *Oxford Dictionary of National Biography* (2009), retrieved 9 January 2019. www.oxforddnb.com/view/10.1093/ref:odnb/9780198614128.001.0001/odnb-9780198614128-e-27122?rskey=2DBey1&result=4.

2　Andrew Hadfield, *Literature, Travel and Colonial Writing in the English Renaissance* (Oxford: Oxford University Press, 1998), p. 1.

3　Esther van Raamsdonk and Alan Moss, 'Across the Narrow Sea: A Transnational Approach to Seventeenth-Century English and Dutch Travelogues', *The Seventeenth Century*, 35.1 (2020):105–124.

4　Anglo-Dutch relations in the West were also of crucial importance in the establishment of America. Alison Games' article is a good example that links Anglo-Dutch relations in the East to the West: 'Anglo-Dutch Connections and Overseas Enterprises: A Global Perspective on Lion Gardiner's World', *Early American Studies*, 9.2 (2011): 435–461. For other works discussing the English and the Dutch in America, see Cynthia J. van Zandt, *Brothers among Nations: The Pursuit of Intercultural Alliances in Early America, 1580–1660* (Oxford: Oxford University Press, 2008), and April Lee Hatfield, *Atlantic Virginia: Intercolonial Relations in the Seventeenth Century* (Pittsburgh: Pennsylvania University Press, 2004).

5　As Christopher N. Warren has explained, globalisation was a term not widely used until the twentieth century, but I am using Dennis O. Flynn's and Arturo Giraldez's argument that we can speak of globalisation when silver from America was traded in China in the year 1571, which would make it a truly early modern concept: Christopher N. Warren, *Literature and the Law of Nations, 1580–1680* (Oxford: Oxford University Press, 2015), p. 1; Dennis O. Flynn and Arturo Giraldez, 'Globalization Began in 1571', in *Globalization and*

Global History, ed. by Barry K. Gills and William R. Thompson (New York: Routledge, 2006): 232–247; *Milton in Translation*, ed. by Angelica Duran, Islam Issa, and Jonathan R. Olson (Oxford: Oxford University Press, 2017).

6 D.K. Smith, "'tis not, what once it was, the world": Andrew Marvell's Re-Mapping of Old and New in *Bermudas* and *Upon Appleton House*', *Seventeenth Century*, 21.1 (2006): 215–248 (p. 217).

7 *CPW*: VIII. 474.

8 Warren Chernaik, 'Waller, Edmund (1608–1687), Poet and Politician', *Oxford Dictionary of National Biography*, retrieved 13 January 2019. www.oxforddnb.com/abstract/10.1093/ref:odnb/9780198614128.001.0001/odnb-97801 98614128-e-28556?rskey=v8qc3R.

9 Martin Dzelzainis, "'. . . ridiculous Pictures, and odious Medails": Visual Propaganda in the Second and Third Anglo-Dutch War', in *Breaking the Image/Image brisée*, ed. by Christian Belin, Agnès Lafont, and Nicholas Myers (Classiques Garnier: in press, forthcoming); *ibid.*, 'Andrew Marvell and the Restoration Literary Underground: Printing the *Painter Poems*', *Seventeenth Century*, 22.2 (2007): 395–410 (p. 396).

10 'Ut picture poesis', literally translated as a poem is like a picture, taken from Horace's *Ars Poetica*, see Joan Faust, 'Blurring the Boundaries: Ut picture poesis and Marvell's Liminal Mower', *Studies in Philology*, 104.4 (2007): 526–555; Nigel Smith, *Andrew Marvell: The Chameleon* (New Haven: Yale University Press, 2012), p. 188; Michael Schoenveldt, 'Marvell and the Designs of Art', in *The Cambridge Companion to Andrew Marvell* (Cambridge: Cambridge University Press, 2011): 87–101 (pp. 98–99).

11 Dzelzainis, 'Andrew Marvell and the Restoration Literary Underground: Printing the *Painter Poems*', p. 396.

12 Warren Chernaik, *The Poetry of Limitation: A Study of Edmund Waller* (New Haven: Yale University Press, 1968), p. 175.

13 Noelle Gallagher, "'Partial to Some One Side": The Advice-to-a Painter Poem as Historical Writing', *English Literary History*, 78.1 (2011): 79–101 (p. 80).

14 George de F. Lord, 'Introduction', in *Poems on Affairs of State, 1660–1714*, 7 vols. (New Haven: Yale University Press, 1963): xxiv–lvi (p. xxxiv). Smith, *The Chameleon*, p. 190; Timothy Raylor, 'Marvell and Waller', in *The Oxford Handbook of Andrew Marvell*, ed. by Martin Dzelzainis and Edward Holberton (Oxford: Oxford University Press, 2019): 636–651 (p. 642).

15 Mary Tom Osborne, *Advice-to-a-Painter Poems 1633–1856: An Annotated Finding List* (Austin: University of Texas Press, 1949), p. 132.

16 John Burrows used a linguistic computational approach in order to determine the authorship of the different Painter Poems. His article has a convincing argument that the *Second* and *Third Advice* and the *Last Instruction* can be attributed to Marvell, but that this is impossible to say about the *Fourth* and *Fifth Advice*, as well as *Further Advice*. John Burrows, 'Andrew Marvell and the Painter Satires: A Computational Approach to Their Authorship', *The Modern Language Review*, 100.2 (2005): 281–297. See for an extended explanation on the different theories on authorship of the *Advice-to-a-Painter Poems*, Nigel Smith, 'Authorship', in *Andrew Marvell: The Poems* (London: Pearson and Longman, 2007): 323–324.

17 Roger L'Estrange, *An Account of the Growth of Knavery, under the Pretended Fears of Arbitrary Government and Popery* (London, 1678), pp. 4–6. For more information on the publication history, and the relationship between L'Estrange and the publication of the Advice-to-a-Painter series, see Martin Dzelzainis, 'L'Estrange, Marvell and the Directions to a Painter', in *Roger L'Estrange and the Making of a Restoration Culture* (Aldershot: Ashgate Publishing, 2008): 53–67.

18 William Speck, 'Britain and the Dutch Republic', in *A Miracle Mirrored: The Dutch Republic in European Perspective* (Cambridge: Cambridge University Press, 1995): 173–195 (pp. 173–174).
19 Van Aitzema, diary 1.10.02, 49.
20 Annabel Patterson, 'The Country Gentleman: Howard, Marvell, and Dryden in the Theater of Politics', *Studies in English Literature, 1500–1900*, 25.1 (1985): 491–509 (p. 494).
21 Edward Holberton, 'Representing the Sea in Andrew Marvell's Advice to a Painter Satires', *Review of English Studies* (2014): 71–86 (p. 72); J.D. Davies, *Gentlemen and Tarpaulins: The Officers and Men of the Restoration Navy* (Oxford: Oxford University Press, 1991); Bernard Capp, *Cromwell's Navy: The Fleet and the English Revolution* (Oxford: Oxford University Press, 1992).
22 Jonathan Israel, *Dutch Primacy in World Trade, 1585–1740* (Oxford: Oxford University Press, 1989), p. 271; see also a letter from De Malines to Joseph Williamson on 27 February in 1665 (NS), revealing intelligence about the Dutch preparation for the Second Anglo-Dutch War, National Archives, SP 84/174 f. 118.
23 Gijs Rommelse, *The Second Anglo-Dutch War* (Hilversum: Verloren, 2006), pp. 64–65.
24 See for some relations between Johan de Witt and England: Ineke Huysman and Roosje Peeters (eds.), *Johan de Witt en Engeland: Een Bloemlezing uit zijn Correspondentie* (Soest: Uitgeverij Catullus, 2019).
25 Steven C. Pincus, *Protestantism and Patriotism* (Cambridge: Cambridge University Press, 1996), pp. 196–198.
26 Holberton, 'Representing the Sea', p. 76.
27 Pincus, *Protestantism and Patriotism*, p. 296.
28 Annabel Patterson, *Marvell and the Civic Crown* (Princeton: Princeton University Press, 1978), pp. 126, 158; Smith, *Chameleon*, pp. 190–192.
29 Holberton, 'Representing the Sea', p. 75.
30 Warren Chernaik, 'Harsh Remedies: Satire and Politics in "Last Instructions to a Painter"', in *The Oxford Handbook to Andrew Marvell*, ed. by Martin Dzelzainis and Edward Holberton (Oxford: Oxford University Press, 2019): 444–462 (p. 445); Holberton, 'Representing the Sea', p. 86.
31 Gallagher, p. 90.
32 Holberton, 'Representing the Sea', p. 74.
33 *The Poems of Edmund Waller*, ed. by G. Thorn Drury, 2 vols. (London: Routledge, 1893), vol. 2, p. 24.
34 David Armitage, *Ideological Origins of the British Empire* (Cambridge: Cambridge University Press, 2004), pp. 109–121.
35 Andrew R. Walkling, *English Dramatick Opera, 1660–1710* (Abingdon: Routledge, 2019), pp. 226–227.
36 Patterson, *Marvell and the Civic Crown*, p. 123.
37 Steven N. Zwicker, *Lines of Authority: Politics and English Literary Culture, 1649–1689* (Ithaca: Cornell University Press, 1993), p. 98.
38 Harold Love, *English Clandestine Satire, 1660–1702* (Oxford: Oxford University Press, 2004), p. 112; Smith, *The Chameleon*, p. 181.
39 Holberton, 'Representing the Sea', pp. 81–86.
40 'Opdam is either sick or so would seem,/ Therefore our Duke is forc't to visit him./ Yet the uncivill Dutch will not look out,/ As if they were all troubled with the gout', Anonymous, *Bellum Belgium Secundum, or, A poem, Attempting something on His Majesties proceedings against the Dutch* (1665), p. 5.
41 P.G. Rogers, *The Dutch in the Medway* (Oxford: Oxford University Press, 1970), p. 14.
42 *The Poems of Edmund Waller*, vol. 2, p. 55.
43 Zwicker, *Lines of Authority*, p. 113.

44   Harold E. Toliver, *Marvell's Ironic Vision* (New Haven: Yale University Press, 1965), p. 207.

45   de F. Lord, p. xliii.

46   Holberton, 'Representing the Sea', p. 85.

47   Chernaik, *The Poet's Time*, p. 69.

48   Denise E. Lynch, 'Politics, Nature and Structure in Marvell's "The Last Instructions to a Painter"', *Restoration: Studies in English Literary Culture 1660–1700*, 16.2 (1992): 82–92 (p. 83).

49   Patterson, *Marvell and the Civic Crown*, p. 497.

50   This is a summarised representation, see for a more complete understanding: Edward W. Said, *Orientalism* (London: Routledge, 1978).

51   Su Fang Ng, 'Dutch Wars, Global Trade, and the Heroic Poem: Dryden's *Annus Mirabilis* (1666) and Amin's *Sya'ir perang Mengkasar* (1670)', *Modern Philology*, 109.3 (2012): 352–384 (p. 352). See also Hans Hägerdal, *Lord of the Land, Lord of the Sea: Conflict and Adaptation in Early Colonial Timor, 1600–1800* (Leiden: KITVL Press, 2012).

52   I will not go into the details of empire and nationhood, and its ambiguous representations in Dryden's, *Annus Mirabilis*, see Su Fang Ng, 'Dutch Wars', pp. 352–384; Laura Brown, 'Dryden and the Imperial Imagination', in *The Cambridge Companion to John Dryden*, ed. Steven N. Zwicker (Cambridge: Cambridge University Press, 2004): 59–74; Sophie Gee, 'The Invention of the Wasteland: Civic Narrative and Dryden's *Annus Mirabilis*', *Eighteenth-Century Life*, 29.1 (2005): 82–108.

53   J. Innes Miller, *The Spice Trade of the Roman Empire, 29 B.C. to A.D. 641* (Oxford: Clarendon Press, 1969); Robert Parthesius, *Dutch Ships in Tropical Waters: The Development of the Dutch India Company (VOC) Shipping Network in Asia, 1595–1660* (Amsterdam: Amsterdam University Press, 2010).

54   Ronald J. Herring, 'How Is Food Political? Market, State, and Knowledge', in *The Oxford Handbook of Food, Politics, and Society*, ed. by Ronald J. Herring (Oxford: Oxford University Press, 2015): 4–29 (p. 8).

55   Robert Markley, *The Far East and the English Imagination, 1600–1730* (Cambridge: Cambridge University Press, 2006), p. 31.

56   Enrique C. Ochoa, 'Political Histories of Food', in *The Oxford Handbook of Food History*, ed. by Jeffrey M. Pilcher (Oxford: Oxford University Press, 2012): 24–35 (p. 25).

57   Jayeeta Sharma, 'Food and Empire', in *The Oxford Handbook of Food History*, ed. by Jeffrey M. Pilcher (Oxford: Oxford University Press, 2012): 242–256 (p. 242); Fabio Parasecoli, 'Introduction', in *Culinary Cultures of Europe: Identity, Diversity and Dialogue*, ed. by Darra Goldstein and Katherine Merkle (Strasbourg: Council of Europe Publishing, 2005): 11–37 (p. 13).

58   Joan Thirsk, *Food in Early Modern England: Phases, Fads, Fashions, 1500–1760* (London: Hambledon Continuum, 2006), pp. 115–118.

59   Thirsk, pp. 92, 317.

60   Stobart writes that Jamaican peppers were already imported to England in the seventeenth century, but I have been unable to find reference to these peppers in literature of the period: Jon Stobart, *Sugar and Spice: Grocers and Groceries in Provincial England 1650–1830* (Oxford: Oxford University Press, 2002), p. 46.

61   This is dated 19 February 2019, and might change slightly when more texts are added onto *Early English Books Online*.

62   Merchants quickly picked up on the market value of these religious associations, and named some of the spices after this belief; spice meleguete pepper, was named 'grains of paradise': Wolfgang Schivelbusch, *Tastes of Paradise: A Social History of Spices, Stimulants and Intoxicants* (New York: Vintage

Books, 1992), pp. 6, 13. The fact that this was sourced from West Africa, and nowhere near India and the supposedly located Garden of Eden, was unknown to the consumer.

63   Schivelbusch, pp. 6, 13.

64   Spice clearly still invokes many associations and is an imagination-sparking subject to write about, demonstrated by the many popular history books published on the subject (see Krondl and Schivelbusch for example). Interestingly, some of these books fall into the same pitfalls of stereotypes and mythologizing seen in travelogues of the period. Krondl, in particular, gives a one-sided view of the Netherlands' past and present, that relies heavily on stereotypes of the country and its people, of which a street scene of 'numberless blond, blue-eyed people' is just one example: Michael Krondl, *The Taste of Conquest: The Rise and Fall of the Three Great Cities of Spice* (New York: Ballantine Books, 2007), p. 189.

65   Eric Song, 'The Country Estate and the East Indies (East and West): The Shifting Scene of Eden in *Paradise Lost*', *Modern Philology*, 108.2 (2010): 199–223 (p. 204).

66   As Nicholas von Maltzahn has shown, Marvell had some interest in countries in the East (and West), shown for example in the interesting expression of '*Indians* poison-pot' in his *Remarks* (*PWAM*: II. 471). This can be traced to a Spanish text about the New World and a Dutch source about Indonesia: Nicholas von Maltzahn, 'Marvell's Indian Poison-Pot', *Notes and Queries*, 60.4 (2013): 535–537.

67   Edward Holberton, *Poetry and the Cromwellian Protectorate: Culture, Politics, and Institutions* (Oxford: Oxford University Press, 2008), p. 124.

68   A.D. Cousins, 'Marvell's Devout Mythology of the New World: Homeland and Home in "Bermudas"', *Parergon*, 30.1 (2013): 203–219 (pp. 203, 216).

69   Smith, '"tis not, what once it was, the world"', pp. 221–222; Patterson, '*Bermudas* and the *Coronet*', p. 488.

70   See for example, Timothy Morton, *The Poetics of Spice* (Cambridge: Cambridge University Press, 2000), p. 71; Lim, *The Arts of Empire*, pp. 208–210.

71   Markley, *The Far East*, p. 33.

72   The merchant ship travels from Turkey to the Greek Islands and Cadiz in Southern Spain. See also Dyani Johns Taff's book chapter 'A Shipwreck of Faith: Hazardous Voyages and Contested Representations in Milton's *Samson Agonistes*', in *Shipwreck and Island Motifs in Literature and Arts*, ed. by Brigitte Le Juez and Olga Springer (Leiden: Brill, 2015): 151–170 (p. 162).

73   Su Fang Ng, 'Pirating Paradise: Alexander the Great, the Dutch East Indies, and Satanic Empire in *Paradise Lost*', *Milton Studies*, 52 (2011): 59–91 (p. 86).

74   Vincent C. Loth, 'Armed Incidents and Unpaid Bills: Anglo-Dutch Rivalry in the Banda Islands in the Seventeenth Century', *Modern Asian Studies*, 29.4 (1995): 705–740.

75   Markley, *The Far East*, p. 51.

76   Van Groesen, 'Global Trade', pp. 169–170.

77   Jonathan Israel, *The Dutch Republic: Its Rise, Greatness and Fall, 1477–1806* (Oxford: Oxford University Press, 1995), p. 942.

78   Hendrik Brouwer, qtd. in Omar Prakesh Chouhan, *The Dutch East India Company and the Economy of Bengal, 1630–1720* (Princeton: Princeton University Press, 1985), p. 16.

79   Su Fang Ng has argued that Satan is a Dutch merchant for different reasons again. She argues that the pun 'hollow', referring to the situation of the Netherlands being below sea-level, draws parallels with Satan's association with marshes, bogs and winds in the epic, 'Pirating Paradise', p. 74.

80   A small snippet of verse: Daar hebben wij gesien langs de Moluckse stroomen/ Hoe schoon het edel kruit,/ De wereld door beroemt, aen jonge nagelboomen/

Uit knop en tacken spruit' (There we saw by the Moluccas' streams/ the
beauty of that noble spice,/ famed throughout the world, from the young
clove-trees/ from bud and branches sprout) (ll. 1–4), 'Op 't eerste boeckx,
sesde hooftstuck', in *Wouter Schouten: Dichter en VOC-Chirurgijn*, ed. by
Marijke Barend-Van Haeften and Hetty Plekenpol (Zutphen: Walburg Pers,
2012): 41–44.

81 'Op 't tweede boeckx, derde hooftstuck', in *Wouter Schouten*, pp. 80–85.

82 See for example Lim, *The Arts of Empire*, pp. 210–218. For critics arguing that
Milton wrote against empire see: David Quint, *Epic and Empire* (Princeton:
Princeton University Press, 1993); Paul Stevens, 'Paradise Lost and the Colonial
Imperative', *Milton Studies*, 34 (1996): 3–21; David Armitage, 'John Milton:
Poet against Empire', in *Milton and Republicanism*, ed. by David Armitage,
Armand Himy, and Quentin Skinner (Cambridge: Cambridge University Press,
1995): 206–225. There are a few other critics who argue for both positive and
negative conceptions of colonialism in Milton, such as J. Martin Evans, *Milton's Imperial Epic: Paradise Lost and the Discourse of Colonialism* (Ithaca:
Cornell University Press, 1996).

83 Eric Song, 'The Country Estate and the East Indies (East and West): The Shifting Scene of Eden in *Paradise Lost*', *Modern Philology*, 108.2 (2010): 199–223;
Barbara Kiefer Lewalski, *Paradise Lost and the Rhetoric of Literary Forms*
(Princeton: Princeton University Press, 1985), p. 181; critics arguing for a
resemblance to the English country house poem genre in the Garden of Eden,
see D.M. Rosenberg, 'Milton's *Paradise Lost* and the Country Estate Poem',
Clio, 18.2 (1989): 123–243; Christopher Wortham, '"A Happy Rural Seat":
Milton's *Paradise Lost* and the English Country House Poem', *Parergon*, 9.1
(1991): 137–150.

84 John B. Broadbent, *Some Graver Subject: An Essay to Paradise Lost* (London:
Chatto and Windus, 1960), p. 183.

85 Robert Markley, '"The destin'd walls/ Of Cambalu": Milton, China, and the
Ambiguities of the East', in *Milton and the Imperial Vision*, ed. by Balachandra Rajan and Elizabeth Sauer (Pittsburgh: Duquesne University Press, 1999):
191–213 (p. 205).

86 For example, a treaty of 1619 divided the spice trade into one third of the
Moluccan spices and half of the Javanese pepper for the English and the rest
for the Dutch, which would inevitably lead to tension: Alison Games, 'Anglo-
Dutch Connections and Overseas Enterprises' 435–461; Marjorie Rubright,
Doppelganger Dilemmas (Pittsburgh, PA: Pennsylvania University Press, 2015),
p. 192; Loth, pp. 719–722; Armitage, *Ideological Origins of the British Empire*,
pp. 109–124.

87 Robert Fallon, 'Cromwell, Milton, and the Western Design', in *Milton and the
Imperial Vision*, ed. by Balachandra Rajan and Elizabeth Sauer (Pittsburgh:
Duquesne Press, 1999), p. 154.

88 Jan L. van Zanden, *The Rise and Decline of Holland's Economy: Merchant
Capitalism and the Labour Market* (Manchester: Manchester University Press,
1993), p. 35.

89 I have located 54 English pamphlets so far that mention the massacre of
Amboyna explicitly in the period 1624–1700. Some examples: Anonymous,
*Nevves out of East India of the cruell and bloody vsage of our English merchants and others at Amboyna, by the Netherlandish gouernour and councell
there. To the tune of Braggendary* (London: s.n., 1624); Anonymous, *A true
relation of the unjust, cruel, and barbarous proceedings against the English, at
Amboyna in the East-Indies, by the Netherlandish Governour & Council there.
Published by authority* (London: s.n., 1651); J.D., *A true and compendious*

narration or, second part of Amboyna, or sundry notorious or remarkable injuries, insolencies, and acts of hostility which the Hollanders have exercised from time to time against the English nation in the East-Indies (London: s.n., 1665).

90 Thomas Myriell, 'To the Right Worshipfull Mr. Maurice Abbott, Governor of the East-India Companie', in *The stripping of Ioseph, or The crueltie of brethren to a brother in a sermon before his Maiestie at White-Hall, by Robert Wilkinson, Doctor in Diuinitie, chaplaine in ordinarie to his Maiestie, and late pastor of Saint Olaues in Southwarke. With a consolatorie epistle, to the English-East-India Companie, for their vnsufferable wrongs sustayned in Amboyna, by the Dutch there. Published and presented vnto them, by Tho. Myriell pastor of Saint Stephens in Walbrooke* (London: s.n., 1625), pp. 1–21; Christopher N. Warren, *Literature and the Law of Nations, 1580–1680* (Oxford: Oxford University Press, 2015), p. 137; Gordon Campbell and Thomas Corns, *John Milton: Life, Works and Thought* (Oxford: Oxford University Press, 2008), p. 25.

91 Leo Miller, *John Milton's Writings in the Anglo-Dutch Negotiations, 1651–1654* (Pittsburgh: Duquesne University Press, 1992), pp. 112–153.

92 Robert Fallon, *Milton in Government* (Pittsburgh, PA: Pennsylvania University Press, 1993), pp. 86–87.

93 Miller, *Anglo-Dutch Negotiations*, pp. 25–30.

94 I am using Miller's reproduction of this document, which includes the original Latin, and a translation: Miller, *Anglo-Dutch Negotiations*, pp. 112–153.

95 'Paper of Demands', in Miller, *Anglo-Dutch Negotiations*, p. 138.

96 Martz makes a similar point about Milton's ambiguity towards empire in his book *Milton: Poet of Exile*, in which he contrasts the elaborate style and glorification of empire in Book 10 of the *Lusiads* with Milton's 'lowered style' at the end of his epic: Martz, pp. 156, 169.

97 Holberton, 'Representing the Sea in Andrew Marvell's *Advice to a Painter Satires*', pp. 71–86; Annabel Patterson, *Marvell and the Civic Crown* (Princeton: Princeton University Press, 1978), p. 123.

98 Anne Barbeau Gardiner, 'Swift on the Dutch East India Merchant: The Context of 1672–1673 War Literature', *Huntington Library Quarterly*, 54.3 (1991): 234–252 (p. 236).

99 Mordechai Feingold, 'Stubbe, Henry (1632–1676)', *Oxford Dictionary of National Biography*, retrieved 24 March 2019. www.oxforddnb.com/view/10.1093/ref:odnb/9780198614128.001.0001/odnb-9780198614128-e-26734.

100 Gardiner, p. 236.

101 See also other publication by Stubbe during the Third Anglo-Dutch War, Dzelzainis, '". . . ridiculous Pictures, and odious Medails"', pp. 19–21.

102 James Thompson argues that Dryden's *Conquest of Granada* could also be seen as part of a similar anti-Dutch movement: James Thompson, 'Dryden's *Conquest of Granada* and the Dutch Wars', *The Eighteenth Century*, 31.3 (1990): 211–226.

103 Rubright, p. 193.

Epilogue

On the 5th of November 1688, William III of Orange landed in Brixham, not far from Exeter, with the intention of becoming the first Dutch king of England. He brought only a small following.[1] His expressed desire was, once again, to join with England to fight for the Protestant cause. The unification that had been desired by the Netherlands during the Eighty Years' War but rejected by Elizabeth I, then suggested by Cromwell in the early 1650s but not on terms acceptable to the States General, had now become a reality.

By this point, Milton and Marvell were both dead, which is why this book (perhaps counter-intuitively) does not track the evolution of Anglo-Dutch relations beyond the seismic shift of the so-called Glorious Revolution. Undoubtedly, this change of political direction altered the currency of images that poets, polemicists and pamphleteers traded in, both of the Dutch rivals and the English sense of self, but this material belongs to a different investigation.[2] New players in the construction and dissemination of images emerged, and the pressing questions discussed in both nations changed. However, no such break is ever clean, and some of the strands of earlier imagery reached far into this new period – which Swift's reference to Amboyna 65 years after the event amply illustrates. It is therefore more than idle speculation to wonder what Marvell and Milton would each have made of William's arrival; their views on nationality, doctrine and righteous authority that I have sought to probe through the preceding chapters would have been tested by this turn of events. What would this change of context bring out what might have been less noticeable in the period before? This short concluding section notes two aspects in particular: Marvell's ironic stance towards essentialist notions of nationality, and Milton's difficult balancing between forms of social power: political structure and religious belief.

In one of his later poems, 'The Loyal Scot' (1667–1673), Marvell lampoons received ideas of nationality, boundaries and linguistic divides.[3] Rather than being timeless, god-appointed entities, Marvell treats nations as human constructions, whose differences may be as slight as clashing accents. The 'shibboleth' that detects foreign speech might be reason enough to exclude or hate another, but such differences are the result and sign of mankind's Fall, and affirm no moral virtue. Nationality and language may be only petty excuses for conflict, and seem poor reasons to claim the favours of providence.

Nation is all but name as shibboleth,
Where a mistaken accent causes death.
In paradise names only Nature showed,
At Babel names from pride and discord flowed;
And ever since men with a female spite
First call each other names, and then they fight.
(ll. 262–267)

Of course, this is at odds with his patriotic satirising of the Dutch in *The Character of Holland*, though even there, as seen in Chapter 1, he mingled common stereotypes with classical allusions and genuine legal disputes, and introduced a crucial note of irony to national chest-beating through his playful insertion of Dutch words and phrases. While he would happily traduce an opposing party, it was not done with the categorical rejection of the other; above all he was able to recognise that the images of 'the other' served a particular purpose. William becoming King of England belied the myth of nations of pure blood or immortal standing, and one suspects Marvell would have seen the humour in it, as the blunt invective against Dutch corruption or injustice, such as Dryden's *Amboyna*, would have been carefully brushed under the carpet. As ever, Marvell's particular allegiances were subtle and pragmatic, so it would be equally incorrect to see him as a robust internationalist. Perhaps what emerges from our examination of his prose and poetry is not a set of fixed ideals, but a longing for an acceptable stability and order. After the chaos and strife of the Civil Wars, the Restoration, and the Anglo-Dutch conflicts, Marvell may have hoped above all for some of the peace and tranquillity of Nun Appleton, even if he was far too worldly-wise to forget the troubles beyond its bounds. If, as in *The Character of Holland*, the United Provinces were merely 'th'off-scouring of the British sand' (l. 2), a Dutch leader could, in the right light, be seen as the return of England's own export. Images are shifting things, as delicate and various as water, with Marvell a master of their changing currents.

A recent discovery has shed unexpected light on Marvell's connections with the Orange family and possible involvement in laying the groundwork for the Glorious Revolution.[4] A copy of *Mr Smirke* with annotations in Marvell's own hand has been found in the Wellcome Library, bound together in the United Provinces with other works, which had been in the likely possession of a certain William Freeman. Freeman was in turn associated with the spy network of Pierre du Moulin. The latter promoted Orangist sympathies in England during the Third Anglo-Dutch War. The implications of this find are yet to be fully understood, not only in terms of Marvell's political sympathies but also for reading his work. Does Freeman's possession of this annotated copy promote the view that Marvell was flirting with the Dutch cause in a more involved way than previously thought, or did his writing merely reflect a useful perspective for Dutch propagandists? How did this Freeman receive Marvell's copy? It is possible that the document will confirm – or further obscure – speculation about Marvell spying for the Dutch, in ways that might further illustrate the raft of material and intellectual connections between the nations. Currently it is too early to draw firm conclusions from this exciting find, though the popular splash made by the announcement points to continued interest in unravelling this complex historical knot, and our own negotiations of European identity, today.[5] These many questions demand further research and consideration, but without doubt they will lead to further evidence being unearthed for the important of Dutch connections in Marvell's life and writing.

More explicit and direct, Milton had already written several tracts on the merits and practicalities of governance without kings. *The Readie and Easie Way to Establish a Free Commonwealth* appeared in February 1660, though by then Charles was already on his way to claim the English throne. Shortly afterwards George Starkey published a retort, *The dignity of kingship asserted: in answer to Mr. Milton's Ready and easie way to establish a free Common-wealth* (late 1660).[6] He argued that the commonwealth Milton proposed was not much different than the constitution of the United Provinces.[7] He used this to undermine Milton's anti-royalism by continuing, 'that the provinces yet as farr as they are capable of it, have a Prince of Orange, who differs little really from a King'.[8] Of course, Milton never endorsed the monarchical aspects of the House of Orange in the Dutch Republic. Even Starkey knew this: '[s]uch a Common-wealth (Mr. Milton,) as Holland is I suppose you could wish, and would help to make England, but there is among them something that you do not so well like and approve of, that is, the house of Nassau or Orange family'.[9] Blair Worden catalogues several specifically anti-Orangist statements in Milton's earlier *Defences*.[10] The Glorious Revolution therefore presented a strange parody of Milton's hopes. The form of government he was endorsing produced, in the rising star of the Prince of Orange, the salvation of the troubled English monarchy he had formerly fought against. It seems already ironic enough that the Dutch republican model he argued for in *The Readie and Easie Way* had harboured the exiled Charles II, before this new inversion of his hopes. We have seen at several points that Vondel, and many others in the Dutch intellectual community, supported the Stuart cause, or at least condemned the Regicide. When the Restoration finally took place, Vondel wrote 'Opgang van Karel Stuart den Tweeden' (Return of Charles II, 1660) to commemorate the journey of Charles back to England, hoping that he would stop in Amsterdam before sailing across the channel, which he unfortunately never did:

> De bloetbant van Oranje en groot Britanje
> Geeft hoope dat, der bontgenooten bant
> Bevestight, elck van beide, op zijn kampanje,
> Braveeren zal wat zich hier tegens kant.
> (ll. 45–48)

The blood ties of Orange and Great Britain,
Give hope, that the companion's bond

Is reinforced, by both, and each on his campaign
Shall brave those who with animosity respond.

What Vondel saw as the joyous hope of rightful kingship restored, bolstered
by further kinship between the countries through Charles II' nephew William, Milton experienced as a crushing defeat. Would he have rejoiced at
the prospect of being ruled by an Orange instead? Probably not, although it
would have been no worse, certainly, than a Stuart. As Starkey noted, Milton preferred a republican over a monarchical institution:

> Mr. Milton comes on the Stage in post hast, and in this juncture of
> time, that he may (if possible) overthrow the Hopes of all Good men,
> endeavours (what he can) to divert those that at present sit at Helme,
> and by fair pretenses, and Sophisticate Arguments, would easily delude
> an inconsiderate Reader into a belief, First, That the Government of a
> Republique is in it self, incomparably to be preferred before Kingship,
> whether we respect men as men, or as Christians.[11]

Perhaps the real question is not whether Milton (or Marvell, for that matter) would endorse a leader from a republic or a monarchy – Dutch or
English – but whether he was Protestant or not. Both wrote against Catholicism and excluded Catholics from the toleration allowed to other doctrines, even though on the individual level they could be more accepting.
William was able to come over to England because the prospect of having
an English Catholic king through James II so appalled a significant party in
government. The anti-Catholic narrative of both English and Dutch identity trumped the fluctuating national concerns of either. In the overlapping
series of images constituting English identity that this book has touched
on, some proved more malleable than others. As noted in the introduction,
the choice of religious (Protestant) identity over national identity might
seem a strange one from the modern perspective of nationalism and the
unity of the state, but here we are considering matters of emerging national
character and conscience, inevitably transnational in nature, to which both
Milton and Marvell gave their personal expression.

   This study has followed one deceptively simple concern: the impact of
Anglo-Dutch relations on the works of two canonical English authors. These
relations were not always direct, or even obvious, but their traces are visible
in the right light. Through each of the chapters, we have seen that the mutual
influence of the United Provinces and England was multifaceted, fluid, and
understood through assorted lenses and biases. The Anglo-Dutch wars
affected disparate layers of society in both countries; scholarly correspondence shaped intellectual environments; the news and print networks carried
controversies swiftly through Protestant Europe; and trading disagreements
with their maritime rivals were frequently at the centre of English foreign policy. Through the close intellectual interactions between the countries, English
and Dutch writers demonstrate striking parallels in their works, whether in

prose, poetry or drama. The authors in this book were responding to similar political developments, such as revolutions, regicide, restorations, or trading conflicts. They shared struggles with Arminianism, toleration, and the futility of the Anglo-Dutch wars. They composed propaganda pamphlets and poetry, yet also indicated admiration for aspects of one another's culture. In such circumstances we should no longer speak of national literary spheres, but of shared and evolving European literary communities.

Every book has its limitations and exclusions. A more complete discussion of other English authors beyond Milton and Marvell, such as John Dryden and Jonathan Swift, would reveal further developments of this Anglo-Dutch literary sphere, as well as examining Anglo-Dutch relations in the later seventeenth and early eighteenth century. A similar argument could be made for the late sixteenth century. Although I have looked at the founding of the Dutch Republic and its influence on English and Dutch rhetoric in Chapter 6, poets such as Philip Sidney and George Gascoigne could illuminate fluctuating English opinions and attitudes about the Dutch. Furthermore, the final chapter of this book took Anglo-Dutch relations beyond the geographical boundaries of Europe to the trading empires of the Far East. Both the English and the Dutch, of course, also had major investments in the West, and their cooperation and conflicts significantly shaped North America's emergence into nationhood. This deserves more attention. While acknowledging these limitations – and opportunities for future research – I hope that the imagological and transnational method demonstrated in this book has offered new readings of Milton's and Marvell's opinions, writing, and lives, establishing their deep-seated interest in, and responsiveness to, their neighbouring country and Europe as a whole. Certainly, as scholars and readers ourselves, such an outlook seems immediately profitable, and too precious to lose.

At the end we can conclude that the Dutch and the English are not wholly different, but have what can be characterised as 'family resemblance'.[12] There is no strict dividing line between the English and the Dutch, nor a single defining characteristic that binds them, but a series of modulating commonalities running through their relations. Each may recognise themselves in the other, both through the noting and exaggeration of differences, and through accepting and analysing similarities. This in a nutshell is the thread running throughout this book: how better than to understand oneself than through encounters with a neighbour, and consequently, how better for modern readers to understand Milton and Marvell than through a transnational lens? The other-self, the *half-anders*, proves a recurring influence in both poets' works.

Notes

1 Scott Sowerby, *Making Toleration: The Repealers and the Glorious Revolution* (Cambridge: Harvard University Press, 2012), p. 171; Steven Pincus, *1688: The First Modern Revolution* (New Haven: Yale University Press, 2009).

2 Helmer Helmers has investigated the turn of public opinion in the Netherlands during the succession of James II in 1685, see '1685 and the Battle for Dutch Public Opinion: Succession Literature from a Transnational Perspective', in *Stuart Succession Literature: Moments and Transformation*, ed. by Paulina Kewes and Andrew McRae (Oxford: Oxford University Press, 2018): 96–113.

3 Annabel Patterson, *Marvell and the Civic Crown* (Princeton: Princeton University Press, 1978), pp. 167–170.

4 Edward Holberton, Martin Dzelzainis, and Steph Coster, 'Andrew Marvell and the Dutch Fifth Column: New Evidence From a Copy of *Mr Smirke* with Authorial Annotations', (Forthcoming). Many thanks to the authors for allowing me to read a draft of the forthcoming article.

5 Edward Holberton, Martin Dzelzainis, and Steph Coster, 'Meeting Mr George: Did Andrew Marvell Spy for the Dutch?', *Times Literary Supplement* (April 10, 2020).

6 Su Fang Ng, 'Pirating Paradise: Alexander the Great, the Dutch East Indies, and Satanic Empire in *Paradise Lost*', *Milton Studies*, 52 (2011): 59–91 (p. 67).

7 George Starkey, *The dignity of kingship asserted: in answer to Mr. Milton's Ready and easie way to establish a free Common-wealth* (London, 1660), pp. 88–89, 104.

8 Starkey, *The Dignity*, p. 103.

9 Starkey, *The Dignity*, p. 106.

10 Blair Worden, *Literature and Politics in Cromwellian England: John Milton, Andrew Marvell and Merchamont Nedham* (Oxford: Oxford University Press, 2008), pp. 202–203.

11 Starkey, *The Dignity*, p. A1.

12 Ludwig Wittgenstein, *Philosophical Investigations*, transl. by G.E.M. Anscombe (Oxford: Blackwell Publishing, 1953), §67.

Bibliography

Manuscript Sources

British Library

'Ambassador Nieuwpoort to States General, 28 March 1659', fol. 136v, in MS 1657–1660 Secret Correspondence, 17677 MMM, British Library.

Hartlib Papers, University of Sheffield

Hartlib, Samuel, *Ephemerides* (1655), Part 4 (13 August–31 December, 1650) [29/5/43A-58A].

National Archives, Kew

E403/2608/36, Calendar of State Papers, Domestic Series, Commonwealth.
SP 18/1/55, fol. 142, 'Sophia to Maurits, 1649'.
SP 84/174 f. 118, 'De Malines to Joseph Williamson, 27 February 1665'. SP 18/33 f. 152, 'John Milton to Lord Bradshaw, 21 February 1653'.

Nationaal Archief, The Hague

1.10.02, 10, diary Lieuwe van Aitzema (1648–1650).
1.10.02, 45, diary Lieuwe van Aitzema (1652).
1.10.02, 49, pieces associated with legislation, Lieuwe van Aitzema (1652).

Primary Sources

Aglionby, William, *The present state of the United Provinces of the Low-Countries, as to the government, laws, forces, riches, manners, customes, revenue, and territory of the Dutch in three books* (London: 1671).
Aitzema, Leo van, *Saeken van staet en oorlogh*, 14 vols. (Amsterdam: 1662).
Anonymous, *A broad-side of the Dutch, with a bounce, a bounce, a bounce* (London: 1672).
———, *A Character of France* (London: 1659).

———, *A familiar discourse, between George a true-hearted English gentleman and Hans a Dutch merchant* (London: 1672).

———, *A true relation of the late cruell and barbarous tortures and execution, done vpon the English at Amboyna in the East Indies, by the Hollanders there residing. As it hath byn lately deliuered to the Kings most Excellent Maiesty* (Saint-Omer: 1624).

———, *A true relation of the vniust, cruell, and barbarous proceedings against the English at Amboyna in the East-Indies, by the Neatherlandish gouernour and councel there. Also the copie of a pamphlet, set forth first in Dutch and then in English, by some Neatherlander; falsly entituled, a true declaration of the newes that came out of the East-Indies, with the pinace called the hare, which arriued at Texel in Iune, 1624. Together with an answer to the same pamphlet. By the English East-India Companie. Published by authoritie* (London: 1624, re-printed in 1632 and 1651).

———, *Amsterdam and her other Hollander sisters put out to sea, by Van Trump, Van Dunck, and Van Dumpe, or, A true description of those so called Hoghens Mogens, set out to the life* (London: 1652).

———, *An Essay upon His Royal Highness the Duke of York his adventure against the Dutch* (London: 1672).

———, *Bellum Belgium Secundum, Or, A poem, Attempting something on his majesties proceedings against the Dutch* (London: 1665).

———, *Dr Dorislaw's ghost, presented by time to unmask the vizards of the Hollanders* (London: 1652).

———, *Englands tryumph, and Hollands downfall* (London: 1666).

———, *Histoire de la Vie et de la Mort des Deux Illustrer Freres, C et J de Witt* (Utrecht: 1707).

———, *Hogan-Moganides, or, the Dutch Hudibras* (London: 1674).

———, *Lucifer faln, or, Some reflections on the present estate of the low-countries* (London: 1672)

———, *Nederlantsche Nyp-tang* (Amsterdam?: 1652).

———, *Nevves Out of East India of the cruell and bloody vsage of our English merchants and others at Amboyna, by the Netherlandish gouernour and councell there. To the tune of Braggendary* (London: 1624).

———, *Poor Robins Character of a Dutch-man* (London: 1672).

———, *Pro Rege et Populo Anglicano Apologia* (Antwerp: 1651).

———, *Sampsons Foxes agreed to fire a Kingdom* (London: 1644).

———, *Strange newes from Holland, being a true character of the country and people* (London: 1672).

———, 'Tegen Vondels Lucifer', in *Apollos Harp* (Amsterdam: 1658): 154.

———, *The Character of Italy* (London: 1660).

———, *The Dutch boare dissected, or a description of hogg-land* (London: 1665).

———, *The Dutch damnified: or, The butter-boxes bob'd* (London: 1665?).

———, *The Dutch drawn to the life* (London: 1664).

———, *The Dutch storm: or, it's an ill wind that blows no-body profit. Being a perfect relation of eighteen ships great and small, taken from the Hogen mogen Stats van Hollandt* (London: 1665).

———, *The Racovian Catechism* (Amsterdam: 1652).

———, *The Seas magazine opened: or the Hollander dispossest of his usurped trade of fishing upon the English seas* (London: 1653).

————, *The 20th of September. The newes which now arrive from diuers parts, translated out of Dutch copies, with some aduertisements sent hither, vnto such as correspond with friends on the other side. In seuerall letters from honourable and worshipfull personages, residing at Skink Sconce, in the leager of his excellencie at Breda, in the campe of Count Mansfield, and from other places* (London: 1622).

————, *Two royal achrostichs on the Dutch in the ditch*. (London: 1672?).

Aristoteles, *Poëtica*, transl. by N. van der Ben and J.M. Bremer (Amsterdam: Athenaeum, 1986).

Arminius, Jacobus, *The Works of James Arminius*, ed. and transl. by James Nicols (London: Longman et al., 1825).

Arnoldi, Henricus, *Vande Conscientie-dwangh, dat is: Klaer ende Grondich Vertoogh, dat de [. . .] Staten Generael in haer Placcaet den 3 Julij 1619 tegen de Conventiculen der Remonstranten ghe-emaneert, gheen Conscientie-dwangh invoeren: Maerallen Ingesetenen der Geunieerde Provincien, van hoedanigen ghelove sy zijn, de behoorlicke ende volcomene vryheydt der Conscientie toe- staen ende vergunnen [. . .]* (Amsterdam: 1629).

Augustine of Hippo, 'St Augustine: On the Holy Trinity, Doctrinal Treatises, Moral Treatises', in *Nicene and Post-Nicene Fathers*, ed. by Philip Shaff (New York: Cosimo, 2007): 3–228.

Baxter, Richard, *Certain Disputations of right to sacraments* (London: 1657).

Beaumont, *The Emblem of ingratitude a true relation of the unjust, cruel, and barbarous proceedings against the English at Amboyna in the East-Indies* (London: 1672).

Beza, Theodore, *Tractationes Theologicae* (Geneva: 1573).

Brome, Richard, *The New Academy* (London: 1658).

————, *The Sparagus Garden* (London: 1640).

Brune, Johan de, *Nieuwe Wyn in oude Le'erzacken* (Middelburg: 1636).

Buchanan, George, *De jure regni apud Scotos, or, A dialogue, concerning the due priviledge of government in the kingdom of Scotland, betwixt George Buchanan and Thomas Maitland by the said George Buchanan; and translated out of the original Latine into English by Philalethes* (London: 1680).

Burmannus, Petrus, *Sylloge Epistolarum a Viris Illustribus Scriptarum*, 3 vols. (Leiden: 1727), vol. 3.

Calvin, Jean, *Institutes of the Christian Religion*, transl. and ed. by Henry Beveridge (Edinburgh: Calvin Translation Society, 1845).

Camões, Luis de, *The Lusiads or the Portugals*, transl. by Richard Fanshawe and ed. by Geoffrey Bullough (London: Centaur Press Ltd., 1963).

Cavendish, Margaret, 'Nature's House' (1651–3?), in *The Country House Poem: A Cabinet of Seventeenth-Century Estate Poems and Related Items*, ed. by Alistair Fowler (Edinburgh: Edinburgh University Press, 1994): 318–319.

Dante, Alighieri, *The Divine Comedy*, transl. and ed. by Robin Kirkpatrick (London: Penguin Classics, 2012).

Dekker, Thomas, *The Shoemaker's Holiday* (London: 1600).

Dekker, Thomas, and Thomas Middleton, *The Roaring Girl* (London: 1611).

D.F., *The Dutch-mens pedigree, or, A relation, shewing how they were first bred and descended from a horse-turd, which was enclosed in a butter-box* (London: 1653).

Diodati, Giovanni, *Pious and Learned Annotations upon the Holy Bible* (London: 1651).

Drayton, Michael, *Poly Olbion* (London: 1612, 1622).

Dryden, John, *Amboyna* (London: 1673).

———, *The Works of John Dryden*, ed. by Edward Niles Hooker and H.T. Swedenberg, 20 vols. (Los Angeles: University of California Press, 1974).

Elizabeth, Tudor, *A Declaration of the causes moouing the Queene of England to giue aide to the Defence of the People afflicted and oppressed in the lowe Countries* (London: 1585).

Estius, Guilelmus, *Annotationes a Ureae in praecipua ac difficiliora Sacrae Scripturae loca* (Cologne: 1622).

Evelyn, John, *Miscellaneous Writings of John Evelyn*, ed. by William Upcott (London: Henry Culborn, 1825).

———, *The Character of England* (London: 1659).

———, *The Diary of John Evelyn*, ed. by E.S. de Beer, 6 vols. (Oxford: Oxford University Press, 1955).

Fanshawe, Sir Richard, 'An Ode upon Occasion of His Majesty's Proclamation in the Year 1630' (9 Sep. 1630), in *The Country House Poem: A Cabinet of Seventeenth-Century Estate Poems and Related Items*, ed. by Alistair Fowler (Edinburgh: Edinburgh University Press, 1994): 123–127.

Felltham, Owen, *A brief character of the Low-Countreys under the states being three weeks observations of the vices and vertues of the inhabitants* (London: 1652).

———, *A Trip to Holland being a description of the country, people and manners: as also some select observations on Amsterdam* (London: 1699).

———, *A true and exact character of the Low-Countreyes; especially Holland or, the Dutchman anatomized, and truly dissected. Being the series of three moneths observations of the country, customes, religions, manners, and dispositions of the people* (London: 1652).

———, *Batavia: or The Hollander displayed Being three weeks observations of the Low Countries, especially Holland. In brief characters and observations of the people and country, the governement of their state and private families, their virtues and vices* (London: 1672, 1697).

———, *Resolves divine, moral, political by Owen Felltham. Brief character of the Low-countries under the states* (London: 1661, 1670, 1677, 1696).

———, *Three weeks of observations of the low country, especially Holland* (London: 1672).

Freitas, Serafim de, *De iusto imperio Lusitanorum Asiatico* (Valladolid: 1625).

Gascoigne, George, 'Gascoigne's voyage into Holland, An. 1572', in *A Hundreth Sundrie Flowres* (1573), ed. by G.W. Pigman (Oxford: Oxford University Press, 2000).

Gomarus, Fransciscus, *Accoort vande Recht-sinnige leere der Voorsienicheyt Gods* (Leiden: 1612).

Grotius, Hugo, *Commentary on the Law of Prize and Booty*, ed. by Martine van Ittersum (Indiapolis: Library Fund, 2006).

———, *De satisfactione Christi adversus Faustum Socinum* (Lyon: 1617).

———, *De veritate religionis Christanae* (Leiden: 1627).

———, *Liber de Antiquitate Reipublicae Batavicae* (Lugdunum Batavorum: 1610).

———, *Mare liberum* (Leiden: 1609).

———, *Ordinum Hollandiae et Westfrisiae pietas* (Leiden: 1611).

———, 'Preface', in *Adamus Exul* (Den Haag: 1601).

——, *Remonstrantie nopende de ordre dije in de landen van Hollandt ende West-vrieslandt dijent gestelt op de Joden*, ed. by Jaap Meijer (Amsterdam: Drukkerij Coster, 1949).

——, *The Rights of War and Peace*, transl. by A.C. Campbell (London: Walter Dunne Publishers, 1901).

Hales, John, *Golden remains* (London: 1659).

——, *A tract concerning schism* (London: 1642).

Hexham, Henry, *A Copious English and Netherduytch Dictionary* (Rotterdam: 1647).

Howard, Edward, *A panegyrick to His Highnesse the Duke of York on his sea-fight with the Dutch* (London: 1666).

Howell, James, *Epistolae Ho-elianae familiar letters domestic and forren divided into sundry sections, partly historicall, politicall, philosophicall, vpon emergent occasions* (London: 1650).

Huygens, Constantijn, *Epimikta, een rouwklacht in het Latijn op de dood van zijn echtgenote (1637–1638)*, ed., transl., and introduced by J.P. Guépin (Voorthuizen: Florivallis, 1996).

——, *Hofwijck*, ed. by Ton van Strien, 2 vols. (Amsterdam: Koninklijke Nederlandse Academie van Amsterdam, 2008).

——, *Korenbloemen* (Amsterdam: 1672).

Huygens, Lodewijck, *The English Journal 1651–1652*, ed. and transl. by A.G.H. Bachrach and R.G. Collmer (Leiden: Brill, 1982).

J.D., *A true and compendious narration or, second part of Amboyna, or sundry notorious or remarkable injuries, insolencies, and acts of hostility which the Hollanders have exercised from time to time against the English nation in the East-Indies* (London: 1665).

J.W., *Brandy-wine, in the Hollanders ingratitude. Being a serious expostulation of an English souldier with the Dutch* (London: 1652).

Kant, Immanuel, *Critique of Judgement*, transl. by Werner S. Pluhar (Indianapolis: Hacket Publishing Company, 1987).

——, *Observations on the Feeling of the Beautiful and Sublime*, transl. by John T. Goldthwait (Berkeley: University of California Press, 1991).

Laet, Johan de, *Notae ad Dissertationem Hugonis Grotii* De Origine Gentium Americanarum: *et Observationes aliquot ad meliorem indaginem difficillimae illius Quaestionis* (Amsterdam: Elzevier, 1643).

L'Estrange, Roger, *An Account of the Growth of Knavery, under the Pretended Fears of Arbitrary Government and Popery* (London: 1678).

Locke, John, *Two Treatises of Government* (London: Everyman's Library, 1978).

Lucretius, Titus, *On the Nature of Things*, transl. by Lucy Hutchinson, in *The Works of Lucy Hutchinson*, ed. by Reid Barbour and David Norbrook (Oxford: Oxford University Press, 2012).

Lupton, Donald, *Englands command on the seas, or, The English seas guarded. Wherin is proved that as the Venetians, Portugals, Spaniard, French, [. . .] have dominion on their seas; so the common-wealth of England hath on our seas* (London: 1653).

Marvell, Andrew, *The Poems of Andrew Marvell*, ed. by Nigel Smith (London: Longman Pearson, 2007).

——, *The Poems and Letters of Andrew Marvell*, ed. by H.M. Margoliouth (revised by Pierre Legouis), 2 vols. (Oxford: Clarendon Press, 1971).

————, *Prose Works of Andrew Marvell*, ed. by Annabel Patterson and Martin Dzelzainis, 2 vols. (New Haven: Yale University Press, 2003).

Milton, John, *Complete Prose Works of John Milton*, gen. ed. Don M. Wolfe, 8 vols. (New Haven: Yale University Press, 1953–1982).

————, *The Complete Shorter Poems*, ed. by John Carey (London: Longman Pearson, 2007).

————, *Complete Works of John Milton*, gen. ed. Gordon Campbell and Thomas Corns (Oxford: Oxford University Press, 2008–2020).

————, *John Milton: Epistolarum Familiarium Liber Unus and Uncollected Letters*, ed., intro., transl. by Estelle Haan (Leuven: Leuven University Press, 2019).

————, *Paradise Lost*, ed. by Alastair Fowler (London: Longman Pearson, 2007).

————, *Private Correspondence and Academic Exercises*, transl. by Phyllis B. Tillyard (Cambridge: Cambridge University Press, 1932).

Milton, John, and Alexander More, *Joannis Miltoni Angli pro Populo Anglicano Densio Secunda: Contra infamem libellum anonymum cui Titulus Regii Sanguinis Clamor Ad Cælum Adversus Parricidas Anglicanos* (Printed by Vlacq, 1654). *Koninklijke Bibliotheek*, Speciale Collecties, KW. 2203 G 19.

Molloy, Charles, *Hollands Ingratitude, or, A serious expostulation with the Dutch* (London: 1666).

More, Alexander, *Alexandri Mori, ecclesiastae, sacrarumque litterarum professoris: Fides Publica contra calumnias Joannis Miltoni Scurrae* (The Hague: 1654).

Moryson, Fynes, *An itinerary written by Fynes Moryson Gent. First in the Latine tong* [. . .] (London: 1617).

Moulin, Pierre du, *Regii sanguinis clamor* (The Hague: 1651).

Mountague, William, *The Delights of Holland: or, A three months travel about that and the other provinces with observations and reflections on their trade, wealth, strength, beauty and policy & c. together with a catalogue of the rarities in the anatomical school at Leyden* (London: 1669).

Muldoon, Paul, *Meeting the British* (London: Faber and Faber, 1987).

Munday, Anthony, *Briefe chronologicall suruay concerning the Netherlands* [. . .] (London: 1611).

Myriell, Thomas, 'To the Right Worshipfull Mr. Maurice Abbott, Governor of the East-India Companie', in *The stripping of Ioseph, Or the crueltie of brethren to a brother in a sermon before his Maiestie at White-Hall, by Robert Wilkinson, Doctor in Diuinitie, chaplaine in ordinarie to his Maiestie, and late pastor of Saint Olaues in Southwarke. With a consolatorie epistle, to the English-East-India Companie, for their vnsufferable wrongs sustayned in Amboyna, by the Dutch there Published and presented vnto them, by Tho. Myriell pastor of Saint Stephens in Walbrooke* (London: 1625).

Nedham, Marchamont, *Of the Dominion, or ownership of the sea* (London: 1652).

Oudaen, Joachim, *De Neergeplofte Lucifer* (Amsterdam: 1659).

Pepys, Samuel, *The Diary of Samuel Pepys*, ed. by Robert Latham William Matthews, 11 vols. (Berkeley: University of California Press, 1971).

Perkins, William, *A Christian and plaine treatise of the manner and order of predestination: and of the largenes of God's grace* (Cambridge: 1606).

Philips, Edward, 'The Life of Mr. John Milton', in *The Early Lives of Milton*, ed. by Helen Darbishire (London: Constable and Co., 1932).

Philips, John, 'The Life of Mr. John Milton', in *The Early Lives of Milton*, ed. by Helen Darbishire (London: Constable and Co., 1932).

Philips, John, *Joannis Philippi Angli responsio* (London: 1651).

Quarles, Francis, *The Historie of Sampson* (London: 1631).

Rabus, Petrus, *Boekzaal van Europa*, 9 vols. (Rotterdam: Pieter vander Slaart, 1695).

Rowland, John, *Polemica, sive Supplementum ad Apologiam Anonymam* (Antwerp: 1653).

Scott, Thomas, *The wicked plots, and perfidious practises of the Spaniards, against the 17: provinces of the Netherlands, before they tooke up arms. Being gathered out of severall Dutch writers, by a lover of truth, and an unfained hater of oppression and tyrannie, the bane of commonwealths* (London: 1642).

Selden, John, *Mare Clausum* (London: 1635).

———, *Titles of Honour* (London: 1614).

Seton, William, *The interest of Scotland in Three Essays* (London?: 1700).

Scaliger, Julius Caesar, *Poetices libri septem* (1560).

Shakespeare, William, *The Complete Works of William Shakespeare*, ed. by Stanley Wells and Gary Taylor (Oxford: Clarendon Press, 2005).

Smith, William, *Ingratitude reveng'd, or A poem upon the happy victory of his majesties naval forces against the Dutch* (London: 1665).

Starkey, George, *The dignity of kingship asserted: in answer to Mr. Milton's Ready and easie way to establish a free Common-wealth* (London: 1660).

Swift, Jonathan, *Gulliver's Travels: Into Several Remote Nations of the World* (London: 1726).

Tacitus, *The Histories of Tacitus* (Cambridge: Loeb Classics, 1931).

Temple, Sir William, *Observations Upon the United Provinces of the Netherlands*, ed. by Sir George Clark (Oxford: Clarendon Press, 1972).

Toland, John, 'The Life of John Milton, 1698', in *The Early Lives of Milton*, ed. by Helen Darbishire (London: Constable and Co., 1923).

Voltaire, *Candide ou l'Optimisme* (France: Gallimard, 2012).

Vondel, Joost van den, *Bespiegelingen van God and Godsdienst; tegens d'Ongodisten, verloochenaars der Godheid of Goddelijke Voorzienigheid* (Amsterdam: 1661).

———, *De werken van Vondel*, ed. by J.F.M. Sterck, et al., 10 vols. (Amsterdam: Wereldbibliotheek, 1927–1937).

Waller, Edmund, *The Poems of Edmund Waller*, ed. by G. Thorn Drury, 2 vols. (London: Routledge, 1893).

Westerbaen, Jacob, *Arctoa tempe: Ockenburgh, woonstede van den Heere van Brandwyck in de Clingen buyten Loosduynen* ('s Gravenhage: 1654).

———, *Minne-dichten* (Amsterdam: 1644).

Wicquefort, Abraham de, *A Relation in the form of Journal*, transl. by William Lower (London: 1660).

Williams, Roger, *The Bloudy Tenent of Persecution, for Cause of Conscience, Discussed in a Conference between Truth and Peace* (London: 1644).

———, *The Letters of Roger Williams* (1632–1682), ed. by John Russel Barlett (Providence: 1874).

Wittgenstein, Ludwig, *Culture and Value*, ed. by G.H. von Wright (Oxford: Blackwell Publishing, 1998).

———, *Philosophical Investigations*, transl. by G.E.M. Anscombe (Oxford: Blackwell Publishing, 1953).

Ziegler, Caspar, and James Schaller, *Caspari Ziegleri Lipsiensis circa Regicidium Anglorum* (Leiden: 1653).

Secondary Sources

Acheson, Katherine O., 'Military Illustration, Garden Design, and Marvell's "Upon Appleton House"', *English Literary Renaissance*, 41.1 (2011): 146–188.

Achinstein, Sharon, '*Samson Agonistes* and the Drama of Dissent', *Milton Studies*, 33 (1997): 133–158.

———, '*Samson Agonistes* and the Politics of Memory', in *Altering Eyes: New Perspectives on 'Samson Agonistes'*, ed. by Joseph Wittreich and Mark Kelley Wittreich (Newark: University of Delaware Press, 2002): 168–191.

Alblas, Jacques B.H., 'Milton's *The Doctrine and Discipline of Divorce*: The Unknown Dutch Translation (1655) Discovered', *Milton Quarterly*, 28.2 (1994): 35–39.

Armitage, David, *Ideological Origins of the British Empire* (Cambridge: Cambridge University Press, 2004).

———, 'John Milton: Poet against Empire', in *Milton and Republicanism*, ed. by David Armitage, Armand Himy, and Quentin Skinner (Cambridge: Cambridge University Press, 1995): 206–225.

Bachrach, A.G.H., *Sir Constantine Huygens and Britain: 1596–1687* (Oxford: Oxford University Press, 1962).

Backhouse, Marcel, 'The Strangers at Work in Sandwich: Native Envy of an Industrious Minority', in *From Revolt to Riches: Culture and History of the Low Countries, 1500–1700*, ed. by Theo Hermans and Reinier Salverda (London: UCL Press, 2017): 61–68.

Bangs, Carl, *Arminius: A Study in the Dutch Reformation* (New York: Abingdon Press, 1971).

Bangs, Jeremy Dupertuis, 'Dutch Contribution to Religious Toleration', *Church History*, 79.3 (2010): 585–613.

Bardle, Stephen, *The Literary Underground in the 1660s: Andrew Marvell, George Wither, Ralph Waller, and the World of Restoration Satire and Pamphleteering* (Oxford: Oxford University Press, 2012).

Barducci, Marco, *Hugo Grotius and the Century of Revolution, 1613–1718* (Oxford: Oxford University Press, 2017).

Barend-Van Haeften, Marijke, and Hetty Plekenpol (eds.), *Wouter Schouten, dichter en VOC-chirurgijn: 36 gedichten bij de Oost-Indische voyagie* (Zutphen: Walburg Pers, 2014).

Barnard, John, 'The 1665 York and London Editions of Marvell's "The Character of Holland"', *The Papers of the Bibliographical Society of America*, 81.4 (1987): 459–464.

Barthes, Roland, 'Myth Today', in *Mythologies* (London: Vintage Classics, 1993): 109–159.

Bauman, Michael, *Milton's Arianism* (Frankfurt: Lang, 1987).

Beek, Pieta van, *The First Female University Student: Anna Maria van Schurman (1636)* (Utrecht: Igitur, 2010).

———, *Klein werk: de Opuscula Hebraea Graeca Latina et Gallica, Prosaica et Metrica* (Ph.D. Thesis, University of Stellenbosch, 2004).

Bekker, Hugo, 'The Religio-Philosophical Orientations of Vondel's *Lucifer*, Milton's *Paradise Lost*, and Grotius's *Adamus Exul*', *Neophilogus*, 44.1 (1960): 234–244.

Beller, Manfred, 'Perception, Image, Imagology', in *Imagology: The Cultural Construction and Literary Representation of National Characters*, ed. by Manfred Beller and Joep Leerssen (Amsterdam: Amsterdam University Press, 2007): 3–16.

———, 'Stereotype', in *Imagology: The Cultural Construction and Literary Representation of National Characters*, ed. by Manfred Beller and Joep Leerssen (Amsterdam: Amsterdam University Press, 2007): 429–434.

Berg, B. van den, 'Boers en Beschaafd in het Begin der 17ᵉ Eeuw', *De Nieuwe Taalgids*, 37 (1943): 242–246.

Berg, J. van den, 'Dutch Calvinism and the Church of England in the Period of the Glorious Revolution', in *The Exchange of Ideas: Religion, Scholarship, and Art in the Seventeenth Century* (Zutphen: Walburg Institute, 1994): 84–99.

Bicknell, E.J., *The Christian Idea of Sin and Original Sin, in the Light of Modern Knowledge* (London: Longmans, 1923).

Blackford, Paul W., 'Preface to Fides Publica and Supplementum', in *Milton: The Complete Prose Works* (New Haven: Yale University Press, 1964), 4, part II: 1082–1085.

Bloemendal, Jan, 'New Philology: Variants in *Adam in Ballingschap* (1664)', in *Joost van den Vondel: Dutch Playwright in the Golden Age*, ed. by Jan Bloemendal and Frans-Willem Korsten (Leiden: Brill, 2012): 489–508.

Blok, F.F., *Isaac Vossius en zijn Kring: Zijn Leven tot Zijn Afscheid van Koningin Christina van Zweden, 1618–1655* (Groningen: Egbert Forsten, 1999).

Boer, William den, *Duplex Amor Dei: Contextuele Karakteristiek van de Theologie van Jacobus Arminius (1559–1609)* (Apeldoorn: Instituut voor Reformatie Onderzoek, 2008).

———, *God's Twofold Love: The Theology of Jacob Arminius (1599–1609)* (Göttingen: Vandenhoeck & Ruprecht, 2010).

———, 'Jacobus Arminius: Theologian of God's Twofold Love', in *Arminius, Arminianism, and Europe*, ed. by Th. Marius van Leeuwen, Keith D. Stanglin, and Marijke Tolsma (Leiden: Brill, 2009): 25–50.

Bork, G.J. van de, and P.J. Verkruijse, 'Pieter Rabus', in *De Nederlandse en Vlaamse Auteurs* (Weesp: De Haan, 1985).

Boswell, Jackson Campbell, *Milton Library: A Catalogue of the Remains of John Milton's Library and an Annotated Reconstruction of Milton's Library and Ancillary Readings* (New York: Garland Publishing, 1975).

Bourne, E.C.E., *The Anglicanism of William Laud* (London: Society for Promoting Christian Knowledge, 1946).

Bowring, John, *Sketch of the Language and Literature of Holland* (Amsterdam: Diederich Brothers, 1829).

Boxer, C.R., *Zeevarend Nederland en zijn Wereldrijk, 1600–1800* (Leiden: A.W. Slijthoff, 1976).

Braudel, Fernand, *La Méditerranée et le Monde Méditerranéen a l'époque de Philippe II*, 3 vols. (Paris: Livre de Poche, 1993).

Bremer, Francis J., 'Williams, Roger (c. 1606–1683)', *Oxford Dictionary of National Biography*, retrieved 21 Mar. 2019. www.oxforddnb.com/abstract/10.1093/ref:odnb/9780198614128.001.0001/odnb-9780198614128-e-29544?rskey=wcjG1y.

Broadbent, John B., *Some Graver Subject: An Essay to Paradise Lost* (London: Chatto and Windus, 1960).

Brown, Cedric C., *John Milton's Aristocratic Entertainments* (Cambridge: Cambridge University Press, 1985).

Brown, Laura, 'Dryden and the Imperial Imagination', in *The Cambridge Companion to John Dryden*, ed. Steven N. Zwicker (Cambridge: Cambridge University Press, 2004): 59–74.

Bruin, C.C. de, *De Statenbijbel en zijn Voorgangers* (Haarlem: Nederlands Bijbelge-nootschap, 1993).

Burnet, John, *Greek Philosophy: Thales to Plato* (London: Macmillan, 1928).

Burrows, John, 'Andrew Marvell and the Painter Satires: A Computational Approach to Their Authorship', *The Modern Language Review*, 100.2 (2005): 281–297.

Butler, W.E., 'Grotius and the Law of the Sea', in *Hugo Grotius and International Relations*, ed. by Hedley Bull, Benedict Kingsbury, and Adam Roberts (Oxford: Oxford University Press, 1990): 210–221.

Calloway, Katherine, 'Milton's Lucretian Anxiety Revisited', *Renaissance and Reformation*, 32.3 (2009): 79–97.

Campbell, Gordon, 'Epilogue on the Multilingual and Multicultural Milton', in *Milton in Translation*, ed. by Angelica Duran, Islam Issa, Jonathan R. Olson (Oxford: Oxford University Press, 2017): 493–497.

———, *A Milton Chronology* (Basingstoke: Palgrave Macmillan, 1997).

Campbell, Gordon, and Thomas Corns, *John Milton: Life, Works and Thought* (Oxford: Oxford University Press, 2008).

Campbell, Gordon, Thomas Corns, John K. Hale, and Fiona J. Tweedie, *Milton and the Manuscript of De doctrina Christiana* (Oxford: Oxford University Press, 2007).

Capp, Bernard, *Cromwell's Navy: The Fleet and the English Revolution* (Oxford: Oxford University Press, 1992).

Carlton, Charles, *Charles I: The Personal Monarch* (London: Routledge, 1983).

Chernaik, Warren L., 'Harsh Remedies: Satire and Politics in "Last Instructions to a Painter"', in *The Oxford Handbook to Andrew Marvell*, ed. by Martin Dzelzainis and Edward Holberton (Oxford: Oxford University Press, 2019): 444–462.

———, *The Poetry of Limitation: A Study of Edmund Waller* (New Haven: Yale University Press, 1968).

———, *The Poet's Time: Politics and Religion in the Work of Andrew Marvell* (Cambridge: Cambridge University Press, 1983).

———, 'Waller, Edmund (1608–1687), Poet and Politician', *Oxford Dictionary of National Biography*, retrieved 13 Jan. 2019. www.oxforddnb.com/abstract/10.1093/ref:odnb/9780198614128.001.0001/odnb-9780198614128-e-28556?rskey=v8qc3R.

Chernaik, Warren L., and Martin Dzelzainis (eds.), *Marvell and Liberty* (Basingstoke: Palgrave Macmillan, 1999).

Chouhan, Omar Prakesh, *The Dutch East India Company and the Economy of Bengal*, 1630–1720 (Princeton: Princeton University Press, 1985).

Cirillo, Albert R., 'Time, Light, and the Phoenix: The Design of *Samson Agonistes*', in *Calm of Mind: Tercentenary Essays on Paradise Regained and Samson Agonistes*, ed. by Joseph Wittreich (London: Western Reserve University, 1971): 209–234.

Colie, Rosalie L., *Some Thankfulness to Constantine: A Study of English Influence upon the Early Works of Constantijn Huygens* (Den Haag: Martinus Nijhoff, 1956).

Como, David R., 'Predestination and Political Conflict in Laud's London', *The Historical Journal*, 46.2 (2003): 263–294.

Connell, Philip, 'Marvell, Milton and the Protectoral Church Settlement', *Review of English Studies*, 62.256 (2011): 562–593.

———, *Secular Chains: Poetry and the Politics of Religion from Milton to Pope* (Oxford: Oxford University Press, 2016).

Conti, Brooke, *Confessions of Faith in Early Modern England* (Philadelphia: Penn-sylvania University Press, 2014).

Corns, Thomas N., 'Milton, Roger Williams, and Limits of Toleration', in *Milton and Toleration*, ed. by Sharon Achinstein and Elizabeth Sauer (Oxford: Oxford University Press, 2007): 72–85.

———, 'Milton's Antiprelatical Tracts and the Marginality of Doctrine', in *Milton and Heresy*, ed. by Stephen B. Dobranski and John P. Rumrich (Cambridge: Cambridge University Press, 1998): 39–48.

———, *Regaining Paradise Lost* (London: Longmans, 1994).

Cotterill, Ann, *Digressive Voices in Early Modern English Literature* (Oxford: Oxford University Press, 2004).

Cotterill, Rodney, *The Material World* (Cambridge: Cambridge University Press, 2008).

Cousins, A.D., 'Marvell's Devout Mythology of the New World: Homeland and Home in "Bermudas"', *Parergon*, 30.1 (2013): 203–219.

Cowan, Brian, 'Millington, Edward (*c.*1636–1703)', *Oxford Dictionary National Biography*, retrieved 23 Mar. 2019. www.oxforddnb.com/view/10.1093/ref:odnb/9780198614128.001.0001/odnb-9780198614128-e-52142.

Cummings, Brian, *The Literary Culture of the Reformation: Grammar and Grace* (Oxford: Oxford University Press, 2002).

Cunningham, Jack, *John Ussher and John Bramhall: The Theology and Politics of Two Irish Ecclesiastics of the Seventeenth Century* (Aldershot: Ashgate Publishing, 2007).

Daley, Koos, *The Triple Fool: A Critical Evaluation of Constantijn Huygens' Translations of John Donne* (Nieuwkoop: De Graaf Publishers, 1990).

Daniels, Paul, 'Kant on the Beautiful: The Interest in Disinterestedness', *Colloquy*, 16 (2008): 198–209.

Danielson, Dennis, *Milton's Good God: A Study in Literary Theodicy* (Cambridge: Cambridge University Press, 1982).

Darbishire, Helen (ed.), *The Early Lives of John Milton* (New York: Barnes and Noble, 1932).

Daugirdas, Kęstutis, 'The Biblical Hermeneutics of Philip van Limborch (1633–1712) and Its Intellectual Challenges', in *Scriptural Authority and Biblical Criticism in the Dutch Golden Age: God's Word Questioned* (Oxford: Oxford University Press, 2017): 220–258.

Davidson, Peter, and Adriaan van der Weel, *A Selection of the Poems of Constantijn Huygens* (Amsterdam: Amsterdam University Press, 1996).

Davies, David W., 'The Geographic Extent of the Dutch Book Trade in the Seventeenth Century', *The Library Quarterly*, 22.3 (1952): 200–207.

Davies, Gwendolyn, *The 'Samson' Theme in the Works of Rembrandt, Vondel, and Milton: A Comparative Study in the Humanities* (Unpublished Masters Thesis, Wayne State University, Detroit, MI).

Davies, J.D., *Gentlemen and Tarpaulins: The Officers and Men of the Restoration Navy* (Oxford: Oxford University Press, 1991).

———, 'Temple, Sir William, Baronet (1628–1699), Diplomat and Author', *Oxford Dictionary of National Biography* (2009), retrieved 9 Jan. 2019. www.oxforddnb.com/view/10.1093/ref:odnb/9780198614128.001.0001/odnb-9780198614128-e-27122?rskey=2DBey1&result=4.

Davies, Julian, *The Caroline Captivity of the Church: Charles I and the Remoulding of Anglicanism, 1625–1641* (Oxford: Clarendon Press, 1992).

Dekker, Evert, *Rijker dan Midas: vrijheid, genade en predestinatie in de theologie van Jacobus Arminius, 1559–1609* (Zoetermeer: Boekencentrum, 1993).

Dijkhuizen, Jan Frans van, and Helmer Helmers, 'Religion and Politics: *Lucifer* (1654) and Milton's *Paradise Lost* (1674)', in *Vondel, Dutch Dramatist in the Golden Age* (Leiden: Brill, 2011): 377–405.

Dikkers, Scott, and Mike Loew, *Our Dumb Century: The Onion Presents 100 Years of Headlines from America's Finest News Source* (Maddison: Three Rivers Press, 1999).

Dimmock, Matthew, Andrew Hadfield, and Margaret Healy, 'Introduction', in *The Intellectual Culture of the English Country House, 1500–1700* (Manchester: Manchester University Press, 2015): 1–10.

Dobranski, Stephen B., *Milton, Authorship, and the Book Trade* (Cambridge: Cambridge University Press, 1999).

———, *Milton's Visual Imagination: Imagery in Paradise Lost* (Cambridge: Cambridge University Press, 2015).

Duke, Alistair, 'The Ambivalent Face of Calvinism in the Netherlands, 1561–1618', in *International Calvinism 1541–1715*, ed. by Menna Prestwich (Oxford: Oxford University Press, 1985): 109–135.

———, *Reformation and Revolt in the Low Countries* (London: Hambledon and London, 1990).

Duncan-Jones, E.E., and Helen Wilcox, 'Marvel's Holt-Fester', *Notes and Queries*, 4 (2001): 395–397.

Dunthorne, Hugh, *Britain and the Dutch Revolt* (Cambridge: Cambridge University Press, 2013).

Duran, Angelica, Islam Issa, and Jonathan R. Olson (eds.), *Milton in Translation* (Oxford: Oxford University Press, 2017).

Durham, John I., *The Biblical Rembrandt: Human Painter in a Landscape of Faith* (Macon: Mercer University Press, 2004).

Du Rieu, W.N. (ed.), *Album studiosorum Academiae Lugduno Batavae MDLXXV-MDCCCLXXV: accedunt nomina curatorum et professorum per eadem secula* (Den Haag: Martinus Nijhoff, 1875).

DuRocher, Richard J., *Milton and Ovid* (Ithaca: Cornell University Press, 1985).

Dust, Philip, 'Milton's *Paradise Lost* and Grotius' *De Jure Belli ac Pacis* (the Law of War and Peace)', *Cithara: Essays in the Judaeo-Christian Tradition*, 33.1 (1993): 17–26.

Dyserinck, Hugo, *Komparatistik: Eine Einführung* (Bonn: Bouvier, 1991).

Dzelzainis, Martin, 'Andrew Marvell and the Restoration Literary Underground: Printing the *Painter Poems*', *Seventeenth Century*, 22.2 (2007): 395–410.

———, 'L'Estrange, Marvell and the Directions to a Painter', in *Roger L'Estrange and the Making of a Restoration Culture* (Aldershot: Ashgate Publishing, 2008): 53–67.

———, 'Marvell and the Dutch in 1665', in *A Concise Companion to the Study of Manuscripts, Printed Books, and the Production of Early Modern Texts*, ed. Edward Jones (Chichester: Wiley-Blackwell, 2015): 249–265.

———, 'Marvell and the Earl of Castlemaine', in *Marvell and Liberty*, ed. by Warren Chernaik and Martin Dzelzainis (Basingstoke: Palgrave Macmillan, 1999): 290–312.

——, 'Milton, Peter du Moulin and the Authorship of *Regii Sanguinis Clamor ad Coelum Adversus Parricidas Anglicanos* (1652)', *Notes and Queries*, 60.4 (2013): 537–538.

——, 'Milton's Politics', in *The Cambridge Companion to Milton*, ed. by Dennis Danielson (Cambridge: Cambridge University Press, 1999): 71–83.

——, '". . . ridiculous Pictures, and odious Medails": Visual Propaganda in the Second and Third Anglo-Dutch War', in *Breaking the Image/Image brisée*, ed. Christian Belin, Agnès Lafont, and Nicholas Myers (Classiques Garnier: in press).

Edmundson, George, *Milton and Vondel: A Curiosity of Literature* (Toronto: Trubner and Co, 1885).

Eisenstein, Elizabeth L., *The Printing Revolution in Early Modern Europe* (Cambridge: Cambridge University Press, 2005).

Ellenzweig, Sarah, '*Paradise Lost* and the Secret of Lucretian Sufficiency', *Modern Language Quarterly*, 75.3 (2014): 385–409.

Evans, J. Martin, *Milton's Imperial Epic: Paradise Lost and the Discourse of Colonialism* (Ithaca: Cornell University Press, 1996).

Eyffinger, Arthur, 'The Fourth Man: Stoic Tradition in Grotian Drama', *Grotiana*, 22.1 (2001): 117–156.

Fallon, Robert, 'Cromwell, Milton, and the Western Design', in *Milton and the Imperial Vision*, ed. by Balachandra Rajan and Elizabeth Sauer (Pittsburgh: Duquesne Press, 1999).

——, *Milton in Government* (Pennsylvania: Pennsylvania University Press, 1993).

Fallon, Stephen, "Elect above the rest": Theology as Self-Representation in Milton', in *Milton and Heresy*, ed. by Stephen B. Dobranksi and John Rumrich (Cambridge: Cambridge University Press, 1998): 93–116.

——, *Milton among the Philosophers: Poetry and Materialism in Seventeenth-Century England* (Ithaca: Cornell University Press, 1991).

——, 'Milton's Arminianism and the Authorship of *De doctrina Christiana*', *Texas Studies in Literature and Language*, 41.2 (1999): 103–127.

——, *Milton's Peculiar Grace: Self-Representation and Authority* (Ithaca: Cornell University Press, 2007).

Faust, Joan, 'Blurring the Boundaries: Ut picture poesis and Marvell's Liminal Mower', *Studies in Philology*, 104.4 (2007): 526–555.

Feingold, Mordechai, 'Stubbe, Henry (1632–1676)', *Oxford Dictionary of National Biography*, retrieved 24 Mar. 2019. www.oxforddnb.com/view/10.1093/ref:odnb/9780198614128.001.0001/odnb-9780198614128-e-26734.

Fleck, Andrew, 'Marvell's Use of Nedham's Selden', *Notes and Queries*, 55.2 (2007): 422–425.

Fletcher, Angus, *Time, Space, and Motion in the Age of Shakespeare* (Cambridge: Harvard University Press, 2007).

Flynn, Dennis O., and Arturo Giraldez, 'Globalization Began in 1571', in *Globalization and Global History*, ed. by Barry K. Gills and William R. Thompson (New York: Routledge, 2006): 232–247.

Fowler, Alistair, 'Introduction', in *The Country House Poem: A Cabinet of Seventeenth-Century Estate Poems and Related Items*, ed. by Alistair Fowler (Edinburgh: Edinburgh University Press, 1994): 1–29.

Fowler, Don, *Lucretius on Atomic Motion* (Oxford: Oxford University Press, 2002).

Freedman, Paul, 'The Medieval Spice Trade', in *The Oxford Handbook of Food History*, ed. by Jeffrey M. Pilcher (Oxford: Oxford University Press, 2012): 325–340.

Freeman, James, *Milton and the Martial Muse: Paradise Lost and European Traditions of War* (Princeton: Princeton University Press, 1980).

Gallagher, John, *Learning Languages in Early Modern England* (Oxford: Oxford University Press, 2019).

Gallagher, Noelle, '"Partial to Some One Side": The Advice-to-a-Painter Poems as Historical Writing', *English Literary History*, 78.1 (2011): 79–101.

Games, Alison, 'Anglo-Dutch Connections and Overseas Enterprises: A Global Perspective on Lion Gardiner's World', *Early American Studies*, 9.2 (2011): 435–461.

Gardiner, Anne Barbeau, 'Swift on the Dutch East India Merchant: The Context of 1672–1673 War Literature', *Huntington Library Quarterly*, 54.3 (1991): 234–252.

Gardiner, Samuel Rawson, *History of the Commonwealth and Protectorate, 1649–1660* (London: Longmans, 1894).

Gasparov, M.L., 'The Rise of Germanic Syllabo-Tonic Verse', in *A History of European Versification*, ed. by M.L. Gasparov, G.S. Smith, and Leofranc Holford-Strevens (Oxford: Oxford University, 1996): 167–208.

Gee, Sophie, 'The Invention of the Wasteland: Civic Narrative and Dryden's *Annus Mirabilis*', *Eighteenth-Century Life*, 29.1 (2005): 82–108.

Geerdink, Nina, *Dichters en verdiensten: de sociale verankering van het dichterschap van Jan Vos (1610–1667)* (Hilversum: Uitgeverij Verloren, 2012).

Gelderen, Martin van, *The Political Thought of the Dutch Revolt, 1555–1590* (Cambridge: Cambridge University Press, 1992).

Gemert, Guillaume van, 'Between Disregard and Political Mobilization: Vondel as a Playwright in Contemporary European Context: England, France and the German Lands', in *Joost van den Vondel: Dutch Playwright in the Golden Age*, ed. by Jan Bloemendal and Frans-Willem Korsten (Leiden: Brill, 2012): 171–200.

Gibbs, G.C., 'The Role of the Dutch Republic as the Intellectual Entrepôt of Europe in the Seventeenth and Eighteenth Centuries', *Bijdragen en Mededelingen Betreffende de Geschiedenis der Nederlanden*, 86.3 (1971): 323–349.

Gimelli Martin, Catherine, *Milton Amongst the Puritans: The Case for Historical Revisionism* (Farnham: Ashgate Publishing, 2010).

Goldenbaum, Ursula, 'Sovereignty and Obedience', in *The Oxford Handbook of Philosophy in Early Modern Europe*, ed. by Desmond M. Clarke and Catherine Wilson (Oxford: Oxford University Press, 2011): 500–521.

Goudriaan, Aza, '"Augustine Asleep" or "Augustine Awake"? Jacobus Arminius's Reception of Augustine', in *Arminius, Arminianism, and Europe*, ed. by Th. Marius van Leeuwen, Keith D. Stanglin, and Marijke Tolsma (Leiden: Brill, 2009): 51–72.

Greenblatt, Stephen, *The Swerve: How the Renaissance Began* (London: Vintage Books, 2012).

Greenslade, Basil, 'Hales, John (1584–1656)', *Oxford Dictionary of National Biography*, retrieved 23 Mar. 2019. www.oxforddnb.com/view/10.1093/ref:odnb/9780198614128.001.0001/odnb-9780198614128-e-11914.

Gregory, Tobias, 'The Political Messages of *Samson Agonistes*', *Studies in English Literature, 1500–1900*, 50.1 (2010): 175–203.

Grell, Ole Peter, *Brethren in Christ: A Calvinist Network in Reformation Europe* (Cambridge: Cambridge University Press, 2011).

———, *Dutch Calvinists in Early Stuart London: The Dutch Church in Austin Friars, 1603–1642* (Leiden: Brill, 1989).

Groesen, Michiel van, 'Global Trade', in *The Cambridge Companion to the Dutch Golden Age* (Cambridge: Cambridge University Press, 2018): 66–186.

Guy, John, *Tudor England* (Oxford: Oxford University Press, 1988).

Haan, Estelle, '*Defensio Prima* and the Latin Poets', in *The Oxford Handbook of Milton*, ed. by Nicholas McDowell and Nigel Smith (Oxford: Oxford University Press, 2011): 292–305.

Hadfield, Andrew, *Literature, Travel and Colonial Writing in the English Renaissance* (Oxford: Oxford University Press, 1998).

Hägerdal, Hans, *Lord of the Land, Lord of the Sea: Conflict and Adaptation in Early Colonial Timor, 1600–1800* (Leiden: KITVL Press, 2012).

Haitsma Mulier, Eco, 'The Language of Seventeenth-Century Republicanism in the United Provinces: Dutch or European', in *The Language of Political Theory in Early-Modern Europe*, ed. by Anthony Pagden (Cambridge: Cambridge University Press, 1987): 179–196.

———, *The Myth of Venice and Dutch Republican Thought in the Seventeenth Century* (Assen: Van Gorcum, 1980).

Hale, John K., Thomas N. Corns, et al., 'The Provenance of *De doctrina Christiana*', *Milton Quarterly*, 31.3 (1997): 67–117.

Haley, K.H.D., *The Dutch in the Seventeenth Century* (London: Thames and Hudson, 1972).

Hall, N.J. van, 'Nederlands Toneel: *Samson of Heilige Wraak* treurspel van Vondel', *De Gids*, 70 (1906): 166–174.

Hamel, A.G. van, *Zeventiende-Eeuwsche Opvattingen en Theorieen over Literatuur in Nederland* (Utrecht: Hes Publishers, 1973).

Hammond, Paul, *Milton's Complex Words: Essays on the Conceptual Structure of Paradise Lost* (Oxford: Oxford University Press, 2017).

Hardie, Philip, 'The Presence of Lucretius in *Paradise Lost*', in *Lucretian Receptions: History, the Sublime, Knowledge*, ed. by Philip Hardie (Cambridge: Cambridge University Press, 2009): 264–279.

Harms, Roeland, Joad Raymond, and Jeroen Salman, 'Chapter 1: The Distribution and Dissemination of Popular Print', in *Not Dead Things: The Dissemination of Popular Print in England and Wales, Italy and the Low Countries, 1500–1820* (Leiden: Brill, 2013): 1–29.

Hatfield, April Lee, *Atlantic Virginia: Intercolonial Relations in the Seventeenth Century* (Pennsylvania: Pennsylvania University Press, 2004).

Haven, Alexander van der, 'Predestination and Toleration: The Dutch Republic's Single Judicial Persecution of Jews in Theological Context', *Renaissance Quarterly*, 71 (2018): 165–205.

Hegarty, J., 'Potter, Christopher (1590/91–1646)', *Oxford Dictionary National Biography*, retrieved 23 Mar. 2019. www.oxforddnb.com/view/10.1093/ref:odnb/9780198614128.001.0001/odnb-9780198614128-e-22607.

Heijden, M.C.A. van der (ed.), *'t Hoge Huis te Muiden: Teksten uit de Muiderkring*, 13 vols. (Utrecht: Uitgeverij Het Spectrum, 1973).

Helmers, Helmer, '1685 and the Battle for Dutch Public Opinion: Succession Literature from a Transnational Perspective', in *Stuart Succession Literature: Moments and Transformation*, ed. by Paulina Kewes and Andrew McRae (Oxford: Oxford University Press, 2018): 96–113.

———, *The Royalist Republic: Literature, Politics and Religion in the Anglo-Dutch Sphere: 1639–1660* (Cambridge: Cambridge University Press, 2015).

———, 'Unknown Shrews: Thee Transformations of the/a Shrew', in *Gender and Power in Shrew-Taming Narratives, 1500–1700*, ed. by G. Holderness and D. Wootton (Houndmills: Palgrave Macmillan, 2010): 123–144.

Herring, Ronald J., 'How Is Food Political? Market, State, and Knowledge', in *The Oxford Handbook of Food, Politics, and Society*, ed. by Ronald J. Herring (Oxford: Oxford University Press, 2015): 4–29.

Hessels, J.H. (ed.), *Epistulae et Tractatus cum Reformationis tum Ecclesiae Londino-Batavae Historiam Illustrantes: Ecclesiae Londino-Batavae Archivum* (Cambridge: Cambridge University Press, 1897).

Hill, Christopher, *The Experience of Defeat: Milton and Some Contemporaries* (London: Verso, 1984).

———, 'From Lollards to Levellers', in *Rebels and Their Causes*, ed. by Maurice Cornforth (London: Lawrence and Wishart, 1978): 49–67.

———, *Milton and the English Revolution* (London: Faber and Faber, 1977).

Hirst, Derek, and Steven N. Zwicker, *Andrew Marvell: Orphan of the Hurricane* (Oxford: Oxford University Press, 2012).

Hoenderdaal, Gerrit Jan, 'The Life and Struggle of Arminius in the Dutch Republic', in *Man's Faith and Freedom: The Theological Influence of Jacobus Arminius* (New York: Abingdon Press, 1962): 11–26.

Hoenselaars, Ton, 'Character: Dramatic', in *Imagology: The Cultural Construction and Literary Representation of National Characters*, ed. by Manfred Beller and Joep Leerssen (Amsterdam: Amsterdam University Press, 2007): 281–284.

Holberton, Edward, 'Marvell and Diplomacy', in *The Oxford Handbook to Andrew Marvell*, ed. by Martin Dzelzainis and Edward Holberton (Oxford: Oxford University Press, 2019): 97–113.

———, *Poetry and the Cromwellian Protectorate: Culture, Politics, and Institutions* (Oxford: Oxford University Press, 2008).

———, 'Representing the Sea in Andrew Marvell's "Advice to a Painter" Satires', *Review of English Studies* (2014): 71–86.

Holberton, Edward, Martin Dzelzainis, and Steph Coster, 'Andrew Marvell and the Dutch Fifth Column: New Evidence From a Copy of *Mr Smirke* with Authorial Annotations', (Forthcoming).

———, 'Meeting Mr George: Did Andrew Marvell Spy for the Dutch?', *Times Literary Supplement* (April 10, 2020).

Horsman, Yasco, 'Psychoananalysis-Law, Theatre, and Violence in *Samson* (1660)', in *Joost van den Vondel: Dutch Playwright in the Golden Age*, ed. by Jan Bloemendal and Frans-Willem Korsten (Leiden: Brill, 2012): 445–459.

Huizinga, J., 'Engelschen en Nederlanders in Shakespeare's tijd', in *Verspreide Opstellen over de Geschiedenis van Nederland* (Amsterdam: Amsterdam University Press, 1982).

———, *Nederlandse Beschaving in de Zeventiende Eeuw* (Groningen: Wolters-Noordhoff, 1926).

Hunter, William, 'Milton's Arianism Considered', *Harvard Theological Review*, 52 (1959): 9–35.

———, 'The Provenance of the Christian Doctrine', *The English Renaissance*, 32.1 (1992): 129–142.

Huysman, Ineke, 'Andrew Marvell and Constantijn Huygens: Common Grounds and Mutual Contacts', *Marvell Studies*, 3.1 (2018): 1–18.

Huysman, Ineke, and Roosje Peeters (eds.), *Johan de Witt en Engeland: Een Bloemlezing uit zijn Correspondentie* (Soest: Uitgeverij Catullus, 2019).

Innes Miller, J., *The Spice Trade of the Roman Empire, 29 B.C. to A.D. 641* (Oxford: Clarendon Press, 1969).

Inwood, Brad, *The Poem of Empedocles* (Toronto: Toronto University Press, 2001).

Israel, Jonathan, *Dutch Primacy in World Trade, 1585–1740* (Oxford: Oxford University Press, 1989).

———, *The Dutch Republic: Its Rise, Greatness and Fall, 1477–1806* (Oxford: Oxford University Press, 1995).

———, 'Religious Toleration and Radical Philosophy', in *Calvinism and Religious Toleration in the Dutch Golden Age*, ed. by R. Po-Chia and Henk van Nierop (Cambridge: Cambridge University Press, 2002): 148–158.

———, 'Toleration in Seventeenth-Century Dutch and English Thought', in *The Exchange of Ideas: Religion, Scholarship, and Art in the Seventeenth Century* (Zutphen: Walburg Instituut, 1994): 13–41.

Jacob, Margaret C., and Catherine Secretan (eds.), *In Praise of Ordinary People: Early Modern Britain and the Dutch Republic* (New York: Palgrave Macmillan, 2013).

Jardine, Lisa, *The Awful End of Prince William the Silent: The First Assassination of a Head of State with a Handgun* (London: Harper Perennial, 2006).

———, *De Reputatie van Constantijn Huygens: Netwerker of Virtuoos* (Amsterdam: Uitgeverij Bert Bakker, 2008).

———, *Gedeelde Weelde*, transl. by Henk Schreuder (Amsterdam: Uitgeverij de Arbeiderspres, 2008).

Joby, Christopher, *Dutch Language in Britain (1550–1702): A Social History of the Use of Dutch in Early Modern Britain* (Leiden: Brill, 2015).

———, *The Multilingualism of Constantijn Huygens (1596–1687)* (Amsterdam: Amsterdam University Press, 2014).

———, '"This is my Body": Huygens' Poetic Response to the Words of Institution', in *Return to Sender: Costantijn Huygens as a Man of Letters*, ed. by Lise Gosseye et al. (Gent: Academia Press, 2013): 83–104.

Jones, Edward, 'Milton's Life, 1608–1640', in *The Oxford Handbook of John Milton*, ed. by Nicholas McDowell and Nigel Smith (Oxford: Oxford University Press, 2009): 3–25.

Jones, J.R., *The Anglo-Dutch Wars of the Seventeenth Century* (London: Longmans, 1996).

Jose, Nicholas, '*Samson Agonistes*: The Play Turned Upside Down', *Essays in Criticism*, 30.2 (1980): 124–150.

Kaplan, Benjamin J., *Divided by Faith: Religious Conflict and the Practise of Toleration in Early Modern Europe* (Cambridge: Harvard University Press, 2007).

———, '"Dutch" Religious Tolerance: Celebration and Revision', in *Calvinism and Religious Toleration in the Dutch Golden Age*, ed. by R. Po-Chia and Henk van Nierop (Cambridge: Cambridge University Press, 2002): 8–26.

Kasa, Deni, 'Arminian Theology, Machiavellian Republicanism, and Cooperative Virtue in Milton's *Paradise Lost*', *Milton Quarterly*, 50.4 (2016): 260–276.

Kasten, Madeleine, 'Translation Studies: Vondel's Appropriation of Grotius's *Sophompaneas*', in *Joost van den Vondel: Dutch Playwright in the Golden Age*, ed. by Jan Bloemendal and Frans-Willem Korsten (Leiden: Brill, 2012): 249–271.

Keeble, N.H., 'Introduction', in the *Complete Prose Works of Andrew Marvell*, ed. by Annabel Patterson, 2 vols. (New Haven: University of Yale Press, 2003): 381–411.

———, *The Literary Culture of Non-Conformity in Later Seventeenth-Century England* (Athens: University of Georgia Press, 1987).

———, 'Why Transpose the Rehearsal?', in *Marvell and Liberty*, ed. by Warren Chernaik and Martin Dzelzainis (London: Palgrave Macmillan, 1999): 249–268.

Keeble, N.H., and Johanna Harris, 'Marvell and Nonconformity', in *The Oxford Handbook of Andrew Marvell*, ed. by Martin Dzelzainis and Edward Holberton (Oxford: Oxford University Press, 2019): 145–163.

Keeble, N.H., and Nicholas McDowell, 'Introduction', in *The Complete Works of John Milton: Volume VI: Vernacular Regicide and Republican Writings* (Oxford: Oxford University Press, 2013): 1–125.

Kelley, Maurice, 'Letter in Times Literary Supplement', *Times Literary Supplement* (29 Apr. 1960).

——, 'Milton's Arianism Again Considered', *The Harvard Theological Review*, 54.3 (1961): 195–205.

——, *This Great Argument: A Study of Milton's De doctrina Christiana as a Gloss upon Paradise Lost* (Princeton: Princeton University Press, 1941).

Kempen-Stijgers, Thea van, and Peter Rietbergen, 'Constantijn Huygens en Engeland', in *Constantijn Huygens en zijn Plaats in Geleerd Europa* (Amsterdam: University Press of Amsterdam, 1973): 77–141.

Kendrick, Christopher, 'Typological Impulses in *Samson Agonistes*', *University of Toronto Quarterly*, 84.2 (2015): 1–30.

Kern, Edith, *The Influence of Heinsius and Vossius Upon French Dramatic Theory* (Baltimore: John Hopkins Press, 1949).

Kerrigan, John, *Archipelagic English: Literature, History and Politics, 1603–1707* (Oxford: Oxford University Press, 2008).

Kerrigan, William, *The Prophetic Milton* (Charlottesville: University Press of Virginia, 1974).

Killeen, Kevin, Helen Smith, and Rachel Willie (eds.), *The Oxford Handbook of the Bible in Early Modern England, c. 1530–1700* (Oxford: Oxford University Press, 2015).

Kingma, J., 'Uitgaven met Verstrekkende Gevolgen. De Elzeviers als Verspreiders van Nieuwe Denkbeelden', in *Boekverkopers van Europa: Het 17de Eeuwse Nederlandse Uitgevershuis Elzevier*, ed. by Dongelmans, Hoftijzer and Lankhorst (Zutphen: Walburg Press, 2000): 107–114.

Kirkconnell, Watson, *The Celestial Cycle* (Toronto: University of Toronto Press, 1952).

——, *That Invincible Samson: The Theme of Samson Agonistes in World Literature with Translations of the Major Analogues* (Toronto: Toronto University Press, 1964).

Knoppers, Laura Lunga, '"England's Case": Contexts of the 1671 Poems', in *The Oxford Handbook of Milton*, ed. by Nicholas McDowell and Nigel Smith (Oxford: Oxford University Press, 2011): 572–588.

——, *Historicizing Milton: Spectacle, Power, and Poetry* (Athens: University of Georgia Press, 1995).

Kocic, Larisa, 'Predestination in Milton's *Paradise Lost* and *De doctrina Christiana*', *The Anachronist* (2003): 65–84.

Kooi, Christine, 'Strategies of Catholic Toleration in Golden Age Holland', in *Calvinism and Religious Toleration in the Dutch Golden Age*, ed. by R. Po-Chia and Henk van Nierop (Cambridge: Cambridge University Press, 2002): 87–101.

Korsten, F., 'De Elzeviers en Engeland', in *Boekverkopers van Europa: Het Zeventiende Eeuwse Nederlandse Uitgevershuis Elzevier*, ed. by Dongelmans, Hoftijzer and Lankhorst (Zutphen: Walburg Pers, 2000): 195–210.

——, *Sovereignty as Inviolability: Vondel's Theatrical Exploration in the Dutch Republic* (Hilversum: Uitgeverij Verloren, 2009).

Krondl, Michael, *The Taste of Conquest: The Rise and Fall of the Three Great Cities of Spice* (New York: Ballantine Books, 2007).

Krouse, E.M., *Milton's Samson and the Christian Tradition* (Princeton: Princeton University Press, 1949).

Lake, Peter, 'Lancelot Andrewes, John Buckeridge, and Avant-Garde Conformity at the Court of James I', in *The Mental World of the Jacobean Court*, ed. by Linda Levy Peck (Cambridge: Cambridge University Press, 1991): 113–153.

Larsen, Anne R., *Anna Maria van Schurman, 'The Star of Utrecht': The Educational Vision and Reception of a Savante* (Abingdon: Routledge, 2016).

Leerintveld, Ad, 'Constantijn Huygens's Library', in *Crossing Boundaries and Transforming Identities: New Pespectives in Netherlandic Studies*, ed. by Margriet Bruyn Lacy and Christine P. Sellin (Münster: Nodus Publikationen, 2011): 11–18.

Leerintveld, Ad, Nan Streekstra, and Richard Todd, 'Seventeenth-Century Versions of Constantijn Huygens' Translations of John Donne in Manuscript and in Print: Authority, Coterie, and Piracy', *Querendo*, 30.1 (2000): 288–310.

Leerssen, Joep, 'Character (Moral)', in *Imagology: The Cultural Construction and Literary Representation of National Characters*, ed. by Manfred Beller and Joep Leerssen (Amsterdam: Amsterdam University Press, 2007): 284–287.

——, 'Image', in *Imagology: The Cultural Construction and Literary Representation of National Characters*, ed. by Manfred Beller and Joep Leerssen (Amsterdam: Amsterdam University Press, 2007): 342–343.

——, 'Imagology: History and Method', in *Imagology: The Cultural Construction and Literary Representation of National Characters*, ed. by Manfred Beller and Joep Leerssen (Amsterdam: Amsterdam University Press, 2007): 17–32.

——, 'Imagology: On Using Ethnicity to Make Sense of the World', *Numéro*, 10 (2016): 13–31.

——, 'Literature', in *Imagology: The Cultural Construction and Literary Representation of National Characters*, ed. by Manfred Beller and Joep Leerssen (Amsterdam: Amsterdam University Press, 2007): 351–354.

——, 'National Character, 1500–2000', in *Imagology: The Cultural Construction and Literary Representation of National Characters*, ed. by Manfred Beller and Joep Leerssen (Amsterdam: Amsterdam University Press, 2007): 63–66.

——, *National Thought in Europe: A Cultural History* (Amsterdam: Amsterdam University Press, 2006).

Leeuwen, Th. Marius van, 'Introduction', in *Arminius, Arminianism, and Europe* (Leiden: Brill, 2009): IX–XXII.

Legouis, Pierre, *Andrew Marvell: Poet, Puritan and Patriot* (Oxford: Clarendon Press, 1965).

Leo, Russ, *Affect before Spinoza: Reformed Faith, Affectus, and Experience, in Jean Calvin, John Donne, John Milton and Baruch Spinoza* (Ph.D. Thesis, Duke University, 2009).

——, 'Grotius among the Dagonists: Joost van den Vondel's *Samson, of Heilige Wraeck*, Revenge and the *Ius Gentium*', in *Politics and Aesthetics in European Baroque and Classicist Tragedy*, ed. by Jan Bloemendal and Nigel Smith (Leiden: Brill, 2016): 75–102.

——, *Tragedy as Philosophy in the Reformation World* (Oxford: Oxford University Press, 2019).

Leonard, John, 'Milton, Lucretius and the "Void profound of unessential night"', in *Living Texts: Interpreting Milton* (London: Associates University Presses, 2000): 198–218.

Levelt, Sjoerd, 'Anthony Munday's "Briefe Chronologicall Suruay Concerning the Netherlands" and the Medieval Chronicle Tradition of Holland in the Early Modern Period: Introduction and Edition', in *The Medieval Chronicle 11*, ed. by Erik Kooper and Sjoerd Levelt (Leiden: Brill, 2018): 258–296.

Levillain, Charles-Édouard, 'England's "Natural Frontier": Andrew Marvell and the Low Countries', in *The Oxford Handbook to Andrew Marvell*, ed. by Martin Dzelzainis and Edward Holberton (Oxford: Oxford University Press, 2019): 115–127.

Lewalski, Barbara, *Milton's Brief Epic: The Genre, Meaning, and Art of Paradise Regained* (Providence: Brown University Press, 1966).

——, 'Milton's *Samson Agonistes* and the "Tragedy" of the Apocalypse', *Periodical Modern Language Association*, 85 (1970): 1050–1062.

——, *Paradise Lost and the Rhetoric of Literary Forms* (Princeton: Princeton University Press, 1985).

Lieb, Michael, *Theological Milton: Deity, Discourse and Heresy in the Miltonic Canon* (Pittsburgh: Duquesne University Press, 2006).

——, '"A thousand fore-skins": Circumcision, Violence, and Selfhood in Milton', *Milton Studies*, 38 (2000): 198–219.

Lim, Walter S.H., *The Arts of Empire: The Poetics of Colonialism from Raleigh to Milton* (Newark: University of Delaware Press, 1998).

Loewenstein, David, *Milton and the Drama of History: Historical Vision, Iconoclasm, and the Literary Imagination* (Cambridge: Cambridge University Press, 2006).

——, *Representing Revolution in Milton and his Contemporaries: Religion, Politics, and Polemics in Radical Puritanism* (Cambridge: Cambridge University Press, 2001).

Lord, George deF., 'Introduction', in *Poems on Affairs of State, 1660–1714*, 7 vols. (New Haven: Yale University Press, 1963), vol. 1 (1660–1678): xxv–lvi.

Loth, Vincent C., 'Armed Incidents and Unpaid Bills: Anglo-Dutch Rivalry in the Banda Islands in the Seventeenth Century', *Modern Asian Studies*, 29.4 (1995): 705–740.

Love, Harold, *English Clandestine Satire, 1660–1702* (Oxford: Oxford University Press, 2004).

Low, Anthony, *The Blaze of Noon: A Reading of Samson Agonistes* (New York: Colombia University Press, 1974).

Lynch, Denise E., 'Politics, Nature and Structure in Marvell's "The Last Instructions to a Painter"', *Restoration: Studies in English Literary Culture 1660–1700*, 16.2 (1992): 82–92.

Major, Philip, '"To wound an oak": The Poetics of Tree-Felling at Nun Appleton', *The Seventeenth Century*, 25.1 (2010): 143–157.

Maley, Willy, '"Neptune to the Common-wealth of England" (1652): The "Republican Britannia" and the Continuity of Interests', *The Seventeenth Century*, 33.4 (2018): 463–483.

Maltzahn, Nicholas von, *An Andrew Marvell Chronology* (Basingstoke: Palgrave, 2005).

——, 'Marvell's Indian Poison-Pot', *Notes and Queries*, 60.4 (2013): 535–537.

——, 'Milton, Marvell and Toleration', in *Milton and Toleration*, ed. by Sharon Achinstein and Elizabeth Sauer (Oxford: Oxford University Press, 2007): 86–104.

Manning, Brian, 'The Levellers and Religion', in *Radical Religion in the English Revolution*, ed. by J.F. McGregor and Barry Reay (Oxford: Oxford University Press, 1984): 65–90.

Margoliouth, H.M., *Andrew Marvell: The Poems and Letters of Andrew Marvell* (Oxford: Clarendon Press, 1971).

Markley, Robert, '"The destin'd walls/ Of Cambalu": Milton, China, and the Ambiguities of the East', in *Milton and the Imperial Vision*, ed. by Balachandra Rajan and Elizabeth Sauer (Pittsburgh: Duquesne University Press, 1999): 191–213.

———, *The Far East and the English Imagination, 1600–1730* (Cambridge: Cambridge University Press, 2006).

Martz, Louis, *Milton: Poet of Exile* (Yale: Yale University Press, 1986).

Masson, David, *The Life of Milton*, 8 vols. (Cambridge: Macmillan Press, 1887).

Mastellone, Salvo, 'Holland as a Political Model in Italy in the Seventeenth Century', *Low Countries Historical Review*, 98.4 (1983): 568–582.

Mathijsen, Marita (ed.), *Boeken onder druk. Censuur en pers-onvrijheid in Nederland sinds de boekdrukkunst* (Amsterdam: Amsterdam University Press, 2011).

McDowell, John, *Mind and Word* (London: Harvard University Press, 1996).

McDowell, Nicholas, 'Family Politics: Or, How John Philips Read His Uncle's Satirical Sonnets', *Milton Quarterly*, 42.1 (2008): 1–21.

———, 'How Laudian Was the Young Milton?', *Milton Studies*, 52 (2011): 3–22.

———, *Poetry and Allegiance in the English Civil War* (Oxford: Oxford University Press, 2008).

Miller, Leo, 'In Defence of Milton's *Pro populo anglicano defensio*', *Renaissance Studies*, 4.3 (1990): 1–12.

———, *John Milton's Writings in the Anglo-Dutch Negotiations, 1651–1654* (Pittsburgh: Duquesne University Press, 1992).

———, *Milton and the Oldenburg Safeguard* (New York: Loewenthal Press, 1985).

———, 'Milton, Salmasius and Hammond: The History of an Insult', *Renaissance and Reformation*, 9.3 (1973): 108–115.

———, 'Milton's *Defensio* Ordered Wholesale for the States of Holland', *Notes and Queries*, 33.1 (1986): 33.

———, 'New Milton Texts and Data from the Aitzema Mission, 1652', *Notes and Queries* (1990): 279–288.

Milton, Anthony, 'Arminianism, Laudians, Anglicans, and Revisionists: Back to Which Drawing Board?', *Huntington Library Quarterly*, 78.4 (2015): 723–742.

———, *Laudian and Royalist Polemic in Seventeenth-Century England: The Career and Writings of Peter Heylyn* (Manchester: Manchester University Press, 2012).

———, 'Marketing a Massacre: Amboyna, the East India Company and the Public Sphere in Early Stuart England', in *The Politics of the Public Sphere in Early Modern England*, ed. by Peter Lake and Steven Pincus (Manchester: Manchester University Press, 2007):168–190.

Milton, Philip, 'Religious Toleration', in *The Oxford Handbook of Philosophy in Early Modern Europe*, ed. by Desmond M. Clarke and Catherine Wilson (Oxford: Oxford University Press, 2011): 571–590.

Mody, Jehangir, *Vondel and Milton* (Bombay: K and J Cooper, 1942).

Mohamed, Feisal G., 'Confronting Religious Violence: Milton's *Samson Agonistes*', *Periodical Modern Language Association*, 120.2 (2005): 327–340.

Monette, Sarah, 'Speaking and Silent Women in "Upon Appleton House"', *Studies in English Literature*, 42.1 (2002): 155–171.

Moolhuizen, Jan Jurien, *Vondel's Lucifer en Milton's Verloren Paradijs* (Ph.D. Thesis, Utrecht University, 1892).

Mortimer, Sarah, *Reason and Religion in the English Revolution: The Challenge of Socinianism* (Cambridge: Cambridge University Press, 2010).

Morton, Timothy, *The Poetics of Spice* (Cambridge: Cambridge University Press, 2000).

Mueller, A., *Milton's Abhaengigkeit von Vondel* (Dissertation, University of Berlin, 1891).

Mueller, Jane, 'The Figure and the Ground: Samson as a Hero of London Nonconformity, 1662–1667', in *Milton and the Terms of Liberty*, ed. by Graham Parry and Joad Raymond (Cambridge: Cambridge University Press, 2002): 137–162.

Myers, Benjamin, 'Prevenient Grace and Conversion in *Paradise Lost*', *Milton Quarterly*, 40.1 (2006): 20–36.

Nadler, Steven, *A Book Forged in Hell: Spinoza's Scandalous Treatise and the Birth of the Secular Age* (Princeton: Princeton University Press, 2011).

Nedo, Michael, *Ludwig Wittgenstein: Ein Biographisches Album* (Munich: C.H. Beck, 2012).

Nellen, Henk, *Hugo de Groot, Een Leven in Strijd om de Vrede* (Amsterdam: Balans, 2007).

———, *Hugo Grotius: A Life-Long Struggle for Peace in Church and State, 1583–1645* (Leiden: Brill, 2007).

Netzley, Ryan, *Lyric Apocalypse: Milton, Marvell, and the Nature of Events* (New York: Fordham University Press, 2015).

Ng, Su Fang, 'Dutch Wars, Global Trade, and the Heroic Poem: Dryden's *Annus Mirabilis* (1666) and Amin's *Sya'ir perang Mengkasar* (1670)', *Modern Philology*, 109.3 (2012): 352–384.

———, 'Pirating Paradise: Alexander the Great, the Dutch East Indies, and Satanic Empire in *Paradise Lost*', *Milton Studies*, 52 (2011): 59–91.

Nierop, H.F.K. van, *Beeldenstorm en Burgelijk Verzet in Amsterdam, 1566–1567* (Nijmegen: Socialistiese Uitgeverij, 1987).

Nijland, Mea, 'Albert Verwey en John Milton', in *Europen Context: Studies in the History and Literature of the Netherlands*, presented to Theodoor Weevers, ed. by P.K. King and P.F. Vincent (Cambridge: Modern Humanities Research Association, 1971): 248–267.

Norbrook, David, 'Women, the Republic of Letters, and the Public Sphere in the Mid Seventeenth Century', *Criticism*, 46.2 (2004): 223–240.

———, *Writing the English Republic: Poetry, Rhetoric and Politics, 1627–1660* (Cambridge: Cambridge University Press, 1999).

Ochoa, Enrique C., 'Political Histories of Food', in *The Oxford Handbook of Food History*, ed. by Jeffrey M. Pilcher (Oxford: Oxford University Press, 2012): 24–35.

Oldman, Elizabeth, 'Milton, Grotius, and the Law of War', *Studies in Philology*, 104.3 (2007): 340–375.

Ormerod, David, and Christopher Wortham, *Andrew Marvell: The Pastoral and the Lyric Poetry of 1681* (Nedlands: University of Western Australia Press, 2000).

Osborne, Mary Tom, *Advice-to-a-Painter Poems 1633–1856: An Annotated Finding List* (Austin: University of Texas Press, 1949).

Osler, Margaret J., *Atoms, Pneuma and Tranquillity: Epicurean and Stoic Themes in European Thought* (Cambridge: Cambridge University Press, 1991).

Osselton, N.E., *The Dumb Linguists: A Study of the Earliest English and Dutch Dictionaries* (Oxford: Oxford University Press, 1973).

Parasecoli, Fabio, 'Introduction', to *Culinary Cultures of Europe: Identity, Diversity and Dialogue*, ed. by Darra Goldstein and Katherine Merkle (Strasbourg: Council of Europe Publishing, 2005): 11–37.

Parker, William Riley, *Milton: A Biography*, 2 vols. (Oxford: Clarendon Press, 1986).

Parkin, Jon, 'Liberty Transpos'd: Andrew Marvell and Samuel Parker', in *Marvell and Liberty*, ed. by Warren Chernaik and Martin Dzelzainis (London: Palgrave Macmillan, 1999): 269–289.

Parry, Graham, *The Arts of the Anglican Counter-Reformation: Glory, Laud and Honour* (Woodbridge: Boydell Press, 2006).

Parthesius, Robert, *Dutch Ships in Tropical Waters: The Development of the Dutch India Company (VOC) Shipping Network in Asia, 1595–1660* (Amsterdam: Amsterdam University Press, 2010).

Partner, Jane, '"The Swelling Hall": Andrew Marvell and the Politics of Architecture at Nun Appleton House', *The Seventeenth Century*, 23.2 (2008): 225–243.

Patrides, C.A., 'Milton and Arianism', *Journal of the History of Ideas*, 25.3 (1964): 423–429.

Patterson, Annabel, *Andrew Marvell* (Plymouth: Northcote House, 1994).

———, '*Bermudas* and the *Coronet*: Marvell's Protestant Poetics', *ELH*, 44.3 (1977): 478–499.

———, 'The Country Gentleman: Howard, Marvell, and Dryden in the Theatre of Politics', *Studies in English Literature, 1500–1900*, 25.1 (1985): 491–509.

———, 'Introduction', in *The Prose Works of Andrew Marvell*, 2 vols. (New Haven: Yale University Press, 2003), vol. 1, xi–liv.

———, *Marvell and the Civic Crown* (Princeton: Princeton University Press, 1978).

———, *Pastoral and Ideology: Virgil to Valéry* (Berkeley: University of California Press, 1987).

Patterson, Annabel, and Martin Dzelzainis, 'Marvell and the Earl of Anglesey: A Chapter in the History of Reading', *The Historical Journal*, 44.3 (2001): 703–726.

Pelt, Robert van, 'Man and Cosmos in Huygens' *Hofwijck*', *Art History*, 4.2 (1981): 150–174.

Perlove, Shelley, and Larry Silver, *Rembrandt's Faith: Church and Temple in the Dutch Golden Age* (Pennsylvania: Pennsylvania University Press, 2009).

Pieters, Jürgen, *Op Zoek naar Huygens* (Gent: Poëziecentrum, KANTL, 2014).

Pincus, Steven C., *1688: The First Modern Revolution* (New Haven: Yale University Press, 2009).

———, *Protestantism and Patriotism* (Cambridge: Cambridge University Press, 1996).

Pollmann, Judith, 'The Bond of Christian Piety', in *Calvinism and Religious Toleration in the Dutch Golden Age*, ed. by R. Po-Chia and Henk van Nierop (Cambridge: Cambridge University Press, 2002): 53–71.

———, 'Vondel's Religion', in *Joost van den Vondel: Dutch Playwright in the Golden Age*, ed. by Jan Bloemendal and Frans-Willem Korsten (Leiden: Brill, 2012): 85–100.

Poole, William, 'Analysing a Private Library, with a Shelflist Attributable to John Hales of Eton, c. 1624', in *A Concise Companion to the Study of Manuscripts, Printed Books and the Production of Early Modern Texts*, ed. by Edward Jones (Chichester: Wiley-Blackwell, 2015): 41–65.

———, *Milton and the Idea of the Fall* (Cambridge: Cambridge University Press, 2005).

———, 'Theology', in *Milton in Context*, ed. by Stephen Dobranski (Cambridge: Cambridge University Press, 2010): 475–486.

Porteman, Karel en Mieke Smits-Veldt, *Een Nieuw Vaderland voor de Muzen: Geschiedenis van de Nederlandse Literatuur, 1560–1700* (Amsterdam: Uitgeverij Bert Bakker, 2009).

Prak, Maarten, *The Dutch Republic in the Seventeenth Century*, transl. by Diane Webb (Cambridge: Cambridge University Press, 2005).

——, 'The Politics of Intolerance: Citizenship and Religion in the Dutch Republic (Seventeenth to Eighteenth Centuries)', in *Calvinism and Religious Toleration in the Dutch Golden Age*, ed. by R. Po-Chia and Henk van Nierop (Cambridge: Cambridge University Press, 2002): 159–175.

Price, J.L., *Holland and the Dutch Republic* (Oxford: Clarendon Press, 1994).

Quint, David, *Epic and Empire* (Princeton: Princeton University Press, 1993).

——, *Inside Paradise Lost: Reading the Designs of Milton's Epic* (Princeton: Princeton University Press, 2014).

Raamsdonk, Esther van, 'Creation in John Milton's *Paradise Lost* (1667) and Joost van den Vondel's *Adam in Ballingschap* (1664) [Adam in Exile]', *Milton Quarterly*, 51.2 (2017): 97–110.

——, 'Did Milton Know Dutch?', *Notes and Queries*, 63.1 (2016): 53–55.

——, 'Vondel's English Lucifer and Milton's Dutch Satan', *Renaissance Studies* (forthcoming).

Raamsdonk, Esther van, and Alan Moss, 'Across the Narrow Sea: A Transnational Approach to Anglo-Dutch Travelogues', *The Seventeenth Century*, 35.1 (2020): 105–124.

Radzinowicz, Mary Ann, 'Forced Allusions: Avatars of King David in the Seventeenth Century', in *The Literary Milton: Text, Pretext and Context*, ed. by Diana Trevino Benet and Michael Lieb (Pittsburgh: Duquesne University Press, 1994): 45–66.

——, *Towards Samson Agonistes: The Growth of Milton's Mind* (Princeton: Princeton University Press, 1978).

Ravenhill, Mark, 'Performance of Voltaire's *Candide*', directed by Lyndsey Turner, Royal Shakespeare Company (2013).

Raylor, Timothy, 'Andrew Marvell: Traveling Tutor', *Marvell Studies*, 2.1 (2017).

——, 'Marvell and Waller', in *The Oxford Handbook of Andrew Marvell*, ed. by Martin Dzelzainis and Edward Holberton (Oxford: Oxford University Press, 2019): 651–636.

Raymond, Joad, 'Books as Diplomatic Agents: Milton in Sweden', in *Cultures of Diplomacy and Literary Writing in the Early Modern World*, ed. by Tracey A. Sowerby and Joanna Craigwood (Oxford: Oxford University Press, 2019): 131–145.

——, 'John Milton, European: The Rhetoric of Milton's Defences', in *The Oxford Handbook of Milton*, ed. by Nicholas McDowell and Nigel Smith (Oxford: Oxford University Press, 2011): 273–291.

——, *Pamphlets and Pamphleteering in Early Modern Britain* (Cambridge: Cambridge University Press, 2003).

Rees, Christine, *The Judgement of Marvell* (London: Pinter Publishers, 1989).

Retallack, Joan, *The Poethical Wager* (Los Angeles: University of California Press, 2003).

Revard, Stella, *The War in Heaven: Paradise Lost and the Tradition of Satan's Rebellion* (Ithaca: Cornell University Press, 1980).

Richard A. Muller, *Post-Reformation Reformed Dogmatics: The Rise and Development of Reformed Orthodoxy, ca. 1520–1725*, 4 vols. (Michigan: Baker Academic, 2003-6).

Rietbergen, Peter, 'Pieter Rabus en de Boekzaal van Europe', in *Pieter Rabus en de Boekzaal van Europa, 1692–1702* (Amsterdam: Holland Universiteits Pers, 1974): 1–109.

Roelofsen, C.G., 'Grotius and International Politics of the Seventeenth Century', in *Hugo Grotius and International Relations*, ed. by Hedley Bull, Benedict Kingsbury, and Adam Roberts (Oxford: Oxford University Press, 1990): 96–132.

Rogers, John, 'Delivering Redemption in *Samson Agonistes*', in *Altering Eyes: New Perspectives on Samson Agonistes*, ed. by Mark R. Kelley and Joseph Wittreich (Newark: University of Delaware Press, 2002): 72–97.

———, *The Matter of Revolution: Science, Poetry and Politics in the Age of Milton* (Ithica: Cornell University Press, 1998).

———, 'Milton and the Heretical Priesthood of Christ', in *Heresy, Literature and Politics in Early Modern English Culture*, ed. by David Loewenstein and John Marshall (Cambridge: Cambridge University Press, 2006): 203–220.

———, 'Ruin the Sacred Truths: Prophecy, Form, and Nonconformity in Marvell and Milton', in *The Oxford Handbook of Andrew Marvell*, ed. by Martin Dzelzainis and Edward Holberton (Oxford: Oxford University Press, 2019): 672–686.

———, 'The Secret of *Samson Agonistes*', *Milton Studies*, 33 (1997): 111–132.

Rogers, P.G., *The Dutch in the Medway* (Oxford: Oxford University Press, 1970).

Romburgh, Sophie van, 'Junius [du Jon], Franciscus [Francis] (1591–1677), Philologist and Writer on Art', *Oxford Dictionary of National Biography*, retrieved 4 July 2018. www.oxforddnb.com/view/10.1093/ref:odnb/9780198614128.001.0001/odnb-9780198614128-e-15167.

Rommelse, Gijs, *The Second Anglo-Dutch War* (Hilversum: Verloren, 2006).

Rooden, Peter van, 'Jews and Religious Toleration in the Dutch Republic', in *Calvinism and Religious Toleration in the Dutch Golden Age*, ed. by R. Po-Chia and Henk van Nierop (Cambridge: Cambridge University Press, 2002): 132–158.

Rosenberg, D.M., 'Milton's *Paradise Lost* and the Country Estate Poem', *Clio*, 18.2 (1989): 123–243.

Rosenblatt, Jason, *Renaissance England's Chief Rabbi: John Selden* (Oxford: Oxford University Press, 2006).

Rubright, Marjorie, *Doppelganger Dilemmas: Anglo-Dutch Relations in Early Modern English Literature and Culture* (Philadelphia: University of Pennsylvania Press, 2014).

Rumrich, John P., 'Milton's Arianism: Why It Matters', in *Milton and Heresy*, ed. Stephen B. Dobranski and John P. Rumrich (Cambridge: Cambridge University Press, 1998): 75–92.

———, 'Milton's God and the Matter of Chaos', *Modern Language Association*, 110.5 (1995): 1035–1046.

———, *Milton Unbound: Controversy and Reinterpretation* (Cambridge: Cambridge University Press, 1966).

Said, Edward W., *Orientalism* (London: Routledge, 1978).

Samuel, Irene, '*Samson Agonistes* as Tragedy', in *Calm of Mind: Tercentenary Essays on Paradise Regained and Samson Agonistes*, ed. by Joseph Wittreich (London: Western Reserve University, 1971): 235–257.

Sanchez, Reuben Marquez, '"The Worst of Superstitions": Milton's *Of True Religion* and the Issue of Religious Tolerance', *Prose Studies*, 9 (1986): 21–38.

Sauer, Elizabeth, 'Pious Fraud: Extralegal Heroism in *Samson Agonistes*', *Studies in English Literature, 1500–1900*, 53.1 (2013): 180–196.

————, The Politics of Performance in the Inner Theater: *Samson Agonistes* as a Closet Drama', in *Milton and Heresy*, ed. by Stephen B. Dobranski and John P. Rumrich (Cambridge: Cambridge University Press, 1998): 199–216.

Schama, Simon, *The Embarrassment of Riches: An Interpretation of Dutch Culture in the Golden Age* (New York: Alfred A. Knopf, 1987).

Schenkeveld-van der Dussen, M.A., 'Duistere Luister: Aspecten van Obscuritas', in *idem.*, *In de Boeken met de Geest: Vijftien Studies van M.A. Schenkelveld-van der Dussen over Vroegmoderne Nederlandse Literatuur*, ed. by A.J. Gelderblom (Amsterdam: Amsterdam University Press, 2002): 153–173.

————, 'Vondel's Work for the Stage Read and Studied over the Centuries', in *Joost van den Vondel (1587–1679): Dutch Playwright in the Golden Age* (Leiden: Brill, 2012): 7–22.

Scherpbier, Herman, *Milton in Holland: A Study in the Literary Relations of England and Holland before 1730* (Amsterdam: Folcroft Library Editions, 1978).

Schivelbusch, Wolfgang, *Tastes of Paradise: A Social History of Spices, Stimulants and Intoxicants* (New York: Vintage Books, 1992).

Schoenveldt, Michael, 'Marvell and the Designs of Art', in *The Cambridge Companion to Andrew Marvell* (Cambridge: Cambridge University Press, 2011): 87–101.

Schöffer, I., 'The Batavian Myth during the Sixteenth and Seventeenth Centuries', in *Britain and the Netherlands: Some Political Mythologies, Papers Delivered to the Fifth Anglo-Dutch Historical Conference* (Den Haag: Martinus Nijhoff, 1975): 78–101.

Schoneveld, Cornelis W., *Intertraffic of the Mind* (Leiden: Brill, 1983).

————, *Sea-Changes: Studies in Three Centuries of Anglo-Dutch Cultural Transmission* (Leiden: Brill, 1996).

Shorto, Russell, *Amsterdam: A History of the World's Most Liberal City* (New York: Penguin Random House, 2014).

Schwartz, Regina M., 'Milton's Hostile Chaos " . . . And the Sea Was No More"', *ELH*, 52.2 (1985): 337–374.

————, '*Samson Agonistes*: The Force of Justice and the Violence of Idolatry', in *The Oxford Handbook of John Milton*, ed. Nicholas McDowell and Nigel Smith (Oxford: Oxford University Press, 2011): 633–648.

Scott, Jonathan, *Commonwealth Principles: Republican Writing of the English Revolution* (Cambridge: Cambridge University, 2004).

Seaward, Paul, 'Marvell and Parliament', in *The Oxford Handbook of Andrew Marvell*, ed. by Martin Dzelzainis and Edward Holberton (Oxford: Oxford University Press, 2019): 80–95.

Seccombe, Thomas, 'Vossius, Isaac (1618–1689), Philologist and Author', *Oxford Dictionary of National Biography*, retrieved 4 July 2018. www.oxforddnb.com/view/10.1093/ref:odnb/9780198614128.001.0001/odnb-9780198614128-e-28356.

Sedivy, Sonia, 'Art from a Wittgensteinian Perspective: Constitutive Norms in Context', *The Journal of Aesthetics and Art Criticism*, 72.1 (Winter 2014): 67–82.

Sellin, Paul, 'John Milton's *Paradise Lost* and *De doctrina christiana* on Predestination', *Milton Studies*, 34 (1996): 45–60.

————, 'The Last of the Renaissance Monsters: The Poetical Institutions of Gerardus Johannes Vossius, and Some Observations on English Criticism', in *Anglo-Dutch Cross Currents in the Seventeenth and Eighteenth Century* (Los Angeles: University of California Press, 1976).

——, 'Lieuwe van Aitzema and John Milton's "The Doctrine and Discipline of Divorce": The Marquette Case', *Dutch Crossing*, 38.3 (Nov. 2014): 235–243.

——, 'P.C. Hooft, Constantijn Huygens, and the *Méditations Chrestiennes* of Rutger Wessel van den Boetzelaer, Baron van Asperen', in *From Revolt to Riches: Culture & History of the Low Countries, 1500–1700*, ed. by Theo Hermans and Reinier Salverda (London: UCL Press, 2017): 167–172.

Serjeantson, R.W., '*Samson Agonistes* and "Single Rebellion"', in *The Oxford Handbook of John Milton*, ed. Nicholas McDowell and Nigel Smith (Oxford: Oxford University Press, 2011): 614–631.

Sharma, Jayeeta, 'Food and Empire', in *The Oxford Handbook of Food History*, ed. by Jeffrey M. Pilcher (Oxford: Oxford University Press, 2012): 242–256.

Sharpe, Kevin, *Image Wars: Promoting Kings and Commonwealths in England, 1603-1660* (New Haven: Yale University Press, 2010).

——, *The Personal Rule of Charles I* (New Haven: Yale University Press, 1992).

Shawcross, John, 'Irony as Tragic Effect: *Samson Agonistes* and the Tragedy of Hope', in *Calm of Mind: Tercentenary Essays on Paradise Regained and Samson Agonistes* (London: Western Reserve University, 1971): 289–306.

——, *John Milton: The Self and the World* (Lexington: University Press of Kentucky, 1993).

——, *The Uncertain World of Samson Agonistes* (Cambridge: Cambridge University Press, 2001).

Sherry, Beverley, 'Lost and Regained in Translation', in *Milton in Translation*, ed. by Angelica Duran, Islam Issa, and Jonathan R. Olson (Oxford: Oxford University Press, 2017): 33–52.

Sierhuis, Freya, *Religion, Politics and the Stage in the Dutch Republic: The Literature of the Arminian Controversy* (Oxford: Oxford University Press, 2015).

——, 'Therapeutic Tragedy: Compassion, Remorse, and Reconciliation in the Joseph Plays of Joost van den Vondel (1635–1640)', *European Review of History*, 17.1 (2010): 27–51.

Simons, John, 'Marvell's Tulips', *Notes and Queries*, 36 (1989): 434.

Slights, Camille Wells, 'A Hero of Conscience: *Samson Agonistes* and Casuistry', *Publications of the Modern Language Association*, 90 (1975): 395–413.

Smith, D.K., '"tis not, what once it was, the world": Andrew Marvell's Re-Mapping of Old and New in 'Bermudas' and *Upon Appleton House*', in *Seventeenth Century*, 21.1 (2006): 215–248.

Smith, Goldwin, 'Andrew Marvell', in *The English Poets, Vol II: The Seventeenth Century: Ben Jonson to Dryden*, ed. by T.H. Ward (New York: Macmillan and Co, 1880).

Smith, Nigel, *Andrew Marvell: The Chameleon* (New Haven: Yale University Press, 2012).

——, '*Areopagitica*: Voicing Contexts, 1643–1645', in *Politics, Poetics and Hermeneutics in Milton's Prose*, ed. by David Loewenstein and James Grantham Turner (Cambridge: Cambridge University Press, 1990): 103–122.

——, 'Best, Biddle and Anti-Trinitarian Heresy', in *Heresy, Literature and Politics in Early Modern English Culture*, ed. by David Loewenstein and John Marshall (Cambridge: Cambridge University Press, 2006): 160–184.

——, 'The Boomerang Theology of Andrew Marvell', *Renaissance and Reformation*, 25.4 (2001): 139–155.

——, 'England, Europe, and the English Revolution', in *The Oxford Handbook of Literature and the English Revolution*, ed. by Laura Lunga Knoppers (Oxford: Oxford University Press, 2012): 30–40.

———, 'Milton and the European Contexts of Toleration', in *Milton and Toleration*, ed. by Sharon Achinstein and Elizabeth Sauer (Oxford: Oxford University Press, 2007): 23–44, (ed.) *The Poems of Andrew Marvell* (London: Longman, 2007).

———, 'The Politics of Tragedy in the Dutch Republic: Joachim Oudaen's Martyr Drama in Context', in *Dramatic Experience: The Poetics of Drama and the Early Modern Public Sphere(s)*, ed. by Katja Gvozdeva, Kirill Ospovat, and Tatiana Korneeva (Leiden: Brill, 2017): 220–249.

Sneller, Agnes A., 'Anna Maria van Schurman (1607–1678) als Literair Persoon en Geleerde Vrouw', *Literatuur*, 10 (1993): 321–328.

Sneller, Agnes A., Olga van Marion, and Netty van Megen (eds.), *De Gedichten van Tesselschade Roemers* (Hilversum: Uitgeverij Verloren, 1994).

Song, Eric, 'The Country Estate and the East Indies (East and West): The Shifting Scene of Eden in *Paradise Lost*', *Modern Philology*, 108.2 (2010): 199–223.

Sowerby, Scott, *Making Toleration: The Repealers and the Glorious Revolution* (Cambridge: Harvard University Press, 2012).

Spaans, Joke, 'Religious Policies in the Seventeenth-Century Dutch Republic', in *Calvinism and Religious Toleration in the Dutch Golden Age*, ed. by R. Po-Chia and Henk van Nierop (Cambridge: Cambridge University Press, 2002): 72–86.

Speck, William, 'Britain and the Dutch Republic', in *A Miracle Mirrored: The Dutch Republic in European Perspective* (Cambridge: Cambridge University Press, 1995): 173–195.

Sprunger, Keith, *Dutch Puritanism: A History of English and Scottish Churches of the Netherlands in the Sixteenth and Seventeenth Centuries* (Leiden: Brill, 1982).

Spurr, John, 'The Poet's Religion', in *The Cambridge Companion to Andrew Marvell*, ed. by Derek Hirst and Steven N. Zwicker (Cambridge: Cambridge University Press, 2011): 158–173.

Staffell, Elizabeth, 'The Horrible Tail-Man and the Anglo-Dutch Wars', *Journal of the Warburg and Courtauld Institutes*, 63 (2000): 169–186.

Stanglin, Keith D., *Arminius on the Assurance of Salvation: The Context, Roots, and Shape of the Leiden Debate, 1603–1609* (Leiden: Brill, 2007).

Stanglin, Keith D., and Thomas H.M. Call, *Arminius: Theologian of Grace* (Oxford: Oxford University Press, 2012).

Stavely, Keith W.F., 'Preface to *Of True Religion*, Heresie, Schism, Toleration', in *Complete Prose Works of John Milton* (New Haven: Yale University Press, 1982), vol. 8: 408–415.

Stevens, Paul, '*Paradise Lost* and the Colonial Imperative', *Milton Studies*, 34 (1996): 3–21.

Stobart, Jon, *Sugar and Spice: Grocers and Groceries in Provincial England, 1650-1830* (Oxford: Oxford University Press, 2002).

Stocker, Margarita, *Apocalyptic Marvell: The Second Coming in Seventeenth-Century Poetry* (Brighton: Harvaster, 1985).

Stone Peters, Julie, 'A "Bridge over Chaos": *De Jure Belli, Paradise Lost*, Terror, Sovereignty, Globalism, and the Modern Law of Nations', *Comparative Literature*, 58.4 (2005): 273–293.

Stoye, John, *English Travellers Abroad, 1604–1667* (London: Yale University Press, 1989).

Strien, C.D. van, *British Travellers in Holland during the Stuart Period* (Leiden: E.J. Brill, 1993).

Strien, Ton van, 'Huygens als vertaler van John Donne', *De Nieuwe Taalgids*, 85 (1992): 247–252.

———, 'Inleiding', in *Constantijn Huygens: Hofwijck* (Amsterdam: KNAW Press, 2008), vol. 2: 1–65.

Sturkenboom, Dorothee, 'Staging the Merchant: Commercial Vices and the Politics of Stereotyping in Early Modern Dutch Theatre', *Dutch Crossing*, 30.2 (2006): 211–228.

Sugimura, N.K., *'Matter of Glorious Trial': Spiritual and Material Substance in Paradise Lost* (New Haven: Yale University Press, 2009).

Swart, K.W., *William the Silent and the Dutch Revolt of the Netherlands* (London: The Historical Association, 1972).

Taff, Dyani Johns, 'A Shipwreck of Faith: Hazardous Voyages and Contested Representations in Milton's *Samson Agonistes*', in *Shipwreck and Island Motifs in Literature and Arts*, ed. by Brigitte Le Juez and Olga Springer (Leiden: Brill, 2015): 151–170.

Tarling, Nicholas (ed.), *The Cambridge History of South-East Asia: Vol I: From Early Times to c. 1800* (Cambridge: Cambridge University Press, 1992).

Taylor, C.C.W., *The Atomists: Lucippus and Democritus* (Toronto: Toronto University Press, 1999).

Thirsk, Joan, *Food in Early Modern England: Phases, Fads, Fashions, 1500–1760* (London: Hambledon Continuum, 2006).

Thompson, James, 'Dryden's *Conquest of Granada* and the Dutch Wars', *The Eighteenth Century*, 31.3 (1990): 211–226.

Todd, Richard, 'Equilibrium and National Stereotyping in "The Character of Holland"', in *On the Celebrated and Neglected Poems of Andrew Marvell*, ed. by Claude J. Summer and Ted-Larry Pebworth (London: University of Missouri Press, 1992): 169–191.

Togashi, Go, 'Contextualizing Milton's *Second Defence of the English People*: Cromwell and the English Republic, 1649–1654', *Milton Quarterly*, 45.4 (2011): 217–244.

Toliver, Harold E., *Marvell's Ironic Vision* (New Haven: Yale University Press, 1965).

Tracy, James, *The Founding of the Dutch Republic: War, Finance, and Politics in Holland, 1572–1588* (Oxford: Oxford University Press, 2008).

Trevor-Roper, H., *Catholics, Anglicans and Puritans: Seventeenth-Century Essays* (Chicago: Chicago University Press, 1988).

———, 'Hugo Grotius and England', in *The Exchange of Ideas: Religion, Scholarship, and Art in the Seventeenth-Century* (Zutphen: Walburg Instituut, 1994): 42–67.

Tuck, Richard, *The Rights of War and Peace: Political Thought and the International Order from Grotius to Kant* (Oxford: Oxford University Press, 2001).

Tyacke, Nicholas, *Anti-Calvinists: The Rise of English Arminianism, 1590–1640* (Oxford: Oxford University Press, 1987).

———, 'Arminianism and the Theology of the Restoration Church', in *The Exchange of Ideas: Religion, Scholarship and Art in the Seventeenth Century* (Zutphen: Walburg Instituut 1994): 68–83.

———, 'The Rise of Arminianism reconsidered', *Past and Present*, 115 (1987): 201–216.

Velema, Wyger R.E., '"That a Republic Is Better Than a Monarchy": Anti-Monarchism in Early Modern Dutch Republican Thought', in *Republicanism*, 2 vols., ed. by Martin van Gelderen and Quentin Skinner (Cambridge: Cambridge University Press, 2002), vol. 2: 1–25.

Vries, Jan de and Ad van der Woude, *The First Modern Economy: Success, Failure, and Perseverance of the Dutch Economy, 1500–1815* (Cambridge: Cambridge University Press, 1997).

Vries, Thieme de, *Holland's Influence on English Language and Literature* (Chicago: Grentzebach, 1916).

Vries, Willemien B. de, *Wandeling en verhandeling: de ontwikkeling van het Nederlandse Hofdicht in de zeventiende eeuw (1613–1710)* (Amsterdam: Uitgeverij Verloren, 1998).

Waddington, Raymond B., *Looking Into Providences: Designs and Trials in Paradise Lost* (Toronto: University of Toronto Press, 2012).

Waite, Gary K., *Jews and Muslims in Seventeenth-Century Discourse* (Abingdon: Routledge, 2018).

———, 'Where Did the Devil Go? Religious Polemic in the Dutch Reformation, 1580-1630', in *Interlinguicity, Internationality and Shakespeare*, ed. by Michael Saenger (Montreal: McGill-Queen's University Press, 2014): 59–73.

Walkling, Andrew R., *English Dramatick Opera, 1660–1710* (Abingdon: Routledge, 2019).

Wallace, John, *Destiny his Choice: The Loyalism of Andrew Marvell* (Cambridge: Cambridge University Press, 1968).

Walsham, Alexandra, *Charitable Hatred: Tolerance and Intolerance in England, 1500-1700* (Manchester: Manchester University Press, 2006).

———, *Providence in Early Modern England* (Oxford: Oxford University Press, 1999).

Warren, Christopher N., *Literature and the Law of Nations, 1580–1680* (Oxford: Oxford University Press, 2015).

———, 'Samson and the Chorus of Dissent', in *Uncircumscribed Mind: Reading Milton Deeply*, ed. by Charles W. Durham and Kristin A. Pruitt (Selinsgrove: Susquchanna University Press, 2008): 276–291.

Weijnen, A., *Zeventiende-eeuwse Taal* (Zutphen: W. J. Thieme, 1955).

White, Peter, *Predestination, Policy and Polemic: Conflict and Consensus in the English Church from the Reformation to the Civil War* (Cambridge: Cambridge University Press, 1992).

Wilde, Marc de, 'Offering Hospitality to Strangers: Hugo Grotius's Draft Regulations for the Jews', *Tijdschrift voor Rechtsgeschiedenis*, 85 (2017): 391–433.

Winkel, Jan te, *De Ontwikkelingsgang der Nederlandsche Letterkunde, Deel 4: Geschiedenis der Nederlandsche Letterkunde van de Republiek der Vereenigde Nederlanden* (Haarlem: De erven F. Bohn, 1924).

Wisse, Kees, 'Samson in Music', in *Samson: Hero or Fool? The Many Faces of Samson*, ed. by E. Eynikel and T. Nicklas (Leiden: Brill, 2014): 161–176.

Witte, John, *The Reformation of Rights* (Cambridge: Cambridge University Press, 2010).

Wittreich, Joseph, *Interpreting Samson Agonistes* (Princeton: Princeton University Press, 1986).

Worden, Blair, *Literature and Politics in Cromwellian England: John Milton, Andrew Marvell and Merchamont Nedham* (Oxford: Oxford University Press, 2008).

———, 'Milton and Merchamont Nedham', in *Milton and Republicanism*, ed. by David Armitage, Armand Himy, and Quentin Skinner (Cambridge: Cambridge University Press, 1995): 156–181.

———, 'Milton, *Samson Agonistes*, and the Restoration', in *Culture and Society in the Stuart Restoration*, ed. by Gerald MacLean (Cambridge: Cambridge University Press, 1995): 111–136.

Wortham, Christopher, '"A Happy Rural Seat": Milton's *Paradise Lost* and the English Country House Poem', *Parergon*, 9.1 (1991): 137–150.

Yoshinaka, Takashi, *Marvell's Ambivalence: Religion and Politics of Imagination in Mid-Seventeenth Century England* (Cambridge: Cambridge University Press, 2012).

Zagorin, Perez, *How the Idea of Toleration Came to the West* (Princeton: Princeton University Press, 2003).

Zanden, J.L. van, *The Rise and Decline of Holland's Economy: Merchant Capitalism and the Labour Market* (Manchester: Manchester University Press, 1993).

Zandt, Cynthia J. van, *Brothers among Nations: The Pursuit of Intercultural Alliances in Early America, 1580–1660* (Oxford: Oxford University Press, 2008).

Zwicker, Steven N., *Lines of Authority: Politics and English Literary Culture, 1649-1689* (Ithaca: Cornell University Press, 1993).

———, 'What's the Problem with the Dutch? Andrew Marvell, the Trade Wars, Toleration, and the Dutch Republic', *Marvell Studies*, 3.1 (2018): 1–12.

Index